Varèse: astronomer in sound

Malcolm MacDonald

Varèse
astronomer in sound

KAHN & AVERILL

First published in 2003 by Kahn & Averill
9 Harrington Road, London sw7 3es

Copyright © 2003 by Malcolm MacDonald

British Library Cataloguing in Publication Data
A catalogue record for this book is available from the British Library

isbn 1-871082-79-x

Set in Monotype Garamond by YHT Ltd., London
Book design by Simon Stern
Printed and bound in Great Britain by
Halstan & Co Ltd., Amersham, Bucks

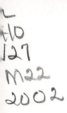
To Morris Kahn, true friend and ideal publisher,
who wanted to see 'what I had to say about Varèse'.

Astronomers are searchers of the arcana of the stars; composers of the arcana of sounds.
EDGARD VARÈSE

Surely the sounds are uttered by the stars...
ARISTIDES QUINTILIANUS (3rd century AD?) On Music

In music the spirit of mysticism puts on flesh; in music aspiration mysteriously attains its end, materializes, as though out of itself, the harmony it strives for.
MARTIN LUTHER

Man is the sun of the world; more than the real sun. The fire of his wonderful heart is the only light and heat worth gauge or measure. Where he is, are the tropics; where he is not, the ice world.
JOHN RUSKIN Modern Painters

ACKNOWLEDGEMENTS

Music examples from Varèse's works are reproduced by kind permission of G. Ricordi & Co Ltd, London, with the exception of the examples from *Un grand sommeil noir*, which are reproduced courtesy of Editions Salabert, Paris. The example from Stravinsky's *Le Sacre du Printemps* is copyright Boosey & Hawkes (Music Publishers) Ltd. I thank the various members of the staff of G. Ricordi in London and Milan who over the years helped to answer my queries, especially those relating to works which were then unpublished, and making available for study a copy of the manuscript of the original version of *Amériques*.

I also wish to record here my gratitude to the many people with whom I discussed individual works and general issues over the period this book was being written. Among them I should mention specifically James Reid-Baxter, who made available his Carpentier material and translated copious passages of Spanish; Robin Freeman for locating writings of Léon Deubel; Anthea Head for advice on astrological matters; Anthony Hill who shared with me some of his Varèse collection and his correspondence with Duchamp; Sue Rose for French translation; and Graham Hatton, Oliver Neighbour, Paul Rapoport, Ronald Stevenson and Richard Tiedman for bringing important information to my attention, answering queries or tracing hard-to-locate items which I had failed to find for myself.

Contents

Introduction

To reveal a new world is the function of creation in all the arts, but the act of creation defies analysis. A composer knows about as little as anyone else where the substance of his work comes from.
VARÈSE
lecturing at Princeton University, 1959

Anyone who does not make his own rules is an ass.[1]
VARÈSE
in interview, 1926

'The world has changed less since the time of Jesus Christ than it has in the last thirty years', wrote the French essayist Charles Péguy. The date was 1913. Edgard Varèse was 30 years old.[1]

There is a tendency to look back on the decades before the First World War as a golden age of social and cultural stability, but they were nothing of the kind. They were an age of mounting social and political tension, destined to culminate (though that destiny need not have

---

[1] To dispense at once with two common biographical confusions: Varèse was born in 1883, not 1885 as stated in many older musical encyclopaedias, and as he himself apparently believed for many years. (The parallel with Beethoven is almost too striking.) Although the French name 'Edgar' is exactly the same as the English form, without a final 'd', 'Edgard' – perhaps reflecting, through his Piedmontaise ancestry, the Italian 'Edgardo' – is the spelling on Varèse's birth-certificate and the one he used until he migrated to the USA. Thereafter he called himself 'Edgar', perhaps to minimize the labour of correcting interviewers and correspondents, until late in life he re-adopted 'Edgard', though with less than total consistency. Many contemporary articles and interviews, therefore, use 'Edgar'. I use 'Edgard' throughout, except when quoting from sources which refer to him as 'Edgar'.

been inevitable) in world war and revolution. Aside from this unrest –
yet lending it motive power – a stream of cultural and technological
innovations were transforming Western man's idea of the world, and
his relation to it. Varèse was born in the year synthetic fibre was
invented. His country upbringing on a Burgundian farm proceeded in
parallel with the creation of the first steam turbine, the first electric
motor, pneumatic tyres, cordite, box cameras and photographic paper.
His move to Turin in 1892 coincided with the invention of the diesel
engine. His first musical work for which we have any evidence – the
childhood 'opera' *Martin Paz* – belongs to the year that the
gramophone record and the cinematograph came into being: the year
before the discovery of X-rays, radio telegraphy and the movie camera.
Freud and Breuer published the first psychoanalytical work, *Studie
über Hysterie*, in 1895, introducing the concepts of the unconscious,
trauma and repression; Freud in 1900 published *The Interpretation of
Dreams*. Varèse returned to Paris, his birthplace, in 1903, the year of
the Wright brothers' first powered flight; and was accepted as a student
at the Conservatoire in 1905, when Einstein first formulated the
Special Theory of Relativity. He was literally a child of the modern age,
and lived to become the most radical pioneer and least tractable father-
figure of 20th-century music.

The original idea for this book arose in the mid-1970s, shortly after
the publication of Louise Varèse's memoir of her husband's life to
1928, *A Looking-Glass Diary*. I was then finishing my volume on
Schoenberg for the JM Dent 'Master Musicians' series. It seemed to me
that the format of that series – unassuming life and works, with
chronology – had proved unexpectedly useful for introducing a
'difficult' modern figure to a wider readership of music-lovers, who
would appreciate the music a great deal better if they were given a
straightforward framework in which to approach it. I was eager to
extend this treatment to Varèse and indeed offered the project to
Dent's as a 'Master Musicians'. I was unsuccessful, but in 1977 Kahn
& Averill accepted the proposal. Clearly I could not, for a different
publisher, exactly reproduce the 'Master Musicians' format, but I was
still contemplating a book along similar lines.

At that stage the only book-length studies in English were primarily
biographical: indeed apart from Louise's memoir the only substantial
work was the English translation of Fernand Ouellette's *Edgard Varèse*,
published the year after the composer's death. Even now, in 2002, these

remain the principal biographical sources. Louise probably knew Varèse better as a man than anyone else; Ouellette had enjoyed his friendship, confidence and co-operation, and his was in a sense the 'authorized' biography. Neither author, however, was a musician. While chronicling the emergence of Varèse's works, Louise says little about them; Ouellette says much, but his descriptions are primarily poetic and impressionistic. They are by no means without insight, and Varèse may well have valued his empathy and enthusiasm far more highly than any conventional analytical skills, but they are of limited use to a reader who wishes his ears to be led to comprehend Varèse's designs.

On the other hand there were several technical studies of Varèse's music, notably those published in various articles by his friend, pupil and sometime amanuensis, the Chinese composer and scholar Chou Wen-Chung. The number of such studies has greatly increased in more recent years, but they have remained confined to critical and musicological journals with the outstanding exception of Jonathan W. Bernard's book *The Music of Edgard Varèse* (1987), so far the most sustained attempt at close analysis of Varèse's scores to determine his working practice and techniques and to propound a theoretical basis for those techniques. A student of Allen Forte, Bernard has developed a mode of graphic representation for portions of Varèse's scores to clarify the workings of pitch- and interval-cells at their various registral levels in what he himself characterizes as a 'reductive analysis'. Despite the excellence of such analytical studies, they have tended to concentrate on a 'core' repertoire within Varèse's already small output. Also they are – as they need to be – hard going for all but dedicated professional musical analysts: who must form, we should hope, only a small sector of Varèse's audience.

In more recent years a number of valuable documentary studies – by Olivia Mattis, among others – have added significantly to our knowledge of how some of Varèse's works came into being. But generally speaking the Varèse literature remains polarized between the biographical and the technical – leaving a yawning gap in the middle-ground where the inquiring but non-academic music lover might hope to find some guidance. This book is for listeners to Varèse's works who have been stimulated to want to know more than they can get from concert programmes and liner-notes. Such listeners – and I imagine them as forming a majority of his audience – may be willing to entertain some analytical concepts, but are more likely to be interested in the broader thrust of Varèse's ideas in action, and in grasping the works as overall designs and dramatic processes. As Schoenberg wrote to Rudolf Kolisch, identifying a crux in understanding *his* music, it is less important to see 'how it is *done*' than 'what it *is*'.

The alert reader will have noted that this book has been in gestation for well over 20 years – during which a multitude of professional and personal interruptions, not to mention a half-dozen other books, intervened to slow its progress. Unsurprisingly, it has evolved into something rather different from the modest volume I originally envisaged.[2] The biographical component is fairly small, except as it impinges directly on discussions of the works, but a running chronology at the head of most of the chapters provides a firm biographical framework. In essence the book is a detailed consideration of Varèse's output, work by work, from the earliest surviving example, the song *Un grand sommeil noir*, to the unfinished *Nocturnal* which was his final utterance. The works are discussed in relation to, and insofar as they illustrate, the remarkable complex of ideas both ancient and modern, mystical and scientific, out of which Varèse fashioned his unique view of music's potential and his characteristic approach to composition. And I have attempted to provide descriptive, rather than deep-structural, analyses which may help to guide listeners through each work – though I have indicated several cases where differing analytical approaches may be equally valid.

Not everyone will approve this manner of proceeding. Jonathan Bernard has opined that 'The kind of landscape description in which a piece is run through and its prominent features mentioned for those who know the piece only slightly or not at all is nearly useless in a serious book'. Clearly I disagree. I have attempted rather more than just 'landscape description', but it is still recognizably the kind of 'musical analysis' that descends from such figures as (the name sounds oddly in this context) Donald Francis Tovey. Some will find this utterly inappropriate for Varèse, but it seems to me – with all possible reservations – to retain considerable utility as a means of explaining

---

[2] I cannot claim this long parturition has bestowed on it either authority or finality. Many sections have been obsessively rewritten, many times; others, no doubt, not obsessively enough. Though often frustrating, the delays eventually had an unexpected benefit: they allowed me to include discussions of *Tuning Up*, *Dance for Burgess* and the original version of *Amériques*, all made public in 1998.

how the music unfolds as a process in time. Despite Varèse's imaginative debt to painters and sculptors, the last thing he thought he was doing was composing static arrangements of notes.

Louise Varèse, Ouellette and Bernard have all given useful accounts of Varèse's aesthetic background: his close relations with leading writers and visual artists which made him in many ways a prime representative of the generation of 20th-century modernism, the most significant musical contemporary of the Cubists and Futurists, of Picasso, Apollinaire and Le Corbusier. He cannot, however, be viewed as belonging to any particular movement within modernism. He was never a follower. His habits of mind were fundamentally eclectic, and insofar as he derived his ideas from the arts and sciences he took what he needed wherever he happened to find it, to synthesize his fiercely individual creative stance. Rather than rehearse his modernist aesthetic credentials at length (I recommend instead the masterly conspectus of Bernard's first chapter) I have emphasized another background presence.

Varèse frequently and deliberately used the language – or at least the rhetoric – of science and scientific analogy to describe his music and its processes. Unquestionably he regarded his works as, in part, a creative expression of the new potentialities that were opening up for mankind during his lifetime, principally through the advances of science and technology. The vital term here, however is 'creative'. Varèse's training in engineering and lifelong interest in technology in no way diminished his sense of the miraculous when he contemplated the scientific discoveries of his time. Rather the reverse. He seems to have found in them an endless source of wonder; to have regarded modern science in a 'magical' sense as an agent not merely of discovery but of human transformation – like the alchemy of the Renaissance, which also appealed to his imagination. Paracelsus, whom Varèse invoked as a kind of tutelary spirit in *Arcana*, has been viewed over the centuries, according to different perspectives, as a pioneer and martyr of hard science or as a charismatic mystagogue. The truth is that he was both, inextricably combined. His work and that of his followers 'reflects strongly both ancient philosophical thought and the opening phases of the Scientific Revolution'.[3] So, in his different way, does Varèse.

---

[3] Allen G. Debus, *The English Paracelsians* (New York: Franklin Watts Inc, 1966), p.10

In the prevailing mythos of 20th-century rationalism, the figure of the scientist came to subsume the prophetic, spiritually authoritative functions of magician and priest. Varèse's works, despite their claims to abstraction and pure manipulation of sound, project a mythos of their own. They are an implied drama of humanity at a crucial point of change in consciousness: a conceptual breakthrough, with new musical means, into a new awareness of Mankind's relationship to his primal instincts, to the forces of nature, and to the vastness of the universe. In this mythos the prophetic function is exercised – consciously or not – by the composer who creates the music that startles audiences into this sudden awareness, whose works embody a new scientific (perhaps better to say *scientistic*) modernity of approach. Underlying Varèse's conceptions are a succession of archetypal figures – searchers after knowledge, speculators of the stars, harbingers and provokers of profound change in the societies around them: Oedipus, Faust, Paracelsus, the Animist shamans of the Mayan mountains and the American desert. It is this which gives his music, rather than that of the many composers who acknowledge his influence and example, the quality that Evan Eisenberg has rightly characterized as 'the urgency of myth'.[4]

From this point of view it is significant that his compositional career in Paris in the 1900s started, if not directly from, then certainly in close proximity with, members of the occult and esoteric fraternities which had been enormously influential in the arts in the 1890s. Though Varèse rejected the trappings of fin-de-siècle occultism, he derived from it important imaginative insights and stimuli which seem to have influenced and underpinned his conceptions of both music and of science throughout his career. As he once remarked: 'The beginning of art is not reason'.

He celebrated the advancing hard sciences and the dynamism of the machine age as forces that would dissolve the stultifying mediocrity of reactionary bourgeois culture, with its formalized canons of good taste. Music, he averred just after completing *Amériques*, was 'the ideal form of expression, since we are living in a mechanical age'. But this was because 'being formless, alone of the arts immaterial' it was 'the antidote to materialism'. Equally vital to his world-view was the new

---

[4] Evan Eisenberg, *The Recording Angel: Music, Records and Culture from Aristotle to Zappa* (London: Picador, 1988), p.111.

awareness being uncovered by anthropology of the timeless, elemental nature of human instinct. A man of explosive moods and strong passions, Varèse was fascinated by the ancient cultures of native peoples – cultures in which magic was taken for granted and which legitimized powerful, primal instincts as part of humanity's common heritage. In hindsight, it seems almost inevitable that he should have made his way to the Americas, literally the 'New World' both in the promise it offered for mankind's future and in its mysteries of a mode of humanity dwelling outside time. In the USA, the most formidable technological progress on earth shared space with a vast continental wilderness. Post-European rationalism had made its habitation on the edge (or perhaps more accurately on the back) of the long-established, sophisticated, shamanic tribal cultures of those whom Busoni called *Der rothaute Amerikas*. Ranging in space – the physical space of the huge, largely empty continent and the imaginative space of the expanding stellar cosmos – Man appeared on the brink of rediscovering his lost identity as the vessel of primal emotions, aroused by unconscious instinct and awe at the magical nature of his universe.

Radical and revolutionary though these ideas might seem, they were of course culturally induced; they were romantic, developing from the artistic agenda of Romanticism since the time of the French Revolution; and they were of European origin. Even as a long-established habitué of New York's Greenwich Village, Varèse remained a French artist – with roots in Beethoven, Berlioz and Debussy – who embodied the ideal of Romantic futurity in its most extreme form and bought it into closest dialogue with the scientific and shamanic realities of the New World. He was most certainly not – as he seemed to his many contemporary critics, and perhaps still seems to some members of the concert-going audience – a determined annihilator of tradition. Jonathan Bernard puts this point with great clarity[5]:

Varèse's declaration that 'the links in the chain of tradition are formed by men who have all been revolutionists!' should serve as a reminder that Varèse was talking about forging continuity, not breaking it. When he spoke of freedom for music, he did not mean irresponsible or unlimited freedom, freedom to do absolutely anything. He meant deliverance from outmoded practices statically

---

[5] Bernard, p.36.

and thoughtlessly perpetuated, from 'bad habits' ('*erroneously* called tradition'), and from restrictions on the use of sound materials that modern technology had made accessible.

So Varèse's 'new worlds' were not spheres of anarchy. In fact, as we shall see, his music depends on a rather limited number of highly individual and self-consistent strategies, applied with painstaking precision, to *suggest* an infinity of the imagination.

If some will be impatient of my emphasis on the 'esoteric' aspects of Varèse's musical cosmos, others may question the amount of space I have devoted to works which no longer survive, or in some cases never existed in any completed form: the lost scores preceding Varèse's migration to the USA in 1915, and the vast unrealized projects which occupied so much of his energies from the 1920s to the 1940s, *The One-All-Alone* and *Espace*. Perhaps the attempt to recover, even in the imagination, something of those missing works is misguided, a mere exercise of pointless speculation. It is not, after all, as if Varèse's surviving oeuvre is in any sense inchoate: it is a tight-knit entity, a creative paradigm of 20th-century modernism. Probably no output so small has established so strong an individual identity, or exercised such a profound effect on the art of music. But it is important to recognize that its air of self-consistent scientific modernity is partly fortuitous, partly the composer's deliberate construct. The music's radicalism is so complete that it seems to emerge out of nowhere, with no immediate recognizable antecedents and few clear contemporary connexions. Still, we should resist the temptation to treat it as a *chose en soi*. The output is so small because so much of it was lost, destroyed, or abandoned incomplete. Varèse composed music for over 60 years, yet his few extant, completed works, on which rests his significance for 20th-century music, were created during much shorter periods within that large span: principally 1920-27 and 1949-57. To give an account of him as a creative artist on that sole basis is like a paleo-anthropologist trying to describe a new stage in human evolution on the basis of a skull, a breastbone and a few fragments of spinal column. Whatever new features displayed by such remains, they are only fully understandable when placed within a sketch, however tentative, of the whole primate.

It was an important aspect of Varese's radicalism that he distrusted all theory, repudiated systems, and deplored 'any form of musical measurement'. He maintained that 'analysis is sterile. To explain by means of it is to decompose, to mutilate the spirit of the work'. Like many of his *obiter dicta*, he wrote those words (in the programme-note for the first performance of *Intégrales*)[6] in a polemical spirit, as much to discourage tiresome and hostile questions as to deflect studious critical inquiry. Though he spoke and wrote extensively about his ideas and his conception of music, he vouchsafed no detailed account of his working practice and propounded no compositional theory. In the main his writings are visionary, powerfully suggestive rather than analytical, liberally laced with visual and scientific analogy, and recur constantly to key concepts – 'projection', 'spatial music', 'the liberation of sound', and so on.[7]

This does not mean, of course, that it is impossible – or improper – to analyse the application of these concepts in his published scores, or to extrapolate a coherent compositional method from close observation of Varèse's practice. No-one can read Chou Wen-Chung's articles, starting with his memorial 'Varèse: A Sketch of the Man and His Music' (*Musical Quarterly*, April 1966) without profit. If Jonathan Bernard's analytical graphs sometimes border upon tautology (like those ever more detailed maps of China which, in Jorge Luis Borges's fable, grew to become 1:1 – scale representations, co-extensive with the Empire they charted[8]) no-one can read his book without an enhanced

---

[6] In fact, he had already honed the latter phrases in his article 'Jerom' s'en va-t'en guerre' (*The Sackbut*, Vol.IV no.5, December 1923, p.147), commenting that listeners 'will never get the meaning of any work by the accumulation of formulas, nor by the exegesis of many doctrines'.

[7] Varèse's exposition of his ideas – scattered through a large number of disparate lectures, articles, interviews, letters and notes – is cogent but hardly systematic. The more developed statements date from the latter part of his career – from the 1930s onward – but self-evidently develop concepts he propounded at a much earlier date. There is no single text that encapsulates all major aspects of his musical philosophy. On the other hand, the number of salient passages crucial to an understanding of his thought are fewer than might be assumed. Once he had arrived at a form of words which satisfied him, he tended to recycle it on different occasions and across different means of presentation, sometimes (but not always) identifying the passage as a self-quotation. Thus identical or near-identical phraseology may be found in several different texts: as witness the previous footnote.

[8] See Borges's 'Of Exactitude in Science' in *A Universal History of Infamy* (London: Penguin Books, 1975, p.131; the piece was first published in Buenos Aires in 1946). It is ironic that Bernard himself uses this image in 'Cracked Octaves, Warped

admiration for Varèse as a musical craftsman, a sculptor in sound.

However, we should be wary of any approach which seeks to understand his works primarily through the way their constituent tones are put together. We must always remember that Varèse came to think of his music 'as organized sound instead of sanctified and regimented notes': for him, even more than for most other composers before and since, the notes on the page are not his music, merely the symbols of it. Since, for the most part, conventional instruments were all he had to work with, he accepted their existing sounds as given, and used conventional notation to project his utterly unconventional designs. But every work strains every fibre to transcend these limitations, to map a universe of sound far beyond what had been historically achieved, to induce in us an awareness of new and infinite possibilities. It is in that spirit of endless inquiry that I have written this book, and recommend it to the next generation of listeners who occupy their minds with the achievement of Edgard Varèse.

STANLEY DOWNTON
April 1999 / March 2002

Perspectives' (*Perspectives of New Music 30/2*, Summer 1992, pp.274-289), as part of his crushing response to Marion Guck's insufficiently focussed but thought-provoking essay 'Varèse Bound' (same issue, pp.244-273).

PART I The past

1910   *Collection Fernand Ouellette*

1 · The lost memory: the enigma of the early music

je ne sais plus rien
je perds la memoire
du mal et du bien
Oh! la triste histoire
PAUL VERLAINE
Un grand sommeil noir

CHRONOLOGY 1883–1914

1883 *22 December: Edgard Victor Achille Charles Varèse is born at 4.00pm at 12 rue de Strasbourg, Paris. He is the eldest of the five children (3 sons, 2 daughters) of the engineer Henri Pié Jules Annibal Varèse, from Pignerol in Piedmont and his 18-year-old wife, Blanche-Marie Cortot, born in Paris of Burgundian stock. (During his lifetime his year of birth will be registered incorrectly, in almost all lexicons, as 1885.)*

1884 *Some weeks after his birth Varèse is entrusted to the family of his Uncle Joseph (brother of his maternal grandfather, Claude Cortot), at the village of Villars in Burgundy. Here he experiences a peasant childhood. 77 years later he will write 'I am a* Bourguignon *... And I have inherited only one thing of value, the memory of my Burgundian grandfather.' Later in the 1880s he attends school in Paris, where Claude Cortot owns a bistro in the Rue de Lancry.*

1890 *Taken by his grandfather to the Paris Exposition, where he hears his first opera, Massenet's* Manon.

1892 *This year (probably) Varèse moves with his parents and grandfather* to Turin, where his father has mining interests. He begins studying music secretly because of the disapproval of his tyrannical father, who intends him to become an engineer; he attends the Technical Institute in the city.

1895 About this time ('when I was eleven') Varèse composes the 'opera' Martin Paz. He hears Debussy's Prélude à l'Après-midi d'un faune, which makes an indelible impression, in Turin. According to Varèse this is his first experience of a symphony concert: it must have been this year at the earliest as Debussy's work was not performed (in Paris) till late 1894.

1897 Death of Varèse's mother, aged 31. On her deathbed she implores the 14-year-old Edgard to protect his brothers from their father, who shortly re-marries.

1900 Visits the Exposition Universelle in Paris. Probably this year Giovanni Bolzoni, director of the Turin Conservatory, begins to take an interest in Varèse and gives him private lessons in harmony and counterpoint.

1903 After beating his father in a fit of rage for maltreating his stepmother, Varèse, aged 19, leaves his family in Turin to pursue his musical studies free of interference. He returns to Paris, where he supports himself as a music copyist.

1904 Through the influence of his cousin, the pianist Alfred Cortot, Varèse gains entry to the Schola Cantorum. Here he studies composition with D'Indy, fugue with Roussel and Medieval, Renaissance and early Baroque music with Charles Bordes, simultaneously working as a librarian in the Schola to pay his fees. A lifelong friendship begins with the Breton composer Paul Le Flem. Unable to abide d'Indy, Varèse takes the examinations for the Paris Conservatoire.

1905 8 January: he is accepted by Fauré as a pupil in Widor's master class at the Conservatoire, where both Widor and Massenet are friendly and supportive. 22 February: Varèse becomes secretary-companion to August Rodin at Meudon. After a few months, however, they quarrel bitterly and Varèse returns to Paris. He lodges with the poet Léon Deubel at the offices of the magazine Rénovation Esthetique on the rue de Fürstemberg and takes private pupils in composition. Probably in this year he composes Prélude à la fin d'un jour, Colloque au bord de la fontaine, Dans le parc, Poème des brumes and Rhapsodie romane.

1906 Varèse founds the Choeur de l'Université Populaire at Faubourg Saint-Antoine, with which he gives concerts at the Château du Peuple.

Spring: fails in the competition for the Prix de Rome. April: he leaves Deubel's apartment and moves to various addresses. He performs a piano version of Rhapsodie romane *at a* Rénovation Esthetique *concert. Editions Roudanez publish Varèse's song* Un grand sommeil noir.

1907 *He receives the Première Bourse artistique de la Ville de Paris at the recommendation of Massenet and Widor. Meets Debussy for the first time. At the Château du Peuple, performs a piano version of his* Apothéose de l'océan *and* Colloque au Bord de la Fontaine. *19 September: obtains exemption from military service through an interview with Clémenceau. 5 November: Varèse marries Suzanne Bing, a student actress also attending the Conservatoire. In the Winter they quit Paris for Berlin, Varèse having meantime left the Conservatoire after 'a rather nasty exchange of unpleasantries with Fauré'.*

1908 *Varèse establishes himself in Berlin, where he stays for the next six years, working as a copyist and giving private lessons but making yearly visits to Paris. Becomes friendly with Ferruccio Busoni and the conductor Karl Muck. Composes* Bourgogne. *Meets Ravel in Paris. Sees Max Reinhardt's production of Hofmannsthal's* Oedipus und die Sphinx *at the Deutsches Theater in Berlin. Winter: meets Hofmannsthal and obtains permission to adapt* Oedipus *as the libretto for an opera; he will work on this project until 1914.*

1909 *January: meets Romain Rolland in Paris, and in the same month founds the Symphonischer Chor in Berlin, which takes part in Reinhardt's productions of* Faust *and* A Midsummer Night's Dream *at the Deutsches Theater. Begins composing* Gargantua. *April: receives a grant from the Paul Kusynski Foundation on the recommendations of Busoni and Muck. May: meets Mahler. Summer: becomes friendly with Richard Strauss.*

1910 *For the next two years Varèse and is mainly supported by financial help from Hofmannsthal. September: Birth of Varèse's daughter, Claude. 7 December: Death of his grandfather Claude Cortot. 15 December: Berlin première (and only performance) of Varèse's symphonic poem* Bourgogne, *by the Blüthner Orchestra conducted by Joseph Stransky.*

1911 *March: Varèse resigns as director of the Symphonischer Chor. He sketches* Mehr Licht.

1912 *Composes* Les cycles du nord. *Early October: Varèse attends the first performance of Schoenberg's* Pierrot Lunaire *at Busoni's house.*

1913 *Suzanne and Varèse agree to separate: Suzanne returns to Paris to pursue an acting career. May: Varèse meets the inventor René Bertrand – the beginning of a long friendship. 12 June: Léon Deubel commits suicide. Summer: Varèse gives up his Berlin apartment and puts most of his manuscripts into storage. To Paris and then (December) to Prague.*

1914 *4 January: Varèse conducts the first concert performance of Debussy's* Le Martyre de Saint-Sébastien *as part of a programme of contemporary French music with the Czech Philharmonic in Prague. The outbreak of World War I forces Varèse to break off work on the almost-completed* Oedipus und die Sphinx. *Varèse introduces Picasso to Cocteau. A proposed collaboration on Cocteau's* Un songe d'une nuit d'été *is discussed well into the next year.*

As far as musical history is concerned, Edgard Varèse bursts into our consciousness at the age of 39, in *Offrandes* and *Amériques*, already a composer quite unlike any of his predecessors, and only tenuously related to his contemporaries. 'Hearing Schoenberg's notorious Five Pieces for Orchestra,' wrote Lawrence Gilman in a famous review—

you will remember that Wagner once lived; hearing Casella's *Alta Notte* you will remember that Schoenberg still lives. Hearing Varèse's *Hyperprism* you remember only Varèse ... It is lonely, incomparable, unique.[1]

This apparent uniqueness and disconnexion from the past were impressions Varèse himself did little to dispel. The pose of self-parturition appealed to one who, as a young man, had declared: '*Moi, je suis l'ancêtre*'. Indeed, perhaps no artist of comparable originality and uniqueness has left fewer clues to his discovery of his chosen path. His development prior to 1920 is a blackness, an absence. Yet largely this is due to tragic accident.

By the time Varèse came to compose the first works by which we know him, he had in fact been writing music – effective and challenging music, to judge by the reactions of his contemporaries – for nearly quarter of a century. Far from being unorthodox, his musical education had followed the time-hallowed pattern for generations of French composers, and was unusual only in that he had undergone

---

[1] Review of the first performance of *Hyperprism*, in the *New York Tribune*, 17 December 1924.

formal training at both the leading establishments in Paris – the Schola Cantorum and the Paris Conservatoire – rather than just one of them. His principal teachers were notable figures to whom an entire generation owed their instruction: Bordes and d'Indy at the Schola, Widor and Massenet at the Conservatoire. Moreover, after he graduated Varèse won the friendship and admiration of three of Europe's leading composers – Debussy, Busoni, Richard Strauss – and two of the most musically-sensitive literary figures of the age: Romain Rolland and Hugo von Hofmannsthal. During that whole period he had been composing: and while the precise total of works is unknown, they included at least a dozen on a comparatively large scale; though only one of these (the symphonic poem *Bourgogne*) was ever performed by the forces for which it was intended.

Yet with one minor (and long unnoticed) exception, utter oblivion has overtaken this substantial early output. Most of Varèse's scores were incinerated in a warehouse fire in 1918; the remainder were lost in various circumstances during the Great War, or – in the sole documented case of *Bourgogne* – destroyed many years later by the composer himself. Among the myriad musical works which, over the centuries, have disappeared into the maw of history, Varèse's early compositions are perhaps our gravest loss. Not necessarily because of their presumed musical quality (at which we can only guess) but because of their inherent aesthetic interest, because of the light they could surely cast on the emergence of such a singularly extreme and uncompromisingly individual artistic personality as Edgard Varèse.

It might seem an impossible task to reconstruct the background of personal artistic development out of which Varèse's works of the 1920s arose. He himself, once it became clear that his earlier music had gone forever, accepted and indeed exploited the fact. He appeared to welcome the opportunity for a totally fresh start in the USA, with a blank sheet that allowed his new works to appear as if from nowhere. He seldom referred to the lost pieces composed in Paris and Berlin. But the very fierceness of his reticence, the wish to blot them from memory, indicates the pain of his loss. If we are to deal justly with Varèse the creator, it is important to give those lost works some substance, some semblance of reality. 25 years of creative activity is no negligible span – least of all for the creator, even if in the end he repudiates all that his work of that time had stood for (and there is no reason to suppose that Varèse did so).

However dimly, the early music must have foreshadowed the concerns of his mature output. In this chapter I shall present a listing of Varèse's early works – those that were known to exist – with a summary of everything that is known about each (which in most cases is little enough). I shall also look in greater detail at the sole, small early work that has survived, the Verlaine song *Un grand sommeil noir*; and afterwards I shall attempt to draw some general conclusions as to the direction of Varèse's musical interests during these forgotten yet crucially formative years of his composing career.

Many of the 'facts' given below are suspect, based on witnesses' fallible memories and authors' personal interpretations of casual remarks or hearsay. Dates especially are vague, most of all for the first few works in the following catalogue. I have attempted to suggest a chronological order, but it will be obvious that for the years 1903–7 several alternative orderings might be proposed. Doubtless, too, Varèse could have worked on several pieces simultaneously (and almost certainly did). Nevertheless, I think the lineaments of a believable pattern of activity, with credible antecedents and tendencies, emerges from a careful sifting of the evidence, such as it is.

MARTIN PAZ *'Opera' with libretto by Varèse after Jules Verne's romance, for boys' voices and mandolin accompaniment. ?1895. (No materials extant; it is unclear to what extent this childhood work was written down.)*

Jules Verne's short novel *Martin Paz* (first published in serial form in 1852 – some sources give the title, incorrectly, as *Martin Pas*) is one of his earliest works of fiction. It was advertised as 'in the style of Fennimore Cooper', and is a rather different kind of book from the vast series of 'Voyages extraordinaires' – whether adventure stories that celebrate scientific progress, or works of predictive science-fiction – for which Verne is best known. Despite its colourful setting it possesses elements of autobiography and wish-fulfillment that must have appealed to Varèse. The action, laid in Peru, is based on a historical incident and was inspired by a series of paintings by the Peruvian artist Merino, whom Verne knew personally. The novel's eponymous hero is an Indian who foments a revolt in Lima against the European domination of his country – and also against his father (Verne, like Varèse, had suffered the influence of a stern and narrow paterfamilias). Eventually Martin Paz dies as a member of an Indian tribe that has taken refuge in the mountains of the Andes. There is a strain of

Catholic religiosity in the book seldom encountered in Verne's later work; but also a strong love-interest in Martin's romance with a beautiful girl who, like Verne's first mistress, Maya Abanes, is of Spanish-Jewish ancestry.

In answer to a question from Gunther Schuller[2] about his most important early musical experiences, Varèse mentioned this childhood work first, commenting that in it 'I was already involved with sonority and unusual sounds'. Louise Varèse reproduces the account Varèse gave her of it:[3]

At the age of eleven I composed what I grandly called an opera. My company consisted of a few musically inclined schoolmates with choirboy voices, my orchestra, and a mandolin my grandfather had given me. I monkeyed with the strings until I managed to get some sounds I liked, not a bit like the silly twiddle of the mandolin – and the frame was my first percussion instrument. ... *Martin Paz* seemed to me a more dramatic and more romantic and therefore a better subject for an opera [than Verne's science-fiction stories]. After all, I lived in operatic Italy!

After *Martin Paz* no further work is heard of until Varèse was a student at the Schola Cantorum, although he began private studies with Bolzoni about 1900; but after 1903, when he left home for Paris, they come thick and fast.

FUGUE *1904. Unpublished; still extant?*

At the end of his life Varèse remarked that 'I still have the fugue, by the way, that admitted me to [Widor's] class at the Conservatoire'[4] Since he was admitted at the very beginning of 1905 this places the fugue in the previous year. We have no further information – whether, for instance, this fugue was for a specific instrument or ensemble or an academic exercise in open-score form; nor whether it still exists. Naturally he would not have regarded it as a serious composition. But the fact that it favorably impressed Widor is good evidence of Varèse's aptitude in this formal contrapuntal discipline. It should be recalled

---

[2] Gunther Schuller, 'Conversation with Varèse', *Perspectives of New Music* 3/2 (1965); p.32; reprinted in *Perspectives on American Composers*, ed. Boretz and Cone (New York: Norton, 1971). Hereinafter cited as Schuller (1965).

[3] Louise Varèse, *A Looking-Glass Diary* (New York: Norton, 1972), p.24. Hereinafter cited as *LGD*.

[4] Schuller (1965), p.32.

that at the Schola he had studied fugue specifically with Roussel, in his way a master of the form.

APOTHÉOSE DE L'OCÉAN *Symphonic poem for orchestra. Period 1904–6. A version for piano was publicly performed by Varèse at the Château du Peuple, Paris, late August 1906. Unpublished; score believed destroyed in warehouse fire, Berlin, c.1918.*

Louise Varèse (*LGD*, p.43) mentions that Varèse preserved a copy of a weekly review reporting on his recital at the Château du Peuple, a free theatre for working-class people, under the auspices of the Université Populaire de Faubourg Saint-Antoine. She calls this source *La Chronique de Paris* and gives no precise date: in fact it was *Le Chroniqueur de Paris* of 30 August 1906 in which the critic 'J.V.B.' wrote enthusiastically: 'Before this audience of simple people, he played – and with what success – his *Colloque au Bord de la Fontaine* and his *Apothéose de l'océan*, a vast symphonic poem, exuberant and magnificently young'.

COLLOQUE AU BORD DE LA FONTAINE *Piece for orchestra (?). Period 1904–5. Varèse played this work in his Paris studio to the journalist 'E.C.' who afterwards published an (untitled) article on the composer in the* Courrier de Bayonne *of 21 September 1905. A piano version was also publicly performed by Varèse at the Château du Peuple, Paris, late August 1906 (see note to* Apothéose de l'Océan*). Unpublished; score believed destroyed in warehouse fire, Berlin, c.1918.*

DANS LE PARC *Piece for orchestra(?). Period 1904–5. Varèse played this work in his Paris studio to the journalist who afterwards published an article on the composer in the* Courrier de Bayonne *of 21 September 1905. Unpublished; score believed destroyed in warehouse fire, Berlin, c.1918.*

POÈME DES BRUMES *Piece for orchestra(?). Period 1904–5. Varèse played this work in his Paris studio to the journalist who afterwards published an article on the composer in the* Courrier de Bayonne *of 21 September 1905. Unpublished; score believed destroyed in warehouse fire, Berlin, c.1918.*

TROIS PIÈCES *For orchestra. c.1905. Unpublished; score believed destroyed in warehouse fire, Berlin, c.1918.*

Though sometimes quoted as a separate composition, it is entirely conceivable that this was merely a collective title for three individual works elsewhere represented in this list: most likely the three just described – *Colloque au bord de la fontaine, Dans le parc* and *Poème des Brumes*. It may be significant that these three titles do not appear in the list of his early works which Varèse gave to Louise (*LGD*, p.100) – whereas the title *Trois Pièces* does.

PRÉLUDE À LA FIN D'UN JOUR *Symphonic poem for orchestra, conceived as a prologue to the poem* La fin d'un jour *from the collection* La Lumière natale *by Léon Deubel. c.1905. Unpublished; the score, entrusted to Léon Deubel, was lost after his suicide in 1913, though said to have been conveyed through the intermediary of the painter Émile Bernard to the novelist Élémir Bourges.*[5]

In a letter frequently quoted, but undated and from an unidentified source, Deubel wrote of Varèse to Émile Bernard: 'He is at the Conservatoire, working in the composition class towards the Prix de Rome ... His works are already remarkable and you would certainly like them. At the moment he is just finishing a *Prélude à la fin d'un jour* for an orchestra of 120 musicians, which is colossal'.[6] The reference to the Prix de Rome puts the letter no later than early 1906.

SOUVENIR *Song for voice and orchestra (?), to a sonnet by Léon Deubel. c.1905. Unpublished; score believed destroyed in warehouse fire, Berlin, c.1918.*

Mentioned by Varèse in his recollections of Deubel; see note to '*Proses rhythmées*'.

---

[5] Élémir Bourges (1852–1925), whose heroic conception of Man and whose enthusiasm for the music of Beethoven, Berlioz and Wagner infuses his ambitious novels, was a perhaps appropriate recipient for Varèse's score, though there is no explanation of why Bernard should have given it to him. It is not known if Bourges knew the composer personally. By the time of Deubel's death he was engrossed in writing *La Nef*, a vast prose-poem on the Prometheus myth.

[6] Most of the information in this entry derives from Fernand Ouellette, *Edgard Varèse, a musical biography* (London: Calder & Boyars, 1968), p.19. Hereinafter cited as 'Ouellette', this is an English translation by Derek Coltman of the original French edition (Paris: Editions Seghers, 1966). Ouellette (p.224, n.18) believes, without having been able to examine the source, that Deubel's letter may have been part of a correspondence with Bernard published in the magazine *Franche-Comté et Monts-Jura* in September 1930.

LE FILS DES ETOILES *Projected opera, after the mystical drama by Sâr Péladan. Period 1906–7.*

Mentioned in the letter of Léon Deubel quoted under *Prélude à la fin d'un jour.* It is unknown to what extent (if any) this opera was composed; it does not figure in the list of titles given to Louise Varèse.

By the time Varèse came to know him, the flamboyant esotericist Joséphin (Sâr) Péladan had been one of the most visible figures in Parisian occult and aesthetic circles for the best part of two decades, best known as the leader of a neo-Rosicrucian movement dedicated to the spiritualization of the arts, the Rose+Croix. His drama *Le Fils des Étoiles*, which he described as a 'Pastorale Kaldéene en 3 Actes', was written in 1891. It was performed the following year (in a programme shared with the *Missa Papae Marcelli* of Palestrina!) at a 'Soirée de la Rose+Croix', with an accompanying score by Erik Satie – that composer's longest work, and itself a document of considerable prophetic importance for 20th-century musicians. Péladan's text, undoubtedly influenced by his worship of Wagner, mingles *fin-de-siècle* decadence with esoteric symbolism. The story, set in the Sumero-Akkadian civilization around 3000 BC, centres on the androgynous poet-shepherd Oelohil, the true 'son of the stars', who like Tannhäuser is torn between spiritual and profane love. He strives to gain the love of lzel, daughter of Goudea, the high priest of Chaldea. During Oelohil's initiation into the mysteries of the Chaldean priesthood he resists various fleshly temptations, and thus achieves purity, lzel, and the powers of a magus.

'PROSES RHYTHMÉES' *For voice and orchestra (?) to specially-written texts by Leon Deubel. c.1905. Unpublished; score believed destroyed in warehouse fire, Berlin, c.1918.*

Varèse himself mentioned these pieces in his tribute to Deubel transcribed by Guillaume Apollinaire for his column *La Vie anecdotique* in the *Mercure de France* of 1 December 1913: 'I set several of his things to music: a sonnet called *Souvenir*, two rhythmic prose pieces, written expressly for me, and which I do not think have been published in any review . . . .'[7] These *Proses rhythmées* may be considered, for our purposes, as forming along with *Souvenir* and

---

[7] *LGD*, p.37; the French text may be found in Odile Vivier, *Varèse* (Paris: Editions Solfèges, 1966), p.16. Hereinafter cited as 'Vivier'.

Prélude à la fin d'un jour a trilogy of works inspired by Léon Deubel. Although no further evidence as to their musical content survives, and though nothing that might correspond to the *Proses rhythmées* appears in Deubel's posthumously published collected works, the other two Deubel texts are in existence, and will require some discussion later (see below, p.33) in relation to Varèse's developing aesthetic.

UN GRAND SOMMEIL NOIR *Song for voice and piano, on a poem by Paul Verlaine. Period 1903–6. Dedication: 'à Léon-Claude Mercerot'. Date of first performance: unknown. First British performance: 26 January 1976, Royal Academy of Music, London, Sara Mousley (sop), Philip Lee (pno). Sara Mousley replaced Linda Rands, advertised as the singer in the programme, at short notice. Autograph lost. Published 1906 by Editions B. Roudanez, Paris;*[8] *reprinted (facsimile of original edition) in 1976 by Editions Salabert, Paris.*

This song was not included in the list of titles Varèse gave to Louise – a fact which casts grave doubt on the list's completeness and raises the possibility that there may have been other works of whose very existence we remain ignorant. As far as is known, he virtually never mentioned the song – even though apparently his first published work. A copy of the printed edition was discovered after Varèse's death by Larry Stempel; its authenticity was confirmed by Varèse's friend and pupil André Jolivet.

(On the Salabert facsimile the composer's name appears in the form 'Edgard-Varèse', which he apparently affected occasionally in his youth. The dedicatee 'Léon-Claude Mercerot' is otherwise unknown. Possibly the last name could be a misspelling of 'Mercereau' – which would indicate a relative of Varèse's writer-friend Alexander Mercereau, a member of the Abbaye de Créteil. For discussion of this work, see below, p.26.)

RHAPSODIE ROMANE *For orchestra. About 1905. Varèse played a solo piano version of this work in his Paris studio at the offices of* Rénovation esthetique, *probably on several occasions and to various audiences, but certainly to Sâr Péladan and to the journalist who afterwards published*

---

[8] Not, therefore, Editions Maurice Senart as stated by Larry Stempel in his pioneering article on this song, 'Not Even Varèse Can Be an Orphan', in *Musical Quarterly* 60/1 (1974), pp.46–60; hereinafter cited as 'Stempel (1974)'.

an article on the composer in the Courrier de Bayonne *of 21 September 1905. Unpublished; score believed destroyed in warehouse fire, Berlin, c.1918.*

Péladan described this work as 'a profane Gregorian chant'. The Bayonnais journalist, referring to 'the medieval spirit of the works of this young artist', found that the *Rhapsodie romane* evoked for him 'Solemn convent bells, shimmering autumnal twilights, ascetic souls in prayer ...' Late in life, Varèse was unusually forthcoming to Gunther Schuller about the imaginative inspiration for this composition:

As a child, I was tremendously impressed by the qualities and character of the granite I found in Burgundy, where I often visited my grandfather. There were two kinds of granite there, one grey, the other streaked with pink and yellow. Then there was the old Romanesque architecture in that part of France: I used to play in one of the oldest French churches – in Tournus – one that was started in the sixth century and built in purest Romanesque style. And I used to watch the old stone cutters, marvelling at the precision with which they worked. They didn't use cement, and every stone had to fit and balance with every other. So I was always in touch with things of stone and with this kind of pure structural architecture – without frills or unnecessary decoration. All this became an integral part of my thinking at a very early stage ... when I composed *Rapsodie romane* I was thinking of Romanesque architecture, not Rome! I wanted to find a way to project in music the concept of calculated or controlled gravitation, how one element pushing against another stabilizes the total structure, thus using the material elements at the same time in opposition to and in support of one another.[9]

The church Varèse refers to is the abbey church of Saint-Philibert in Tournus, Burgundy, which made an indelible impression on him as a child.

In connexion with this work it is surely not out of place to recall the Tenth Organ Symphony of his teacher Widor, the *Symphonie romane*. Widely esteemed at the time as Widor's masterpiece, this had been published as recently as 1900, and was intended to reflect in music the architecture of the Romanesque church of St-Sernin at Toulouse. The *Symphonie* is based on a number of Gregorian chants, principally the Easter Day plainchant *Haec dies*: which Widor introduces, daringly for his time, in free rhythm and which exercises its influence in the work's

---

[9] Schuller (1965), p.34

unusually slow rate of harmonic change, leading to passages of virtual stasis. Widor is generally considered a highly conservative composer, and Varèse never seems to have mentioned any direct influence from his music. Yet he freely admitted to his affection and admiration for Widor – alone among his teachers – both as man and musician, and he surely took note of the *Symphonie romane*. (The generic form *Rhapsodie romane* is something of an anomaly among Varèse's titles: maybe even a deliberate allusion.) If nothing else we may wonder whether its 'chant-like' aspect – which apparently was also a component of *Bourgogne*, another work partly inspired by church architecture – may have owed something to Widor's example.

On the other hand Varèse talked to Schuller in the altogether more modern terminology of 'projection' of 'calculated or controlled gravitation'. If he really did conceive his aesthetic aim in these terms at such an early period – his language anticipates by several years the similar terminology of Rodin's *Les Cathédrales de France* (pub. 1914) – this was certainly a novel and original idea of 'architecture in music'. (There is no reason, of course, to presume that the resemblance to Rodin's thought is entirely coincidental, since Varèse had been a member of the sculptor's household at Meudon in early 1905.) In the same interview Varèse also let fall general observations on his early works which may well have applied with particular force to *Rhapsodie romane*. Noting that his later music showed an increased interest in internal rhythmic and metrical relationships, he remarked that the early works were 'more architectonic':

I was working with blocks of sound; calculated and balanced against each other. I was preoccupied with volume in an architectural sense; and with projection. ... I think I would characterize my early music as granitic![10]

(LA) CHANSON DES JEUNES HOMMES *For orchestra (?). Period 1905–7. Unpublished; score believed destroyed in warehouse fire, Berlin, c. 1918.*

Vivier (p.16) says only that this work was 'sketched' during the period of Varèse's involvement with the various Deubel-inspired compositions. Its presence on the list of titles he gave Louise argues for its completion.

---

[10] Ibid.

LE DÉLIRE DE CLYTEMNESTRE *'Tragèdie symphonique' for voices and orchestra. Text by Ricciotto Canudo. 1907. Unpublished; lost (probably destroyed in warehouse fire, Berlin, c.1918)*

This work does not figure on the list of titles that Varèse gave Louise, and its existence seems only to have been properly documented by Ouellette in the revised and expanded version of his Varèse biography which appeared in 1989.[11]

The Italian poet and critic Canudo (1879–1923), a thoroughgoing esotericist, settled in France in 1902 after being initiated into the mysteries of Theosophy in Florence. He was a member of the experimental artistic commune of L'Abbaye de Créteil, an exponent of the musico-mystic aesthetic of Orphism, and founder of a religion whose creed included the worship of Beethoven. He wrote the text of *Le délire de Clytemnestre* specifically for Varèse, presumably as an opera libretto, but the result was a *'tragédie symphonique'* (Varèse's term). On the other hand, given Canudo's passionate admiration of Beethoven's Choral Symphony, the 'symphonic' aspect may already have been anticipated in his text. According to a letter of Canudo's, the work was completed and constituted 'a new realization of musical drama, a kind of highly flexible synthesis of lyric drama and the new aesthetic necessities revealed by the *musique de scène* of a modern drama'.[12]

To judge by the title, the action was a modern updating of Greek tragedy, presumably the *Eumenides* of Aeschylus in particular; thus the work may well be considered a forerunner of Varèse's principal effort in modernized Greek tragedy, *Oedipus und die Sphinx*.

BOURGOGNE *Symphonic poem for large orchestra. 1908. Dedicated to 'Mon grandpère, Claude Cortot'. First performed 15 December 1910, Berlin, Blüthner Orchestra c. Josef Stransky. Score destroyed by Varèse*

---

[11] *Edgard Varèse. Edition revue et augmenteé par l'auteur precedeé de 'Varèse, l'exception' et suivi d'une bibliographie et discographie entièrement remise à jour par Louis Hirbour* (Paris, 1989). Hereinafter cited as Ouellette (1989).

[12] Ouellette (1989), p.40. See pp.37 below for further remarks on Canudo. Varèse visited the Abbaye de Créteil and was friendly with most of its fraternity. For Varèse and the Orphists see Bernard, pp.14–16 – with no mention of Canudo but an example of 'Orphic' poetry for performance by 18 voices by Varèse's friend Henri Barzun. The texts which we know Varèse actually set at this period – by Verlaine and Deubel – were considerably more conventional.

c.1961 ('about a year ago' according to Louise Varèse in a letter to Odile Vivier dated 10 December 1962).

As its title implies, *Bourgogne* was inspired by the landscape of Burgundy – and probably to some extent by its church architecture, like *Rhapsodie romane*. Both these works may possibly be regarded as contributions to a contemporary assertion of 'Burgundian' cultural identity in music, harking back to the glories of the Burgundian school of Renaissance choral writing. The chief exponents of this movement were the critic Émile Vuillermoz and the composer, musicologist and pedagogue Maurice Emmanuel, a generation older than Varèse and destined to be the teacher of Olivier Messiaen. Emmanuel, who had started his career in the cathedrals of Beaune and Dijon, composed his *Sonatine bourgoignonne* on Burgundian folksongs and dances as early as 1893, and at the time Varèse composed *Bourgogne* he was working on his *Trente chansons bourguignonnes du pays de Beaune*, the collection of folksong settings which awoke Messiaen to the potential of modal composition.

For a variety of reasons, but principally because it received a prestigious and much-noticed public performance, we know more about *Bourgogne* than any other of Varèse's missing early works. The score was also examined by a number of discerning writers. Romain Rolland, to whom Varèse showed it in search of an honest opinion, responded by letter on 19 January 1909 with a number of interesting (and tantalizing) observations (quoted here in Louise Varèse's translation, *LGD* p.58):

I do not like to judge an orchestral work without first hearing it played; I believe an audition is necessary even for the most prolific readers. ... [Nevertheless] you seem to me to be remarkably gifted for the orchestra; and your orchestral matter seems light, supple, alive and full. The composition in general remains valid from beginning to end; and it is very limpid and clear. In spite of the influence of Strauss in the general movement (not to mention a few Debussy traits in the beginning) it seems to me very French in feeling and nearer to d'Indy than Strauss. That is probably due to its calm and religious nature, but also to its clarity, with that figure of triplets, so characteristic, alternating with the *phrase carrée*. The development seems to me to be more in the orchestra, in the colour, than in the conception or the spirit; and passion is always a little in the background, or to one side, as though exterior to the subject. It is true that your subject is really BURGUNDY and not yourself ...

Rolland also mentioned the work in a letter he wrote to a friend on 24 January 1910 (*ibid.*, p.60), saying that it

Seemed to me interesting, and remarkably written, in particular from the point of view of orchestral colour.

It is of course difficult to extract much from these prevailingly generalized comments. (Varèse might not have been flattered by the comparison with d'Indy.) In drawing a distinction between 'the beginning' and 'the general movement', Rolland perhaps hints that *Bourgogne* was a binary structure with a clearly defined preludial section. His remark about the alternation of triplets with a '*phrase carrée*', which I take to be something foursquare, in common time, is at least suggestive of a certain kind of chant-like metrical scheme. But even this may read too much into his words.

Later Karl Muck, recommending Varèse for a grant from the Paul Kusynski Foundation, spoke of 'a symphonic poem' (presumably *Bourgogne*) 'which shows a rich and personal inventiveness, a vivid imagination and a complete mastery of his technical means' (*ibid.*, pp.86–7). Richard Strauss, of course, was sufficiently impressed to be instrumental in persuading Stransky to mount the Berlin première. The work's reception in concert was something of a *scandale*, without much *succès* attached. The 'calm and religious nature' Rolland discerned in the score was not apparent to the critics Willy Renz and Bruno Schräder. Reviewing the concert in *Die Musik*, Renz found Varèse's work 'an almost monstrous impressionistic splotch of colours', while Schräder called it 'an infernal din, mere caterwauling'. But Alfred Kerr – significantly, a *literary* rather than a music critic, though a very influential one – found it 'full of beautiful things'.

In the audience was the pianist Eduard Steuermann, then a pupil of Busoni and soon to become a disciple of Arnold Schoenberg. Half a century later, in conversation with Gunther Schuller, Steuermann recalled one passage of *Bourgogne* that still lingered in his memory,

... for terrifically divisi strings – I don't know how many individual parts – that made a tremendous forest of string sound.[13]

---

[13] Gunther Schuller, 'Conversation with Steuermann', *Perspectives of New Music* 3/1 (1964); reprinted in Boretz and Cone (ed.), *Perspectives on American Composers* (New York: Norton, 1971). Cited from p.210 of the latter edition.

When Schuller relayed this observation to Varèse the composer volunteered:

I was trying to approximate the kind of inner, microcosmic life you find in certain chemical solutions, or through the filtering of light. I used these strings unthematically as the background behind a great deal of brass and percussion.[14]

It has recently been suggested[15] that Varèse had in mind the phenomenon known as 'Brownian Motion', the random continuous motion of plant spores when suspended in a fluid medium, discovered by the botanist Robert Brown in 1827. Around the turn of the century Einstein and others had proved that this was caused in turn by the movement of the molecules of the fluid.

Ouellette quotes H.H.Stuckenschmidt as stating in his book *Modern Music*[16] that 'Edgard Varèse has, for example, been able to point out that as early as 1910 he had introduced combinations of sevenths and ninths into his compositions which established a sort of counterpoise between the twelve semitones'. Ouellette and others have linked this observation to the harmonic language of *Bourgogne*, but it perhaps applied more directly to some of the scores which came after. In any case it should be referred to Busoni's proclamation of the theoretical equality of the twelve semitones in his *New Aesthetic*, published in 1907 (see p. 67).

GARGANTUA *Symphonic poem for orchestra. 1909?. Not completed. Unpublished; score believed destroyed in warehouse fire, Berlin, c.1918.*

When Varèse took the score of *Bourgogne* to Romain Rolland in January 1909, he was already speaking of his next project – a symphonic poem after Rabelais's teeming and coprophagous satire *Gargantua* – and may indeed have begun composing it. The subject itself would seem to require a colourful programmatic treatment with much orchestral narrative and anecdotage, so we are perhaps justified in regarding this work as Varèse's nearest approach to Richard Strauss's tone poems. In his letter of 19 January quoted above, Rolland urged

---

[14] Schuller (1965), pp.33–4.

[15] John D. Anderson, 'Varèse and the Lyricism of the New Physics', *Musical Quarterly* Volume 75, Number 1 (Spring 1991), p.38.

[16] Ouellette's source is *Musique nouvelle*, a French translation (Paris: Correa Buchet-Chastel, 1956), p.107.

Varèse: 'Don't describe, *be* Gargantua' and three days later he wrote that it seemed 'an ideal subject, alive and popular (in the sense of an entire people)'. Rolland was especially enamoured of this project because the hero of his famous composer-novel *Jean-Christophe*, on which he was working at exactly this time, had also begun composing a *Gargantua*. From Varèse's correspondence with Hofmannsthal we know that he was devoting his principal creative energies to this symphonic poem in the latter half of 1909 – but according to the list of titles he gave Louise, it was never finished.

Ouellette (p.30) records the strange detail that Yvette Guilbert's husband, M. Schiller, tried to persuade Varèse to turn the piece into a double-bass concerto for Serge Koussevitsky, better known at that period as a virtuoso of the instrument than as a conductor. It is perhaps not over-bold to remark that, in order to be suitable for, or to have suggested, such an adaptation, this symphonic poem must have featured a fair amount of clearly-defined melodic writing. One is tempted to speculate further that it may already have included a prominent part for the double-bass, which could have impersonated the giant Gargantua in the same way that the cello takes the character of Don Quixote, and the viola that of Sancho Panza, in Richard Strauss's *Don Quixote*.

(WORKS FOR PERCUSSION, WITH OR WITHOUT VOICES?)
Speaking to Gunther Schuller (op.cit., p.35) about his much later percussion piece *Ionisation* Varèse remarked, almost by the way.

But this was not my first percussion piece. I had already done some in Berlin and Paris, especially in connection with the choruses I conducted in Berlin. These works used special percussion instruments that I had collected myself, which the singers often played themselves.

The terms 'some', 'especially' and 'often' provide no indication of how many pieces in total we are dealing with. I have found no other reference to these early percussion pieces: they seem not to figure in the list of lost early works that Varèse gave to Louise. It would seem that the majority of them involved voices, and it is remotely possible that, for instance, the piece called *Chanson des jeunes hommes* was one of them. They should probably be fitted into the period stretching from 1906, when he founded the Choeur de l'Université Populaire, to early 1911, when he resigned from the conductorship of the Symphonischer

Chor. It is possible that some pieces were composed for the productions at the Deutsches Theater in which the latter choir took part; even – though this is mere speculation – that Varèse's proposed musical contribution to the projected Cocteau production of *Un Songe d'une Nuit d'été* (see below, p.24) would have been related to a percussion piece he might have written for Max Reinhardt's 1909 *Midsummer Night's Dream* production.

OEDIPUS UND DIE SPHINX *Opera in 3 acts. Libretto adapted by Varèse and Hugo von Hofmannsthal from Hofmannsthal's drama of the same title (pub. 1906). Composed 1909–14. Not completed? Unpublished; score of Acts 1 and 2 believed destroyed in warehouse fire, Berlin, c.1918. Score (or draft) of Act 3 untraced – last heard of shortly before the outbreak of World War I, when Varèse sent it to a Dr. Merton in Switzerland.*

Hofmannsthal's voluble poetic treatment of the myth of Oedipus stresses the unconscious motivations of the main figures, especially Oedipus and Jokaste. In Act 1, cursed by the gods and fleeing from his supposed parents in Corinth, Oedipus encounters his real father Laios, King of Thebes, on the road and kills him in a rage. After the deed he experiences a terrific feeling of liberation. Act 2 finds Kreon, brother of Laios's widow Jokaste, trying to engineer his own acclamation as the new King, but Jokaste takes an oath to marry and crown whoever can deliver the city from the curse of the Sphinx. Oedipus arrives and takes up the challenge. The people acclaim him as their deliverer and Kreon offers to lead him to the Sphinx's mountain lair, hoping the monster will devour this foreign rival. In the manner of Greek tragedy, the confrontation with the Sphinx occurs offstage. In the final act Kreon is preparing to murder Oedipus on the mountainside should he give up the attempt, but is amazed to hear the dying scream of the Sphinx. Realizing Oedipus has been victorious, he acclaims him as a godlike conqueror. Oedipus, however, is devastated by the fact that the Sphinx greeted him by name: it means he is still being hunted by the gods. Jokaste nevertheless accepts him as husband and King; there is a strong suggestion that she realizes, subconsciously, that she is marrying her son.

Written between July 1903 and December 1905, *Oedipus und die Sphinx* was closely associated with Hofmannsthal's virtually contemporary translation of Sophocles's *King Oedipus*, and indeed partly intended as a prologue to it. Moreover, it followed immediately upon the completion of Hofmannsthal's most famous reworking of an ancient Greek dramatic subject, *Elektra* (1903) – most famous because it was no sooner staged by Max Reinhardt than seized upon by Richard Strauss as the libretto of his fourth and, perhaps, greatest opera, completed in September 1908. Though Strauss's first opera to a Hofmannsthal text, *Elektra* was not a collaboration between composer and librettist in the way that *Der Rosenkavalier* and subsequent stage works became. Strauss set Hofmannsthal's existing stage play largely as it stood, with only a few textual changes from the playwright.

The parallels and temporal conjunctions with Varèse's lost opera are remarkable. Though *Oedipus und die Sphinx* was first staged on 2 February 1906 at the Deutsches Theater, Berlin, produced by Max Reinhardt, it was Reinhardt's 1908 production which Varèse saw and which convinced him the play was the ideal basis for an opera. (In fact, Hofmannsthal's drama seems to have been conceived with the possibility of an operatic treatment in mind; certainly his notes on production specify the tempo of certain scenes and the quality of voices in a very 'operatic' manner.) It seems likely that Varèse, already a firm admirer of Strauss, was aware of the existence of *Elektra*, although that opera was as yet unperformed and he had not yet made Strauss's personal acquaintance. In his resolve to create an opera from Hofmannsthal's very next drama in classical form Varèse may consciously have been pursuing a 'Straussian' path – as he may also have been with the symphonic poem *Gargantua*.

Varèse approached Hofmannsthal for permission, readily granted, to turn *Oedipus* into an opera (despite Romain Rolland's grave doubts about the suitability of the play, which he considered 'very dreary and erudite' and 'overrefined'). Varèse visited Hofmannsthal at his home in Rodaun near Vienna in May 1909. A close friendship sprang up between composer and playwright; Hofmannsthal began cutting and editing the play as a libretto, but this seems largely to have been confined to the first act; in September he turned over the later stages of this task almost entirely to Varèse, writing on 12 September:

... frankly I believe that it would be better if you were to do the whole thing yourself. I think you should so penetrate the work that you will finally know what use to make (or not to make) of Kreon, better than I would myself – and understand the *Motiv* and *Gegenmotiv*.[17]

---

[17] *LGD*, p.83.

Varèse carried out his injunction, and eventually submitted the results for Hofmannsthal's approval, which was forthcoming (unfortunately, on an undated postcard):

It is excellent, especially your suppressing everything from page 170. I am very *pleased* with the way you have penetrated the drama.[18]

It should be remembered that this opera, the largest and most ambitious of Varèse's early works, constituted his principal creative effort throughout the five years 1909–14. Its importance requires a separate discussion, for which see p.63.

MEHR LICHT *For orchestra. 1911. Unpublished, perhaps unfinished; score believed destroyed in warehouse fire, Berlin, c. 1918.*

Varèse told Gunther Schuller this was based 'on a Goethe poem ... At that time Goethe was very important to my thinking, as was Hoéné Wronsky [*sic*] ... who was also a physicist and philosopher'.[19] There is, however, no Goethe poem with this title. '*Mehr Licht!*' (More light!) was the version of the dying Goethe's last words popularly disseminated in Romanticized accounts of his life.[20]

Ouellette (p.37) states that Varèse accorded the phrase a different significance, 'as though it were a question of filtering the raw material of sound in order to make it more luminous'. (Compare Varèse's comment to Schuller that in *Bourgogne* he was concerned with the 'inner, microcosmic life you find ... through the filtering of light'.) Ouellette also avers that *Mehr Licht* 'progressed no further than the sketch stage at this time, though later on, in 1912, it became *Les Cycles du Nord*, a work inspired by the wonder of the Aurora Borealis'. Whatever the relationship between these two works, the fact that they were noted separately in the list of titles which Varèse gave to Louise[21]

---

[18] Ibid, p.84. Louise adds that Varèse retained two copies of the original 1906 Fischer printing of the play. One contains cuts and changes to Act I in Hofmannsthal's handwriting; the other, which was Varèse's working copy, is marked up by Varèse throughout, apart from a few pencilled suggestions by Hofmannsthal.

[19] Schuller (1965), pp.32–33.

[20] And even fairly judicious ones such as G.H. Lewes's *The Life and Works of Goethe* (1855). Though not exactly apocryphal, the appeal loses something of its agonized prophetic quality when set alongside the most trustworthy record. The actual words were 'Open the second shutter, so that more light can come in'.

[21] They also appear separately, as late as 1947, in the list of works published in *Possibilities I* (see Chapter 9, n.25).

suggests that *Mehr Licht* may in fact have passed beyond the sketch stage, and perhaps existed as a completed score.

LES CYCLES DU NORD *For orchestra. 1912–3. Dedicated to Hugo von Hofmannsthal. (Perhaps a recomposition of Mehr Licht, above – see the notes on that work.) Score probably lost in post in transit to Béla Bartók, a few days before the outbreak of World War I* (LGD, p. 102).

This must be the 'symphonic poem which promises well' that Varèse said he was finishing in a letter to Hofmannsthal in late 1912, and which on 25 February 1913 he asked the poet's permission to dedicate to him. Ouellette's comment about the inspiration Varèse received from the Aurora Borealis, quoted above, makes certain the identification of this work (rather than *Mehr Licht*) as the one whose inspiration Varèse described to Louise in the following terms (*LGD*, pp. 100–101):

He told me that once watching a display of the aurora borealis he felt an 'unbelievable exaltation – an indescribable sensation' and that as he watched those 'pulsating incandescent streamers of light' he 'not only saw but *heard* them'. As soon as he returned home he wrote down the sounds that had accompanied the movements of the light.

Varèse, in his memoir of Busoni (see *LGD*, p. 49), recalled showing this, his 'latest score' – if it was not part of *Oedipus und die Sphinx* – to Busoni, whom he had known by that time 'for three years or more'. Busoni suggested various modifications which Varèse adamantly refused to accept; the difference of opinion in fact marked a new closeness in their friendship, since Busoni thenceforth treated Varèse as an equal.

UN SONGE D'UNE NUIT D'ÉTÉ *Music (probably only projected) for circus orchestra, for a production by Jean Cocteau of Shakespeare's* A Midsummer Night's Dream. *1915.*

Cocteau, with the impresario-director Gabriel Astruc, envisaged this as a collaborative project, involving the Cubist painters Albert Gleizes and Albert Lhote (possibly Picasso as well), and five composers including Varèse and Erik Satie. The production of Shakespeare's play, 'literally translated' by Cocteau (more likely adapted from an existing French translation, given his inadequate English) with extensive cuts, was to have been staged at the Cirque Medrano, Montmartre, featuring real circus clowns. Preparations were under way from March 1915: to some extent Cocteau's idea was an anti-German riposte to Max Reinhardt's announcement earlier in the year of his intention to revive his famous Berlin production of 1910 with Mendelssohn's music. (The chorus-director then had been Varèse.) New music, to be performed by the circus orchestra under Varèse's direction, was requested from Satie, Florent Schmitt, Ravel, Stravinsky and Varèse himself: it seems Varèse had overall musical responsibility and assigned the various sections to their composers, intending the result to be a 'pot-pourri de musiques françaises'.

The only concrete result was Satie's suite for small orchestra *Cinq Grimaces pour une songe d'une nuit d'été*, whose draft is dated 2 April 1915; this was subsequently orchestrated on the basis of a piano reduction made by Darius Milhaud.[22] The other composers were required to write one piece each; in an unpublished interview with Gilbert Chase, recorded in 1961, Varèse recalled that these four pieces were to be interpolated between Satie's five movements, his own coming last, before Satie's final 'Pour sortir'.[23] Apparently none of these other pieces was written. The production never materialized, and was definitively abandoned in November 1915, shortly before Varèse left France for the USA. Cocteau's 'translation' has never been found. It was in connexion with this project that Cocteau was introduced to Picasso – by Varèse, who had known the painter since his student days. The meeting led indirectly to the famous Cocteau-Picasso-Satie collaboration of 1917, the ballet *Parade*.

---

[22] We should note Louise Varèse's statement (*LGD*, p.117) that the *Cinq Grimaces* was partly orchestrated for Satie by Varèse. There appears to be no evidence for this in the surviving manuscript materials listed by Robert Orledge in *Satie the Composer* (Cambridge University Press, 1990), p.310. In fact Satie's final movement remained unfinished, and was completed by Milhaud in 1925. Satie apparently knew of Varèse's claim to have assisted in the orchestration, and resented it. On 6 February 1916, replying to Varèse's request for a score of the *Cinq Grimaces* to perform in New York, Satie sent instead his own fastidious orchestration of a piano piece by his totally unknown pupil, the perfume manufacturer Albert Verley (Orledge, op. cit., pp.122–4 and 350–1 n.29).

[23] Cited by Olivia Mattis, 'Theater as Circus: "A Midsummer Night's Dream" ', *Library Chronicle of the University of Texas at Austin*, 23/4 (1993), p.59. On Satie's role in the project see now Steven Moore Whiting, *Satie the Bohemian: From Cabaret to Concert Hall* (Oxford: Clarendon Press, 1999), pp.462–66.

As we have seen, the sole survivor of this impressively fertile early epoch of Varèse's creativity is the song *Un grand sommeil noir*, published in 1906 by Editions Roudanez and presumably written in or shortly before that year. Composed merely for voice and piano (though it would be possible to imagine an orchestral version – indeed, the piano part occasionally resembles a piano reduction from an orchestral original),[24] it seems to have been forgotten by its creator – perhaps deliberately – and is clearly untypical of his works of the period, both in its limited forces and its small dimensions (33 bars, occupying three pages in Salabert's rather blotchy reprint of the original printed edition). Yet unless some fantastic chance has spared *Les cycles du nord* or the last act of *Oedipus und die Sphinx*, so that they emerge at a future date from some obscure corner of Europe, this little song constitutes our only concrete evidence about the formative period of Varèse's musical language.

Un grand sommeil noir has been discussed very thoroughly by Larry Stempel, who first called attention to its existence and significance.[25] He notes, first, apropos the choice of text, the fact that Verlaine was the poet most often set by Debussy: and that this famous poem from *Sagesse* (which Debussy did not set) 'reveals a surreal trope that haunted the composer throughout his career'.

Un grand sommeil noir	*A great black sleep*
Tombe sur ma vie:	*Falls upon my life:*
Dormez, tout espoir,	*Sleep, all hope,*
Dormez, toute envie!	*All desire!*
Je ne sais plus rien,	*I no longer know anything,*
Je perds la mémoire	*I lose the memory*
Du mal et du bien ...	*Of good and evil ...*
O la triste histoire!	*Oh, melancholy story!*
Je suis un berceau	*I am a cradle*
Qu'une main balance	*Rocked*
Au creu d'un caveau:	*In the hollow of a vault:*
Silence, silence!	*Be silent, silent!*

---

[24] An orchestration of *Un grand sommeil noir* by Anthony Beaumont was performed in Amsterdam on 24 August 1998 by the Royal Concertgebouw Orchestra under Riccardo Chailly.

[25] Stempel (1974).

'... it is now clear', Stempel remarks,

that there is a netherworld of human consciousness (sleep, dark, night, etc.) pervading [Varèse's] work that stirs first with *Un grand sommeil noir*, moves his thinking from the sleeping Seine that opens *Offrandes* to the 'oscura noche' of Saint John of the Cross that closes the sketch to *Espace*, and expires only with *Nocturnal* and *Nuit*.[26]

Second, he compares Varèse's setting with the treatment accorded to this same poem by six other composers – three famous and three forgotten – over half a century: Ravel (1895), Gustave Sandre (1897), Raoul Laparra (1909), Stravinsky (1910), Dirk Foch (1921) and Honegger (1947). Noting that Verlaine's three-stanza form seems to demand the introduction of 'disparate elements' for the setting of its second stanza, he observes that only Sandre (in his *Trois Mélodies*, op. 56) and Stravinsky (in the first of his op.9 Verlaine Songs) do in fact provide the stanza with a differentiated musical character. Whereas the young Varèse, uniquely among these seven settings, not only introduces new musical elements for that stanza, but successfully integrates these elements with the return of the opening ones in his treatment of the third and last stanza: a small but accomplished compositional feat which suggests a closer and more imaginative 'reading' of the poem than any of its other composers gave it.

Most revealing of all is an examination of the music itself. Stempel approaches it via its motivic properties; I prefer to look in the first instance at its harmonic ones, but either approach will take us to the same goal, for we soon find that, even this early in Varèse's career, his music is working through the development and elaboration of a harmonic/motivic 'cell', and one not unfamiliar from his later music. Within the little song's restricted scope, he appears impressively aware of his orientation and his individual direction.

The preludial bars of *Un grand sommeil noir*, for piano alone (Ex.1), appear at first glance to present a straightforward (and typically Debussian) succession of chords of the bare fifth and octave, without a third in sight: an austere, hieratic invocation of darkness, moving in Impressionist *organum*. Then we look at the key-signature, and realize we are mistaken. In the key of E flat minor, C is flattened while F is

---

[26] Ibid, p.54. For the reference to 'the sketch to *Espace*' (Stempel means *Etude pour Espace*) see below, p.314.

not; conjunct movement upwards from the bare-fifth E♭/B♭ therefore produces, not a parallel fifth, but a flattened one – the tritone, *diabolus in musica*.

This opening explores with masterly economy the effect of that intrusive discord within such neo-mediaeval consonance, building it into increasingly wide-spread, cumulatively dissonant chords. The result is austere indeed, but it has a dark tang, an acidulous severity, that concisely evokes the element of nightmare in Verlaine's 'black sleep'. The vocal writing is austere also, strictly syllabic, half-chanting, in the manner of Debussy's contemporary songs.

With the end of the first verse a new element enters the music, equally stark and simple in its effectiveness – a rising arpeggio, '*mystérieux et lointain*', outlining in slow triplets the bare-fifth component, and later the minor third, of the key. The triplet rhythm paves the way for the two-against-three cross-rhythms of the accompaniment which Varèse establishes for the second stanza, the left hand insistently tolling two repeated triplet-crotchets with the syncope of a third triplet-crotchet rest, like the beating of a distant drum; or a heart (Ex.2).

From the end of this stanza the song moves directly to the last, with the direction '*pressez et animez*': Ex.1 returns in the piano, but poised now on the dominant of G flat rather than of E flat, and a beat earlier in the bar, transforming its tonal and rhythmic profile. The voice enters a full nine beats earlier than before, and the opening line 'Je suis un berceau' brings back the arpeggio-pattern that introduced the second stanza, assimilated now as a left-hand bass pattern beneath the first-stanza music. At 'au creux d'un caveau' the accompaniment reduces itself to a hollow, tolling B♭; then the Ex.1 music returns more explicitly, at its original pitch, while the voice intones 'Silence, silence' also on a low B♭. The final bars, for piano alone, grow organically out of the last bar of Ex.1; but, as Stempel has pointed out, the result so closely reproduces the end of Act IV of Debussy's *Pelléas et Mélisande* that it has the effect of a deliberate paraphrase (though in dynamic reverse): see Ex.3.

Even so, the effects which Varèse draws from Debussy's cadential formula are strikingly different: not fast and dramatic, but slow and suggestive of nocturnal despair, the dynamic climax occuring earlier and ebbing away to the borders of audibility, to that silence which the poet craves.

We can see, therefore, that Varèse's *Un grand sommeil noir*, modest though it is, takes one of the basic principles of Debussian impressionism – the harmonic sensation of parallel motion – and distils from it a new 20th-century austerity. Moreover, in a manner faintly parallel to that which Schoenberg was beginning to explore in Vienna, it finds means of projecting its harmony into the motivic sphere, initiating a process of organic development in both horizontal and vertical dimensions. The perfect fifth/tritone opposition of the chords in Ex.1 yields a motivic shape, outlined first by the middle voice of the left-hand chords – which stand out precisely because their movement does not parallel the upper and lower ones – and then by the uppermost voice of the right-hand chords. This is a melodic-harmonic cell (or 'matrix', to use Stempel's term) involving 'the minor second, the tritone, and the perfect fourth that is their difference, and/or its inversion, the perfect fifth that is their sum'[27]: see Ex.4. It is remarkable to find it here, however unremarkable it may appear in these post-Impressionist surroundings. This cell is destined – in quite different textures and spacings – to remain one of the most characteristic elements of the works of Varèse's maturity.

The cell itself has an ancestry: Stempel traces it, significantly enough, to a Verlaine setting by Debussy – the motto of *L'Ombre des arbres*, third of the older composer's *Ariettes oubliées* of 1888 – and he concludes, after an analysis of that work, that 'the harmonic vocabulary that will become explicit in the later work of Varèse is implicit not only in *Un grand sommeil noir* but also clearly foreshadowed in the Debussy chanson'.

Jonathan Bernard has suggested[28] that Larry Stempel attaches more significance to *Un grand sommeil noir* than it can reasonably be made to bear; but as we have seen, several interesting features emerge very clearly from a close examination of this song – as long as we treat any deductions from those features with due caution. At the very least, this sole surviving early work of Varèse, from his years in Paris, strongly suggests that his mature music grows out of an underlying stratum of Debussian Impressionism. It betrays no sign of d'Indy or his Conservatoire teachers (except perhaps in the terraced resonances of some of the superimposed chords, reminiscent of an organist like Widor). Rather it presents a composer who is steeped in the more radical musical language of the immediate Parisian past – Impressionism, and especially its foremost begetter and living

---

[27] Ibid, p.56

[28] Jonathan W. Bernard, *The Music of Edgard Varèse* (New Haven: Yale University Press, 1987), p.241. Hereinafter cited as 'Bernard'.

practitioner, Debussy – and who is beginning to isolate certain elements of the Impressionist vocabulary, within strict formal limitations that Debussy himself might have observed. The particular elements Varèse chose to isolate may have been suggested by, and merely tailored to, the dark, unquiet imagery of Verlaine's poem: but it cannot be without significance that they include a melodic/harmonic cell that recurs and becomes the basis of astonishing developments in his later work. Instinctively or no, Varèse was selecting elements that he felt personally drawn to.

Over and above this, *Un grand sommeil noir* is of course a 'minor' work; but it is gratifying to find that it is such an elegant performance. Varèse sets himself strict limits, but within them achieves all that might be asked of him: a powerful evocation of the mood of Verlaine's poem, a musical correlative gravid with expressive resonance. At 22 or 23, the composer 'Edgard-Varèse' already thoroughly knew his business.

2 · 'Further and beyond': aspects of Varèse's developing aesthetic

A l'heure qui est mienne en marche vers la nuit,
A la ville aux frontons de granit où s'inscrit,
Moribonde clarté, ton rayon lapidaire
Au dernier vol corbant son arc à l'horizon
A la flamme qui brûle aux vitres des maisons,
Salut! Je suis le Soir, vainqueur de la Lumiere!
LÉON DEUBEL
La Fin d'un Jour

Un grand sommeil noir, taken together with the exiguous evidence for Varèse's other early scores, seems to tell us a good deal about his pre-1914 music. We can never reconstruct the sounds, the scoring, the structural experiments and formal innovations which the orchestral and dramatic works might have revealed to us.[1] But we can make some intelligent guesses as to the kind of composer the young Varèse was; what he hoped to achieve; to which traditions he felt most aligned.

Yet in some ways *Un grand sommeil noir* is almost too perfect a foundation for our speculations. It prefigures the later composer so clearly that, had we wanted to extrapolate an example of his musical apprenticeship from what we know of his later works, it is almost exactly the kind of piece we might have hypothesized. The song's technical features and aesthetic standpoint undeniably point to Varèse's future style, and they are rooted in the best – or what our later 20th-

---

[1] The contemporary English composer Benedict Mason's homage to Varèse, an imaginative fantasy for two pianos entitled *Fragment of 'Bourgogne'*, is a generalized essay in ultra-late-Romantic harmonic afflatus, without reference to the descriptions of *Bourgogne* given by Rolland, Steuermann and Varèse (cf. pp.18–19).

century taste has come to regard as the best – near-contemporary models: Debussy for music, the haunted and powerfully concise Verlaine for text.

But another poem that Varèse set at this period survives, though unfortunately not the music he set it to. And it is more difficult to imagine these lines accommodated to the dissonant and impressively sculptural idiom of *Un grand sommeil noir*.

> *Garde mon souvenir comme un bouquet donné*
> *Un jour, par le chemin qui mène à mon village.*
> *Un bel adolescent viendra, comme un roi mage,*
> *Offrir la douce myrrhe à mon nouveau né.*
>
> *Un jour tu souriras à mon front coronné,*
> *Alourdi sous le poids des lauriers et de l'âge,*
> *Et ton coeur dédiera les plus chers paysages*
> *Au repos éternel de notre amour fané.*
>
> *Alors, à la lueur pensive de ta lampe,*
> *Mes vers te salueront en inclinat leurs hampes*
> *Comme des étentards levés dans le Passé.*
>
> *Tu fermeras les yeux. Et l'Amour et la Gloire,*
> *Pareils à deux flambeaux veillant à un trépassé*
> *Consacreront mon nom à ta chère mémoire.*

(Keep my memory like a nosegay of flowers
presented on the road to my village one day.
A handsome youth will come, like a wise man
With a gift of sweet myrrh for my newborn child.

One day, you will smile at my crowned brow
Bowed beneath the weight of laurels and old age,
And your heart will consign our fondest scenes
To the eternal rest of our faded love.

Then, in the contemplative glow of your lamp
My lines will salute you, by tilting their poles
Like standards raised in times gone by.

You will close your eyes. And Love and Glory,
Like two torches watching over one departed
Will consecrate my name to your beloved memory.)[2]

This is 'the sonnet called *Souvenir*' – its actual title is *Le Souvenir* –
which Varèse mentioned to Apollinaire in 1913 as one of the poems by
Léon Deubel for which he had supplied music. The preciousness of the
language and the element of fin-de-siècle decadence remind us that
Varèse emerged from a Parisian circle that remained heavily in thrall to
the spirit of the aesthetic and alchemical 1890s. Leading figures of that
previous decade – such as Sâr Péladan and Emile Bernard – were still
active forces. Of the French composers who embodied the spirit of that
time, Debussy and to a lesser extent Satie were vital figures for Varèse,
and we may see parallels too in the nature-mystic Koechlin and the
religious mystic Tournemire.

It is possible to persuade ourselves that Varèse merely set *Souvenir* as
a gesture of friendship to Deubel, but its prophecy of future
achievement and celebrity may well have appealed to him. He told
Apollinaire that Deubel was 'hungry for fame'. It was a hunger that
Varèse shared. The fact that his setting was apparently for voice and
orchestra suggests he found it worth expending real labour on it.
However, no mere debt of friendship could have called forth the
Prélude à la fin d'un jour, the substantial work for large orchestra
intended as a prologue to the long poem *La fin d'un jour*, which
Deubel published in his collection *La lumière natale*.

For its time and place this is a very curious piece of verse. A
consciously artificial production in Alexandrines, *La fin d'un jour* harks
back to the 18th or even 17th century both in metre and in its
evocation of the conventions of pastoral masque.[3] The poet engages in
dialogue with a gallery of characters and personifications – the Day, a
Faun, a Shepherd, a Small Hill, the Moon, the Hour, the Spring, and

---

[2] Léon Deubel, 'Le Souvenir' from *Poèsies* (1906). I am indebted to Robin Freeman
for locating and transcribing the text for me, and to Sue Rose for the English verse
translation given here. The phrase 'like a wise man' refers, obviously, to the Three Wise
Men (as we call them in English) who came from the East to present their gifts to the
newborn Christ. Deubel's 'comme un roi mage' evokes their conventional appellation
in French, *Les trois rois mages* – so a literal translation would be 'like a magician-king'.

[3] The full text occupies pp.148–156 of Deubel's posthumous *Poèmes*.

the Evening – during the course of the waning afternoon and the arrival of night. The atmosphere is one that might have been evoked by Poussin. The Varèse who responded to this mannered effusion in such apparently enthusiastic orchestral terms was surely no single-minded modernist.

Yet on a closer reading the poem contains elements which could well have stirred his imagination. For all its decorative formality it treats the coming of night as a cosmic event, and the landscape is an animate one, even if peopled by abstractions. The stars in the sky are '*fleuves d'argent*', the moon looks down from the '*balustres d'or des constellations*', the winds make music at the coming of Night '*qui préside à la Mort*'. The spirit of pantheism peoples the evening with Deubel's various speakers, even though their characterization is the flimsiest literary device. The Day expires with the hope of a '*demain radieux*' on its lips. There are copious references to music, most striking perhaps in these lines where the Spring speaks of:

> *Le maître qui m'apprit les claires sonatines*
> *Et l'innombrable lied qui plaît aux amoureux*
> *Est mort dans l'ombre errante aux desseins ténébres.*
> *Chochote, interrogeuse, ô ma voix clandestine!*
> *Arcane inviolé qu'on n'interprète pas ...*

Mere similarity of title has led commentators to expect that Varese's *Prélude à la fin d'un jour* in some way resembled Debussy's *Prélude à l'après-midi d'un faune*, though it should now be clear that Deubel's poem stands far removed from Mallarmé's. The evidence of *Un grand sommeil noir* allows us to speculate with some confidence that Varèse's score did exhibit some Debussian traits. But its overall conception must have been very different. Deubel may not have been inaccurate when he described it as 'colossal'. It seems highly unlikely that it evoked in intricate detail the imagery and various speakers in the poem. But the underlying event: the ineluctable passage of time, the fading of the radiant colours of a summer day through evening twilight to the coming of night, the rising of the moon and the stars, and the promise of a new tomorrow, seem likely to have furnished Varèse with a controlling musical image and form which he probably found highly congenial. Thus it is a fair possibility that *Prélude à la fin d'un jour* was the first of in a series of 'astronomical' works that continued in *Les cycles du nord* and eventually climaxed in *Arcana*.

Yet the 'dated' and somewhat decadent aspects of Deubel's verse apply a useful check on our natural tendency to see the young Varèse as simply an apprentice version of the radical modernist he became: a tendency, as I suggested above, perhaps too neatly validated by *Un grand sommeil noir*. We tend to forget that all the great modernist movements – Expressionism, Futurism, Cubism, Surrealism, Dada – grew, sometimes in violent reaction, sometimes in more or less logical development, out of what immediately preceded them: Symbolism, Impressionism, Fauvism, Decadence, Art Nouveau, the whole rich aesthetic-alchemical amniotic soup of the 1890s. These earlier movements in fact overlapped, in their latter stages, with the new; and many of their leading figures were still active and available – above all in Paris in the first decade of the 20th century. It would therefore be a severe mistake to begin any consideration of Varèse's aesthetic by comparing him with the Cubists, who began to have significance for him a decade later. Just as Cubism was rooted in the abandonment of realistic perspective by such artists as Odilon Redon, Émile Bernard and the later Gauguin, so Varèse's revolutionary rethinking of musical syntax is unthinkable without Debussy's renunciation of traditional aspects of functional tonality.

Deubel's *La fin d'un jour* bears a dedication to, precisely, Émile Bernard: his friend and patron – and the recipient, we recall, of his letter about Varèse's *Prélude* quoted on p.11. Bernard (1868–1941) was founder and editor of *La Rénovation: Revue de l'art le meilleur*, which appeared from 1905 to 1909 and whose offices were Varèse's home during the early part of that period. Painter, theorist, aesthetician, 'Catholic writer', omnivorously interested in the arts, religion and philosophy, Bernard was a significant creative figure in his own right and had been active for nearly a quarter of a century before Varèse came into contact with his circle. Friend of Van Gogh and Redon, disciple – and, in his own opinion, instructor – of Gauguin, Bernard was seen in his own time as one of the leaders of the reaction against Impressionism, abandoning naturalism and concentrating on the essence (*la notion*) of a picture. His development of non-naturalistic forms and irrational perspective, in an important series of paintings done in Brittany, certainly gave new impetus to Gauguin's adoption of similar methods. In Bernard's own work it culminated in such powerful and still startling canvases as *Moisson au bord de la mer* (Harvest by the sea), of 1891, where he rejects all hint of the picturesque and creates a rhythmic pattern between the figures of the harvesters, the bales of corn, and the landscape in which they work. The people and the fruits of their harvest assume an architectural quality, as if the menhirs of a stone circle, in a symbiotic relationship with the land itself.

Shortly after he painted this work Bernard experienced a religious crisis and began his association with Sâr Péladan, exhibiting at his Salons de la Rose+Croix and exploring more esoteric aspects of art. In addition to his occult activities Péladan was a tireless promulgator of the cult of Ancient Greek and Italian Renaissance art, and by the time Varèse encountered Bernard the artist's own work had become much more classical in conception. Still, the pages (and the offices) of *La Rénovation* allowed practising artists and esoteric theorists to meet on common ground. Bernard combined both roles in his own person. While his journal was principally devoted to the visual and literary arts, the only composer accorded entry to the canon of 'spiritual' creators being the inevitable Wagner, Bernard himself was keenly interested in music. In 1909 he published an article, 'Théorie des correspondances' in another esoteric arts magazine, *Entretiens idéalistes*, speculating on the relationship of the tones of the musical scale to the spectrum of colours, and exploring the harmonic implications of their correspondence.[4] *La Rénovation* was sympathetic to contemporary developments, and Varèse's piano recitals of his own music were enthusiastically reviewed. Certainly, it was under Bernard's aegis that Varèse came into contact with such occultist illuminati as Péladan and Ricciotto Canudo – to name two who went so far as to provide him with libretti.

Canudo has been described as a Nietzschean, and his writings on music as poetic 'but in the worst sense'.[5] Nevertheless, there were clearly aspects of his thought and poetry that Varèse found congenial. A writer who, as early as 1911, could publish an article on the cinema as the birth of 'a new Muse, presiding over the Sixth Art ... the magnificent conciliation of the Rhythms of Space (the plastic arts) and

---

[4] Apart from agreeing that A is Green, Bernard's arrangement bears no relation to the famous 'colour keyboard' of Scriabin; both systems, in the end, are mere episodes in a long tradition of attempted equivalences between colour and tone.

[5] Joscelyn Godwin, *Music and the Occult: French Musical Philosophies*, 1750–1950 (University of Rochester Press, 1995), p.207.

the Rhythms of Time (music and poetry)' must have appealed to Varèse's sense of modernity.[6] Naturally, too, though at a far deeper musical level, Varèse shared the enthusiasm for Beethoven with which Canudo opposed the prevailing worship of Wagner. Canudo was developing the case for Beethoven's greatness, so forcibly and recently presented by Romain Rolland in his book about the composer published in 1903, in entirely esoteric and mystical directions, but these were directions Varèse may well have found fruitfully suggestive.

Scattered throughout Canudo's intoxicated eulogy of Beethoven, *Le livre de la genèse* (1905), are concepts which – however slender their sense – surely resonate with ideas embodied in Varèse's mature aesthetic.

... Music represents the maximum of vibrations in matter before it turns into light. In the perpetual effort of *subtilization*, which comes out of the bowels of the Earth and takes on its surface the various aspects of minerals, vegetables, animals, sentiments and thoughts, Music is at the summit of man's sentiment and intelligence. As matter in vibration, it masks the last limit between thought and fire ... In the hierarchy of 'densities' of matter, it represents the beginning of fire ...[7]

This movement from the mineral to the spiritual world, which Canudo terms the 'metaphysical determinism' of Beethoven's music, is the central doctrine of Hermetic magic: 'as above, so below'[8] – the fundamental correspondence between the archetypal world of ideas and the material world. Canudo also saw Beethoven's works as embodying the ancient Hermetic-alchemical idea of the two polarized forces of existence: the centripetal force of compression, which he identifies with harmony, and the centrifugal force of expansion, which

---

[6] Ibid., p.205. Canudo was later to collaborate in a ballet with Arthur Honegger and Fernand Léger.

[7] Ricciotto Canudo, *Le Livre de la genèse: la IXe symphonie de Beethoven* (Paris: Editions de la plume, 1905). Quoted from Godwin, op. cit., p.205. Canudo's book was the first part of a trilogy of esoteric musical speculation, continued in *Le Livre de l'évolution: l'homme (psychologie musicale des civilisations)* (1907–8) and concluded in *La musique comme religion du futur* (1913).

[8] See footnote 9 on p.55 for the source of this famous saying. Canudo's curious terminology in the quotation just given is deeply infused by the ancient Hermetic/Neoplatonic cosmology, in which fire, by reason of its upward motion, is 'already escaping bodily nature' (Plotinus) and on the way to becoming pure spirit.

he identifies with melody. Varèse's desire for a music 'that expands into space' immediately comes to mind. None of Canudo's assertions is backed up by any close observation of Beethoven's actual musical procedures. But perhaps that was their very attraction for Varèse: he was left free to imagine what might realize the authentic musical expression of such ideas, without being limited to any aspect of Beethovenian sonata dialectic.

Despite his reputation as an intransigent modernist, Varèse's knowledge of the music of earlier ages was impressive by any standard, as his own words and the programmes he conducted testify. In spirit at least he came to feel very close to the purity and intensity of some of the remoter masters – notably certain Medieval and Renaissance composers, whose music he knew much better than did many of his contemporaries. Naturally his appreciation was of an entirely different order from that of an amateur like Canudo. Yet the way he expressed it does not always entirely discard esoteric concepts, if only – but is it only? – as metaphor. An example is this moving tribute to his predecessors, from a lecture he gave at Princeton in 1959:

My fight for the liberation of sound and for my right to make music with any sound and all sounds has sometimes been construed as a desire to disparage and even to discard the great music of the past. But that is where my roots are. No matter how original, how different a composer may seem, he has only grafted a little bit of himself on the old plant. But this he should be allowed to do without being accused of wanting to kill the plant. He only wants to produce a new flower. ... Many of the old masters are my intimate friends – all are respected colleagues. None of them are dead saints – in fact none of them are dead – and the rules they made for themselves are not sacrosanct and are not everlasting laws. Listening to music by Pérotin, Machaut, Monteverdi, Bach or Beethoven we are conscious of living substances; they are 'alive in the present'.[9]

The idea of music as a 'living substance', sometimes with the strange implication that it is also a sentient substance, runs through many of Varèse's pronouncements. It seems to have taken root in his imagination very early, and its source is surely to be sought in the speculative intellectual milieu he frequented as a student in Paris. The esoteric element in his early circle of acquaintance has not, I feel, been

[9] 'The Liberation of Sound' (excerpts from lectures by Varèse complied by Chou Wen-Chung), *Perspectives of New Music* 5/1, pp.14–15.

accorded its proper significance. As I hope to show in later chapters, though his mature works overtly suggest, through their titles and processes, a compositional approach inspired by 20th-century 'hard science', his understanding of the physical universe – and therefore his musical expression of it – appears to retain a profoundly occult colouring. This metaphysical outlook, absorbed *after* his teenage scientific training,[10] was almost certainly crystallized during the mid-1900s, when he consorted with people such as Bernard, Canudo, Deubel, Péladan and the Paracelsus translator Pelletier. It may well offer a further avenue to understanding his lost works of this period.

VARÈSE AND DEBUSSY

It is now fairly well established that Debussy – perhaps *the* commanding contemporary master for the young Varèse – partook in, and derived inspiration from, the esoteric ferment of 1890s Paris, although some of his links to the protagonists in that movement remain speculative.[11] Varèse's links a decade later – sometimes with the selfsame figures – are much more firmly established, and are the more striking because he was simultaneously in personal contact with Debussy. They surely constitute a significant element of aesthetic orientation, shared between the young composer and his mentor.

As he explained to Gunther Schuller, among his elder contemporaries Varèse admired Debussy, whose music he had known since the 1890s, first and above all ('especially for his *Pelléas*'); then Strauss (citing the final scene of *Salome* and the Recognition scene in *Elektra*) and Busoni. Secondarily he mentioned the orchestral works of Scriabin and the music of Satie (the Kyrie of his *Messe des Pauvres*, said Varèse, 'always reminds me of Dante's *Inferno* and strikes me as a kind of pre-electronic music').[12]

---

[10] Is it worth speculating that this training – undertaken at the command of his hated father – could only be freed from the parental taint once it was transmuted by the arcane mysteries of alchemy?

[11] The painter, Catholic mystic and philosopher of music, colour and number Maurice Denis (1870–1943), who was a friend and champion of both Debussy and André Gide, an associate of Bernard and a protégé of Péladan, may have been an important nexus. Denis produced an illustrated edition of Verlaine's *Sagesse*, the collection from which Varèse set *Un grand sommeil noir*.

[12] Schuller (1965), p.33.

We have already noted the profoundly Debussian orientation of *Un grand sommeil noir* – in choice of poet, in technique; even, in its closing bars, in its near-reminiscence of *Pelléas et Mélisande*. The titles of Varèse's other works from this period only strengthen the suggestion of affinity with Debussy. Precisely what relationship Varèse's *Apothéose de l'océan* may have borne to that archetypal 'apotheosis of the ocean', the older composer's *La Mer*, will remain unknown;[13] but the title is certainly suggestive – just as the titles *Colloque au bord de la fontaine* and *Dans le parc* ineluctably recall Debussy's explorations in song of the world of Verlaine's *Fêtes galantes* (e.g., *Colloque sentimentale* and, perhaps, *L'ombre des arbres*). Likewise Varèse's terms *Proses rhythmées* for his Deubel settings suggest a parallel with Debussy's *Proses lyriques*; and the *Poème des Brumes*, less precisely, brings to mind *Nuages* from Debussy's *Nocturnes*.

We should not accord mere verbal correspondences more weight than they can bear – we have already seen how different was the poetic basis of *Prélude à la fin d'un jour* to that of *Prélude à l'aprés-mide d'un faune*. These various pieces of Varèse may not, overall, have sounded much like Debussy (though *Un grand sommeil noir* makes it extremely likely they explored aspects of Debussian technique and vocabulary). But they were surely the work of a composer who cultivated a Debussian cast of mind and had Debussian models before him. In purely technical terms our discussion of *Un grand sommeil noir* has indicated that these models certainly included *Pelléas* and possibly Debussy's own Verlaine setting *L'ombre des arbres*; while the organum-like nature of the piano writing could have been suggested by several Debussy piano pieces, such as the Sarabande in *Pour le Piano*. (The roots of this style, of course, are equally imbedded in the early 'Rosicrucian' works of Satie.)

'I admired Debussy', Varèse told Schuller,

primarily for his economy of means and clarity, and the intensity he achieved through them, balancing with almost mathematical equilibrium timbres against rhythms and textures – like a fantastic chemist.[14]

---

[13] Debussy presented a copy of *La Mer*, with his own autograph revisions, to Varèse in 1908, by which date *Apothéose de l'océan* was certainly in existence. But Varèse would have known the piece since its première in October 1905.

[14] Schuller (1965), p.33.

That tribute is couched in terms he liked to apply to his own music, including the favourable image of the composer as a kind of scientist. But there is no doubt that it was primarily Debussy who initiated the approach to music which Varèse was to extend and explore in his mature works. Debussy, indeed, was arguably the most truly revolutionary figure in the music of the later 19th and early 20th centuries, more fundamentally so than either Schoenberg or Stravinsky – in his impatience with conventional formulae, his disregard of classical harmonic function, his glorification of the chord as self-sufficient sensation, his passion for tone-colour and timbre, his interest in oriental percussion musics with their apparent suspension of time, and above all in his call for a music of 'continuous arabesque' that should reject traditional structural models and create its own forms continually anew.[15] An apparent sensualist and aesthete, there was no more exacting and painstaking practitioner of his art.

The composer who felt suffocated by the mediocrity of his contemporaries, who wrote that 'Music ... is a dream from which the veils have been lifted. It's not even the expression of a feeling, it's the feeling itself', who desired 'the courage to go on living one's dream! And the energy to go on searching for the Inexpressible which is the ideal of all art'[16], could not help but excite Varèse's admiration. And when Debussy wrote that

Every sound you hear around you can be reproduced. Everything that a keen ear perceives in the rhythm of the surrounding world can be represented musically

– he seems especially prophetic of Varèse's own approach to music as sound. In *La Mer*, perhaps above all, the fusion of nature and art, the transcription of wind- and wave-patterns and painterly conceptions of

---

[15] In his remarks on the 'old masters' quoted above, Varèse could well have added the name of Berlioz, whose more monumental works – such as the *Grande Messe des Morts* – he enormously admired, and who of all previous French composers, with the possible exception of Debussy, most anticipated his own attitudes to sound and to musical space. Indeed we may place Berlioz–Debussy–Varèse in a direct line of descent, the Revolutionary tradition of French music from the early 19th century to the later 20th.

[16] Debussy in a letter of February 1893 to André Poniatowski; translated by Roger Nichols in *Debussy Letters* selected and edited by François Lesure and Roger Nichols (London: Faber and Faber, 1987), pp.37–38.

light into a symphonic argument via music's powers of symbolism, was surely an abiding inspiration to a composer who wished to 'approximate the ... inner, microcosmic life you find in certain chemical solutions, or through the filtering of light' and 'the qualities and character' of Burgundian granite. Equally striking in this connexion is Debussy's comment in a letter of 1898 to Georges Hartmann, provoked by his detestation of the architecture of the Opéra-Comique:

These people seem to know nothing about light, and consequently about the whole theory of luminous undulations, the mysterious harmony that links up the different parts of an edifice ...[17]

Among Debussy's later works, Varèse conceived an abiding admiration for what he described as the 'constant tension' of *Jeux*, that ballet-score later to be hailed by Pierre Boulez and others as a cornerstone of musical modernism. Though it is highly unlikely that Debussy, had he lived on to compose in the 1920s and 30s, would have produced works at all resembling Varèse's, they would undoubtedly have remained at one in their exploratory attitude to their art, and in making their art their means of inner exploration. 'Shall I ever regain my power of working?' wrote Debussy after undergoing radium treatment in his last illness, 'my desire always to go further and beyond which for me is the bread and wine of life?'[18]

Varèse and Debussy (unlike many composers) shared keen interest and appreciation of the other arts; painters, writers and other kinds of artists and thinkers outnumbered musicians among their close acquaintances. Indeed, though Varèse was a generation younger, their circles of acquaintance overlapped in some important areas. Among these – though they came at it from different backgrounds and from the standpoints of different generations – was the large category of esoteric speculation which we may gather under the convenient term of 'the occult'.

This is a subject with which musicologists, in general, feel very uncomfortable. Understandably so: it is so far from intellectual respectability, surrounded by so much secrecy and mystification, and

---

[17] Quoted in Roy Howat, *Debussy in Proportion: A Musical Analysis* (Cambridge University Press, 1983), p.172.

[18] Letter to Robert Godet, quoted in Edward Lockspeiser, *Debussy: His Life and Mind*, Volume 2 (London: Cassell, 1965), p.196n.

so inextricably entwined with a large proportion of rubbish that it tends to resist any sensible assessment. Many of its practitioners and devotees have been unimpressive advertisements for the beneficent effects, occult powers, ancient traditions and inner mysteries of the practices they profess. Enormous basic confusions surround the subject even today: witness the routine tabloid and Fundamentalist Christian equation of every division in an enormously diverse field – ritual magic, number mysticism, esoteric spirituality, witchcraft, extra-sensory perception, astrology, alchemy, divination, mediumship and so on – with Black Magic or Satanism.

There are few professional plaudits to be gained by bringing such stuff into serious artistic discussion, and any attempt to do so properly involves acquiring a great deal of curious knowledge that is literally arcane (i.e., difficult of access) and much of it maybe not worth having. As a result the 'occult interests' of many artists are often conveniently ignored, or simply dismissed as the decadent nonsense of a bourgeois 'society on the brink of collapse'. (The controlling image here is Freud's 'black tide of mud – of occultism', though as far as Freud was concerned the 'tide' included practically all religion and a much respectable philosophy as well).

If 'the occult' proves to have had an intimate and unquestionable connexion with the artist's creative development, the critical strategy is a little different. In that case (as with Satie's Rosicrucian period) the phenomenon can be carefully delineated as a somewhat unfortunate though surprisingly fruitful 'phase' the artist was going through, or sometimes adduced (as with Scriabin's millennial Theosophy, or Cyril Scott's vegetarian version) as evidence of mental instability.

Such negative approaches, I suspect, are deeply unhelpful, founded as they are on a fundamental misconception of the role which esoteric speculation performed in the arts at the turn of the century. The more one investigates, the more difficult it becomes to find significant figures who were *not* in some fashion and measure affected by the occult, however widely defined. With all the attractions of the secret and mysterious, it was a visible and palpable component of the intellectual climate. While esoteric knowledge and spirituality was certainly merely a fashion of the time among many artists and writers (particularly, in France, those involved with the Symbolist movement), the very fact it could become a fashion shows how ubiquitous its presence was.

In fact the esoteric ferment in the Western World of the late 19th century (signalized by the success of such organizations as the Theosophical Society, the Golden Dawn and various Rosicrucian fraternities) was, in part, an attempt to address spiritual questions and aspirations which were not being satisfied by the old – and, in the view of many intellectuals, moribund – religious and philosophic conventions. The search for new forms of old wisdom was instrumental in bringing to birth many aspects of the modern movement in the arts. In similar fashion the Hermetic, Cabbalistic and Alchemical ferment of the early Renaissance (a direct progenitor of the 19th-century movement[19]), by positing a new relationship between Man and the Cosmos, helped to create the exact and experimental sciences that in time gave birth to the Enlightenment.[20]

Yet in neither case should we complacently imagine that a 'modern', rational and correct cast of mind simply replaced and made obsolete a more primitive, 'superstitious' and fallacious one which then withered away. The esoteric represents *another path*, a fundamentally different mode of perceiving the world: not rational (though it may in its own terms be logical) but intuitive, instinctual – not a process of experiment but a striving towards illumination.

And what kind of illumination is vouchsafed? I shall venture here a large and simple generalization. Though doubtless vulnerable to innumerable qualifications, it should be adequate for the matter in hand, namely the imaginative environment in which Varèse first found himself as a composer. At the heart of practically all species of magical and esoteric speculation, then, is the revelation of an animate, not to say animated, universe: a cosmos in which everything has its proper

---

[19] According the esotericist-poet Victor-Émile Michelet (quoted in Howat, op.cit., p.167), Debussy 'let himself be thoroughly impregnated with Hermetic philosophy' in the early 1890s.

[20] The importance of the great Renaissance Hermeticists, Cabbalists and other magi – figures such as Ramón Lull, Marsilio Ficino, Pico della Mirandola, Giordano Bruno, Thomasso Campanella, John Dee and Robert Fludd – as thinkers, and as encouragers of scientific and artistic speculation and of a liberal religious outlook, has been much more widely recognized in recent years, largely due to the work of Francis Yates; her most important studies include *Giordano Bruno and the Hermetic Tradition* (1964), *The Art of Memory* (1966), *The Rosicrucian Enlightenment* (1972), and *The Occult Philosophy in the Elizabethan Age* (1979). A reappraisal of the significance of Renaissance alchemy was pioneered by C.G. Jung.

mode of life and being, where matter itself is not inert, in which the chain of creation extends upward beyond the physical world onto ethereal realms of energy and spirit (the 'inner planes', as modern occultism names them) of which the visible world is merely the outer veil. Upon those planes (but still within our world if we know how to find them) move other sorts of being, other intelligences, be they discarnate spirits, elementals, daemons, devas, angels or whatever, each with their specific powers and spheres of operation.

Most esoteric beliefs come down to the conviction that what happens on the Inner affects the Outer, and vice versa: which is the meaning of the ancient saying 'as above, so below'. Acts of magic, so called, rest on the belief that the powers of the Inner can be used to bring about desired changes in the Outer world – by those, of course, who are sufficiently adept or illumined: who have undergone whichever training is necessary to know which rituals or meditations to perform, which names to name, the power of secret numbers, the workings of the particular model of Creation taught by their brand of Occultism, and the proper spirit in which to make use of this knowledge. The acts themselves may be reading cards or throwing yarrow-stalks to divine the future; healing by sympathetic magic or understanding the influence of the stars; or it may be converse with the souls of the dead, the commanding of spirits, the invocation of archangels. But all these actions rest upon a view of the universe that transcends merely physical boundaries; which proclaims that there are more things in Heaven and Earth than are dreamt of in conventional science, religion and philosophy, and that in all imaginable dimensions, there are things that may be done and performed.

Now it seems to me that except for the most dedicated adepts of the various esoteric schools, the literal, objective truth of such claims is less important than the glamour – the poetry – of the world-view itself.[21] It appeals powerfully to our faculties of imagination and fantasy. (The idea that we might communicate with beings of radiant spirituality, even if now we picture them as aliens descending to earth from a shining spacecraft, has as popular an appeal today as when Dr. Dee or

---

[21] I leave out of account the fundamentally important question of whether various forms of magic function precisely because of, or only in the presence of, belief in their efficacy; and the fact that most magical processes are directed towards transformation of consciousness, which does not lend them to objective measurement.

William Blake talked with archangels.) And thus it can give an enormous impetus to those arts which principally affect our imagination and fantasy – for what is the experience, with rapt attention, of a profound work of art but a guided meditation, and transformation (however temporary) of consciousness? As Mallarmé observed in a letter of 1890:

Occultism is the commentary on the pure signs obeyed by all literature, the immediate projection of the spirit.[22]

How much more 'immediate' in its workings is music, which communicates directly with its audience without the interposition of language! And how appropriate is Mallarmé's comment to Varèse, who was concerned throughout his life with the 'projection' of sounds which, as we shall see, he treated as (I do not say he believed they were) animate entities.

Mention of Mallarmé returns us to Paris, in its 'alchemical Nineties' – the Paris of Eliphas Lévi's occult speculation, Papus's researches into the Tarot, the Rosicrucian orders of Péladan and others; of Strindberg's *Inferno*, Huysmans' *Là-Bas*; even of MacGregor Mathers (establishing in that decade a Parisian temple of the Golden Dawn), who was closely involved with Debussy's friend, the occultist-poet Jules Bois. A decade later, these circles still intersected the merely chronologically more 'modern' outlook of Varèse's early Paris years. Many of the same figures were still active in the mid-1900s – among them Sâr Péladan and Debussy himself. Debussy's interest and involvement in the esoteric seems to have been deeper than that of many of his contemporaries. From his childhood encounters with the cabbalist Charles de Sivry (Verlaine's brother-in-law) to his tenure as Grand Master in the secret Rosicrucian order of the Prièuré de Sion, his course is spottily but by now quite well documented; and according to Maggie Teyte[23] he was still involved in the occult, including the esoteric aspects of Egyptology, late in the first decade of the 20th century, about the time he was most in contact with Varèse.

Some readers may feel slightly scandalized that I should drag the name of Varèse into this miry vicinity: Varèse, the uncompromising

---

[22] Quoted in Howat, op.cit., p.168.

[23] Reported in ibid., p.170. Howat's pp.163–171 provide a good summary of Debussy's occult and esoteric connexions, with especial reference to his use in his music of Golden Section (of which more anon).

prophet of the modern, the first virtuoso of musical electronics, the very titles of whose works proclaim his allegiance to the disciplines of mathematics, crystallography, biology and atomic physics. Yet at the start of his career the occult was a part of his imaginative world. Like his modernist friends in the other arts – Picasso, Modigliani, Apollinaire, Max Jacob – he reacted against it, partly because it seemed to belong to the fin-de-siècle; but perhaps because of his association with Debussy and Satie, Varèse did not reject it outright. It seems to have helped shape attitudes which carried through into his mature music – and, indeed, influenced the way in which he viewed the 'hard' sciences of his time.[24] In any case, he never troubled to conceal the fact that he had early encounters with esoteric figures and writings, even though his later public attitudes were sometimes deprecatory of them. And one thing known by practically any lay music-lover who enjoys Varèse's music is that one of his greatest works, *Arcana*, takes its title and prominently displays a mystical epigraph from the works of the prince of all Renaissance alchemists, Paracelsus.[25]

Although Varèse experienced a more rational and rigorous upbringing in science and engineering than most of the artists of the previous generation, in Paris he was surrounded – and certainly affected – by the 'alchemical' atmosphere. On his own admission, around 1905 he was initiated into the writings of Paracelsus when he befriended the young Latin scholar Maurice Pelletier, who was engaged in translating them into French. Ouellette[26] is quick to assure us that 'Varèse did not actually believe in alchemy as such, any more than in any of the other branches of occult knowledge'. Quite so, if we mean he surely disbelieved that either the Philosopher's Stone or the elixir of Eternal Youth could be created by following Paracelsus' apallingly obscure recipes, involving undefined 'spagyric substances'. On the other hand Ouellette admits he was 'amazed' by Paracelsus' description of the transmutation of elements: suggestive indeed to the imagination

---

[24] A simple illustration: a passage in 'New Instruments and New Music', one of Varèse's Santa Fe lectures of 1936, describes his (proto-electronic) conception of music in a quasi-scientific vocabulary, mentioning 'Zones of Intensities', 'opacities', 'rarefactions', 'resultants' and 'oxygenation' – but his conclusion is that this would be 'An entirely new magic of sound!'

[25] 'One star exists, higher than all the rest ...', etc. See p.190 for the correct source of this quotation.

[26] Op. cit., p.17.

of a composer whose music has a great deal to do with 'transmutation' in other senses.

I shall have more to say of Paracelsus, and in particular of his 'hermetic astronomy', when I come to discuss *Arcana*, but for the moment it is enough to say that it would have been highly surprising if Varèse had not become interested in this mysterious and potent figure, hermetic philosopher and experimental scientist in one, founder of modern medicine, student of mercury and magnetism, practitioner of alchemy and astral magic, and inspiration to the original Rosicrucian fraternities.

3 · 'All'illustro futuro': Wronski to Busoni

WRONSKI AND 'INTELLIGENT SOUNDS'

It was also in his early years in Paris, and in the same esoteric milieu, that Varèse encountered the ideas of the Polish savant whom he usually referred to as 'Hoëne Wronsky': the mathematician, philosopher and inventor Joseph-Maria-Hoëne Wronski (1776–1853).[1] Wronski's mathematical work – he was the originator of the so-called 'Wronskian' coefficients for the series expansion of functional equations – was long dismissed and derided, but has undergone a revaluation in recent decades: it is now admitted he achieved some brilliant insights. When Varèse came across him he was principally remembered as a disciple of Kant and for his messianic philosophy, which he proclaimed in lectures and writings for half a century after he experienced an ecstatic vision of 'the Absolute' in 1803. By all accounts he was a difficult, combative,

---

[1] The name of this personage is very variously reported in different sources. Son of the architect to the last King of Poland, he was born Jozséf Marja Hoëne. He served heroically in the defence of Warsaw against the Russians and Prussians in 1794, later became an artillery officer in the Russian army, and only adopted the name Wronski after he settled in Paris c. 1810.

self-obsessed man. Yet Varèse always maintained that Wronski's ideas and definitions were crucial in helping him to form his own conception of music.

When I was about 20, my own attitude towards music – at least towards what I wanted my music to be – became suddenly crystallized by Hoëne-Wronsky's definition of music. It was probably what first started me thinking of music as spatial – as bodies of intelligent sounds moving freely in space, a concept I gradually developed and made my own.[2]

Wronski's major contribution to musicology was probably his firm separation of the science of acoustics from aesthetics. He was only incidentally a philosopher of music insofar as he was a philosopher of everything, yet his lectures set so eminent an authority as Josef Fétis on the path which transformed him into a great theorist and pedagogue.[3] Wronski's musical writings were not published in his lifetime and are partly lost. The primary surviving material consists of an extract from his lost essay *Philosophie absolue de la musique* and a letter on the subject dated 3 January 1850. Both were published by his disciple, the musicologist Camille Durutte, in his *Esthétique musicale: Technie, ou lois générales du système harmonique* (1855). Varèse probably derived his knowledge of Wronski from Durutte's later and very similarly titled *Esthétique musicale: résumé élémentaire de la 'Technie harmonique'* (1876), which quotes extensively from the former work. But he could also have derived it from Durutte's texts as they were incorporated in the encyclopedic work *Wronski et l'esthétique musicale* (1887) by the mathematician, and leading esotericist, Charles Henry (1859–1926).

Henry, who has been described as the very last Renaissance Man, and as a modern alchemist,[4] worked on nothing less than a unifying theory of matter, energy and consciousness. His theories of colour and the geometry of aesthetic perception made him an important influence on the Symbolist movement. He garnered admirers from the entire

---

[2] Edgard Varèse, 'Spatial Music', from a lecture given at Sarah Lawrence College in 1959 and incorporated in the version of 'The Liberation of Sound', compiled and annotated by Chou Wen-Chung, published in Barney Childs and Elliott Schwartz, eds., *Contemporary Composers on Contemporary Music* (New York: Holt Rinehart, 1967), p.204. (The *Perspectives of New Music* version of 'The Liberation of Sound', cited elsewhere, does not include the 'Spatial Music' section.)

[3] Fétis, incidentally, taught Widor, who taught Varèse.

[4] Godwin, op.cit., p.116.

artistic spectrum of Paris, including Paul Valéry and the surrealist Albert Gleizes (who became a friend of Varèse in Paris and later in New York). It is generally supposed that Debussy was familiar with Henry, at least by reputation, and they certainly had friends in common, such as Eugène Ysaÿe, who commissioned Debussy's *Nocturnes*. Henry's advocacy of the whole-tone scale as a new harmonic resource, and specifically his suggestions (in an 1892 lecture, 'Une transformation de l'orchestre') for a much-reduced orchestra of individual chamber soloists, and for whole-tone harp glissandi, may well have inspired features of Debussy's *Prélude à l'après-midi d'un faune* (1892–4). It is therefore quite possible that Varèse interested himself in Henry's speculations, founded as they were on Wronski's work.

As Joscelyn Godwin has remarked, Wronski and Henry were esotericists – but not speculative amateurs, ignorant of science. On the contrary, they were genuine 'scientists and technologists, but they differed from others of their time by their acceptance of immaterial realities, and – which is much more rare – by their refusal to exclude these from their scientific thought. Henry is perhaps best understood as a modern alchemist, working to reconcile spiritual facts with laboratory experiments'.[5] This scientific attitude embracing the occult may well be what aroused Varèse's interest in Wronski, and perhaps in Henry too.

Wronski, who considered the first principle of music to be 'the aesthetic modification of time' by means of rhythm, and who rejected the need for equal temperament or indeed for any tuning except one entirely derived from rational numbers, was certainly an original thinker by any standard. But the aspect of his musical philosophy which seems to have made the deepest impression on Varèse is encapsulated in the phrase which he quoted from Wronski in many different articles and lectures: *la corporification de l'intelligence qui est dans les sons* – the object of music is 'the embodiment of intelligence in tones'. That at least is how the phrase is commonly translated, as if suggesting that in the act of composition the (human) intelligence embodies its ideas in sound. But Wronski's original French certainly implies that 'intelligence' is an inherent quality of the musical tones themselves; and only a few sentences further on in this passage (first published by Durutte in 1855), he mentions the modification of time

---

[5] Ibid.

'which alone constitutes *a priori* an embodiment of the spirit or the intelligence forming the object of music'. Varèse was therefore perfectly accurate to translate, as he consistently did, 'the corporealization of the intelligence that is in sound'.[6]

This interpretation opens the door to the intensely esoteric idea that sounds are 'intelligent' entities in their own right – in some manner alive and aware. Varèse extended and developed the image, customarily describing his music as consisting of 'bodies of intelligent sounds moving freely in space' (see, for instance, the quotation on p.51 above). His frequent references to sound as 'organic matter' and suchlike (cf. his characterization of the music of former masters as 'living substances', p.39 above) are of a piece with this idea – which became, in fact, the cornerstone of his musical thinking.

By conceiving sounds as 'intelligent ... moving freely in space', Varèse clearly had in mind an analogy with the spirit-world of esoteric speculation. He imagined that space as constituted in several dimensions, by the tessitura of the instruments, the duration of the performance, the acoustical environment, the intensity of the dynamics – and the movement of the sounds themselves, projected outwards as, figuratively speaking, the spirits or elementals which inhabit the space.

The parallels with the Swedenborgian vision of the cosmos, relayed to Arnold Schoenberg in Balzac's mystical novel *Seraphita* – that mystically sounding space with neither right nor left, nor up nor down, wherein circle souls, genii, stars, gods and angels – are remarkable. One version of that vision is the subject of Schoenberg's unfinished oratorio *Die Jakobsleiter*, a cardinal document in the evolution of the music of the Second Viennese School. It is now generally accepted that this Swedenborgian idea of heaven had some influence, as a potent image, on Schoenberg's new conception of the horizontal and vertical dimensions of music, from which he extrapolated the 12-note method of composition. But Swedenborg's vision is in important respects circular, closed, hierarchical – as are the central doctrines of serial music. Varèse, by contrast, was more attracted by the idea of movement that was utterly free, the ability of his 'intelligent sounds' to go anywhere.

---

[6] For instance, in a lecture given at Yale in 1962, and in Schuller (1965), p.33, where Varèse calls it 'a phrase I never forgot'.

In conversation with Gunther Schuller, Varèse specifically linked his interest in Wronski with the fact that 'Goethe was very important to my thinking'. He had just mentioned his symphonic poem *Mehr Licht*, 'on a Goethe poem' (see p.23 above), and may have connected Goethe with Wronski because the two were contemporaries. But in this context it sounds as if he found Goethe especially stimulating not as a poet, but in his role as an esoteric theorist of light, optics and plant morphology.[7]

In addition to Wronski's musical philosophy, Varèse at this same period studied some of the most ancient Greek musicological writings, seeking to follow the art back to its origins. Ouellette reports that he read particularly Aristotle (actually the musical sections of the pseudo-Aristotelian *Problems*) and Aristoxenus of Tarentum, the supreme ancient authority on harmony and – perhaps even more important for Varèse – on rhythm. Both these writers were affected by the Pythagorean mystical view of music as an acoustical paradigm of the cosmos ('The Music of the Spheres'), and a means of harmonizing the body and the soul.

Which brings us back, perhaps, to Varèse's projected opera on *Le Fils des Etoiles*, the 'Chaldean pastoral' by that prominent occultist, Rosicrucian and mystagogue, Sâr ('High Priest') Péladan. There seems no conclusive evidence that Varèse ever wrote a note of this work; some have expressed scepticism that he could ever have considered involving himself with such a document of *fin-de-siècle* decadence. Doubt is reinforced by Péladan's reputation as (in the phrase of Debussy's biographer Edward Lockspeiser) 'an incorrigible poseur'. It is all too easy to envisage the flamboyant and eccentric Sâr – the '*Grand Maitre*' of the second of Satie's *Sonneries de la Rose+Croix* – precipitately forcing his ritual drama upon Varèse. But Varèse does appear to have given it serious thought.

He may partly have been attracted by the historic connexion with Satie. Indeed the organum-like progressions and tritone harmonies of the first of the three *Préludes* Satie composed for Péladan's play in 1892 (which Varèse presumably knew) might be considered a further model for the opening measures of his own *Un grand sommeil noir*. But the

---

[7] Goethe's theories were possibly derived from the original Rosicrucian writings, and in their turn became a key element in the development of Rudolf Steiner's Anthroposophic philosophy. See further pp.70–1 below.

actual esoteric content may have fired him too, in such pronouncements as this:

> That which is above is like that which is below;
>   And that which is below
> Is like that which is above to accomplish
>   The miracles of will.
> Will rises from the earth to the sky
> And then descends once more onto the earth
> Receiving the strength of superior and inferior things.[8]

This is, of course, a high-flown restatement of the cardinal axiom of
ancient alchemy, 'As above, so below',[9] affirming the unity of the
physical and spiritual worlds, microcosm and macrocosm – and thus
also symbolically proclaiming the unity of body and soul in man. It
may be that at precisely this time the young and deeply self-divided
Varèse felt the inner core of esoteric spirituality – however suspicious
he may have been of its meretricious outer trappings – to offer a
unifying force that he needed within himself. After all the real or inner
meaning of alchemy is work upon and perfection of the soul, for which
the transmutation of elements is only a metaphor or symbolic
correlative. *Le fils des Etoiles*' theme of ritual initiation, of difficulties
overcome in order to become a complete magus and possess hidden
knowledge (knowledge, indeed, 'of the stars'), would have rather
obvious attractions for him.

There is no evidence that Varèse became any kind of formal
member of Péladan's Rose+Croix fraternity (if indeed it was still in
existence as a functioning group). At a later date – perhaps quite soon
– he came to reject the more decadent and self-indulgent brand of
esotericism which it represented. Many years later he recalled the
course which he had followed instead, apropos of his links with the
Futurist painters (a very different aesthetic orientation):

---

[8] As quoted in Pierre-Daniel Templier, *Erik Satie* (MIT Press, 1968, trs. E.L. and
D.S. French), p.13.

[9] In full, 'What is below is like that which is above, and what is above is like that
which is below. Together they work to accomplish the wonders of the One Thing'.
This is Precept 2 from the so-called *Precepts of Hermes Trismegistus*, a late-classical
alchemical text also known as *The Emerald Tablet (Tabula Smaragdina)*. I quote the
translation of George Luck in *Arcana Mundi* (Johns Hopkins University Press, 1985),
p.368.

I became a sort of diabolic Parsifal, searching not for the Holy Grail but for the bomb that would make the musical world explode and thereby let in all sounds, sounds which up to now – and even today – have been called noises.[10]

Varèse's imagery here seems chosen as a deliberate repudiation of such *fin-de-siècle* figures as the foppish Sâr Péladan – whose organization was called in full the 'Order of the Catholic Rosy Cross, the Temple and the Grail', and who, as a devout Wagnerian, proclaimed that his 'genius as a tragedian was made in Bayreuth' (where he had attended a performance of *Parsifal* in 1888). Yet there was surely enough to Péladan that could, if only for a short time, have engaged Varèse's interest. After his own fashion, the man was an energizer and enlivener of the arts. From 1892 to 1897 his annual 'Salons de la Rose+Croix' had attempted 'to ruin realism, reform Latin taste and create a new school of idealistic art' and to encourage the depiction of subjects drawn from legend, myth and dream. Thus Péladan had exhibited and proselytised for the work of many Symbolist painters – among them, as we have seen, Émile Bernard of the *Rénovation aesthetique*.

Péladan was also immensely and curiously learned, and well able to discuss the finer points of music. Apparently his musical theories, in esoteric parallel to Varèse's own researches in ancient writers, derived mainly from Pythagoras and Plotinus, and thus from the mystical traditions of number and numerology. Roy Howat has speculated that it may have been Péladan who led Debussy towards the employment of Golden Section as a form-building device.[11] That Debussy was, in fact, well aware of Pythagorean theory is illustrated by his defence of Rameau's scientific approach to music, which he described – in a manner that would surely have delighted Varèse – with reference to

the old Pythagorean theory that music should be reduced to a combination of numbers: it is the 'arithmetic of sound' just as optics is the 'geometry of light'.[12]

---

[10] Translated from an autobiographical article, 'Le Destin de la musique est de conquérir la liberté', printed in *Liberté 5* (1959), p.280. (The title of Varèse's article is a paraphrase of Busoni's famous dictum in the *Sketch for a New Aesthetic of Music*: 'Music was born free; and to win freedom is its destiny'.)

[11] Howat, op.cit., p.170.

Varèse was always firm in his later pronouncements that music should be considered primarily an art of sound – albeit one which, in his case, derived significant inspiration from the latest discoveries of the physical sciences in his time. But those sciences, including acoustics, rest upon mathematics; and for that reason he was bound to be familiar with the traditions of music as number – which includes the Pythagorean tradition of magical numbers.

GOLDEN SECTION: UN GRAND SOMMEIL NOIR AGAIN

Part of that tradition is the above-mentioned proportional structure known as Golden Section (or Golden Mean, Golden Ratio). Recognized in ancient times from its occurrence in such natural organisms such as fir-cones and nautilus shells, it was explicated by Euclid and other classical mathematicians, and has since found application in the arts of painting, sculpture and architecture. Golden Section (hereafter GS) divides a line of known length in two at the point where the geometric ratio of the shorter part to the longer matches the ratio of the longer part to the whole. The longer part, therefore, is the geometric mean of the smaller part plus the total length. If this longer span is then likewise divided by GS, the second GS point will divide the whole length by GS in the other direction. No other ratio has this property, and the system can be extended by any number of further subdivisions of the separate spans, to produce a hierarchy of interlocking GS divisions in both directions.

Like *Pi*, GS is an irrational number (0.618034 ..., continuing for an infinite number of decimal places). But perhaps because of its origins in the organic world it has been held to confer a special authority of 'naturalness', beauty and physical perfection on designs constructed according to it. Credited as far back as the Pythagoreans with magical and health-giving powers, it was thus early caught up in the long esoteric tradition of 'sacred geometry', by which magical workings are made possible through the use of correct (perfect, holy, secret and above all *harmonious*) proportion. As previously mentioned,

---

[12] *Debussy on Music* compiled and ed. François Lesure, translated by Richard Langham Smith (London: 1977). Debussy's piano piece *Hommage à Rameau* is one of the works which Howat's analysis reveals to be of Golden Section construction.

construction by GS proportion has long been practised in architecture: the Great Pyramid of Giza and the Parthenon in Athens both appear to incorporate it. A striking modern instance is Le Corbusier's architectural grid, the *modulor*, which relates GS proportions to those of the human body. Varèse and Le Corbusier were to meet in the 1920s, and three decades later their collaboration would lead to Varèse composing *Poème électronique*.

There is a long (though until recent times neglected) history of certain composers employing GS proportions – for instance, of duration in performance, or number of beats or bars – to determine the position of important structural events in musical works. From the Classical Era onward it has been available, to those who knew of it, as a kind of secret alternative to the proportions of sonata form or various kinds of symmetry.[13] In view of the young Varèse's keen interest in Medieval and Renaissance music – an interest in which Debussy had preceded him – it is perhaps significant that Masses by Obrecht and works of Dunstable, Machaut and Dufay have proved susceptible to GS analysis. Mozart, Beethoven, Schubert and especially Haydn also seem to have made occasional use of GS. The Hungarian musicologist Ernö Lendvai was the first to demonstrate a thoroughgoing employment of GS technique in a major 20th-century composer, namely Béla Bartók; and Roy Howat has done the same for Debussy, who is shown to have employed it in a number of major works, most notably *La Mer*. Satie, too, experimented with GS – precisely in his 'Rose+Croix' period.[14]

It might seem that, as a purely mathematical principle, GS is available to any composer to deduce or discover; the mere fact of its use carries no esoteric implications. Yet it has long flourished under the

---

[13] A mathematically simpler analogue to GS is the Fibonacci number series (called after the medieval mathematician Leonardo da Pisa, nicknamed 'Figlio Bonaccio'). This is a 'summation series': each number equals the sum of the two preceding numbers – thus 2, 3, 5, 8, 13, 21, 34, 55 ... But each number in the series also gives (to the nearest whole number) the GS of the sum of the numbers preceding and following it. (Thus 13 is approximately the GS of 29 [8+21]; the larger the numbers, the nearer the ratio approaches 0.618034.)

[14] Bartók: see Ernö Lendvai, *Béla Bartók: An Analysis of his Music* (London: Kahn & Averill, 1971). Debussy: see Howat, op.cit. Satie: See Eric Gillmor, *Erik Satie* (Boston, Twayne Publishers, 1988).

wing of 'occult' studies, which have fostered the tradition of its special beauty and efficacy, its truly 'golden' properties. It seems rather likely that it was in occult circles that Debussy, for one, first became aware of this intriguing and, in his hands, aesthetically effective, system of proportion. Moreover he seems to have regarded it as a 'secret' not for public knowledge. Debussy in fact left no explicit written testimony that he employed such a system. He may, or may not, have initiated colleagues of perception and discretion into his secrets; even if he did not, his techniques are detectable by numerological analysis, and presumably were equally detectable in his own time to musicians who possessed a similarly speculative intellectual background.[15]

Was one of those musicians Varèse? We saw in the previous chapter how the song *Un grand sommeil noir* yields clues and indications as to the young Varèse's compositional habits in a profusion out of all proportion to its size. A further examination discloses that on the largest structural level the little work is shaped by GS proportions.

My previous description (pp.27–30) implied it has a ternary form, corresponding to the three stanzas of Verlaine's poem. So indeed, on the most obvious thematic level, it has, with new material introduced for the second stanza and the two types of material combined in the third. But on the tonal level the piece divides into two. Stanzas 1 and 2 form a unit, seemingly immovably fastened to E flat or its dominant. The one major structural division occurs at the start of stanza 3 with its decisive move to the dominant of G flat, though modulating back to E flat well before the end of the song.

Varèse achieves this in an interesting way. Bars 20–22, which I quote below along with bar 19 as Ex.1a, correspond to bars 1–3, quoted in Ex.1 of the previous chapter and given again below as Ex.1*b* for comparison. We see that the correspondence is inexact: bar 1's motivic content is suppressed in bar 20. Instead a different tonal shape in the piano's left hand, the crescendo and the motion of the voice all give bar 20 an essentially cadential character which bar 1 does not possess – a cadence onto the D flat chord at the beginning of bar 21. This chord is also the beginning of the new section, into which the

---

[15] Howat (op.cit., pp.192–3) makes the interesting point that Fauré's song 'Reflets dans l'eau', op.113 no.2, written the year after Debussy's death to a text which, by implication, pays homage to him, is – uniquely in the song-cycle of which it is a member, and perhaps uniquely in Fauré's output altogether – a GS structure.

cadence is dovetailed. As I noted earlier (p.28) this music is shifted forward by one crotchet value so that the D flat chord falls on the strongest beat of its bar, lending it the decisive sense of defining a new tonal area which the corresponding B flat chord in bar 2 was never called upon to supply.

This D flat chord therefore marks the principal structural division of *Un grand sommeil noir*: a chord which falls upon the 81st beat of a song that comprises in total 132 crotchet beats. By this time it hardly seems necessary to observe that the GS of 132 is 81, more or less (actually 81.5804). That fact is considerably less likely to be a coincidence when we reflect that the chord in question would not sit astride the GS had not Varèse deliberately brought it, and the music it introduces, one beat forward from their analogous place at the song's beginning (and changing the music's rhythmic profile in consequence).

Though achieved with some compositional subtlety this is a very simple, indeed elementary application of GS proportion to supply the principal division of a binary movement (albeit one on which an implied ternary form is superimposed). Can it be pushed further? If the two parts, of 81 and 51 beats respectively, were further subdivided by GS we would expect some similarly definite indication of closure or division around the 31st or 50th beat of the longer opening portion, and of the 19th or 31st beat of the shorter concluding portion (the 100th or 112th beats of the song as a whole). It is in fact possible to assign some significance to beats 31, 100 and 112 (beat 50, in the midst of the arpeggios that introduce the second stanza, discloses no special importance). A minor structural division – the B flat chord in the piano's right hand, concluding the setting of the poem's first two lines – falls on the 31st beat: this is followed by low left-hand octaves on B flat. At the 100th beat the 'arpeggio element' comes to an end on a low monotone B flat, destined to be repeated several times against the words 'au creux d'un caveau': this is an implied reflection of the earlier B flat octave passage, though much transformed. But the 112th beat is more interesting, for upon it falls the B flat chord corresponding to the crucial D flat chord in Ex.1*a*, which corresponds in turn to the B flat chord in Ex.1*b*; this third passage is shown as Ex.1*c*. Once again the music has been shifted one beat forward, changing the rhythmic profile; the 112th beat is an upbeat, introducing the singer's last words – the impressively sepulchral 'Silence, silence' – and the ensuing climactic coda.

I am unwilling to press these conclusions too far. However, the major GS division of the song into two parts at the 81st beat is clear enough, and indications of GS subdivisions of these two parts are suggestive (if not definitive). Beat 31 is at least far more plausible as a GS point than beat 50; about as plausible as beat 100, though I find this in turn less striking than the claims of 112, because of the latter's relation to beat 81. Tentatively, therefore, I suggest that *Un grand sommeil noir* is a GS construct of $31+50+31+20=132$, as outlined in the figure given below.

I do not propose to speculate further as to where Varèse derived the idea of using GS proportion in his music at this early date, but the fact that he did so, once accepted, is unsurprising. His scientific and mathematical bent, his studies in ancient proportional theory, his friendship with Debussy and Satie and his contact with the esoteric circles that they themselves frequented, all provide possible avenues. It will be more fruitful to observe to what extent GS affected his mature music; and if we find (as we shall) that it was certainly not consistently

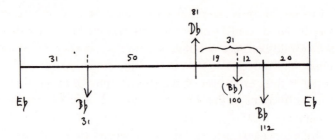

pursued, the quest will at least alert us to the presence of other kinds of proportionality, such as the use of exact symmetry which is evident, for instance, in *Ionisation*.

STRAUSS AND OEDIPUS

Such mathematical concerns seem entirely appropriate for an ex-engineer who, in his first major works – or at least the first not obviously related to any Debussian/Satiean aesthetic – also concerned himself with 'the concept of calculated or controlled gravitation ... volume in an architectural sense' (*Rhapsodie romane*) and 'the kind of inner, microcosmic life you find in certain chemical solutions, or through the filtering of light' (*Bourgogne*). But very shortly a different aesthetic orientation becomes perceptible in the early works, one clearly influenced by Varèse's admiration for and contacts with Richard Strauss. No doubt already the sheer virtuosity of the orchestral scoring in *Bourgogne* owed much to a desire to emulate Strauss as well as Debussy, as Romain Rolland picked up from a perusal of the score. Varèse's next symphonic poem, *Gargantua*, with its possible obbligato role for double bass, suggests a work with parallels to Strauss's tone poems,[16] particularly those deriving from other classics of satirical fiction – *Till Eulenspiels lustige Streiche* and *Don Quixote*. Even in Varèse's mature orchestral works there is a grandeur, an aggressive largeness of gesture, a virile monumental brass-dominated sound which owes more to Strauss – and perhaps especially to the most hubristic of Strauss's orchestral works, *Also sprach Zarathustra* and *Ein Heldenleben* – than to anything in Debussy.

---

[16] Satie's *Trois petites pièces montées* for orchestra, with their own whimsical allusions to Rabelais's giants Gargantua and Pantagruel, were not composed until another decade had elapsed.

But when he came to essay *Le délire de Clytemnestre* Varèse began to encroach upon Strauss's own exactly contemporary subject-matter. Canudo's text must have reworked some aspect of the Electra myth, just as Hofmannsthal had reworked Sophocles' *Elektra*, to produce his modern, psychologized version, with its vampiric Clytemnestra. If Varèse's 'tragédie symphonique' should indeed be dated to 1907, it was written within the time-frame of Strauss's *Elektra*, composed 1906–1908, by which the older composer transferred Hofmannsthal's drama to the musical stage, creating a Klytaemnestra of overpowering, indeed suffocating, presence. And as soon as 1908, before Strauss's opera had even been performed, Varèse had determined to make an opera of Hofmannsthal's very next updating of violent Greek myth: *Oedipus und die Sphinx*.

It is important to remember that it was the play, not the identity of its author, which first attracted him to the subject. Varèse saw and was struck by Reinhardt's 1908 Berlin revival of his original 1906 production, and it was this rather than any Straussian connexion which prompted him to make contact with Hofmannsthal and propose a collaboration. (The result was, in fact, rather more of a collaboration than occurred in *Elektra*, with which Hofmannsthal had not been directly involved. Apparently with *Oedipus* he did some refashioning of the first act, at least, as a libretto, though thereafter Varèse proceeded on his own, merely showing the results to Hofmannsthal and winning his approval.) It was the drama inherent in the myth, and the effectiveness of Hofmannsthal's presentation of it, that made the vital impact on him.

But why *this* of all myths as the subject for the work that was clearly a culmination of all his early development: almost certainly the largest score he ever composed, and one to which he was prepared to devote several years of his time with no track-record as an opera composer and no immediate prospects of a production? It is fatally easy to fall into a mode of amateur psychologizing over composers' choice of subjects, but in this case the temptation can hardly be resisted, not least because the Oedipus myth has played a significant role in the development of psychology itself. Everyone knows that Freud interpreted the story of Oedipus in terms of a childhood fixation on the parents: a son's feelings of sexual rivalry with his father and desire for the mother engender the fantasy of killing the father and replacing him as the mother's lover. This complex, according to Freud, can be responsible for much unconscious guilt in later life, and if children remain fixated at the Oedipal level they will tend to choose sexual partners who resemble their parents.

Freud first asserted the existence of the Oedipus Complex in *Die Traumdeutung* (*The Interpretation of Dreams*), published in 1900. Hofmannsthal's *Oedipus und die Sphinx* was the first post-*Traumdeutung* retelling of the Oedipus myth. The dramatist was certainly aware of Freud's theories, which were widely publicized and popularized by Hofmannsthal's friend Arthur Schnitzler; and though he would not have considered *Elektra* and *Oedipus und die Sphinx* as 'Freudian interpretations' of the classic Greek tragedies he did conceive them as laying bare the unconscious motivations of their archetypal characters – the primal instincts of their blood. Elektra, fixated on the figure of her dead father, has displaced her sexuality into lust for vengeance on his murderers – a lust potentially incestuous when she encounters her long-lost brother Orestes, in whom she finds the instrument of her revenge. Hints of this interpretation may be discerned in the Electra plays of Aeschylus, Euripides, and especially Sophocles, who was Hofmannsthal's principal model. But no classical drama survives of Oedipus's parricide and encounter with the Sphinx, and Hofmannsthal accordingly had a greater field for free invention of incident and detail.[17]

Hofmannsthal's Oedipus has foreknowledge of the prophecy that he will kill his father and marry his mother. The King and Queen of Corinth, who adopted him as their son when he was found as a baby, abandoned by his real father to die in the mountains, are all the parents he knows. He has left home not merely to escape the prophecy but because he already discerns it working out in his blood: he feels a sexual attraction for the Queen, whom he believes to be his mother. He has, in fact, a mother-fixation, and when he comes to Thebes he half-recognizes Jokaste as the mother he shall marry. Already, in killing Laios in towering anger when the Theban king tries to force him off the road, Oedipus already suspects it is this King, and not Polybos in Corinth, who is the father he is destined to slay, but he is powerless before the force of his own rage and feelings of rejection. Jokaste in

---

[17] Although, since he intended his play as a prologue to Sophocles's *King Oedipus*, he was constrained by that play's gradual revelation of Oedipus's past history, which provided him with the basic material of his drama.

turn half-recognizes him; and at the play's end even the Theban crowd, as they acclaim Oedipus and Jokaste, hand in hand, as King and Queen after he has slain the Sphinx, half-recognize that their coupling will be incestuous. By this time Oedipus knows that there is nowhere he can flee the workings of the curse: the Sphinx knew who he was and greeted him by name even as it died. He is caught in the net of the Gods – 'the whole world is their net', in which he writhes naked, unable to escape his fate.

It is important to see that all this was only partially relevant to Varèse, and it is probably significant that he appears to have curtailed Hofmannsthal's text towards the end, reducing the role of Jokaste and cutting out her union with Oedipus and their acclamation by the Theban people. The figure of Oedipus probably attracted him especially as a disruptor, a solitary, fated seeker after truth who breaks all social taboos. No-one has ever suggested Varèse had a mother-fixation; he seems to have regarded his own mother as more pitiable than desirable. But the other aspect of the Oedipus's predicament – the killing of the father – had a relevance so powerful Varèse could hardly have resisted it. Raised in Burgundy by his mother's parents, who took the place of his mother and father, he was at length sent far away to Turin to the stranger-father he grew to hate, and eventually attack. Varèse's childhood and adolescence thus resonate with parallels to the young Oedipus: parallels more specific than, and differently oriented to, those assumed in Freud's psychological model.[18] His hatred for his brutal, indifferent father was an eruptive, dominating force, born of internalized feelings of emotional rejection and alienation – a terrific unresolved rage and anger which Varèse himself felt was responsible for his many crippling depressions throughout his life.

He had resolved the situation in the short term when he resorted to physical violence, thrashed his father, and left home, but in the longer term it was not resolved. The son had fled, not ejected the father from the home and from his position, even if diminished, as head of the household. Late in life, Varèse would still say he should have killed him. Throughout his career Varèse had to struggle against his personal

---

[18] Varèse's circumstances were also very different from Freud's personal experience as the family favourite, the apple of his mother's eye. Freud was devastated by grief at the death of his father, who had occupied a less dominant position within the household than Henri Varèse did in his.

demons: not guilt so much as rage, loneliness, emotional despair, fear of loss of creativity. In *Oedipus und die Sphinx* he must have seen a perfect vehicle for acting out his anger against his father and his sense of rejection. It was this aspect, I speculate, which made the play such an attractive choice for the opera which he surely intended as his *chef d'œuvre* to date.

But he must also have been attracted to it as dramatic spectacle, with its memorable images of Oedipus killing Laios in Act 1, the crowd scenes and political interplay of Act 2 as Oedipus's approach and arrival impinge upon Jokaste and her scheming brother Kreon, ambitious for the crown, and Act 3 where Oedipus meets and kills the Sphinx upon the mountainside, confounding Kreon – who had meant to kill him and now instead hails him as conqueror and king. Oedipus's archetypal role as a lone seeker, a creator of a new order who stands between the common people and a monstrous threat or prodigy – in his case the Sphinx – finds parallels, as we shall see, with the astronomer-protagonist of Varèse's huge projected stage-work of the 1920s, *The One All Alone*. Varèse may have been attracted, too, by those shaman-like figures who appear in Act 2 of Hofmannsthal's drama: not only Tiresias, the traditional blind prophet of the Theban mythos, but Hofmannsthal's invention, the dying mage Anagyrotidas, whom Kreon tries to enlist in his attempt to seize the throne. Though the atmosphere of the play is both 'decadent' and 'post-Freudian', it is also in truth considerably more 'magical' than *Elektra*. The magical element culminates in the demonic entity of the Sphinx: who is not presented directly on stage by Hofmannsthal, but whose dying scream echoes down from the mountainside to amaze and terrify Kreon. One would dearly like to know how Varèse represented that scream, and whether – however imprecisely – it foreshadowed the final cry of the disembodied voice that sounds towards the end of *Poème électronique*.

Oedipus discourses with the supernatural and outrages convention, correctness and good taste: we might regard this as his parricide projected onto the whole world of ideas. Thus his myth spoke powerfully to the iconoclastic nature of Varèse's creativity. Varèse did not reject the great masters of the past: they were 'respected colleagues'. But he rejected utterly the moribund conservatism that sought to regard them as 'dead saints'. He sought new approaches in music that would allow him to express the primal emotion which conventional decorum would deny.

BUSONI, GOETHE AND FUTURISM

He had found models, or at least highly suggestive means of proceeding, in Debussy and in Strauss (perhaps more accurately in a mix of Strauss and Hofmannsthal). A further constellation of ideas that propelled him towards the unknown future was provided by Busoni, with whom he was in closest contact throughout the period he composed *Oedipus und die Sphinx*. In fact it is worth considering whether it was his reading of Busoni's *New Aesthetic*, rather than his admiration for Strauss, that pointed Varèse in the direction of Hofmannsthal – for Busoni concludes his revolutionary pamphlet with a Hofmannsthal quotation about the desirability of a new language for poetry, without which further artistic progress will be impossible:

... a language not even one of whose words I know, a language in which dumb things speak to me, and in which, it may be, I shall at last have to respond in my grave to an Unknown Judge.[19]

At the very beginning of the *New Aesthetic* stands another quotation, from Busoni's opera-libretto *Der mächtige Zauberer* (The Mighty Magician) based on a story by Gobineau: an opera for which he never composed the music:

> What seek you? Say! And what do you expect?
> I know not what: the Unknown I would have!
> What's known to me, is endless; I would go
> Beyond the end: The last word still is wanting.[20]

---

[19] This is from Hofmannsthal's 'Chandos-Brief' of 1902. It does not in fact appear in the original (1907) edition of Busoni's *New Aesthetic* but was only added in the English edition of 1911 (New York: G.Schirmer – the translation is by Theodore Baker). Perhaps, instead, this was an example of Varèse influencing Busoni. Busoni, however, also knew Hofmannsthal personally, from 1911 if not earlier.

[20] Varèse quoted these lines in a lecture he gave at Princeton University in 1959 (cf. 'The Liberation of Sound', p.17), attributing them by some oversight to the Danish poet Oelenschlager (whom Busoni had set in the choral finale of his Piano Concerto). *Der mächtige Zauberer*, along with the libretto of *Die Brautwahl* (after ETA Hoffmann) was published in the original edition of the *Entwurf einer neuen Ästhetik der Tonkunst* (Trieste: Schmidl Verlag, 1907). Varèse's accounts consistently suggest it was in late 1907, just before he went to Berlin, that he read the *Entwurf* – although that volume

In the *New Aesthetic* itself, Varèse read that music was a child compared to the other arts, full of unrealized potential, of which Bach and Beethoven are only the beginning; that the true 'absolute music' should be an art released from every material consideration, which reflects 'that music which pervades the universe ... Music is a part of the vibrating universe'. Busoni went on to define the true creative artist as one who does not obey laws but brings new principles spontaneously into being. Having earlier dispensed with the necessity for major and minor modes, he deplores the limitations of tonality, the academic division of harmonies into consonances and dissonances 'in a sphere where no dissonances can possibly exist!', and the imperfections of the tempered system. He proposes infinite division of the octave into third-tones, quarter-tones, sixth-tones and so on; a more liberal use of the existing 12 semitones; and outlines 113 possible new 'modes', unused scales of equal importance to diatonic major and minor. Finally he speculates on the possibility of electronic instruments able to play the infinite range of intervals, and he reports on the 'Dynamophone' invented by the American Thaddeus Cahill ('a comprehensive apparatus which makes it possible to transform an electric current into a fixed and mathematically exact number of vibrations'). In his closing paragraphs Busoni quotes from Nietzsche's *Beyond Good and Evil* and concludes that music is one path to this Nirvana:

A way to the very portal. To the bars that divide Man from Eternity – or that open to admit that which was temporal. Beyond that portal sounds *music*. Not the strains of 'musical art'. – It may be, that we must leave earth to find that music ...

It is easy to see how greatly Varèse must have been stirred by this potent mixture of technical observation and poetic, indeed mystical aspiration towards a new view of music, all of it summed up in Busoni's ringing pronouncement, which Varèse loved to quote: 'Music was born free; and to win freedom is its destiny'.

(Footnote contd.)

seems to have had a very limited circulation, and according to some commentators (cf. Vivier, p.20) Varèse was still unable to speak German on his arrival in Berlin, and he conversed with Busoni in Italian and French. That does not necessarily mean he was unable to make his way through a German text. Yet he seems never to have referred to Busoni's libretti, except for this misattributed quotation.

Busoni seems to have taken a closer and more practical interest in the progress of the young composer than either Debussy or Strauss. Clearly Varèse found him a charismatic presence, but Busoni adroitly avoided the dangerous role of father-figure by treating Varèse as an equal and intimate. When Varèse belligerently refused to accept certain modifications which Busoni wanted him to make to a score (it may have been *Oedipus und die Sphinx*) the older man was sensitive enough to back off, saying 'From now on it is no longer *Maestro* but *Ferruccio* and *Tu*'.[21]

Busoni actively supported Varèse, examined and criticized his scores, discussed the future direction of musical developments with him; and in later life Varèse paid him generous tribute:

I owe an enormous debt of gratitude to this extraordinary man – almost a figure out of the Renaissance – not only one of the greatest pianists of all time, but a man of wide culture, a scholar, thinker, writer, composer, conductor, teacher and *animateur* – a man who stimulated others to think and do things. Personally, I know that he crystallized my half-formed ideas, stimulated my imagination, and determined, I believe, the future development of my music. Treating me as he did, as a colleague and a friend, he was as fructifying to me as the sun and rain and fertilizer to soil.[22]

All this although Varèse confessed himself unable to understand how Busoni's tastes, and his own works, remained so conservative in comparison to his visionary ideas. ('It was as though his heart, loyal to the past, refused to follow his adventurous mind into so strange a future.')

Since *Oedipus und die Sphinx* absorbed most of Varèse's creative energies up to 1914 it is difficult to detect if during this period Busoni exercised any compositional influence or dramatically changed Varèse's creative direction. Yet Busoni's chief creative efforts in 1906–11 were also being lavished on a 'first' opera, the ambitious theatrical fantasy *Die Brautwahl*, with its good and bad magicians.[23] It is easy to imagine that the composers must have discussed their respective operas, and

---

[21] from Varèse's memoir of Busoni, published in *Columbia University Forum* 9/2 (Spring 1966), cited by Louise Varèse in *LGD*, p.49.

[22] Ibid, p.50.

[23] His very early operatic effort, the fairy-tale *Sigune* (1885–89) never proceeded beyond a short score.

that Varèse's *Oedipus* may have stood in some subtle relationship to *Die Brautwahl*, as well as to Strauss's *Elektra*. Moreover, Busoni was becoming increasingly concerned with his plans for an opera on the theme of Doctor Faust; and the Oedipus of Hofmannsthal's play is certainly in one aspect a Faustian seeker after power and truth. (At one stage Busoni even proposed that Hofmannsthal should work with him on the *Faust* libretto.)

It is therefore suggestive that the next major work Varèse attempted, *Mehr Licht*, in 1911, draws its title from Goethe. Given Busoni's profound and lifelong study of Goethe – and his *Faust* opera is indebted to Goethe's *Faust* even as it goes back beyond it to the ancient puppet-plays – it may be that this poet too came to occupy Varèse's attention because of Busoni's advocacy, though Max Reinhardt's Berlin *Faust* productions were probably an equally important encouragement. If there was ever any direct Busonian compositional influence upon Varèse's music it would have registered in works which are lost to us: *Oedipus*, and the symphonic poems *Mehr Licht* and *Les Cycles du Nord*. The inspiration of the latter – in the sounds Varèse claimed he 'heard' in the lights of the Aurora Borealis – strikes another Faustian chord.

If any weight can be attached to Varèse's brief remarks to Gunther Schuller apropos *Mehr Licht* (his phrasing is notably loose, including that work among 'an enormous amount of music' written 'by the time I was twenty'), they raise fascinating questions about his sources of inspiration for these two symphonic poems (if they were really two: in this context he does not mention *Les Cycles du Nord* at all). The importance of 'Goethe' (not Goethe's poetry) for his 'thinking', in conjunction with Goethe's contemporary Wronski, hints that Varèse's attention may have been directed to Goethe's scientific writings – so unusual a manifestation of his genius, and so unpalatable to scientific orthodoxy from his day to ours.

As an organic outgrowth of his creative endeavours, Goethe's scientific work has tended to exert more stimuli on fellow creative artists. J.M.W. Turner's late paintings employing Goethe's colour theories are well known, and in music it is now widely accepted that Anton Webern's refinement of 12-note method was partly inspired by his appreciation of Goethe's work on plant morphology. In *Mehr Licht*, Varèse could have been thinking of Goethe's work on light and colour in the *Beiträge zur Optik* (*Contributions to Optics*) (1791) and *Farbenlehre* (*Theory of Colour*) (1810), and of his passionate dispute with Newtonian optical theory, which he considered a deadening reductionism that totally failed to describe – or indeed explain – light and colour as we experience them. Varèse's description of the light of the Aurora Borealis (above, p.24) tends to support the idea that he was exploring the idea of aural equivalents for optical phenomena.[24]

This does not necessarily invalidate his statement that *Mehr Licht* was written 'on a Goethe poem'. Many of Goethe's poems express the phenomenological perceptions he codified in his scientific works: thus 'The Metamorphosis of Plants' (1789) is a poetic summary of the principles outlined in the *Pflanzenlehre*. Since *Mehr Licht* is not the title of a poem, it might seem virtually impossible to identify a suitable candidate among Goethe's enormous output. Perhaps, however, we need not look very far. One poetic text by Goethe which Varèse certainly knew was *Faust*, the archetypal drama of the magus and wonder-worker – for he had taken part, as conductor of the Berlin Symphonischer Chor, in Max Reinhardt's lavish productions at the Deutsches Theater. Thus if nothing else, he would have known the choruses very well. Reinhardt's 1909 production had been only of *Faust Part 1*; *Part 2* followed in 1911 – the very year, apparently, in which Varèse was composing *Mehr Licht*. And *Faust Part 2* begins with a choric prologue, where Ariel, in dialogue with a chorus of Spirits, describes to the exhausted Faust the change in landscape from twilight, through night-time, to dawn. This draws to an end with a remarkable evocation of the idea of light engendering sound:

> Hark! The storm of hours draws near,
> Loudly to the spirit-ear
> Signs of coming day appear.
> Rocky gates are wildly crashing,
> Phoebus' wheels are onward dashing
>
> *(A wonderful noise proclaims the approach of the sun)*
>
> Light doth mighty sounds beget!
> Pealing loud as rolling thunder,

---

[24] A topic much in the air in 1911–12 owing to the international success of Scriabin's symphony *Prometheus* (*The Poem of Fire*), which related pitch to colour and included a part for a 'light-keyboard', intended to project the music's changing colours into the auditorium. (Varèse, we remember, told Schuller he found Scriabin's orchestral works 'simply overwhelming'.)

Eye and ear it fills with wonder,
Though itself unconscious yet,
Downward steals it, 'mongst the flowers
Seeking deeper, stiller bowers,
'Mongst the foliage, neath the rock;
Thou'lt be deafened by the shock![25]

I propose this identification simply as a useful hypothesis that may fit
the pitifully few facts as we know them. But if correct, it would help
to 'place' *Mehr Licht/Les Cycles du Nord* as a work or works dealing with
the cosmic processes of night and day, as did the *Prélude à la fin d'un
jour*, likewise on a poem in the form of a dramatic dialogue. We could
also speculate that this was Varèse's first 'Faustian' musical conception;
it would not be his last. Finally, it directs us on, to his last musical
project before he left Europe. Goethe's introduction here of
Shakespeare's Ariel reminds us of the satirical 'Walpurgisnachtstraum'
in Faust Part 1, subtitled 'Oberon and Titania's Golden Wedding', with
its phantasmagoric re-use of characters from *A Midsummer Night's
Dream*. From such a Goethean perspective, a production of
Shakespeare's play with circus clowns would be an eminently
appropriate enterprise.

It is certainly hard to ascribe any 'Busonian' features to Varèse's
surviving works from *Amériques* on, just as Busoni's compositional
personality is less easy to describe in terms of specific technical features
than that of Debussy or Strauss. But it is pertinent to note that the
years when Varèse was in closest contact with Busoni were those of the
older composer's most pronounced compositional radicalism: the years
of the *Berceuse élégiaque* (Varèse treasured a score of this that Busoni
had inscribed in 1910 '*All'illustro Futuro – l'amico Varèse*'), the
Sonatina Seconda for piano and the orchestral *Nocturne symphonique*,
both conceived as studies for *Doktor Faust*. Traces of these works –
especially the *Nocturne* – are perhaps still detectable in the first,
transitional scores that Varèse composed in the USA, most clearly in
the original version of *Amériques*. And in the *Berceuse*, the *Sonatina* and

---

[25] Translation by E.A.Bowring, from *The Poems of Goethe translated in the Original
Metres* (New York: Lovell, Coryell & Company, 1882). I have no idea who Bowring
was, and his version is not exactly abounding in felicities: yet 'Light doth mighty
sounds beget!' is the simplest rendering I have seen of Goethe's *Welch Getöse bringt das
Licht!*, even if it unduly domesticates the din or racket or roar suggested by *Getöse*.

the *Nocturne* we find possibly the clearest embodiments of the ideal of musical form which Busoni had promulgated in the *New Aesthetic*: an ideal (expressed in language reminiscent of Goethe's plant morphology studies) which plainly influenced Varèse in such later works as *Hyperprism*, *Intégrales* and *Octandre*:

Every motive – so it seems to me – contains, like a seed, its life-germ within itself. From the different plant-seeds grow different families of plants, dissimilar in form, foliage, blossom, fruit, growth and colour. Even each individual plant belonging to one and the same species assumes, in size, form and strength, a growth peculiar to itself. And so, in each motive, there lies the embryo of its fully developed form; each one must unfold itself differently, yet each obediently follows the law of eternal harmony. *This form is imperishable, though each be unlike every other.*[26]

Clearly there were also affinities of personal character. Varèse spoke approvingly of Busoni's vein of occasionally cruel humour, his 'Florentine' sarcasm, which balanced his more mystical and speculative tendencies. It may also be that he responded to Busoni specifically as an *Italian*, a fellow-Latin in quasi-exile within the overwhelming cultural apparatus of Wilhelmine Germany. When together, they spoke French and Italian. In addition to Varèse's patrimony as a Parisian and *bourguignon*, there was an Italian element in his make-up, or at least an instinctive feel for the Italian personality and culture, to which his Piedmontaise ancestry and his adolescence in Turin obviously contributed. Busoni and he were alike fascinated by Leonardo da Vinci as the type of ideal man and artist, and in Paris Varèse had several Italian artist-friends, notably Modigliani. It was only natural that he should have become interested in Futurism, which in its origins was principally an Italian artistic movement, and Futurism also engaged Busoni's attention at this time.

During his lifetime Varèse was often to be popularly termed a 'Futurist composer' – a label he always indignantly rejected. Yet it is easy to see how the misconception arose: the aggressive, percussive aspects of his music almost seem the ideal embodiment of the violent, disruptive approach to art called for in the various Futurist Manifestos. He was familiar with these, and especially the writings of Marinetti,

---

[26] *Sketch of a New Aesthetic of Music* (1911 edition, reprinted NY: Dover Publications Inc, 1962), p.81.

who had called for an art that would celebrate 'the frenetic life of our great cities' and 'glory in our day to day world splendidly transformed by victorious science'; who had also declared in the first Futurist Manifesto of February 1909 that 'no work without an aggressive character can be a masterpiece'.

Varèse knew Marinetti personally and retained a long-standing friendship with Luigi Russolo, the Futurist most directly involved with music as a builder of new instruments and exponent of *l'arte di rumori*, the 'art of noise'. He came to reject most of Futurist art – as early as 1917 he was dismissing the Futurists, at least in the musical sphere, for 'slavishly imitating only what is superficial and most boring in ... our daily lives', and Louise Varèse notes that he would often say: 'The futurists imitate, an artist transmutes'. Yet she also records that before World War I he was 'in enthusiastic accord' with many of Marinetti's pronouncements.[27] Indeed many elements of the Futurist approach – especially in the visual arts – provide suggestive parallels with the later evolution of Varèse's musical ideas. If they did not directly influence him they must be counted among part of the fermenting culture of nascent artistic modernism within which he moved, and which his own works came to realize in such a decisive and individual fashion.[28]

Apart from Marinetti's deliberate desire to shock and gain notoriety for his movement with his hyperbolical assertions of the need to do away with all previously established artistic traditions,[29] if one concern distinguished the Futurists from the many competing modern art movements (such as Cubism) it was their concern with dynamic motion: motion in space. Expressed at its crudest in Marinetti's apotheosis of sheer speed – the speed of the motor-car – it was developed by several of the gifted painters who assembled under his banner and issued the Futurist Manifesto on Art in April 1910, into a theory of paintings organized around 'lines of force'. For the Manifesto of 1913 Carlo Carrà produced an essay on 'Plastic Planes as Spherical Expansions in Space', a title immediately reminiscent of Varèse's words

---

[27] *LGD*, p.106.

[28] Jonathan Bernard has much the best general examination of Varèse's relations with Futurism (Bernard, pp.23–31); my discussion pursues only a few salient topics.

[29] As Bernard has pointed out, Marinetti's thirst for 'blowing up all the traditions, like rotten bridges' (*Let's Murder the Moonshine*) resonates with Varèse's youthful search 'not for the Holy Grail but for the bomb that would make the musical world explode' (above, p.56).

about his own music. These ideas of force and space reached a highly developed form in the writings and art of Umberto Boccioni, perhaps the most gifted of the Futurist painters.

Virtually all the Italian Futurists began their creative careers as painters in the 'Divisionist' style – Divisionism being a native Italian art movement parallel to, rather than imitative of, Post-Impressionism.[30] This had led several artists – not uninfluenced by Goethe – to research in optics and theories of colours which they felt led naturally towards what one of them proclaimed as 'a whole new aesthetic' of painting.[31] The most fully-developed exposition of the techniques of this 'new aesthetic' appeared as late as 1906 in the *Principi scientifici del Divisionismo: La Tecnica della Pittura* by Gaetano Previati. This had a tremendous impact on the young Boccioni, who consulted with Previati and wrote a monograph about him in 1916. In Previati he found a master who had 'reduced classic form to luminous masses and volumes, which deform atmospheres and bodies according to the artist's will'.

Developing Divisionist ideas in the Futurist manifestos on art and in his commentaries on his own paintings in the decade before World War I, Boccioni asserted that 'objects never end; they intersect with innumerable combinations of attraction and innumerable shocks of aversion'. He described this process as the 'interpenetration' or 'compenetration' of planes. In his paintings of 1910–11 he was searching for 'the unique form that expresses its continuity in space': such works as *Visioni Simultanee* (*Simultaneous Visions*) and *La Strada entra nella casa* (*The street enters the house*) develop a technique of interpenetrative spatial disruption, 'the dislocation and dismemberment of objects, the scattering and fusion of details, freed from accepted logic, and independent from one another'. Of *Gli Adii* (*The Farewells*, first panel of his major triptych *States of Mind*) he wrote

---

[30] This style of painting evolved out of the optical principle that the two complementary colours juxtaposed in dots rather than mixed on the canvas would, at a certain distance, fuse into the intended mixture in the eye of the spectator. The technique offered increased luminosity and a more accurate portrayal of natural light. Yet the Divisionist were interested not just in complimentaries but in many gradations of hue and colour similarity – striving to produce, ideally, a faithful rendering of all kinds of light and lighting effects.

[31] Vittore Grubicy de Dragon, 'Tecnica e Estetica divisionista' (1896). Grubicy was the patron of Carrà.

that 'the mingled concrete and abstract are translated into *force lines* and rhythms in quasi musical harmony'.[32]

Some of these comments strikingly anticipate elements of Varèse's writing on his own compositions. Whether or not he had read them all, he certainly knew the 1910 Futurist Art Manifesto, which was largely composed by Boccioni, and he must certainly have been aware of him as a painter since Busoni was acquainted with Boccioni and esteemed his work.[33] We know that Busoni received Boccioni in Berlin (in company with Marinetti, who was an admirer of the *Sonatina Seconda*) and listened politely to their Futurist polemics. These early contacts ripened into friendship, crowned in June 1916 when they spent several weeks together at Pallanza, where Busoni began to compose the score of his *Doktor Faust* and Boccioni painted the sombre and probing portrait, *Maestro Ferruccio Busoni*, which is generally considered his masterpiece. (Two months more and Boccioni was dead, killed by a fall from his horse after military call-up, and Busoni was writing a memorial article in the *Neue Zürcher Zeitung*.)

How much of Boccioni's work Varèse knew is open to question, but one very large, very characteristic painting must have been familiar to him. Painted in 1910–11, it was exhibited in Berlin in 1912 and purchased by – Busoni. On the huge canvas, in a vast flamboyant swirl of activity, labourers struggle to restrain enormous horses that convey an overwhelming sense of dangerous animal vitality and are apparently in the act of sprouting wings. In the distance, massive buildings are under construction in a maze of scaffolding. As Christopher Butler has commented,

the light of the sun conducted along the central horse's mane is an overpowering force within the painting, as Boccioni adapts divisionist technique to convey the impression of a huge magnetic field activated by light.[34]

---

[32] Boccioni's italics. This and most of the other quotations are from Christopher Butler, *Early Modernism* (Oxford University Press, 1994), pp.144ff.

[33] '... at last, after a lengthy interval, an Italian painter of historical significance' – Letter from Busoni to Jella Oppenheimer, in *Ferruccio Busoni: Selected Letters*, translated and edited by Antony Beaumont (London: Faber & Faber, 1987), p.248.

[34] Butler, op. cit., p. 144.

Boccioni viewed this work of his as 'erecting a new altar to modern life vibrant with dynamism ... one no less pure and exalting than those raised out of religious contemplation of the divine mystery'. The painting is entitled *La Città sale* (*The City Rises*).

PART 2 New worlds

1921 (silverpoint drawing by Joseph Stella)   *G. Ricordi & Co Ltd*

4 · From the Seine to Brooklyn Bridge

*J'ordonnerai la saturnale sur Brooklyn-Bridge face aux
  sky-scrapers étonnés*
VARÈSE
Oblation

CHRONOLOGY 1915–1918

1915 *April: Mobilized in the French army, as a bicycle messenger
stationed with the 25th Staff Headquarters at the Ecole de Guerre in Paris,
but invalided out after six months owing to double pneumonia. Lung
trouble, and a feeling of inability to breathe, trouble him for the rest of his
life. Decides to look for work in the USA. 18 December: sails for New York
on the* Rochambeau, *arriving 29 December.*

1916 *In New York, Varèse is unsuccessful in finding work. ('Musical
organizations were run entirely by society ladies, who certainly did not
want to hear any modern music.') But he finds congenial company among
other exiled French artists – notably Marcel Duchamp, the photographer
Alfred Steiglitz and the painter Albert Gleizes. He is befriended by Fritz
Kreisler, and also comes to know Eugène Ysaÿe, Isadora Duncan, the poet
Walter Arensburg and the novelist Djuna Barnes. He frequents the
Metropolitan Opera, attending rehearsals.*

1917 *1 April: conducts a performance of Berlioz's* Grande Messe des
Morts *at the Hippodrome, New York 'in memory of the dead of all
nations'. Close association with the Cubist painter and poet Francis*

Picabia: Varèse contributes to his magazine 391. During the summer he and Picabia move into an apartment rented from the translator Louise Norton, who is a friend of Duchamp. After she returns from a six-month absence out West she and Varèse become friends, and soon lovers.

1918 *Friendship with the harpist-composer Carlos Salzedo. 17 March: Varèse conducts the Cincinnati Symphony Orchestra as a guest artist, but a planned tour with the orchestra is cancelled because of his 'scandalous' association with Louise Norton (who is separated from her first husband). Probably this year begins work on* Amériques.

1919 *Founds the New Symphony Orchestra, specifically for the performance of modern music. Its first programme, conducted by Varèse on 11 and 12 April at Carnegie Hall, features Bartók, Casella, Debussy and Dupont (every work a US première) and the music is assailed by the critics for the very fact of its modernity. After protests, Varèse resigns the conductorship.*

1920 *Spends part of this year in Chicago, where he acts in a number of silent films, including* Dr. Jekyll and Mr. Hyde *with John Barrymore.*

1921 *31 May: with Salzedo, Varèse founds the International Composers' Guild. Composes* Offrandes *and probably completes* Amériques.

1922 *19 February: first concert of the International Composers' Guild. Varèse spends the spring in Berlin, where he sees Busoni once more. He also learns of the destruction of all the pre-war manuscripts he had left in storage. With Busoni as President he helps to found an Internationale Komponisten Guild on the pattern of the ICG, establishing through Arthur Lourié an affiliation with the Collective of Composers in Moscow. 23 April: Carlos Salzedo conducts the première of* Offrandes *at an ICG concert in New York. 1 November: the first concert of the IKG in Berlin includes* Offrandes' *European première. Begins composing* Hyperprism.

THE AMERICAN SCENE

America was a new start. That much is clear, although some years elapsed, apparently, before Varèse began to compose again. When he did, it was in a new spirit. Varèse often tried to play down the significance of his titles, but they tell us much about the attitudes he wanted to convey. *Amériques, Hyperprism, Intégrales* and so on immediately proclaim new worlds and the new scientific awareness of them, and their manner of expression evokes the teeming, raucous life of the modern city. They are intensely urban music. Whatever may have been prophetic in the lost works of Varèse's European period, their titles (and even at this late stage we had better recall that in most cases the titles are all we have) speak of the sea, of mists, conversations in the park, the onset of evening, the Burgundian landscape, cathedral architecture, the starry night. Pretty nearly the whole Post-Impressionist agenda, in fact.

In this, as in the physical evidence of *Un grand sommeil noir*, the young Varèse had revealed himself as a follower of Debussy. Although Rodin, Monet and Cezanne gave birth to the modern movement in the visual arts through the new ways they apprehended the physical world, their work constitutes the last great efflorescence of the pastoral, figurative images of nature which had dominated art since the Renaissance. Debussy's music, likewise, remains rooted in evocations of nature – unprecedentedly vibrant in its illusion of direct auditory transcription from the sounds and rhythms of the physical world, yet that world is still conceived, if only in the imagination, as essentially pastoral and even on occasion *faux*-Hellenic.

This is the tradition within which the young Varèse composed. If, during that time, he was a musical revolutionary *in potentia*, it was only when he came to the USA that he became a revolutionary in fact. It is the relation of potential to fact that is important. His 'new start' was not a complete break with the past, nor a rejection of it. The hard sciences arose from the speculative experimentation of alchemy, and belief in magic gave birth to the machine, the 'magical' aid to overcome the brute constraints of the physical universe. Varèse's urbanized, machine-age music must still have developed out of his previous works, and to some extent in tandem with contemporary developments in the other arts.

If in his first Paris sojourn he had already formulated a conception of music as the projection of sounds (intelligent or not) in space, then he was rethinking musical perspective in a manner comparable to Picasso's and Braque's development of Cubism – apparently at the same time, around 1907–8. But clearly the conception was only fully put into effect a decade later, after Varèse's first years in New York. He had already known some of the Cubists, notably Albert Gleizes and Fernard Léger, in Paris, but it was in New York that he was thrown for a while into close association with these fellow-exiles, and with Picabia and Duchamp, who were developing Dadaism from Cubism. Varèse did not accept the Dadaist aesthetic,[1] but he certainly shared their excitement in the new urban age of technology, to which New York and the USA generally – a city and country practically synonymous with modernism, run on modern production methods and unburdened by the freight of history – seemed the natural home.

Metal, machines and mass-production inspired Picabia, Léger and Duchamp in different ways. Picabia viewed man's creation, the machine, as a kind of self-portrait, and represented human relationships (sex, predominantly) as repetitive mechanical processes. Duchamp's famous *Nude Descending a Staircase* (1912), derived from the sequential images of cinematography, had interpreted the human figure as an erotic machine. At the time he and Varèse were in closest contact, Duchamp had begun work on his enigmatic, never-finished *Large Glass* (*The Bride Stripped Bare by Her Bachelors, Even*), which has been described as the 'Grand Arcanum of modern art' and as a parody 'of the language and the forms of science without the slightest regard for scientific probability cause and effect'.[2] It is probably significant that the *Large Glass* can also be interpreted in mystical, alchemical or even cabbalistic terms, reminding us that Duchamp too frequented the same esoteric Parisian circles as the young Varèse.

Varèse's own outlook was probably closer to that of Léger, whom he had helped to release from harsh military service in the trenches. Léger turned his back on abstraction and the more academic and self-regarding aspects of Cubism to celebrate the dynamism of the new century and the modern city in broad, bold strokes intended to be intelligible to the widest possible audience. In a painting like the *Card Players* of 1917, men and machines are alike delineated with steely precision, in almost symbiotic union. Throughout his long career Léger remained an optimist about technology, his art dedicated to the proposition that man should live in the present, not the past, and be in harmony with the world he has made. Society, functioning with the precision and inevitability of the machine, will attain that harmony. If people are dwarfed by their huge buildings and constructions, as by the

---

[1] Louise Norton (soon to be Louise Varèse) and her first husband knew Picabia and Duchamp, on whose behalf they founded and edited a Dadaist magazine, *Rogue*, in 1916 (it did not last out the year).

[2] Robert Hughes, *The Mechanical Paradise* (1980).

forces of nature, they are still responsible for them, and remain in command.

Machine imagery as such is less central to Varèse's music,[3] though he eagerly embraced noise-making machines – sirens – for their sonic potential, and in his first American interview declared that

Musicians should take up this question [of instrumentation] in deep earnest with the help of machinery specialists ... What I am looking for is new mechanical mediums which will lend themselves to every expression of thought and keep up with thought.[4]

Machinery, then, as the handmaid of creation, not its subject. In his music, he would always strive to parallel the thrust and dynamism of the new technological world-view, rather than merely illustrating it in the onomatopoeic fashion of Honegger's *Pacific 231*, Mossolov's *Zavod*, or Villa-Lobos's *Assobio a Jato*. But perhaps – though it is a big perhaps – he did once experiment with that illustrative, 'Picabian' mode in a work teasingly chronicled in the Dadaist press during 1917. This is the *Danse du Robinet froid* (generally referred to in English as 'Cold Faucet Dance').

Such existence as we can infer for the piece is confined to three allusions from Picabia. In 391 No.3, 'M. Varèse has almost completed the orchestration of his *Danse du Robinet froid*'; but in No.8 'the *Danse du Robinet froid* is still not yet finished'; while in *Dada* no.7 'the *Robinet froid* is going to be purchased for the botanical gardens'. Most commentators have been disposed to view this project, if such it was, as a mere joke or figment of Picabia's imagination. Certainly no such piece appears to survive, even in incomplete form. Yet it is difficult to believe that Varèse, previously extremely productive, really spent the years 1915–18 without attempting any new compositions, and for that reason alone some reality may lie behind the magazine pronouncements. The report about Varèse completing the orchestration looks objective enough in form and, in view of the probably extensive dance component of the *Songe d'une nuit d'été* project (to say nothing of the much later *Dance for Burgess*), we can hardly reject the idea that Varese would compose a dance. Perhaps

---

[3] Not, at any rate, until later in his career, when he drew directly on factory sounds for *Déserts* and *Poème électronique*.

[4] *New York Telegraph*, March 1916.

specifically a *Tap Dance* ('faucet' is after all an Americanism; the possibility of a pun on 'tap' rises more readily to the British mind) with all the percussive connotations of that genre as well as its associations with the circus and the Music-hall. If the piece existed at all it may well have been nothing more than a parodic entertainment, a musical correlative for some of the sillier Cubist-Dadaist ideas, just as the poem *Oblation*, dedicated to Picabia, which Varèse wrote during an evening's drinking with Picabia on Brooklyn Bridge and contributed to 391 No.5 (June 1917), is a parody of Dadaist verse. The title *Danse du Robinet froid* suggests a marriage of music and technology (in this case the technology of plumbing), while pouring cold water on some of the wilder and more sentimental excesses of the Dadaists' faith in the machine.

* * *

Just as in the visual arts, the USA had become the Mecca and home to a new kind of music, developing in many varied aspects. Its rhythms and dissonances were born of the big city experience of multiplicity, mass movement and machines; the intoxication and alienation of industrial power, which opened limitless possibilities while making possible new levels of barbarism and violence; scientific sophistication and the new primitivism; jazz and blues. Varèse would soon emerge as the most absolute representative of this musical current; and though his idiom and achievement were unique, it is salutary to remember the extent to which he *was* representative, part of a wider movement involving both 'indigenous' Americans and European immigrants.

The most radical musical mind in the Americas, Charles Ives, was at this time virtually unknown as a composer, despite the visible commercial success of his New York insurance business. Scion of an old New England puritan family, Ives took his inspiration as much from childhood memory, pastoral reverie and hymnody as he did from the teeming cities of the present. But some of his most boldly exploratory music enshrines a graphic urban component, including a directly imitative and demotic impulse (*Central Park in the Dark*, *Over the Pavements*, the steamboat explosion of *The General Slocum*, the crowds awaiting the train in *From Hanover Square North* ..., the subway system in *Tone Roads No.3*) that Varèse would never adopt. In its fierce dissonance and polyphonic multiplicity, its superimposed layers of texture, its bold use of percussion ensembles in complex metres (Symphony No.4), and its attempt at stereophonic placement of different ensembles (*The Unanswered Question, From the Steeples and the Mountains*), Ives's music offers some of the most suggestive contemporary parallels to Varèse, despite their profound differences of aesthetic orientation. The mystical side of Ives's work, deriving from the New England Transcendentalists (*The Unanswered Question, Concord, The Celestial Railroad, From Paracelsus*) resonates, too, with the esoteric strain in Varèse's. When he eventually came to know Ives's work, in the 1920s and 30s, Varèse strongly admired it, though sadly the esteem does not seem to have been mutual.

Ives's friend and fellow-New Englander Carl Ruggles was still struggling to forge his personal idiom, but would soon begin, in *Angels* for six trumpets, to establish a granitically hewn polyphony that resembled the principles of 'dissonant counterpoint' already being developed by the theorist and ethnomusicologist Charles Seeger. Though himself only a small composer, Seeger was very influential as a thinker, especially in proposing a dissonantly-based style which would be free of the weaknesses, as he saw them, of the tonally-based dissonant styles of such European avant-gardists as Scriabin and Schoenberg: a true 'modern American' idiom, in fact. His ideas were perhaps to be most perfectly realized in the remarkable chamber compositions of his wife, Ruth Crawford Seeger (though her creative gifts encompassed much more than mere reproduction of her husband's theories).

In one sense, all these composers were still involved with more traditional compositional concepts than was Varèse – even if their angular counterpoint evokes steel girders and skyscrapers rather than peacefully flowing rivers. Counterpoint *per se* was to have less function in his music than the individual identities of tones within dissonant harmonic constructions, and while Seeger or Ruggles tended still to accept musical tones as their given materials, Varèse was being drawn to the exploration of sound in a yet rawer state.

In this if little else he was close to some of the younger generation of Americans, notably Henry Cowell from California (the newest part of the New World). By 1917 the 20-year-old Cowell had studied with Seeger; he was to become a key figure in new music promotion and publishing in the 1920s and 30s, performing prodigies on behalf of Ives, Ruggles, Varèse and many others. Fabulously prolific from the age of 15, without benefit of academic training, Cowell had already experimented with sirens. (He would later employ Native American percussion such as thundersticks, and explore the development of electronic keyboard instruments.) He was producing boldly experimental piano music, which opened up a whole new range of resonance from the instrument: harmonics, glissandi and drumbeats on the strings, the intense dissonance of cluster chords. In works such as the *Quartet Romantic* (1915–17), which would remain beyond the capacity of players for half a century, he was seeking to demonstrate what he considered the 'physical identity between rhythm and harmony' – which he also sought to prove in his treatise *New Musical Resources* (already partly written, though not to be published until 1930).

Younger even than Cowell, the teenage George Antheil was almost ready to embark on the brash, self-promoting career of a virtuoso modernist piano composer that would take him in the opposite direction to Varèse – from New York to Paris. There his various flirtations with surrealism, Dadaism, Ezra Pound, and Picabia climaxed in collaboration with Léger on *Ballet mécanique*. But even by 1920, in Trenton, New Jersey, Antheil was adumbrating a 'mechanistic' aesthetic of music in pieces such as *Lithuanian Nights* for string quartet and the *Airplane Sonata* for piano. He was to proclaim himself a 'Musico-Mechanist', an enemy of sentiment and illusion. His works were 'time mechanisms' operating in 'time-space'. Antheil averred that 'the environment of the machine has already become a spiritual thing', and he manipulated rhythmic and harmonic blocks of material in the manner (at least in his estimation) of a Cubist painter: 'hard musical objects ... so fast and unalterable that they are hard as stone, indestructible fragments for all ages'.[5] Antheil may have been a superficial musical thinker, a callow adapter of current artistic ideas (then again, he may have been something more substantial). But if so, the importance of his ideas and slogans lies precisely in the fact that they *were* current, that they fulfilled certain avant-garde expectations of the role of music in the new machine age.

Antheil consciously marketed himself to his first concert agent as a 'fiery ultramodern' pianist in the mould of Leo Ornstein, eight years his senior – a Russian immigrant who came to the USA as a child and sprang from New York's Lower East Side as one of the most remarkable

---

[5] Quotations from Antheil's unpublished letters and papers as cited by the Antheil specialist Linda Whitesitt in her notes to Albany TROY 146: 'George Antheil: Bad Boy of Music'.

pianist-composers of his time. From 1911 onward Ornstein's recitals introduced many works by Ravel, Scriabin, Busoni, Bartók and Schoenberg to America, while his own pieces, some of them furiously dissonant and percussive, glorying in unremitting, machine-like rhythms, tone clusters, crushed seconds, gong effects and irregular metres, won glowing reviews from the more modern-minded critics. 'Always one senses the pavements stretching between steel buildings, the black hurrying tides of human beings', wrote Paul Rosenfeld, later to be a friend and champion of Varèse. Ornstein was dubbed a 'Futurist' musician. His *Danse Sauvage* and *Suicide in an Airplane* (both 1913) are direct precursors of Antheil's *Sauvage* and *Airplane* Sonatas from the early 1920s. Henry Cowell, whose first piano work with chord-clusters also dates from 1913, considered studying with Ornstein before he went to Seeger.

Ornstein was perhaps the most visible and notorious of the 'immigrant' modernists whose impact on music in the USA compounded that of the 'indigenous' Americans in the period when Varèse first arrived there. He began to withdraw from the concert platform in the early 1920s, while still at the peak of his career, and by the 1930s his music and influence was beginning to be forgotten.[6] Others were to be more closely associated with Varèse, or to parallel aspects of his musical innovations. A year after Varèse's arrival New York received another Parisian composer-conductor into American musical life – Daniel Chennevière, better known by his assumed name Dane Rudhyar, who came to supervise a festival of avant-garde music and ritual at the Metropolitan Opera and stayed on once the US had entered the Great War. Eleven years younger than Varèse, Rudhyar too had been befriended by Debussy and was an exponent of musical modernism with an occult and esoteric tinge, influenced by the theosophical ideas of Scriabin. With Varèse, Rudhyar was a founder-member of the International Composers' Guild, and as a penetrating writer on music – from an essentially esoteric standpoint – was to be one of Varèse's most consistent champions in print.

Unlike Varèse, who wrote no solo piano music apart from arrangements, most of Rudhyar's important works were piano pieces. But he conceived of the piano in very unconventional terms, asking

---

[6] In February 2002, before this book went to press, Leo Ornstein died in Wisconsin at the reputed age of 110.

performers to think of the instrument as 'a resonant mass of wood and metal, a sort of condensed orchestra of gongs, bells and the like'. His works of the 1920s carry polytonality to extremes of rock-like dissonance, and titles such as *Paeans, Stars, Granites, Pentagrams, Ouranos* reflect an enthusiasm for elemental forces not dissimilar to Varèse's own. The protean Rudhyar was also a painter, poet and novelist – though his most enduring legacy may not be in any of these fields, nor in music, but as the architect of a 20th-century reconstitution of astrology, uniting that ancient symbol-system with depth psychology, which he established in some 35 books and countless articles.

More immediately significant for Varèse was Carlos Salzedo (1885–1961), the harpist and composer, with whom he co-founded the International Composers Guild. French-born and Paris Conservatoire-trained, Salzedo had been resident in the USA since 1909, when he became principal harpist of the Metropolitan Opera. An enthusiast for modernism in music and his instrument's particular role in it, Salzedo pioneered new methods of writing for the harp, including percussive effects both on the strings and the body of the instrument. These he explored in his own compositions and clearly also influenced Varèse's harp-writing in *Offrandes* and *Amériques*.

* * *

Within this welter of modernist musical activity in the USA, therefore, *Offrandes* and *Amériques*, the two works which Vaèse composed in the period 1918–21 – his first two works to survive, apart from *Un grand sommeil noir* – emerge as representative rather than unique. Representative of their time and place, of an exciting period of new possibilities, of new ways of representation, in the arts generally and in music in particular. Representative of change, and of the changes in Varèse's own life as he crossed from the Old World to the New. Though already they could hardly be mistaken for the work of any other composer, they are in the fullest sense transitional pieces, still abounding in reference to the European past and open to a wide range of contemporary influence.[7] They are the last stages on the road to the

---

[7] Though it is impossible to know whether this had any relation to the works' lingering 'European' characteristics, at the time he composed *Amériques* and *Offrandes* Varèse still believed most of his early output was intact and waiting for him to reclaim it from the Berlin warehouse.

attainment of his unique personal idiom, which would soon burst out with tremendous force in *Hyperprism*, *Octandre* and *Intégrales*.

Offrandes is strictly speaking the later work, conceived and written in a relatively short time when *Amériques* was nearing completion after a much lengthier parturition. Within its much smaller space it is also stylistically more unified and 'advanced', nearer to the fully realized 'Varèse sound' of the works of 1922–5. From most points of view, including the strictly 'evolutionary', it might therefore seem logical to discuss *Amériques* in advance of *Offrandes*. I have decided on the opposite course. This is partly because *Offrandes* introduces us to a number of Varèse's salient compositional techniques in a relatively compact design – though there are other ways in which it, too, is untypical of his extant output as a whole. It was the first work which Varèse completed in the New World, and his first to be performed there, several years in advance of *Amériques* – and he went on working at and revising *Amériques* for a considerable period after its official completion date of 1922. Also, though it is not an unimportant piece in the history of 20th-century music, Varèse himself regarded *Offrandes* as a comparatively minor work. He poured an immense amount of himself into *Amériques*, which remained one of his most-loved pieces, despite (or because of) the paucity of performances during his lifetime.

OFFRANDES

Offrandes is a diptych of two songs for soprano and chamber orchestra, composed in 1921. Varèse seems never to have commented on the precise significance to be attached to the title (which means, of course, 'Offerings') and perhaps intended only the obvious one. Originally he called it *Dédications*, and this was the title under which it was first performed. The two songs, 'Chanson de Là-haut', to lines by Vicente Huidobro and 'La Croix du sud', to a poem by José Juan Tablada, are in fact dedicated respectively 'à Louise' (whom he had just married) and to his harpist-composer friend Carlos Salzedo.

This miniature song-cycle received its première on 23 April 1922 in New York, at the Greenwich Village Theater, as part of a concert of the International Composers' Guild which Varèse, with Salzedo, had been largely responsible for founding. Salzedo conducted the ensemble (in which Varèse played the cymbals) with the Russian soprano Nina

Koshetz as soloist. It was not published until 1927, by C.C. Birchard & Co., Boston; Varèse made a few (but significant) revisions for the new edition brought out by Franco Colombo's Colfranc Edition, New York, in 1960.

Thus before the rediscovery of *Un grand sommeil noir* this was, as far as anyone knew, the only available starting-point for a consideration of Varèse's musical identity. He himself seems to have down-played its significance, describing it as 'a very small-scale work, a purely intimate piece'. Yet many of its sounds and gestures are dramatic, even violent, rather than intimate in any conventional sense. Even so, *Offrandes* has tended to receive surprisingly little attention. Commentators prefer to accord it only a cursory glance on the way to their in-depth studies of the more obviously radical works of a few years later. That in itself tells us something: that the piece's radicalism – though certainly an important aspect of it – is neither so total, nor so pronounced, as in Varèse's other compositions of the 1920s. The corollary, often unspoken, is that many features of *Offrandes* can be clearly if not always comfortably related to tradition, and to contemporary European compositional practice: and this is indeed the case. The work implies an expressive background that is still largely familiar to any listener conversant with the general run of early 20th-century music. The divergences from that background therefore stand out with especial clarity, enabling us to see precisely what kind of powerful, piquant, and beautiful 'new music' is here taking shape.

The chosen form is one with clear antecedents – a small song-cycle (lasting about 8 minutes in all) for a chamber orchestra whose composition is not too different from the kind of reduced ensemble that composers had been finding increasingly appealing since around the turn of the century. The texts themselves have certain affinities with the symbolist poems to which many other composers had already been drawn. Although both poets were Spanish-speaking, they wrote their texts in French. So these are Varèse's last settings of his native language (with even a topographic reference to his beloved Paris) – and his approach generally conforms to the syllabic and declamatory manners of word-setting pioneered especially by Debussy. There is little attempt at any direct pictorial or onomatapoeic representation of the texts; but unquestionably certain phrases have suggested certain specific musical ideas. These songs' ancestry – spiritual if not literal – certainly includes the *Poèmes de Mallarmé* of Ravel, Stravinsky's

Japanese Lyrics, perhaps Schoenberg's *Pierrot Lunaire*; and further back probably Ravel's *Shéhérazade* and, indeed, Debussy's *Pelléas et Mélisande*. (Webern's op.13 songs for voice and chamber orchestra, composed a few years earlier, still lay unpublished.)

The 'traditional' features are however unevenly distributed between the two songs, which form a strongly contrasted diptych. 'Chanson de Là-haut' is the one which manifests them most strongly (which perhaps explains why it was actually encored by popular acclamation at the première), while also containing significant pointers to the future. 'La croix du sud' brings that future much closer: as a total conception it is much more original, although many aspects remain essentially familiar.

Varèse's chamber orchestra calls for piccolo, flute, oboe, clarinet, bassoon, horn, trumpet, trombone, harp, and a string quintet of 2 violins, viola, cello and double bass (the string strength may, at the conductor's discretion, be increased to a maximum of 6.4.4.2.2). Thus far the layout is almost conventional – but to this he adds a percussion section requiring up to eight players. The first song employs triangle, tambourine, cymbals (one suspended, and a clashed pair), two gongs (medium and low), a snare drum, and a bass drum which the score specifies should be of 'Mammoth' size. In the second song, these are augmented by castanets and a ratchet. If this seems a decidedly large complement in relation to the rest of the ensemble, it is as nothing to the percussion demands of later Varèse scores; but it is – along with the highly detailed and idiomatic use to which this section is put – a strong indication of one direction in which his interests were moving.

Varèse's choice of texts may have been casual (both poets were personal acquaintances), but in retrospect it feels highly significant, if not symbolic. The poets were Latin Americans, citizens of the exotic, Spanish-speaking South and Central America which so captivated Varèse's imagination. In the first generation of their countries' literary modernists, they were his contemporaries and also, like himself, culturally displaced persons. Huidobro (1893–1948), a Chilean, had exiled himself in Paris to escape his aristocratic Catholic upbringing; the Mexican Tablada (1871–1945), an acute critic of modern art, had been living in New York since 1914, self-exiled from the dictatorship of Victoriano Huerta. Their two poems hymn a magical sense of new possibilities, Huidobro's from the perspective of the Old World, Tablada in the New.

'Chanson de Là-Haut' (Song from on high) is Varèse's own title for a section which he extracted and slightly adapted from a much larger poem by Huidobro, *Tour Eiffel*, published in 1917.

> *La Seine dort sous l'ombre de ses ponts*
> *Je vois tourner la terre*
> *Et je sonne mon clairon*
> *Vers toutes les mers.*
>
> *Sur le chemin de ton parfum*
> *Toutes les abeilles et les paroles s'en vont.*
> *Reine des Vents que fâne l'Automne.*
>
> *Dans ma tête un oiseau chante toute l'année.*

> (The Seine is asleep in the shadow of its bridges.
> I watch earth spinning,
> And I sound my trumpet
> Toward all the seas.
>
> On the pathway of her perfume
> All the bees and all the words depart,
> Queen of the Polar Dawns,
> Rose of the Winds that Autumn withers!
>
> In my head a bird sings all year long.)[8]

In fact the Eiffel Tower is not mentioned by name in the lines of Varèse's song, but it is unmistakably a very specific 'là-haut' from which the French girl[9] looks out over the earth. Paris is spread below her, the Seine 'asleep in the shadow of its bridges'. Before the construction of the Eiffel Tower in 1889, only a balloonist could have seen this view. The great attraction which the Tower offered the French public from its opening was *Paris vu d'en haut*. The highest man-made structure on earth, crafted from a modern industrial material – steel – the Tower was, as Robert Hughes has pointed out,[10] 'the great metaphor of [modernism's] sense of change – its master-image, the one

---

[8] The uncredited English translations of Huidobro's and Tablada's texts which appear in the published score of *Offrandes* are presumably the work of Louise Varèse.

[9] The lines which Varèse extracted are a response to Huidobro's question: 'Jacqueline/Fille de France/Qu'est-ce que tu vois là-haut?'

[10] Op. cit.

structure that seemed to gather all the meanings of modernity together'. Eight years before Huidobro wrote his poem, the world's first regular radio broadcast system was installed on the Tower. The poet, in lines not set by Varèse, calls it 'guitar of the sky/Your wireless telegraphy/Draws words to you/As a rose-arbour draws bees ... telescope or bugle ... a beehive of words ... A bird calls/in the antennae/ of the wireless ... It is the wind from Europe/The electric wind'.

These phrases immediately clarify aspects of Varèse's chosen text. Despite the pastoral imagery (shall we call it 'Post-impressionist'?), Huidobro is talking of electricity and radio-waves. The Tower itself is the trumpet sounding, the bird singing, the bees buzzing, broadcasting to the world, to all points of the compass. (I take the 'Queen of the Polar Dawns', by the way, to be the Aurora Borealis, itself an electrical phenomenon, and already the subject and inspiration of Varèse's lost *Les Cycles du Nord*.) All this, and the Parisian *mis-en-scène* from which the fragment sets out, must have attracted him strongly. Strongest of all, perhaps, the sounding of the trumpet towards all the seas. Later, composing *Arcana*, he would dream of angels blowing trumpets over water (see p.196); and Louise observed a 'lump in his throat' when Nina Koshetz first sang '*Je sonne mon clairon vers toutes les mers*'.[11] It seems those words formed the springboard for the entire song.

For it opens with a muted but stabbing trumpet-call, echoed by the oboe; beneath them muted violins and violas undulate in rocking sextuplets, a solo cello keens with a repeated rising third (Ex.1):

Ex.1

Trumpet and oboe form in effect a single line, and Varèse already shows the acuteness of his ear for timbre in making one instrument sound like the other. They stress, insistently, the single pitch D♮.

---

[11]   *LGD*, p. 176. (It may also have been a reaction to hearing his music peformed in public for the first time in 12 years.)

Against this (and against each other), the two types of activity in the strings seem designed to establish the idea of an interval – the major or minor third. But throughout these opening bars an increasing number of new pitches is being sounded, filling up the total chromatic: and we may note (without drawing any firm conclusions from the fact – we have as yet far too little evidence to establish a meaningful context for it) that with the horn's F♮, arriving at the start of bar 6, all 12 tones have been sounded. The actual sonorities would not be greatly out of place in an Impressionist score, but Varèse has with great economy already set up four polarities: pitch against interval; single pitch as against multiple pitches; the hard, metallic sound of the winds against the softer chiaroscuro of the muted strings; and the contrast between stable rhythms in the strings and the winds' irregular subdivisions of the beat, emphasized by unexpected accents.

No sooner has the twelfth pitch arrived than the previously D♮ fixated trumpet gives tongue to a five-note motif, and launches out, unaccompanied, into a species of declamatory, fanfare-like, faintly oriental melodic statement – an anacrusis up to a high, insistent, irregularly repeated pitch – which is not like *any* Impressionist composer, but is a unique, unmistakable finger-print of Varèse (Ex.2).

The effect is of the same phrase, three times repeated: but the repetitions, exact as to pitch, are subtly varied in rhythm each time: there is a tension of stasis, yet there is movement within the stasis itself, driving the trumpet eventually to a sixth pitch, B♮, its highest yet. But it is clear by now that the oft-sounded D♮ is in some sense the predominating pitch of the music: not its 'key', but the thread around which it is being woven.

The arrival of the high B♮ brings a downward-swooping clarinet flourish, and more 'traditionally' Impressionist sounds – a Debussian shimmer of harp glissandi, underpinned by gong, bass-drum and cymbals: the percussion thus makes its first entry unobtrusively, and in a comparatively 'normal' manner. The drums then enter softly, with what we shall learn to recognize as more characteristic Varèsian march-rhythms, while further impressionist elements make their appearance: chromatic eddies in clarinet, horn and bassoon, high violin harmonics in parallel fifths above a weeping oboe figure.

All splinters of a familiar vocabulary: and so is the soloist's first entry, low in her register, singing the opening line in a simple *parlando* phrase centred around the pitch F♮. The Debussian harp-glissandi swirl back, and introduce a new *Animé* passage with a more prophetic – and certainly proclamatory – ring to it. The trumpet still centres on D♮; while the other instruments develop its rhythms from Ex.1 in harsh repetitions, it takes on a new rhythmic profile that suggests the spirit of jazz. Yet what it plays is, very clearly – and appropriately in the context of the poem – a phrase from Rouget de Lisle's *La Marseillaise*: 'Aux armes, citoyens! Formez vos battalions'. The trumpet sounding to the four corners is a reveille to wake the Seine out of its sleep.

The soloist seizes the trumpet's last D♮ and uses the *Marseillaise* phrase to launch a declamatory setting of '*sonne mon clairon vers toutes les mers*' that climbs, over active double-bass and percussion, to land on a high G♯, D♮'s tritonal opposite. This provokes a shattering *fortissimo* tutti: two bars of mechanistic march-rhythm involving the full forces – one component of which is a strident, almost unrecognizable development of the strings' undulating thirds from Ex.1.

Within this tutti complex – which forms the song's central climax – all 12 pitches are being sounded almost continually, yet the one most prominent to the ear is the G♯, taken over by the trumpet and blared out in the tutti's principal rhythm. But a gruff, *pesantissimo* recitative-figure for strings and bass drum in rhythmic unison lands the music suddenly on a new crop of sustained D♮'s, long-held and resonating two octaves apart. The tempo slows almost to stillness.

Flute and bassoon continue to hold the D♮'s, while the harp repeats a soft, neutral chord against them and other instruments, equally softly, hold a static harmony on the pitches A, C♯, and G♯. Flute and bassoon use the D♮'s as the central point of an oriental-sounding, chant-like theme – a development of Ex.2. Surrounded by this texture the soprano sings 'Sur le chemins de ton parfum' on a rising phrase from B♭ to A, then perhaps illustrates the departing bees on a lazy, wayward chromatic descent from there, beginning with a quarter-tone flattening of the A.

The flute suddenly steps down from its D♮ to a G♯; the clarinet uses that as the first pitch for a reminiscence of its flourish, landing on a low

Ex 4

F♮, resonated by horn. With a compressed recall of the sonorities that introduced the soloist's first entry, the voice swoops down from its highest point – B♭ – in the invocation of the Queen of the Polar Dawns. The texture which accompanies this is the most iridescently impressionistic, almost Ravelian, in the entire song (Ex.4, opposite). The pitch D♮ has almost disappeared, except as a passing-note; instead the pulsating F♮ of the woodwind and harp assumes a temporary importance.

Yet this texture dissolves into stillness: there is a flutter of birdsong on the piccolo, subtly related to the trumpet-call Ex.2 and ending in a high repeated G♯ that is echoed by the violins; and the soloist, centred on a low G, intones the last line of text *sans couleur*, in the same matter-of-fact *parlando* style with which she began.

Among José Juan Tablada's achievements are the fact that he introduced the *haiku* into Spanish poetry, but 'La Croix du sud' is no such example of poetic discipline. Though it can be regarded as a sonnet, it is one whose form has deliquesced, under the pressure of its fantastic imagery, into a kind of surrealist rhapsody.

> *Les femmes aux gestes de madrépore*
> *Ont des poils et des lèvres rouge d'orchidée.*
> *Les singes du Pôle sont albinos*
> *Ambre et neige, et sautent*
> *Vêtus d'aurore boréale.*
> *Dans le Ciel il y a une affiche*
> *D'Oléomargarine.*
> *Voici l'arbre de la quinine*
> *Et la Vierge des Douleurs.*
> *Le Zodiaque tourne dans le nuit de fièvre jaune*
> *La pluie enferme tout le Tropique dans une cage de cristal.*
> *C'est l'heure d'enjamber le crépuscule*
> *Comme une zèbre vers l'îlle de jadis*
> *Où se réveillent les femmes assassinées.*

(Women with gestures of madrepores[12]
Have lips and hair as red as orchids.

---

[12] Soft, waving coral: the *Madreporia* are 'an order of stony anthozoan corals, often greatly branched, the chief reef-building corals of tropical seas' (*Webster's International Dictionary*).

> The monkeys at the pole are albinos,
> Amber and snow, and frisk
> Dressed in the aurora borealis.
> In the sky there is a sign,
> Oleomargarine.[13]
> Here is the quinine tree
> And the Virgin of Sorrows.
> The Zodiac revolves in the night of yellow fever.
> The rain holds the tropics in a crystal cage.
> It is the hour to stride over the dusk
> Like a Zebra toward the Island of Yesterday
> Where the murdered women wake.)

Of all the (few) texts that Varèse set to music, this one comes closest to the New York Surrealist aesthetic with its chaotic and ironic stream of consciousness. Whereas in 'Chanson de Là-Haut' Europe was confidently beaming its technological message out across the world, in 'La Croix du Sud' the four corners of the globe are presented as fantastic, exotic places, heedless of any laws but their own. Primal, mysterious, illogical as an opium dream, they are the source of strange creatures and plants, of inexplicable violence and mind-expanding substances. Nevertheless Tablada's poem echoes Huidobro's lines in various ways – especially in its cosmic imagery, mention of the Poles and (again) the Aurora Borealis. The Zodiac revolves, just as the planet spun in 'Chanson de Là-Haut'. And the line 'C'est l'heure d'enjamber le crépuscule' could almost come from Deubel's *La fin d'un jour*.

Just as the text is more exuberantly and assertively free in association, so is Varèse's setting of it. The proportion of 'radical' to traditional elements is quite differently balanced, and apparently weighted much more towards the former: 'apparently', because different aspects of tradition are here brought into play.

However, the opening bars – a malefic, hissing rattle of percussion noise combined with rapid, booming glissandi in the harp's lowest octave and the rasp of a trombone pedal-note – are clearly a statement of radical intent. (The trombone's pitch, B♭, will recur at several salient points, without quite assuming the cardinal importance of the trumpet D of the first song.) Here we have encountered the first real appearance

---

[13] i.e. margarine – 'in the US extended by statute to include butter substitutes made from fats and oils derived from certain animals and plants' (Ibid.).

of the typical 'Varèse sound', poised on the borders of sheer noise yet vibrant with musical possibilities.

The percussion then settles into what we shall come to know as a typically complex, polyrhythmic pattern (Ex.5):

This has several functions. Illustratively, it helps create an exotic and fantastic atmosphere. Kinetically, it subjects each bar to a myriad rhythmic subdivisions and cross-accents, while nevertheless containing enough stable (or only slightly varied) elements to maintain a feeling of inevitable rhythm. And on a larger scale the whole of Ex.5 forms a 3-bar unit that is immediately repeated (again with slight variation), followed by a third appearance of its first 2 bars.

Above this dense but stable rhythmic formula, strings and woodwind hold hot clusters of three notes a semitone apart; and harp and bassoon play a scrambling sextuplet semiquaver figure. As the percussion continue the upper strings and woodwind begin a high, plangent polyphony while the soloist makes her first entrance (Ex.6):

As can be seen, the vocal writing has now assumed a much more wide-ranging, legato, cantabile character – and indeed the·whole texture, though more fiercely dissonant and strange in sound, is a good deal less fragmented than that of the first song. Here, continuity is stressed. There are far fewer fluctuations of tempo; and apart from the frequent irruptions of the percussion ensemble, the music tends to be rhythmically simpler, too. This helps to make the piece's radical sounds easier to assimilate. It also helps Varèse to keep the delivery of text continuous – as he needs to do with a longer poem, and with its continuous outpouring of imagery.

The low B♭ on trumpet and cello shown at the end of Ex.6 coincides with the disappearance of the percussion pattern of Ex.5, and may serve to remind us of the pedal B♭ at the start of the song. The same pitch resonates on in the violins, while the soloist continues in a kind of free counterpoint with lower strings and woodwind, against sparse percussion noise (and a grotesque low quarter-tone on the harp for the albino monkeys' leap).[14]

When Tablada's text arrives at the great margarine advertisement in the sky, the music arrives at an almost-normal, rather Stravinskian 'orchestral' texture, with a short motif repeated over a motoric ostinato in harp and low strings – maybe to match the banality of the image. But the mention of the quinine tree brings back the percussion pattern of Ex.5 and rushing waves of chromatic glissandi in low strings, brass, and clarinet. The appearance of 'La Vierge des Douleurs' is greeted by a severe chromatic fanfare (Ex.7) – a particular formula that sounds through many of Varèse's later scores:

It also brings a sudden quickening of pace. The initial figure x is immediately taken up by other instruments and repeated in imitation, creating a spinning effect appropriate to the revolving Zodiac. This works up to an extremely brief but truly 'feverish' climax (the entire passage from the start of Ex. 7 is in fact a quotation from *Amèriques* – see Ex. 8 in the discussion of that work – reduced for *Offrandes*' much

---

[14] The effect is produced – clearly on the advice of Carlos Salzedo – by holding the pedal half-way between two notches. Stravinsky (in 'Some Composers', *Musical America*, June 1962, p.11) paid it this compliment: 'the most extraordinary noise in all Varèse is [this] harp attack ("heart attack", I almost said and that is what it almost gives one)'.

smaller ensemble). It is suddenly cut off, leaving the soloist to sail on with the word *'jaune'* (yellow) against a new figure in the clarinet – a stutter of repeated semiquavers and an oscillating semitone. New percussion patterns sound quietly underneath it, and the figure itself is soon pitchlessly mimicked by the side-drum (Ex.8).

While the soprano sings of the crystal cage, shorter versions of this same figure pass from harp to muted strings to horn, with a little motoric woodwind ostinato over the top of it. The horn's version lands us back on B♭, and with it a 2-bar return of the harp, percussion, and trombone sound with which the song began. The Ex.5 percussion complex returns too, and over this the soprano sings the last three lines of text to a melodic line closely similar to her first entry in Ex.6, but with only attenuated shadows of the original woodwind accompaniment. She ascends to a high, *pianissimo* G♮. Perhaps in response to the thought of murder (*'assassinées'*), flute, piccolo and clarinet give an angular shriek, and *Offrandes* ends on a loud, long-held chord-complex spread through the orchestra (with B♭ at the bottom in trombone and bassoon, surrounded by a violent glissando-vibrato in the harp), which gradually echoes into silence against the clicks and rattles of the percussion, like the fading of a strange, disturbing dream.

AMÉRIQUES

Versions and editions

If *Offrandes* is a comparatively 'minor' work – though in many respects highly characteristic, and prophetic of Varèse's future development – *Amériques* is in every sense a major one, one of the compositional peaks of his entire output. Extending the dominant musical form he had pursued in the pre-War years, it is a kind of symphonic poem for large orchestra. He wrote it between 1919 and 1921, though the original manuscript is dated '1922', and no doubt Varèse was finalizing the orchestration into that year. The manuscript bears the dedication: 'To my unknown friends of the Spring of 1921'. As Louise Varèse has explained,[15] this is a tribute of thanks to the anonymous admirers who provided the composer with a substantial cheque at that time, through the medium of a lawyer, when his financial situation was anything but secure.

The title signifies *Americas* – not one America, not three (North, Central and South) – but rather an infinite number of imaginary Americas, new worlds of wonder and potentiality. In this sense the work explores on the largest scale the possibilities indicated within the smaller compass of *Offrandes*. In a note explaining the title, Varèse gave a succinct account of the imaginative world inhabited by this teeming, sometimes raucously affirmative music.

I was still under the spell of my first impressions of New York, not only New York seen but more especially heard ... As I worked in my Westside apartment ... I could hear all the river sounds – the lonely foghorns, the shrill peremptory whistles – the whole wonderful river symphony which moved me more than anything ever had before. Besides, as a boy, the mere word 'America' meant all discoveries, all adventures. It meant the unknown ... new worlds on this planet, in outer space, and in the minds of man.

Later, he would back away from this specificity of time and place, saying he could as easily have called the piece *The Himalayas*. But there seems no reason to doubt that the original inspiration was indeed New York as New World, and especially the 'river symphony' of the Hudson so reminiscent and yet so different from that of the Seine evoked in *Chanson de Là-haut*. Louise Varèse has pertinently drawn attention to her husband's close association with the Italian painter Joseph Stella at this time, and their 'kindred – creative – passion for New York' which issued in Stella's pictures of skyscrapers and Brooklyn Bridge. She also quotes Stella's commentary on his New York oils, which echoes – or finds its echo in – Varèse's note on *Amériques* quoted above:

Many nights I stood on [Brooklyn Bridge] ... crushed by the mountainous black impenetrability of the skyscrapers – here and there lights resembling suspended falls of astral bodies or fantastic splendor of remote rites ... at times

---

[15] *LGD*, pp.156–7. The principal benefactor was Gertrude Vanderbilt Whitney, acting at the suggestion of Julianne Force.

ringing as alarm in a tempest, the shrill voice of the trolley wires – now and then strange moanings of appeal from the tug boats, guessed more than seen, through the infernal recesses below – I felt deeply moved, as if on the threshold of a new religion ...[16]

Amériques was published in 1925 by J.Curwen & Sons Ltd., London. The world premiere was given on 9 April 1926 at the Academy of Music, Philadelphia, by the Philadelphia Orchestra conducted by Leopold Stokowski, repeated the next evening, and performed in New York by the same artists on 13 April. The first Philadelphia audience received the work with boos and hisses, but in a pugnacious newspaper interview of 12 April Varèse declared himself well pleased with the performance, declaring of his score 'It stands as it is! I don't want to change one note!'[17] Nevertheless, despite this defiant attitude, in the summer of 1927 he considerably revised the work, reducing the orchestration as well as recomposing several passages. This revised version was published by Editions Max Eschig, Paris in 1929 and premièred at the Maison Gaveau on 30 May of that year by the Orchestre des Concerts Poulet under the baton of Gaston Poulet.

We have, therefore, an original version, published and performed – and then superseded by a revised version, issued by a different publisher. (There was no separate manuscript of the revised version: Varèse made his revisions on two printed copies of the Curwen edition.) This apparently straightforward situation remained in force during Varèse's lifetime, not least because there were no subsequent performances of *Amériques* after 1929, even though the composer retained a lively affection for the work. Only in 1966 was the score (in the 1927 revision, naturally) revived by Maurice Abravanel and the Utah Symphony Orchestra, who went on to record it on disc. For two more decades performances remained sparse, most likely because of all Varèse's extant works it calls, even in the 1927 revision, for the largest forces; and because it was deemed 'early' and 'uncharacteristic'. Pierre Boulez, among others, nevertheless helped to build up a performance tradition, and in recent years *Amériques* has been performed and recorded with increasing frequency. It has taken its rightful place as one

---

[16] Ibid., p.158.

[17] 'Varèse Answers "Amériques" Critics', *Philadelphia Evening Bulletin*, 12 April 1926, p.3.

of the supreme virtuoso orchestral showpieces of the early 20th century, along with Mahler's symphonies, Debussy's *La Mer* and Stravinsky's *Sacre du Printemps*. Increasing interest directed attention to the deficiencies of the existing editions: both the 1925 Curwen and 1929 Eschig editions, apparently only cursorily checked by Varèse, are riddled with errors. The perceived need for a standard text of this complex work has, in time, brought about a textual situation scarcely less confusing than that of some of Bruckner's symphonies.

In 1973 a new edition of *Amériques*, 'revised and edited by Chou Wen-Chung', was issued by the Colfranc Music Publishing Corporation of New York. This is a corrected version of Varèse's 1927 revision, prepared on the basis of the autograph manuscript (of the original '1922' version), both the Curwen and Eschig editions, and sundry corrections, additions and deletions made to the Eschig edition by the composer at various times between 1929 and the 1960s. In some cases, as Chou has noted, Varèse was himself misled by errors and misprints, which he mistakenly incorporated in these annotations. The 1973 Colfranc edition is thus the 'best text' of the revised (1927) *Amériques*, and has been the basis for most modern performances and recordings until the 1990s; but interest in the original (1922) version, with its differing content and substantially larger orchestra, has grown in recent years. In 1991 the German musicologist Klaus Angermann prepared an edition of the 'original version', taking as his basic text the 1925 Curwen score; he published various passages from it his dissertation *Edgard Varèse: Amériques. Ein analytischer Vergleich der beiden Fassungen*,[18] with cogent arguments for the original's revival. Yet according to Chou Wen-Chung the Curwen score 'simply could not serve as the basis for any new editions because of the enormous number of mistakes – large and small – throughout the score' as compared with Varèse's own manuscript.

In 1996 therefore Chou himself, under a joint commission from the Royal Concertgebouw Orchestra, the Decca Record Company, and G. Ricordi, went back to the manuscript and edited it for performance as part of Riccardo Chailly's project to record Varèse's complete works for Decca.[19] The first performance of the 1922 version in modern times,

---

[18] Submitted to the Technische Universität Berlin, and published in edited form as *Work in Progress. Varèses Ameriques* (Munich, Musikprint, 1996).

[19] For more on this project, which also resulted in the first recordings of *Tuning Up* and *Dance for Burgess*, see p.316.

in Chou's 'facsimile performance edition', was given by the Concertgebouw under Chailly in December 1996 during recording sessions in the Grote Zaal of the Concertgebouw, Amsterdam. The public première of this edition – and the European première of the 'original' *Amériques* – was given in the same venue on 24 August 1998.

We may summarize the textual situation as follows, therefore:

1922   Varèse's manuscript (original version)

1925   Curwen Edition (of original version; faulty)

1927   Revised version (prepared on Curwen scores)

1929   Eschig Edition (of revised version; faulty)

1973   Colfranc Edition (ed. Chou; corrected edition of 1927 revised version)

1991   Angermann edition (Ricordi, Munich: an attempt to return to 1922 version through the 1925 edition)

1996   Ricordi, Milan edition (ed. Chou; corrected 'facsimile performance edition' of 1922 manuscript, processed for hire 2001)

Essentially however we need concern ourselves only with the 1973 Colfranc Edition and Chou's 'facsimile performance edition', as the best texts of Varèse's revised version of 1927, and his original version of 1922 respectively. Chou has said that the revised version, as represented by the Colfranc Edition, 'should continue to be available (in accordance with Varèse's wishes)'. However the original version, because of its intrinsic interest and substantive differences from the 1927 version, should now also be available as an alternative to it. It seems highly likely that, in future, both versions will be performed, depending on the available resources and programming requirements of orchestras. Indeed it is the 1922 version which reveals how essentially *Amériques* is a transitional work, stylistically still owing much to French impressionism in its actual musical fabric, just as *Offrandes* does in its texts.[20]

---

[20] The tangling of this textual web has impinged upon the present chapter. Originally it was written (in the 1980s) as an account of the 1927 version, as reflected in the 1973 Colfranc score, at that time the only version available. Preparing this book for press in 1998 I have had to weigh the claims of the recently-reinstated original version, in Chou's performance edition. Not only because future readers of this book may well encounter it in the concert hall and on disc, but also because of its great intrinsic interest, some account of it is vitally necessary. Although the following

The first obvious difference between the two versions is in their orchestration. Even in its 1927 form, *Amériques* calls for the largest orchestral apparatus of any work that Varèse completed: 2 piccolos, 2 flutes, alto flute in G, 3 oboes, cor anglais, heckelphone, E♭ clarinet, 3 B♭ clarinets, bass clarinet, 3 bassoons, 2 double bassoons; 8 horns, 6 trumpets, 3 tenor, 1 bass and 1 contrabass trombones, tuba and contrabass tuba; two harps, 2 sets of timpani, strings, and a huge percussion battery, immensely larger than that encountered in *Offrandes*. In fact the *Offrandes* percussion complement, though large in proportion to the rest of the ensemble, contains nothing especially unusual by the standards of many other late-19th- or early 20th-century composers. It is in *Amériques* that we first become aware of the unique importance of percussion instruments in Varèse's sonic universe. The 1927 version requires at least nine (and ideally 10) percussionists. In addition to such standard or only slightly uncommon instruments for the age of Mahler, Strauss, Ravel and Stravinsky as xylophone, glockenspiel, celesta, chimes, triangle, sleigh bells, low rattle ('affixed to a solid base'), whip, tambourine, tam-tam, 2 bass drums, triangle, castanets, crash cymbal, suspended cymbals, a pair of cymbals and snare drum, Varèse calls for the Lion's Roar (a friction drum with a rosined cord pulled through the membrane, producing the sound from which it takes its name) and two 'deep and very powerful' sirens. Both of these unusual elements would become characteristic of his orchestration in larger ensembles. It is worth remark, nevertheless, that this line-up does not include any instruments of South American origin, which would shortly seize his imagination.

Large though this orchestra is in total, that for the original version of *Amériques* is very significantly larger. The flutes comprise 3 piccolos and 4 standard flutes in addition to the alto. The number of oboes is increased to 4; Varèse originally wrote parts for an oboe d'amore and an oboe in E flat as well (the latter doubled by oboe IV), but deleted them, apparently before the first performance. Clarinets are increased to 4 (two in B♭ and two in A), with a contrabass clarinet supplementing the bass. There is also a fourth bassoon. The basic brass complement is

account continues to take the 1927 version as the 'principal' form of *Amériques* – as this is still the form in which it is likely to be most often encountered – I have therefore enlarged the chapter to include parallel consideration of the 1922 version, and especially those aspects in which that version differs from the later one.

similar to that of 1927, with an extra tenor trombone and contrabass tuba (but no contrabass trombone). Moreover this is augmented by a secondary brass group which Varèse designated '*fanfare intérieure*': 2 trumpets in E♭, 2 in D, 2 tenor trombones and a bass trombone, which add an almost operatic dimension to the score. They remain offstage throughout most of the piece, only joining the rest of the orchestra near the end: at which point *Amériques'* brass forces number 8 horns, 10 trumpets, 8 trombones and 3 tubas. The string strength is specified as 16-16-14-10-10.

The requirements for timpani and harps remain the same as in 1927, but the percussion line-up shows several major differences. The 1922 manuscript specifies celesta, glockenspiel, xylophone, sleigh-bells, string drum, a 'big rattle', snare drum, 2 bass drums (one described as 'mammoth'), 2 cymbals, crash cymbal, triangle, castanets, tambour de Basque, fouet (whip) and tam-tam. So far, this closely corresponds to the 1927 score. But in addition there is a Cyclone Whistle, Steamboat Whistle, Hand Siren ('same as used by New York Fire Department on fire engines', is Varèse's stipulation), Crow Call and Rute (the bunch of birch-twigs first added to the orchestra by Mahler in his *Resurrection* Symphony). Chou Wen-Chung advises that all these instruments 'must be authentic rather than modern substitutes', and that the tam-tam should be at least 36″ in diameter.

The presence of the Steamboat Whistle and a specifically NY Fire Department siren – although these instruments are partly a reflection of Varèse's musical modernism, extras that allow him to use raw sounds unfiltered through centuries of orchestral tradition – suggest that at least in its original form *Amériques* was more anecdotal in inspiration than Varèse would later allow, more closely intended as an expression of a particular time and place: the city of New York at the dawn of the 1920s, and especially the river area round Brooklyn Bridge. 'The whole wonderful river symphony', in fact. (The '*fanfare intérieure*' also points in this direction, with its evocations of distant revelry.) Of course the work's significance and its imaginative range are much wider than that, and in this sense Varèse's application of his title to 'new worlds' of every kind is fully justified. But while resolutely resisting the temptation to treat any aspect of the work as programmatic, it does the music no injustice to view it as a kind of phantasmagoria of impressions of city life – especially night life – at the cutting edge of the modern industrial revolution.

We may also say of the percussion demands – not merely the size of the percussion ensemble but the way it is employed, almost continuously – that this is the single most decisively original element in Varèse's music, setting it apart from his predecessors and elder contemporaries in a way that the rest of the score, with its huge and colourful Mahler-Strauss orchestra, does not. Short solo percussion passages in other composers' works (Strauss's *Ein Heldenleben*, for example, the second scherzo of Mahler's Tenth Symphony,[21] Stravinsky's *Petrushka* and *L'Histoire du Soldat*) had been largely pictorial or onomatopoeic in effect, and cannot be held comparable. Not only does Varèse call for a much larger array of instruments and more players than any earlier composer – thus making possible percussion writing of a previously unapproached timbral variety and polyrhythmic intricacy – but the percussion's role is conceived in an entirely new way. Certainly at many points it provides colour and rhythmic support for the activities of the rest of the orchestra. But for much of the time it functions as an independent element, equally as important as wind or strings, going about its own clicking, rattling, pulsating business even if the other instruments are silent.

A footnote which Varèse affixed to the score towards the end of *Amériques* has ramifications far beyond the particular section to which it applies: *Percussion: dans le sentiment de monotonie et de prèsque indifférence – épousant toutefois le dynamisme de l'orchestre.* What this underlines is an *emotional separation* or dissociation between the rest of the orchestra and the percussion, which functions as an aloof, machine-like continuum with its own internal dynamic and rhythmic structures. Clearly Varèse felt he needed to add to the traditional instrumental palette a new, distancing, 'objectifying' sonic resource: and at this stage he found it in a new conception of the percussion ensemble. In the same Philadelphia newspaper feature which followed the first performances of *Amériques*, he made the point explicitly, in regard to the sirens and whistles, in terms of his exploration of the potential of 'pure sound' as against musical tone:

I employ these instruments with a definite, fixed pitch to serve as a contrast in pure sound. It is surprising how pure sound, without overtones, re-

---

[21] Which was of course unknown to Varèse: Deryck Cooke's 'performing edition' of this movement would not be unveiled until 1960.

interprets the quality of the musical notes with which it is surrounded. Actually, the use of pure sound in music does to the harmonics what a crystal prism does to pure light. It scatters it into a thousand varied and unexpected vibrations.[22]

It was the same impulse which would lead him to explore the possibilities of electronic instruments – and when, 30 years later, he was eventually able to create music directly on tape, it was his percussion writing above all which provided him with a model. *Amériques* therefore stands at the beginning of a line of development that leads straight to Varèse's electronic music.

* * *

The form of *Amériques* may loosely be described as episodic: so are all of Varèse's works, insofar as they reject the strong thematic and tonal patterning of sonata and other classically-derived forms, and rely instead on the dramatic succession of contrasting musical events. Sometimes (as for instance in *Hyperprism*) there may be a general ternary shape, with some implication of the return of opening material; certain sections may repeat, more or less exactly, at different points of the works; there may even be a single dominating idea, reappearing throughout in identifiable guises. More often, the 'episodic' progress appears more freewheeling and open-ended, but by no means random. Generally speaking, a composition by Varèse will tend to create the impression of a mosaic through the juxtapositioning of its ideas, but will end up somewhere very different from where it set out.

This is certainly the case with *Amériques*. But this particular score, remarkable in Varèse's output for its physical size and orchestral demands, is likewise unique in the prodigal nature of its thematic invention – the sheer number of ideas which Varèse elects to work with. Not only that, but very few of these ideas is an isolated occurence (as often happens in later works). Practically everything recurs at least once, and some ideas many times. Comparatively few of the recurrences are literal repetitions (outside the opening section, where literal repetition is part of its preludial, form-building function). Instead, themes engender other themes, bearing more or less of a family resemblance to one another; they are themselves metamorphosed, in processes still recognizable as 'development',

---

[22] 'Varèse Answers "Amériques" Critics' (loc.cit, footnote 17).

growing and changing at each appearance. The mosaic becomes very complex and highly coloured, but rich in unexpected elements of patterning.

A large number of the work's salient ideas make their first appearance during the opening, introductory section of *Amèriques*, as represented by the first 14 pages of the 1973 Colfranc edition. The 1922 and 1927 versions are here virtually identical in content, despite myriad variations in instrumentation owing to the larger orchestra of the original. At the very outset (Ex.1) the music consists of just three elements: (*a*) a languorous, repeated phrase given to the alto flute, (*b*) a monotonous oscillating semiquaver pattern in the harps, discreetly reinforced by percussive impacts on their sounding-boards, and (*c*) a little 4-note curl of rising chromatic scale on solo bassoon.

All three figures stem recognizably from the Debussy-Stravinsky tradition of impressionistic evocation, though the flute phrase itself has an exotic flavour, oriental or Amerindian. In terms of pitch, figures *a*, *b* and *c* occupy quite distinct areas[23] and between them they encompass 11 of the 12 different pitches of the chromatic scale. Varèse is careful, though, not to throw too much information at his listeners too quickly. In the first three bars, a fresh element is added for each

---

[23] Apart from the G common to figures a and c.

repetition of figure *a*; and after that there are no further additions: he varies the time-signature, and the length and entry points of the alto flute's figure, allowing the three to appear in various rhythmic relations and effecting a slight *accelerando*. Otherwise there is no alteration in the materials, nor in their pitch. They remain in a mutual harmonic stasis, giving the music a gentle, somewhat hypnotic sense of immobility.

The calm is ripped apart by a sudden barbaric, dissonant fanfare (Ex.2). Apart from the percussion – still to make their appearance – this uses practically all the orchestral instruments except for the four employed in Ex.1; and whereas Ex.1 had contrived to state only one repeated set of 11 chromatic tones in the space of seven bars, this fanfare delivers two separate 11-note complexes within a single 5/4 measure.

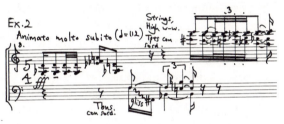

With no transition of any kind, the music immediately reverts to Ex.1, but now with an intricate rhythmic underlay contributed by the percussion; and this time it persists for only two bars before a distant, Debussian dance-figure (Ex.3) breaks in on trumpets and trombones.[24]

This, in its turn, is contradicted by a dark, heavy cadence-figure consisting of two pairs of impassive chords on trombones (Ex.4*a*),

---

[24] Marked '*dans le lointain*' in the 1927 version, in the original of 1922 this is literally in the distance, as Varèse gives it to his offstage 'fanfare interieure'.

introducing a veiled, sonorous theme on six horns, bassoon, and contrabassoon (Ex.4*b*) – the whole with a continuation of the percussion underlay.

Varèse is familiarizing us with his harmonic and melodic language: both its richness and its restrictions. Ex.4*b*, it will be observed, merely gives rhythmic shape to the oscillation of two chords, and those chords are essentially expansions of the trombone 'cadence-figure' Ex.4a.

Ex.1 (or rather, figures *a* and *b* of it) now returns for three bars, only to be replaced by a complex, florid polyphony of solo woodwind instruments over a long-held bass drum and cymbal roll. This peters out and Ex.1*a* and *b* are heard again, this time merely as an introductory bar to a delicate and spine-tingling web of 'impressionist' sound. Soft polyrhythmic percussion patterns (still essentially the pattern of the percussion's first appearance, after Ex.2) are enwrapped by muted, *sul ponticello* string textures, harp glissandi (echoed by glissandi in the inner parts of the strings) and the return of the little chromatic figure Ex.1c – not a bassoon solo now, but a plaintive chorus of nocturnal cries on celesta doubled by first violins, in harmonics and *div a 3*. This purely impressionistic scoring is succeeded by rapid chromatic swirls of demisemiquavers in the lowest strings, rising and falling like sudden gusts of cold wind. These string figures form a transition from impressionistic romantic evocation to modern, 'realistic' presentation – and to an 'instrument' that is infinitely chromatic, all glissando, and has no fixed pitch at all. For the siren now first lifts up its clamant, urban voice in a long rising-falling sonic curve, against a chiming, mechanistic background of celesta, glockenspiel and xylophone, soon taken over by the percussion ensemble, with a single baleful growl from the Lion's Roar. This weird event provokes a squealing, sardonic fanfare-figure (Ex.5, opposite).

The alto flute returns yet again with its figure *a*, landing on the motif's final B♮ and holding onto it with repeated, irregularly rhythmicized attacks. The siren begins to wail again, and a new

Ex.5

element breaks in: the bass instruments and bass drums combine in a heavy, pounding, *pesantissimo* rhythm:

(X)

This rhythm persists, urging the music to a culmination in a huge, wide-spaced *ffff* chord in all wind and brass, dying away to reveal a web of polyrhythmic percussion patterns similar to those we have heard before. The siren continues to rise and fall; in the original version of the score the Steamboat Whistle is first sounded here. The sardonic fanfare-figure Ex.5 is heard again, its upper component split up now into two halves, the first on flutes and piccolos, the second on trumpets and xylophone. The three elements – percussion, siren, fanfare – all swell out together in a swift crescendo that cuts off suddenly to leave a single trumpet exposed on a high A. From this pitch it essays, not Ex.1*a*, but a recognizable variant of that figure (I have given it in the lower half of Ex.1 as a^2).

Although this initial, 'expository' section of *Amèriques* is much shorter in performance than this description of it is to read, and although it consists of so many disparate and constantly-changing musics, the many recurrences and unchanging nature of Ex.1*a* impart to it a strong sense of consistency and stability. The trumpet's appropriation of a form of that motif is the first time that it occurs in any version distinct from Ex.1*a* (minor rhythmic differences apart), and the first time it has been heard on any instrument save alto flute. And in fact the Ex.1*a* form, which has so far been a constant thread in the argument — counting its various repetitions in the opening bars it has been heard 11 times – is never heard again, although more or less altered versions of it will recur on several occasions (two of these forms are given in Ex.1 as a^3 and a^4). The trumpet's intervention at this point signals that the music is about to move on from the initial premises that Varèse has painstakingly set up.

The immediate result of the trumpet solo is a brief but tumultuous outburst for full orchestra marked *Vivo quasi cadenza*. Basically this is a V-shaped scamper downwards and then up again in small note-values, incorporating a practically verbatim restatement of the wild fanfare Ex.2, and landing upon a dense, wide-spread chordal complex. Larry Stempel[25] sees the first two bars of this *Vivo* (recapitulated exactly later in the work) as a 'direct reference' to the opening of the fourth of Schoenberg's Five Orchestral Pieces, op.16 – a score Varèse certainly knew well by this time. Whether or not the 'reference' is intentional, it is certainly very close, especially with regard to the second bar in both passages, cf. Ex.6.

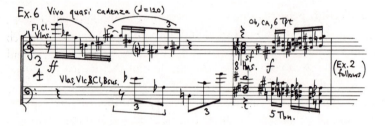

The tempo suddenly switches to *Presto*, crotchet=192. Here we encounter the first substantial difference between the versions of 1922 and 1927. In the former, Varèse proceeds immediately to the music starting with Ex.7 below. But in the later version he has inserted a 15-bar episode of stark registral oppositions, strings and woodwind reaching up to a high, long-held F♮ while brass and low wind descend to a deep D♭, resonated by timpani, fleshed out with trills and minatory footfalls of percussion. While the D♭ persists like a deep pedal, the siren lifts its voice, the E♭ clarinet essays a further variant of Ex.1*a*, a trumpet peals a high A and flutes and piccolos, *fff*, drill the B♭ a minor ninth and seventeenth above into the listener's ear. More characteristic of his music of the later 1920s, this episode certainly creates an enhanced sense of orchestral space, with entities moving within it.

We now hear a rather sinister ostinato-figure on strings and muted harp (Ex.7), which is clearly a development of the harp ostinato Ex.1*b* from the work's opening.

---

[25] Stempel (1974), p.52 and n.18.

This alternates with a strident music on eight horns developed from
Ex.4*b*, an explosive block-chord, and the sardonic fanfare Ex.5;
meanwhile full percussion, including the siren, make contributions
both weighty and agitated.

This rapid alternation of elements works up to a massive
polyphonic combination of them: see Ex.8 (on p.118). Here the
woodwind and four trombones develop the chromatic curl Ex.1*c* (itself
virtually identical to the opening gesture of Ex.5), against Ex.6
(developed from Ex.1*b*) in strings and harp, and another distortion of
Ex.1*a* in the trumpet. The elements in horns and tubas appear new,
but perhaps they relate to one of the fanfare-figures, Ex.2 or Ex.5, both
of which include similar gestures.

This grand outburst is cut off suddenly, to be replaced by a *Poco
Lento* of much more delicate, fragmentary scoring. Wisps and shreds of
new themes are heard in tremolo, *sul ponticello* violas, flutes, solo
bassoon, and double-basses. The two timpani enter into a quiet,
intricately rhythmic dialogue, against a soft background of percussion.
The familiar elements return: the Debussian dancing trumpets of Ex.3
are heard again in a new, extended form (Ex.9).

To this immediately succeed, as to Ex.3 on its original appearance,
Ex.4*a* and *b* – the dark trombone chords and the horn music, now
more richly scored but without their original percussion backing. The
outcome is a new, processional *Lento* idea (Ex.10) of crotchet
harmonies in contrary motion over an angular ostinato in the bass,
richly and luminously scored.

Ex. 8

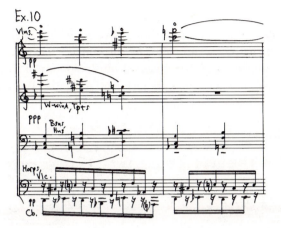

Ex.10

Debussy or Stravinsky might have made much of this element, which so suddenly appears as a fully developed entity (its closeness to certain passages of Debussy's *Jeux* is remarkable); but Varèse characteristically abandons it after just four bars in favour of a slow, oscillating, chant-like melody (Ex.11) in rhythmic unison on oboe, cor anglais, clarinet, bass clarinet and bassoon.

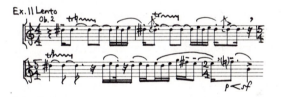

Ex. 11 Lento

Again, the force of this idea is as something quite new, although it might perhaps be regarded as a slow expansion and elaboration of the horn music Ex.4*b*. It never occurs again exactly; but it seems to be the seed of several later, similar melodic ideas.

Varèse now leaves the *Lento* tempo, and whips up the motion with more rapidly-passing fragments on woodwind, trumpets and strings. Before long everything stills (despite a new *Presto* tempo-marking) on a long, pulsating E♭ tremolo in the violas. Through this, the side-drum beats out a military-sounding march-rhythm; and over it, the sombre cadential chords of Ex.4*a* return again – this time much more massively scored, first for full brass and woodwind and then for low woodwind and eight horns. These towering vertical complexes seem to be taking on the character of looming skyscrapers. The first and third horns take up the violas' E♭ – and this now flowers into a comparatively long, nostalgic-sounding horn solo entwined within spellbindingly ethereal string harmonies amplified by harp and celesta chords and soft percussion support. The dark, magical impressionism of this passage (Ex.12) relates not so much to Debussy as to the Busoni of the *Nocturne Symphonique*.

This eerily beautiful passage fades, and a brief transition section (including distorted developments of Ex.6 in the strings, and the chromatic Ex.1*c* in the woodwind) whips up the excitement and leads to a new *Presto* section. Despite the percussion support and fragmentary figures in the wind, this is one of the comparatively few occasions in *Amèriques* where the strings come to the fore: they dominate the scene in powerful octave unison with a furious, oriental-sounding monody marked *sauvagement* (Ex.13).

This tune seems fairly clearly a descendant from the chant-like Ex.11, by way of the horn melody in Ex.12. It leads to a rather slower tempo, and an excited, rapid chromatic swirling in the full orchestra – a clear expansion of the 'impressionist' swirls of the opening section, further embellished and thickened out by rising and falling glissandi in brass, upper strings, and harps, and also raised in dynamics – its final stage is marked *Immensamente crescendo*.

It will be remembered that this kind of swirling chromatic music led in the first section of the work to the introduction of the siren, and the same thing happens here. Indeed the next short episode is virtually a solo for siren, rising and falling against a nagging, stumbling rhythm in low strings, low woodwind and the two timpani. It dies away into a sudden *Subito Lento*[26] with rapid repeated notes in piccolos, flute, and celesta, reinforced by tremolo violas; this seems to relate in less fragmentary fashion to the equally unexpected *Poco Lento* shortly before Ex.9; and serves now to bring about a passage of rapid 'recapitulation' of familiar materials. Even within it, a clarinet *très en dehors* gives out a new version of Ex. 1a – see a^3. First a version of the fanfare Ex.2;[27] then the sombre trombone chords of Ex.4*a* (very loud this time), followed by a scrap of the Ex.4*b* horn music; then three bars of the Debussian Ex.10 complex, in rather more attenuated scoring.

An accelerating upward sweep now initiates an *Allegro moderato* tutti passage, involving almost the whole orchestra in a loud and deliberate movement of chromatic scales in contrary motion, descending from the highest registers and rising from the lowest. The passage is repeated with intensified scoring and embellished with trumpet calls, reaches a climax, and is then cut short.

Here again the two versions of *Amériques* temporarily diverge. In the original version, the next 11 bars are occupied by a new brass fanfare from the offstage '*fanfare intèrieure*' – the trumpets' chromatic descent against 'sombre' trombone triads is vaguely reminiscent of Debussy's *L'après-midi* or the second of his *Nocturnes* – with following string and woodwind flourishes, interjected percussion patterns and the sounds of the steam whistle. In 1927 Varèse substituted a 9-bar section which is far removed from this impressionist revelry. Now orchestral trumpets and trombones hold a static chord against which horns have a primitive-sounding scrap of tune (Ex.14).

Ex.14

[26] In the manuscript Varèse's direction is *Plötzlich: Sehr Ruhig-LANGSAM*. One effect of the 1927 revision seems to have been to suppress all trace of the 1922 version's occasional use of German.

[27] Only in the 1927 version. The original extends the tremolo descent which concluded the previous passage.

Just like the episode in the earlier version, this seems to have only a tenuous connexion to what has gone before – but its relative textural simplicity dissipates some of the tension of the previous bars. It introduces a splintered music of woodwind flourishes, sinister muted brass, and percussion patterns surmounted by the siren – all related to the florid polyphony heard near the start of the work. Ex.5's mocking fanfare bursts in once more on trumpets and high woodwind, and from this point the two versions of *Amériques* are once again in agreement.

The first trumpet, solo, now essays its variant of Ex.1*a* – the one I have designated a^2 – a tone higher than on its original appearance. As before, it leads to the *Quasi cadenza* music, which is repeated with only minor changes (and generally slightly higher in pitch), and is then extended into a orgiastic, pulsatingly rhythmic tutti. But this soon dies out, with string tremolos and percussion writing being pitted against tutti wind chords, the last of which dies away to almost nothing. The tempo slows and, in the 1927 version, trumpets in octaves give out a new, harshly augmented variant of Ex.1*a* – see a^4. (In fact it is 'new' in a chronological as well as developmental sense, substituting for a shorter offstage brass link in the original.) This summons a return of the uncanny 'Busonian' episode, Ex.12, but with its soulful tune transferred to most of the woodwind in resonant octaves, and underpinned by triplet pulses in the two timpani, the string parts now in sheeny harmonics.

The tempo switches to *Animé*, crotchet=112, and Varèse begins to whip up the tension in a swift-moving sequence whose focus is almost entirely rhythmic: it is dominated by ostinato figures in woodwind, strings and percussion, and by fanfare-type motifs in the heavy brass which have some relation to the oscillating melodic components of Exx. 11, 12 and 13. The excitement steadily rises until, at *Più ritenuto* (figure 25 in the 1927 score), the trumpets cover themselves with glory in one of the great climactic moments of *Amériques*, and of Varèse's output as a whole.

One reason this climax is so striking (among so much bizarre and inventive sonic exploration) is the relative orthodoxy of its texture. For once, we hear an extended melodic line over a largely accompanimental orchestral background – and both elements, whether by intention or not, relate strongly to the idioms of Big Band jazz. But the sheer virtuosic élan of the melody, and the rhythmic effervescence generated by the accompaniment, carries the passage far beyond the conventional: it is an exhilarating explosion of sheer orchestral power.

The ostinato-patterns of the preceding section are developed by the orchestra as a whole, sometimes in blocks or in superimposed layers, and with sycopated chordal elements, notably in the six horns. The trumpets (four of them in unison to begin with, later all six, marked *jubilantes*) ride above the entire orchestral texture with a wild and gleeful development of the theme they had originally introduced as Ex.3, shorn now of all its echoes of Debussian pastoral nocturne and thrust triumphantly into the heart of the big city. It stands revealed as an archetypal urban music – and more, an American urban music, as evocative of New York as is Gershwin's *Rhapsody in Blue* (not to be composed for another three years or more). In the middle of the tune there is just one bar of delighted, communal choric response from woodwind and glockenspiel, before the trumpets – having taken a very necessary breath – launch into the even more stunning second half, the eight horns now accompanying them with bells in the air. Finally they unite with the rest of the orchestra (siren included) on a vast culminatory *ffff* tutti chord spanning a range of six octaves, embellished with swooping glissandi from the five trombones. Strings and woodwind spiral rapidly up into sudden silence, punctuated only by a sinister *ppp* rattle of percussion, and an ironic half-vocalized laugh from the fourth trombone (Ex.15).

This is, of course, a version of the sardonic Ex.5. Its mockery is presumably directed at the glorious big-city sound and fury that has gone before, but there is nothing cynical about it – it strikes one, rather, as simply a different aspect of Varèse's explosive high spirits and anarchic humour: a Mephistophelean spirit that denies, perhaps – but a *human* spirit, determined not to be overawed by the naked power of the modern industrial cosmos, nor by its musical expression. Ex.15 is the signal for the music to dissolve once more, via 'Impressionist' harp glissandi and a *Subito lento* slowing of tempo, into soft horn music (distantly related to Ex.4*b*) that leads, through a Debussian descending figure in woodwind and celesta, to quietly tolling chords in brass, F♯ bell, and low percussive harp attacks.

It is at this point, virtually the geographical centre of *Amériques*, that the 1922 and 1927 scores diverge most markedly. Save for one short episode shared by both versions, the music heard in the next four to five minutes is entirely different, depending on which text is followed. In Varèse's original version, the impressionistic textures persist, and indeed are elaborated by flutes, glittering pitched percussion and swirling harp glissandi, against sinister muted brass. Out of this emerges a solo cor anglais – hesitant, recitative-like – which soon begins to reminisce around Ex.1*a* from the work's opening. A flute takes up the line, then an oboe and finally a viola accompanied by alto flute, in a succession of free-floating solos and duets above a phosphorescent orchestral accompaniment. The viola solo even includes quarter-tones, with a sustained high C quarter-sharp which Varèse directs to be played *sfff heulend* ('howling'), yet the mood is more picturesque than anguished, and the Debussian echoes, strong throughout this passage, become overwhelming as pizzicato basses and castanets hint at the rhythm of a Habanera. For a moment we are nearer the alleys of *Ibéria*, with their night perfumes, and the enchanted tennis-courts of *Jeux* than the streets of New York.

The flute takes the lead again as the diaphanous textures swirl and eddy in sinuous dance rhythm. Offstage fanfares compete with passionate string melody, then a ruminative bass recitative. A sudden tutti, whose descending phrases perhaps go back to Ex.10, is surmounted by an urgent call from the four trumpets in unison, then angry horn trills presage a snapping, irregularly repeated tutti chord, interspersed with a new figure on clarinets and violas. A rejoicing music breaks in from offstage on the '*fanfare intèrieure*'. Basically it is another variation of Ex.3 – an augmentation of the whirling trumpet music of the big tutti preceding Ex.15 into a kind of distant processional, the sense of marching crowds intensified by the regular beat of the drums and castanets. The siren wails again as we are catapulted into another tumultuous tutti. Elements of the Ex.2 fanfare, the *Vivo quasi cadenza*, and especially the chromatic curl of Ex.1*c* developed in contrary motion on virtually the full orchestra may all be discerned here, though they flash by so quickly the listener is unlikely to make the connexions except subliminally.

Typically, this is cut off short: a rhythmically-pulsing bar for horns and trumpets and another brief burst of trumpet fanfare from off-stage (the procession recedes?) gives way to a series of sinuous woodwind soli, begun by a trilling, acrobatic clarinet and featuring an impressionistic flute rhapsody over clicking and chiming percussion writing and iridescent strings. Trombones, whose block chords and glissandi feature quarter-tone inflections, lead the way into a soft, exfoliating, complexly glittering passage for almost the full orchestra (see Illustration, Ex.16). The horns take the lead in this highly involved texture (at least they do in Chailly's Decca recording) with a line which may be regarded as a continuation of the previous florid woodwind solos. Varèse directs that now the brass players of the '*fanfare intèrieure*' should make their way on stage and take their places with the rest of the orchestra. Stumbling bassoon arpeggii, a snatch of fanfare, brief clarinet and flute solos, capped by the strings restating the a^3 form of Ex.1*a*, brings to an end this eventful central span.

So it went in 1922. Before looking at what happens over the same span in the 1927 version, we should consider some aspects of Varèse's original. It is marvellous music – haunting, colourful, evocative. But it is also perhaps the most 'backward-looking' portion of the score. As pointed out, the Debussian ambience is particularly strong, making the music more 'Old World' than 'New World' in effect. Despite some pages of punchy, aggressive modernism, especially around the big central tutti, the general flavour is more Impressionistic/Late Romantic than in any other surviving score of Varèse. To that extent, though undoubtedly seductive, it is stylistically somewhat incongruous; it's entirely explicable that he should have wanted to bring this portion of the work more 'up to date'. However it also concentrates our minds on the *roots* of Varèse's music, in a very revealing way. Those roots are overwhelmingly in Debussy. We have earlier noted resemblances to Debussy's late ballet score for Diaghilev, *Jeux* (1912). They are especially close here, and they far outweigh the passing similarities with works of Schoenberg and Stravinsky. On his own testimony, Varèse knew and strongly admired *Jeux*. Not for nothing did Debussy's marvellous '*poème dansée*', long neglected and misunderstood in the inter-War period, come to be regarded in the 1950s as a key work of musical modernism, its special qualities analysed by, among others, Pierre Boulez. *Amériques* as a whole – even more in its form than in its idiom – can plausibly be understood as a direct descendant of *Jeux*. True, Debussy's work is veiled and mysterious in atmosphere, with

Ex. 16: a page from the original version of 'Amériques', in Varèse's hand (by kind permission of G. Ricordi Ltd., London) none of Varèse's harsh dissonance and aggressive, dionysiac expression. But the way that Debussy creates a large, kaleidoscopic form out of many short sections, out of the ebb and flow and juxtaposition of small melodic and harmonic units, with continual fluctuations of tempo and rhythm and orchestral perspective, is perhaps more prophetic of Varèse's methods in *Amériques* – and through *Amériques* into his later music – than almost any other work one can think of apart from *Le Sacre du Printemps*.

This 'post-Debussian' formal aspect continues to operate in the 1927 *Amériques*, of course, but the actual content of this central span is very different. Above all, the 'impressionist' textures largely disappear, and Varèse's personal voice is much clearer, without any mediation from his late friend and mentor. In his revision, the music with the tolling F♯ bell is torn apart by a sudden chordal complex – high secundal clashes in woodwind and strings, low wide-spread harmony in brass, harps, timpani and basses. This is the same chord that occurred in the opening section of the work, shortly after the rhythmic example X, only raised a semitone in pitch. As before, it dies gradually away to reveal exactly the same polyrhythmic percussion pattern, embellished by the siren's wail. But in the way it is approached, high woodwind vaulting up to the top of the chord, bass instruments slumping downward a minor ninth, also establishes a link with the new passage of registral oppositions Varèse had composed earlier in the work before the appearance of Ex.7.

The tempo changes to *Vif*; the ensuing music is marked *pp ma distintissimo*. Here, in fact, begins the one passage of this central span which the two versions of *Amériques* have in common (but the revision arrives at it much more quickly): what we hear is the rejoicing brass music which, in the 1922 version, was coming from offstage. Varèse has transferred it to his available brass onstage and elaborated the texture with an agile wind and string counterpoint largely in triplet values. The ensuing tumultuous tutti ensues and, just as in 1922, is cut off short to make way for a harshly rhythmical horn and trumpet music: but this itself is different from 1922, and leads (with the E♭ clarinet reprising its variant of Ex. 1*a* from the 'registral oppositions' passage added in 1927) to high, long-held dissonance in wind and strings and low tremolo rumblings in double bassoons and basses. Then a stark complex of brass and woodwind polyphony, like the interlacing girders to support a great building, soars up to one of the work's biggest climaxes – a pulverising *Più animato* that locks most of the orchestra into a shuddering dotted rhythm reminiscent of the Nibelungs' anvil-battering hammers in Wagner's *Ring* (many years later Varèse would make this explicit in his rewriting of the passage for *Tuning Up*) while horns, trumpets and trombones blast forth with an angry fanfare in a conflicting rhythm.

The trumpets project this fanfare onward, within two huge *Largamente* chords from the rest of the orchestra, and introduce a short passage of recapitulation. It is signalled by a fairly literal reprise of the 'barbaric' Ex.2. Percussion patterns familiar from the work's opening (topped off with the siren), lead on to a new theme shown here as Ex.17, immediately memorable in its grave, sonorous scoring for woodwind choir in octaves. On the one hand it seems a development of Ex. 1*a*; on the other it could be viewed as an elaboration of the horn tune Ex.14 (which itself, we recall, was only created in the 1927 revision).

Ex.17

A continuation of this melody on unison strings, followed by warm brass harmony that imparts a sense of cadence, serve to conclude this eventful central span of *Amériques* in its 1927 version. From this point, for the final third of the work, the versions of 1922 and 1927 are again reunited in musical substance, with a few more minor divergences still to be noted.

The last span has distinctly the character of a finale, and it operates in a different manner from the rest of the work. Certainly it concerns itself – often in fairly obvious fashion – with motifs that have by now grown quite familiar; certainly it may be divided into a number of sections. But those sections are now few, and large. The constant changes of texture and subject-matter are renounced, and continuity is ensured by sustained ostinato rhythms, melodic repetition and development. In mood, this is the most exhilarating, 'primitive' portion of Varèse's vast virtuosic orchestral canvas, yet it suggests a certain stability of purpose, a deliberate, triumphant advance to a fully-envisaged goal.

It begins *Presto* with a developing pattern of two alternating, very short staccato quaver chords shared among virtually the whole orchestra (strings in pizzicato double-stopping) except for high woodwind. The percussion also have a role in this, starting simultaneously with a self-absorbed polyrhythm of their own, but rapidly coming to provide additional ictus and support for the orchestra's chords, which fall thicker and faster as the pattern gains in complexity. But all this is merely – and very obviously – an accompaniment. The high woodwind (piccolos, flutes, oboes, E♭ clarinet) meanwhile launch into a very long florid tune in shrill octave unison. It is a straight, but enormously extended, development of the *sauvagement* melody we have previously met in the strings as Ex.13. (In the 1922 score Varèse now gives it the expression-mark *Ruvido e âcre* – 'rough and pungent'.) As it proceeds, the tune becomes more and more agitated and intense, its ornamental shakes and roulades longer and more elaborate and occurring closer together, until the whole melodic line deliquesces into a molten stream of accelerating demisemiquavers. Meanwhile the chordal accompaniment in orchestra and percussion attains a peak of excitement in a continuously battering passage marked *Tutti cresc. moltissimo*.

The woodwind soar up to a high, long-held unison E and the texture begins to break apart, though the tempo remains the same *Presto*. Fragments of the previous accompaniment rhythm are heard; and then the full orchestra engages in an antiphonal contest with the full percussion body. The orchestra lays down enormous tutti block-chords, slowly crescendoing from *pp* to *fff*, whereas the percussion simultaneously, and in the extended spaces between the chords, provides a rhythmic tattoo of its own.[28] The huge chordal blocs, rearing up like gaunt skyscrapers against the skyline, are the ultimate development of the 'cadential' chords of Ex.4a. Out of the last chord emerges once more the voice of the siren (brilliantly resonated in the lower regions of the orchestra by contrabassoon), and this sparks off the ultimate development of the swirling, chromatic, 'impressionistic' textures that have been encountered at various points in *Amériques*. It is in fact closely modelled upon the similar episode that occurred immediately after the first appearance of the *sauvagement* tune Ex.13,

---

[28] This passage is much more extended in the 1922 version, which has nine of these chords, including several short, abrupt ones, to the four of the 1927 revision.

but is now lengthened (and greatly elaborated in detail) into a shifting web of rising/falling chromatic *glissandi* in various regions of the orchestra. Finally it evanesces into two still *pianissimo* bars deceptively marked *Più calmo*: while they sound, the tempo slows to a broad crotchet=60, and it is at this deliberate pace that the ultimate, climactic explosion of *Amèriques'* orchestral power takes place.

The passage – we can think of it as a huge coda – is marked *Grandioso*: Varèse may fairly be said to have earned by this stage the right to a little boastful musical rhetoric. However it is also among the least characteristic music in the work: by which I mean that its rhythmic insistence, and to some extent its material, remind us ineluctably of a quite different composer. To be specific, the music seems full of echoes, deliberate or not, of Stravinsky's *Le Sacre du printemps*; and its main motif, to be more specific still, closely resembles that of Stravinsky's 'Cortêge du Sage' (cf. Ex.18*a* and *b*).

It also directly develops the *pesantissimo* pounding rhythm from *Amériques'* exposition (Example X), which is now revealed as a first foretaste of this coda. This stamping, obstinate, chant-like figure, which moves swiftly and yet with a heavy deliberation, is ceaselessly repeated – usually with small variations but without ever losing its recognizability. It is the backbone of the whole passage, entrusted to the 8 horns, 4 trombones, and tuba; and against it Varèse plays off a welter of other elements, both rhythmic and melodic, more characteristic of the work as a whole. Indeed, several of these are forms of previously-familiar motifs, and the one which comes to predominate is the mocking fanfare Ex.5. But it is Ex.18*a* which provides the motive power, and like some gigantic reciprocating engine, the music comes to accumulate an enormous machine-like energy, terrible and splendid in its strength and wild abandon. The entire orchestra is constantly involved, and the texture ranges from the fragmented to the very full indeed. The music's sense of forward drive and decisiveness signals that we are approaching the end of this sonic adventure.

Abruptly, these imperious sounds are cut off, and in their place we hear the ostinato string-figure Ex.7. Indeed Varèse now brings back a varied repetition of the music originally heard on Ex.7's first appearance, at the beginning of the central section of *Amériques*. The principal difference here is the excision of the horn-music and the substitution of clipped, heavily rhythmic *sfff tutti* chords which themselves develop out of the preceding music. But the fanfare Ex.5 blares out for one last time in zany grandeur, and the elements shown earlier on Example Page A – including the 'chromatic curl' Ex.1c on woodwind and trombones and the trumpet's distortion of Ex.1a – all return in precisely the same relationship to one another, through slightly differently scored and transposed bodily upward by a major third.

It is unclear whether Varèse's intention here is primarily to stress thematic connexions, or pattern-making on a larger scale: probably both at once. Although he uses this whole musical complex like a free-standing block, the fact that it contains ideas deriving directly from the work's opening means that, in effect, the end of *Amériques* is in its beginning. After this last outburst the work concludes with a stark, invigorating display of physical energy. A single chordal complex, broken up into incisive rhythms, resonated by percussion and the clamorous siren, pounds its way to the end. Finally it stabilizes into a long-held *fff* chord that swells out to *sffff* in an accompanying roar of tremolo percussion, the trumpets, horns and trombones raising their bells up to project the sound triumphantly into the ambient air.

To be accurate, the last vast chordal crescendo is found only in the 1927 revision. Varèse's original shows only three huge clipped *ffff* chords, separated by silences, and a single last empty bar, surmounted by a fermata, for the sounds to ring on into. This is the first example of a feature found in many of his mature scores: after all the sound and fury, the music will swallow itself in a composed silence. At the end stands the place and date – 'N.Y. City MDCCCCXXII' – at which this amazing music was given birth.

*   *   *

This one huge score of Varèse, a viscerally exciting experience in the concert hall, is endlessly fascinating and stimulating, and as triumphant a statement of the modernist vision, in its full glory, as any artist has achieved. Yet Jonathan Bernard, in performing his close analytical work on Varèse's music, was not necessarily wrong virtually to exclude *Amériques* from consideration. As he has noted, it 'proves extremely problematic when approached with the methods developed in [his] book, suggesting it has some aspects of a transitional work'.[29] Not only is it transitional, but the rewriting or substitution of some passages during revision is likely to have further disrupted the compositional framework from an analytical standpoint.

Since the composer was so adamant, in 1926, that not a note of *Amériques* needed to be changed, it remains to ponder the reasons for, and the effect of, the 1927 revision. What happened in a single year to change his mind? The simple answer is probably that this was the year in which he wrote the bulk of his next major orchestral work, *Arcana*. The *Amèriques* revisions followed swiftly upon that great creative outburst. Working again with a large orchestra, and producing a work at once less rhapsodic and more stylistically self-consistent than *Amériques*, he must have experienced a measure of dissatisfaction with the more 'backward-looking' parts of the earlier score, especially its central span. The new passages that Varèse composed are in his fully mature, constructivist idiom of the later 1920s. They radically reduce the overtly 'Impressionist' component in *Amériques*, and – as we have seen – they establish musical links not only with the existing material but with each other. Thus they make it, to some extent, a tauter and stronger work, even though they may also be said to slightly reduce its spectrum of colour. The reduction in the size of the orchestra – roughly to the same dimensions as *Arcana* – and the abandonment of the off-stage brass group *may* have been a capitulation to the sheer practicalities of performance, but that was seldom Varèse's way. More likely it was also a means of tightening and refining the original vision.

We can doubtless agree that the revised *Amériques* of 1927 is the more artistically unified and consistent work. Yet the original of 1922 possesses a different consistency: the totality of the expressive impulse as Varèse first realized it, which included the less fully developed aspects of his musical language and the references back to his pre-war

---

[29] Bernard, p.243, n.34.

compositional influences, to which he was that much closer in time. If we add to this the different, more dramatic conception of orchestral space supplied by the '*fanfare intèrieure*', and the very much larger orchestral apparatus with its more anecdotal elements, it seems less an 'unsuccessful' first attempt at a particular musical goal than another route to that goal. Perhaps it helps to think of the two versions as two Cubist-era canvases, *Amériques I* and *II*, to be hung separately or side by side: both depicting Brooklyn Bridge and the New York skyline, but from slightly different perspectives and at a different night-time hour. One of them incorporates, Dada style, a couple of industrial artifacts, yet alludes more explicitly to the artist's roots in Cézanne; in the other some of the shapes have taken a further step towards abstraction; but each of them is a glorious work of art.

5 · Flowering crystals

... in the twenties ... I said that my music was organized sound and that I was not a musician, but a worker in frequencies and intensities.
VARÈSE IN CONVERSATION (1963)[1]

CHRONOLOGY 1923–25

1923 *4 March: Varèse conducts the première of* Hyperprism *at a Guild Concert in New York, causing a near-riot. In response to the audience outcry he immediately repeats the work. (Several newspaper critics indulge the metaphor of a 'menagerie'.) The performance leads nevertheless to Varèse's music being taken on by the British publisher Kenneth Curwen. The ICG affiliates to Casella's Corporazione delle nuove Musiche in Italy. Six Guild members (Arthur Bliss, Louis Gruenberg, Leo Ornstein, Claire Reis, Lazare Saminsky and Emerson Whithorne) secede to form the League of Composers. Varèse reorganizes the Guild under a Technical Board consisting of himself, Carl Ruggles, Salzedo, Casella and the conductor Walter Straram.*

1924 *13 January: Robert Schmitz conducts the première of* Octandre *at a Guild Concert in New York. May: Varèse returns to Paris, staying in the studio of Fernand Léger and working on the composition of* Intégrales.

---

[1] 'Edgard Varèse on Music and Art: a Conversation between Varèse and Alcopley' in *Leonardo*, Vol. 1 no.2, p.194.

Visits London in June and again for the European première of
Hyperprism, *conducted by Eugene Goossens in a BBC Concert on 30 July*
entitled 'From Bach to Varèse'. Returns to New York at the end of
September. Stokowski performs Hyperprism *in Philadelphia in November,*
and again in one of his Carnegie Hall concerts in December.

1925 *January:* Intégrales *completed. 1 March: Leopold Stokowski*
conducts the première in an ICG concert in New York. Varèse irritable and
depressed. May: after several years renting a variety of apartments, Varèse
and Louise buy a house in 188 Sullivan Street, New York. September:
leaving Louise in NY, Varèse returns to Paris to seek advice on prostate
trouble from a doctor who treated him the previous year. Working on
Arcanes *(original title of* Arcana*) but destroys much of what he writes.*
Returns to New York in early December. 18 December: Octandre
performed in Mexico, conducted by Carlos Chávez.

The three works Varèse composed and introduced to the public
between 1922 and 1925 – *Hyperprism, Octandre, Intégrales* – were
those which established his reputation as an ultra-modernist of
formidable gifts. No longer transitional in style, they consolidated his
musical idiom and ideas in particularly cogent form, and they – or at
least *Octandre* – have remained ever since among the most frequently
performed of his scores.

They are, therefore, the first works we may regard as the wholly
authentic expression of their composer's highly individual approach to
music. This is not to say that they contain no references to the past, or
reveal no evidence of his stylistic roots. But whereas in *Offrandes* and
Amériques this evidence may still be found near the surface, in terms of
identifiable influence, now in *Hyperprism, Octandre* and *Intégrales* all
such traces of other composers are entirely subordinated to Varèse's
uniquely forceful and individual syntax, and his fiercely original
sound-world. The three works constitute a kind of trilogy, exploring
the now-achieved idiom from different angles and in different
instrumental and formal contexts.

One is struck immediately by the change in scale and perspective.
Gone are the cityscapes, the onomatopoeia, the profuse, ocean-
spanning imagery of new worlds. Instead there is a sense of
concentration on the basic elements of music, the organic life of sound
itself. Throughout Varèse's mature output, we encounter these swings

between macrocosm and microcosm, extrovert and introvert, magical and scientific: between works which, in some measure, evoke the vastness of terrestrial or cosmic landscape, and those which seem instead to suggest an analysis of the very roots of matter. In this sense, too, *Hyperprism*, *Octandre* and *Intégrales* are a kind of trilogy, and perhaps reveal their individual natures most clearly when performed as such.

Compared to *Amériques*, these are scores of short duration and for small forces: essentially, groups of wind and percussion in *Hyperprism* and *Intégrales*, and seven solo wind instruments plus string bass in *Octandre*. (The exclusion of all string instruments, save for that one bass, immediately makes for a starker, more characteristically 'Varèsian' sound.) The percussion requirements, maintaining the range and complexity unveiled in *Amériques* and *Offrandes*, are certainly large in comparison to almost all of Varèse's contemporaries. The preponderance of wind instruments has its contemporary parallels in the works of Stravinsky, Hindemith, Kurt Weill and others, but no other composer was as strongly committed to them as his principal melodic and harmonic agents as Varèse. Yet they are not, in themselves, large bodies if we think, for example, of Stravinsky's *Symphonies of Wind Instruments* (1920) and some of Hindemith's *Kammermusik* series (1922–27). External measurements, in any case, can be deceptive. Compared to these three works, *Amériques* is diffuse, discursive, anecdotal: while they are concentrated, essentialized and – within their reduced dimensions – its expressive equal in sheer explosive power.

The very titles signal a newly 'scientific' approach to sound. In place of the romantic, evocative or topographical titles of his earlier works we now have references to crystallography (*Hyperprism*), the structure of plants (*Octandre*) and higher mathematics (*Intégrales*). They suggest a new logic, and an absence of sentimentality or affect. Yet the difference in attitude is more apparent than real. A change in focus does not change the object in the telescope or microscope, though it may help us to see it more clearly. Though hard scientists and esoteric theorists remain at odds, both will acknowledge that the matter of the physical and impalpable universe is – like acoustics – determined by rates of vibration. At the atomic and sub-atomic levels, everything is in motion; matter is anything but inert. At such levels, sounds are as alive, as 'intelligent', as crystals, or plants. The only expressions available to science to describe and manipulate such phenomena are mathematical. Music and mathematics go hand in hand: music, as an 'art-science' (Varèse's term) that deals in the physical reality of acoustical structures, can be seen as a symbol of the union of the mystical and the scientific at the root of matter. Varèse did not put it quite like that, but he did say to Gunther Schuller, sharply distinguishing his view of music from that of the post-War serialists, 'I want to be *in* the material, part of the acoustic vibration, so to speak'.[2]

Perhaps this is to read too much into Varèse's titles. The programme note he wrote for the first performance of *Intégrales* is largely an elaborate disclaimer that any extra-musical significance should be attached to this or any other of his works, or that his titles should be taken to suggest such significance.

The music is not a story, is not a picture, is not psychological nor a philosophical abstraction. It is quite simply my music. It has definite form which may be apprehended more justly by listening to the music than by rationalizing about it. I repeat ... analysis is sterile. To explain by means of it is to decompose, to mutilate the spirit of the work. As to the title of a score, it is of no importance. It serves as a convenient means of cataloguing a work. I admit that I get much amusement out of choosing my titles – a sort of parental pastime, like christening a newborn child, very different from the more intense business of begetting. I find no fun in family names. I often borrow from higher mathematics or astronomy only because these sciences stimulate my imagination and give me the impression of movement, of rhythm. For me there is more musical fertility in the contemplation of the stars – preferably through a telescope – and the high poetry of certain mathematical expositions than in the most sublime gossip of human passions. However there are no planets or theorems to be looked for in my music. Music being a special form of thought can, I believe, express nothing but itself.[3]

We will encounter similar disavowals when we come to consider the next work Varèse wrote, *Arcana*. But they are not quite the last word on the subject that they seem. There is plenty of 'sublime gossip' in *Amériques* and *Offrandes*. On another occasion, in conversation with Georges Charbonnier, Varèse averred that there was no 'pure' music, all

---

[2] Schuller (1965), p.36.
[3] Quoted from *LGD*, pp. 227–228.

music being in some sense representational. Louise Varèse has remarked that the *Intégrales* programme note was 'plainly ... a protest and in answer to monotonous questionings'. For the moment I shall simply note that a title is only 'a convenient means of cataloguing a work' when it is a generic one, of the order of 'Symphony No.3' or *Piece in Two Parts for Six Players*. Titles which are *sui generis*, like *Jeux*, *Hyperprism* or *I met Heine on the rue Fürstemberg*, draw attention to themselves, invite us to consider them in direct or oblique relation to the music they subsume under their rubric. And Varèse's titles are, in fact, part of our experience of his music: they are instantly memorable signs under which it was written, and impart a specific aura that somehow reflects back on the works themselves.

And as works, *Hyperprism*, *Octandre* and *Intégrales* encapsulate, in a comparatively small space, the essential features of Varèse's developed musical language. He would extend these features on a larger scale in later years, and accrete to them a limited number of other techniques. But the abiding characteristics of his mature idiom are already in place, and it is worth summarizing them here before we proceed. The paradox of Varèse's oeuvre is not only that he seems to create a whole new universe of sound with such a small number of works, but that those works deploy a really quite limited number of elements, revolutionary though those are in effect. To him this was not a paradox at all. Describing his music in terms of what became his favourite analogy – that of crystallization – he was content to note that 'in spite of the relatively limited variety of internal structures, the external forms of crystals are almost limitless'.[4]

Most of the features have already been encountered in *Offrandes* and *Amériques*, but in this instrumental trilogy they may be considered for themselves, apart from any poetic or picturesque descriptive context. These are perhaps the first scores that wholly justify his frequent references to his own music as 'organized sound'. One overriding context in which they must be considered, however, is Varèse's idea of 'projection' in music. In their different ways *Hyperprism*, *Octandre* and *Intégrales* show this key concept in action.

---

[4] Lecture given at Princeton University, 1959, reprinted in 'The Liberation of Sound', pp. 16–17. The same comment appears word for word in the Conversation with Alcopley (this chapter, footnote 1) with the misprint – or Freudian slip – of 'interval' for 'internal'.

Varèse traced it back to a performance of Beethoven's Seventh Symphony he heard in the earliest years of the century in Paris, in the Salle Pleyel:

Probably because the hall happened to be over-resonant ... I became conscious of an entirely new effect produced by this familiar music. I seemed to feel the music detaching itself and projecting itself into space. I became conscious of a third dimension in the music. I call this process 'sound projection' or the feeling given us by certain blocks of sound. Probably I should call them beams of sound, since the feeling is akin to that aroused by beams of light sent forth by a powerful searchlight. For the ear – just as the eye – it gives a sense of prolongation, a journey into space.[5]

The relation of this concept to the one which Varèse derived from Wronski, of 'intelligent sounds moving in space', is so close it hardly requires pointing out. Here is a vision of music as sounds in motion in a three-dimensional space, being projected in certain directions according to the composer's desire, and creating a profound emotional effect thereby. 'Space' itself seems to be many things: the literal three-dimensional space of the concert hall, the 'vertical' space of instrumental register from the lowest to the highest available tone, the 'horizontal' direction of the sounds' onward progress through time, and also – by implication – an imagined interplanetary or interstellar space within which the music, like all human activity, is ultimately taking place. Varèse put it another way, in one of his most famous pronouncements:

I think of musical space as open rather than bounded, which is why I speak about projection in the sense that I want simply to project a sound, a musical thought, to initiate it, and then let it take its own course.[6]

In these terms, 'projection' is a fairly loose concept. (Perhaps after initiation of the sound one can 'let it take its own course' precisely because it is 'intelligent'?) But speaking of *Intégrales* many years after his polemical programme-note disparaging its analysis, Varèse gave a much more detailed account of 'projection', at least as far as it applied to that work.

---

[5] 'Varèse envisions "Space" Symphonies', *New York Times*, 6 December 1939, section 2, p.7.

[6] Schuller (1965), pp.36–37.

Intégrales was conceived for spatial projection – that is, for certain acoustical media not yet available but which I knew could be built and would be available sooner or later ... While in our musical system we deal with quantities whose values are fixed, in the realization that I conceived the values would be continually changing in relation to a constant. In other words, this would be like a series of variations, the changes resulting from slight alterations of the form of a function or by the transposition of one function into another. A visual illustration may make clear what I mean: Imagine the projection of a geometrical figure on a plane, with both figure and plane moving in space, each with its own arbitrary and varying speeds of translation[7] and rotation. The immediate form of the projection is determined by the relative orientation between the figure and the plane. By allowing both the figure and the plane to have motions of their own, a highly complex and seemingly unpredictable image will result. Further variations are possible by having the form of the geometrical figure vary as well as the speeds.[8]

So 'projection' may simultaneously affect several musical ideas, in several dimensions and at several speeds. The result is a kind of polyphony: not of melodic lines but of what Varèse liked to call 'sound-masses' or 'planes' – areas defined by pitch, register and instrumentation.

He set out the compositional vision that gave rise to this polyphony most fully in a lecture he gave in New Mexico in 1936, so important it is worth quoting here *in extenso*. Although the passage is couched in the future conditional, as an account of what he *would* be able to do when the means existed, it is also a description of what he was attempting to do, with the means at his disposal, in the music he had already written.

When new instruments will allow me to write music as I conceive it, taking the place of the linear counterpoint, the movement of sound-masses, of

---

[7] 'lateral movement' in 'Mind over Music'.

[8] I quote this text basically as reproduced by Louise Varèse in 'Statements by Edgard Varèse', *Soundings* 10, summer 1976. Another version was broadcast in 'Mind over Music', a radio interview with Fred Grunfeld on station WQXR, New York, 13 December 1953. Yet another appears in *Poème éleectronique Le Corbusier* (Paris: Editions de Minuit, 1959), p. 192. All are closely similar in wording but this seems to me the clearest in expression. I have filled in an apparent lacuna in the *Soundings* text by importing from 'Mind over Music' the words 'By allowing both'.

shifting planes, will be clearly perceived. When these sound-masses collide the phenomena of penetration or repulsion will seem to occur. Certain transmutations taking place on certain planes will seem to be projected onto other planes, moving at different speeds and at different angles. There will no longer be the old conception of melody or interplay of melodies. The entire work will be a melodic totality. The entire work will flow as a river flows.

We have actually three dimensions in music: horizontal, vertical, and dynamic swelling or decreasing. I shall add a fourth, sound projection – that feeling that sound is leaving us with no hope of being reflected back, a feeling akin to that aroused by beams of light sent forth by a powerful searchlight – for the ear as for the eye, that sense of projection, of a journey into space.

Today with the technical means that exist and are easily adaptable, the differentiation of the various masses and different planes as well as these beams of sound, could be made discernible to the listener by means of certain acoustical arrangements. Moreover, such an acoustical arrangement would permit the delimitation of what I call Zones of Intensities. These zones would be differentiated by various timbres or colors and different loudnesses. Through such a physical process these zones would appear of different colors and of different magnitude in different perspectives for our perception. The role of color would be completely changed from being incidental, anecdotal, sensual or picturesque; it would become an agent of delineation like the different colours on a map separating different areas, and an integral part of form. These zones would be felt as isolated, and the hitherto unobtainable non-blending (or at least the sensation of non-blending) would become possible.

In the moving masses you would be conscious of their transmutations when they pass over different layers, when they penetrate certain opacities, or are dilated in certain rarefactions. Moreover, the new musical apparatus I envisage, able to emit sounds of any number of frequencies, will extend the limits of the lowest and highest registers, hence new organization of the vertical resultants: chords, their arrangements, their spacings, that is, their oxygenation. Not only will the harmonic possibilities of the overtones be revealed in all their splendor but the use of certain interferences created by the partials will represent an appreciable contribution. The never before thought of use of the inferior resultants and of the differential and additional sounds may also be expected. An entirely new magic of sound![9]

---

[9] 'New Instruments and New Music', a lecture at Mary Austin House, Santa Fe, 1936 (printed in 'The Liberation of Sound' pp. 11–12). Note that part of the second

There are many issues in this crucial pronouncement, with its echoes of Futurist and quasi-scientific terminology ('oxygenation'!); but for the moment it is enough to note that Varèse clearly regarded 'projection' as taking the place of polyphony in more traditional music and allowing sounds or ideas to expand and grow through any or all of the musical 'dimensions' open to them – through melody, harmony, rhythm, timbre, attack, dynamics, register and actual acoustical space – and by their growth to determine the overall form of the piece.

We can see these ideas coming to fruition and being applied throughout *Hyperprism*, *Octandre* and *Intégrales*. In the melodic sphere, Varèse's most typical strategy is to create 'themes' which focus on a single pitch: stabbing repeated notes, leapt up to by an anacrusis, or decorated by semitonal slides above and below – see the initial utterances of *Hyperprism* (tenor trombone) and *Intégrales* (E flat clarinet). This is projection made palpable as sound directed along a straight line, like a searchlight beam, with the 'ornaments' functioning to intensify the salient pitch and almost literally push it along.

These piercing, aggressively travelling sounds move within the space created by a plangently dissonant harmony, spread out through the available instrumental registers. Its fundamental elements are a projection into the vertical sphere – by octave displacement – of the tight-knit semitonal clusters that decorate and push at the 'searchlight' pitch. Thus the predominant intervals are major sevenths and minor ninths, as well as tritones: see for example Ex.2 of *Hyperprism* and Ex.2 of *Intégrales*. Traditional harmony interprets these intervals as extreme dissonances. In the music of diatonic tonality, up to the end of the 19th century, they created unsustainable tensions that demanded resolution – a tonal cadence onto the stability of a tonic triad. But in the radical music of the 20th century – in, for example, Schoenberg, Webern and Varèse – harmonies built on these intervals *replace* the tonic triads: themselves innately unstable, they become the basic elements of the musical language and thus guarantors of a different kind of stability, an unchanging continuum in a music of perpetual change. Their innate tension, their potential to 'go anywhere', is the prerequisite for new kinds of growth, beyond the traditional formal archetypes of sonata, rondo and so on.

paragraph was recycled verbatim three years later in 'Varèse envisions "Space" Symphonies' (above, footnote 5).

In Varèse, then, both melody and harmony are essentially static. Chords – sometimes heavy and insistently repeated – tend to recur at the same pitch-level, or to contain the same tones even if their vertical hierarchy is shuffled. Varèse's chordal and pitch collections are not concerned to 'harmonize', even in the broadest sense, the musical material to a controlling tonic, and the modal inflections of major and minor have no relevance. There is no sense of cadence or indeed any of the general characteristics of 'functional' harmony. Instead, each tone has value in itself as a distinct sound, its individual identity stressed and enhanced by instrumentation and dynamics. Ideally, the intensity of each tone should be independent of all the others, and this intensity should be continually varying as the tone continues to be 'projected'.

The key to the effectiveness of this approach is orchestration: treating the quality and timbre of each sound as its vital essence, inseparable from its pitch. In fact Varèse seems not to have viewed himself as composing pitches which he then 'clothed' in instrumentation, but as composing directly with sounds whose constituent pitches were mere *post hoc* abstractions. For him, instrumentation *was* the music just as much as the tones he wrote down for the instruments to play:

... orchestration is an essential part of the structure of a work. Timbres and their combinations – or better, quality of tones and tone compounds of different pitch, instead of being incidental become part of the form, colouring and making discernible the different planes and sound-masses, and so create the sensation of non-blending. Variations in the intensity of certain tones of the compounds modify the structure of the masses and planes. Contrasting dynamics are based on the play of simultaneously opposing loudnesses – loudness as defined by Harvey Fletcher as 'the magnitude of sensation'.[10]

The result is at least an approach towards what Varèse clearly felt to be a highly desirable state and which he called, slightly awkwardly, 'the sensation of non-blending'. (See also his reference to 'the hitherto unobtainable non-blending' in his 1936 lecture, above, p.141.) The positive outcome of that negative formulation is a music in which all sounds or sound-groups are treated as individual entities with their own internal life, in complete opposition to the upholstered homogeneity of the late-19th century symphony orchestra or the

---

[10] Answer to Kurt List in *Possibilities 1* (Winter 1947/8), p.97.

standard chamber ensembles. Thus, as he said, his attitude to timbre was

precisely the reverse of the symphonic. The symphony orchestra strives for the utmost blending of colors. I strive to make the listener aware of the utmost differentiation of colors and densities.[11]

The prolongation of these sounds in vertical agglomerations of pitch subverts the natural desire for tonal closure, keeping the music, instead, 'open rather than bounded'. Such proceedings are much more accurately described as 'atonal' than is the music of Arnold Schoenberg, whose view of harmonic function remained conditioned by tradition, no matter how esoterically embodied in his totally-chromatic and serially organized scores. Varèse's dissonances, his incandescent pitch-clusters, are always in one sense mere symbols of the sounds he did not have the means to produce.

Varèse liked to employ the extreme high and low registers of his instruments, and also the highest and lowest sectors of the tonal range that his combinations of instruments made available to him. Very deep and very high sustained tones helped to extend and define the vertical acoustical space, often six or seven octaves in altitude, into which his sounds, projecting outward from tiny initial cells, expand as if into a vacuum, attempting to fill it by a spreading of the total chromatic through the whole available gamut.

The resulting 'space-filling' gestures – the rapid verticalization of many horizontal projections by the building-up or piling-up of sustained tones, generally rushing upwards from bottom to top of the register and forming a huge climactic chord with a crescendo – is one of the most characteristic, essentially 'Varèsian' features of his music. Ex.2 of *Intégrales* (below, p.178) is a simple instance. Another is Ex.4 of *Arcana* (below, p.197), which I mention because of Varèse's choice of terminology: he specifically referred to this latter example as a 'fanfare'. Though one can see the relevance in the music's brassy, proclamatory character, the effect does not have the insistent rhythmic quality of the conventional brass flourish for ceremonial purposes which most listeners would recognize as 'fanfare'.

In fact Varèse also writes figures and passages which come nearer to

---

[11] Quoted in Alfred Frankenstein, 'Varèse, Worker in Intensities', *San Francisco Chronicle*, 28 November 1937.

this more conventional idea of 'fanfare'. These are rapid, stuttering or pulsing repeated-note groupings whose function is both rhythmic, in that they subdivide the musical pulse into small, sometimes irrational units (quintuplets, for example), and 'projectional', for the reiterations intensify the projection of the tones or pitch-clusters they consist of. Were the word not so archaic, I would be tempted to call these signal-like patterns 'tuckets', for onomatopoeic convenience.[12] In the ensuing discussions I will tend to call them 'fanfares', and the more vertically-based space-fillers 'build-ups'; if I occasionally resort to Varèse's habit and call these latter 'fanfares', I hope context and description will make clear which kind I mean.

These 'tucket'-like rhythmic figures bear an intimate relationship to the activities of the percussion, often appearing as a projection of the percussion's unpitched rhythms into the sphere of pitch. In the much reduced instrumental context of *Hyperprism* and *Intégrales* (the percussion-less *Octandre* is a unique exception in Varèse's ensemble output) their extensive percussion requirements bulk huge indeed. Varèse uses the percussion in many ways – not least as a continuum of sound already 'liberated' from specific pitch, a 'sound-mass' that moves and shifts against the tonal structures being projected by the conventional instruments. But this 'sound-mass' moves of its own volition by the action of the extremely intricate percussion rhythms which are its life. Through their internal dynamics and the distinct tone-qualities of each percussion instrument, these interlocking rhythms create elaborate structures, polyrhythmic webs that divide and measure the music's metrical units with fine discrimination. (*Offrandes* Ex.5 – see p.101 above – provides a fairly simple example.) They can be strident, aggressive, battering – or delicate and tintinnabulous as a scattering of raindrops. They are Varèse's principal means of bringing about that 'aesthetic modification of time' which Wronski had asserted to be rhythm's proper function.

The relationship between pitched instruments and unpitched percussion is therefore sometimes contrapuntal – simultaneous streams flowing side by side – and sometimes antiphonal, the 'vertical' tone structures and chord-complexes of the pitched instruments alternating with or juxtaposed against percussion 'breaks' which create the sense of

---

[12] 'Let the trumpets sound the tucket sonance and the note to mount' – Shakespeare, *Henry V*, Act IV sc.2.

horizontal extension by their linear telling-off of time. It is this interplay between contrasting elements, rather than the rhythmic figures themselves, which creates the larger rhythm of the piece of music. For from his pronouncements on the subject, Varèse clearly related rhythm to structure, to overall form:

Rhythm is too often confused with metrics. Cadence or the regular succession of beats and accents has little to do with the rhythm of a composition. Rhythm is the element in music that gives life to a work and that holds it together. It is the element of stability, the generator of form. In my own work rhythm derives from the simultaneous interplay of unrelated elements that intervene at calculated but not regular time lapses. This corresponds more nearly to the definition in physics and philosophy as a 'succession of alternate and opposite or correlative states'.[13]

Succession, alternation, opposition are basic conditions of the large-scale structure of Varèse's works. As for correlation – used apparently in the biological sense, as the evolution of reciprocal relationships in the occurrence of different structures and processes – this is the result that these other characteristics serve to bring about. It is clear to any listener that Varèse's music depends, at its most basic level, on the abrupt juxtaposition and alternation of blocks of material, each block distinguished by having its own identity in terms of register, rhythm, instrumentation, and often its own pitch-content.

The laying-out of musical ideas as self-contained entities, as in a collage or mosaic, each idea directly abutting the next without sense of closure or smoothly-composed transition, directly subverts the purposeful, organic, *durchkomponiert* symphonic architecture which had been considered paramount throughout the 19th century. It may be viewed, indeed, as the manifestation of a general revolution in attitudes to musical structure in the early 20th century – a revolution engendered by the changing world-view of an increasingly urbanized and mechanized Western culture, and paralleling comparable revolutions in the other arts. From Debussy to Stravinsky, to the 'factory'-inspired works of early Soviet composers, to the starkly gestural evocations of geological forces in the music of the Icelander Jón Leifs, to the abrupt fissures introduced by Havergal Brian into

---

[13] 'Rhythm, Form and Content', lecture given at Princeton University 1959, cited from 'The Liberation of Sound', pp. 15–16.

symphonic architecture itself, composers had begun to explore the potential inherent in 'creative discontinuity' as a strategy of form. To the more modernistically-minded among them, a music of multiple, unmediated statements seemed to offer a more intense and primal artistic experience than anything taught in the Conservatoires.

As we have seen, this was already Varèse's strategy in *Amériques*, and the opening pages of that work provide a palmary example of it in action. If such formal thinking was at that time relatively new in his music (how one would love to test this assertion by evaluating the procedures of *Bourgogne* or *Les cycles du nord!*), he could have come to it by a number of routes. I have suggested Debussy's *Jeux* as the work's most obvious direct ancestor, but it is pointless to ignore the many passages in *Amériques* which seem to recall, sometimes even rephrase, parts of Stravinsky's *Le Sacre du printemps*. At the time Varèse wrote his work, *Le Sacre* was the single most revolutionary example of music composed in discrete blocks and by layering several contrasting elements within those blocks. Though the elements of *Amériques* are juxtaposed more abruptly than anything in *Le Sacre* there seems no doubt that he had studied Stravinsky's score closely and been profoundly affected by it – even if it was not, of itself, crucial to the formation of his ideas.[14] The visual analogies of collage and mosaic are especially appropriate in his case in view of his close contacts with art world, and it is clear that his view of musical structures took some of its colouring from Cubism and Futurism.

It is often assumed that discontinuity in music is essentially non-developmental (in the manner, say, of Satie's *Entr'acte cinématographique* of 1924). This need not be the case. Abrupt breaks and juxtapositions close off traditional routes of steady growth, but in some composers they encourage exploration of byways and inspired leaps across chasms. Debussy's *Jeux* is in many ways a strongly developmental score, its fragmented ideas subtly drawing together in its final pages to find their communal apotheosis in its magnificently long-breathed waltz-climax. Stravinsky's *Sacre* finds no matchingly revelatory nexus in its 'Danse Sacrale', an explosive (and detachable) final block laid at the end of all the others, though certainly one that takes to a climax the rhythmic-barbaric tendencies observable

---

[14] *Les Noces* and the *Symphonies of Wind Instruments* present further developments of Stravinsky's techniques of discontinuity, but at the time he composed *Amériques* Varèse could not have known either of them.

throughout the work. The final stages of *Amériques*, however, despite their clear echoes of *Le Sacre*, do form a culmination of disparate elements heard before: layered, simultaneous, placed in new relationships and welded into a climactic statement. Through all the intercutting and juxtaposition, the material has changed in recognizable ways; the discourse has been driven to a conclusion. In discontinuity, a subtle continuity has been maintained throughout the entire work and engendered a sense of purposeful growth.

In his later statements on this matter, therefore, Varèse avoided the analogy of collage or mosaic or any suggestion that his music was merely concerned with 'a rearrangement of musical patterns'. Instead he favoured a mineralogical analogy. In his most celebrated pronouncement, he defined musical form 'as a *resultant* – the result of a process'.

Each of my works discovers its own form ... There is an idea, the basis of an internal structure, expanded and split into different shapes or groups of sound, constantly changing in shape, direction and speed, attracted and repulsed by various forces. The form is the consequence of this interaction. Possible musical forms are as limitless as the exterior forms of crystals ... Form and content are one. Take away form, and there is no content, and if there is no content there is only a rearrangement of musical patterns, but no form ... the content of what is called program music ... is still only music. ... To reveal a new world is the function of creation in all the arts, but the act of creation defies analysis.[15]

He illustrated this by quoting 'the crystallographic description given me' by Nathaniel Arbiter, professor of mineralogy at Columbia University:

'The crystal is characterized by both a definite external form and a definite internal structure. The internal structure is based on the unit of crystal which is the smallest grouping of the atoms that has the order and composition of the substance. The extension of the unit into space forms the whole crystal. But in spite of the relatively limited variety of internal structures, the external forms of crystals are limitless. Crystal form itself is a *resultant* rather than a primary attribute. [It] is the consequence of the interaction of attractive and repulsive forces and the ordered packing of the atom.'[16]

---

[15] 'The Liberation of Sound', p.16.

[16] Ibid. Despite their seemingly limitless repertoire of shapes, all crystals may be

Crystals are inanimate, yet they grow through the action of terrific forces of heat and pressure. Growth, of a similarly powerful kind, is at work in Varèse's scores.

Yet even this analogy is inadequate, for Varèse's music is still a process that unfolds in time – not an exercise in three-dimensional geometry. As listeners, we can only experience the musical events in a particular, fixed order. At any given moment our attention will be engaged in the musical events of that moment, while we simultaneously engage in an involuntary act of memory, relating what we hear at that moment to what has gone before. As we put it together for ourselves, between our ears and our brains, we realize it is no mere collage or pattern because it has growth and climax and relaxation. 'Abstract' or not, Varèse's music impresses itself on our consciousness as a narrative of events, a drama whose *personnages* are 'different shapes or groups of sound'. No composer was more skilled in the composition of beginnings, middles and ends. Aristotle would have been proud of him.

For a composer who, as suggested above, viewed himself as working directly with *sounds* rather than *pitch*, the standard orchestral instruments were, in a powerful sense, as much an encumbrance as the 19th-century orchestras in which they all took their place. Throughout his career, Varèse felt this deprivation very keenly indeed. He wished for new instruments, new means of sound-production, not only for their own sake but as a means of escaping from music's equally desperate imprisonment within the 12-equal tempered scale that had been standard since the 18th century. Busoni had experienced these desires, but Varèse had to grapple with them as creative issues and felt their effects much more keenly.

'We need new instruments very badly', he said in 1916 in an interview for the *New York Telegraph*. '... In my work I have always felt the need of new mediums of expression ... What I am looking for is new mechanical mediums which will lend themselves to every expression of thought and keep up with thought'. Writing in *391*, he developed this idea:

---

classified according to only seven categories of symmetry, differentiated by the axes, the angle at which the axes radiate from the crystal's central point of intersection, and the planes in which the axes lie.

I dream of instruments obedient to thought – and which, supported by a flowering of undreamed-of timbres, will lend themselves to any combination I choose to impose and will submit to the exigencies of my inner rhythm.[17]

Varèse told Gunther Schuller that this desire already went back at least a decade, to his time at the Conservatoire.

I was already disenchanted with the tempered system ... and could never understand why we should be limited to it when our instruments can give us anything we want, and why it should be imposed as a prescriptive, as if it were the final stage of musical development.[18]

It was at this same time, at the *Marché aux Puces*, that he acquired his first two small sirens, intrigued by Helmholtz's description (in *Die Lehre von Tonempfindungen als physiologische Grundlage für die Theorie der Musik*, 1894) of his experiments with sirens:

With these, and using also children's whistles, I made my first experiments in what I later called spatial music. The beautiful parabolas and hyperbolas of sound the sirens gave me and the haunting quality of the tones made me aware for the first time of the wealth of music outside the narrow limits imposed by keyboard instruments.[19]

As far as we know, Varèse did not actually include sirens in an orchestral score until *Amériques*, when courtesy of the New York Fire Department he was able to weave his 'parabolas and hyperbolas of sound' into the very fabric of his grandiose evocation of the modern American city (and substitute a powerful steamboat whistle for the children's whistles). The siren clearly fascinated him both by the 'parabolic' shape of its swooping glissandi, and its absolute incapacity to be tied to single defined pitches, instead roving through the entire spectrum via a seamless continuum of micro-intervals.

Almost inevitably, sirens went on to be a frequent component of his instrumental apparatus; but they were of course rather primitive and limited in their capabilities. Varèse continued to search for more flexible means of sound-production. Kenneth Curwen reported in

---

[17] 391, No. 5 (June 1917). Translated from the French by Louise Varèse.

[18] Schuller (1965), p.32.

[19] 'Spatial Music', lecture at Sarah Lawrence College, 1959. I take it Varèse means 'outside 12-tone equal temperament', whose predominance is essentially a keyboard convenience.

1925 that 'he dreams of new electric instruments that will give him the precise number of vibrations per second that he asks, and no harmonics'.[20] His continuing interest in Russolo's noise-making machines is thus entirely explicable, though he made no use of them in his own music. In the 1930s he was to employ true electronic instruments, the Theremin and Ondes martenot (in *Ecuatorial*); but not until the 1950s, in his seventies, was he to have access to the techniques and technology of electronic filtering to produce true electronic music on tape for stereophonic reproduction, whether combined with conventional instruments (*Déserts*) or not (*Poème électronique*).

So most of Varèse's music is for conventional instruments, written in standard notation for the tempered scale. He had to accept their tonal production as it existed, and to organize the pitches they produced, because despite his ceaseless search for new media they were, for most of his life, all he had to work with. In the process he wrote for them as a master orchestrator; he extended their techniques; and he evolved methods of pitch organization uniquely tailored to his expressive requirements. Yet, questioned by John Cage about the nature of the music of the future, Varèse reiterated his faith that it would be 'surely *beyond* notes and based on sound'.[21] Always he hungered to go beyond the physical restrictions and encumbrance and baggage of the 19th century orchestra, which is, even now at the start of the 21st century, the dominating performance medium for serious music.

Thus in one sense his methods of tonal organization, no matter how intricate and finely adjusted, are only an approximation of what he felt he could achieve with an unrestricted sound-spectrum. For him, even more than most composers, a score was 'only a blueprint'.[22] Though they inhabit an authentic and pungent instrumental idiom, the extent to which Varèse's concert works aspire to the condition of electronic composition, far ahead of the technological development that would make this possible, is a fundamental aspect of their nature. Sometimes we may imagine that we hear, as one shade of the scores' emotional life, the sheer sense of frustration this fact engendered.

---

[20] 'Personalities. IV. Edgar Varèse', *The Sackbut*, February 1925.

[21] *Possibilities 1* (see footnote 10), ibid.

[22] Alcopley conversation (see footnote 1), p. 187.

HYPERPRISM

Varèse composed *Hyperprism*, a single short movement for wind instruments and percussion, between November 1922 and the early spring of 1923 – though doubtless its conception had been germinating for some time beforehand, probably even during work on *Amériques* and *Offrandes*. He dedicated it to José Juan Tablada (the poet of 'La croix du sud') and his wife Nena. Varèse himself conducted the première – in which the great battery of percussion was played by the Faculty and pupils of the Dalcroze School of Eurythmics – on 4 March 1923 at the Klaw Theater, New York, as part of a concert of the International Composers' Guild. The work provoked a near-riot: the audience formed into pro- and anti-Varèse camps of hissers and counter-hissers, and fights broke out at the rear of the auditorium. Not at all disconcerted by the reaction – rather, delighted that at least some people seemed to appreciate his music – Varèse immediately gave it a second performance.

In the audience that evening was the British publisher Kenneth Curwen, who immediately accepted *Hyperprism* for publication. The score appeared in 1924, the first of several that Curwen was to issue in the next few years and the first work of Varèse to be printed since *Un grand sommeil noir* in 1906. (The score was reissued in 1966 by Franco Colombo's Colfranc Music Publishing Corporation of New York, and 20 years later, in 1986, Colfranc published a new edition revised and edited by Richard Sacks. A prominent feature of Sacks's edition is the logical distribution of the enormous percussion battery between nine players and the provision of a part for an optional tenth player to ease the transition between instruments in certain passages.) On 30 July 1924, presumably as a result of Curwen's advocacy, *Hyperprism* achieved a broadcast on the fledgling BBC, conducted by Eugene Goossens – arousing considerable publicity but probably even less appreciation than it had received in New York. As Dion Gow recalled in *Radio Times* ten years later, 'almost everybody treated it as a huge joke'.[23]

Hyperprism is no joke. It is a brilliant achievement, fresh (and dateless) in its manner of expression, with a stunning musical impact out of all proportion to its size. Within its four minutes duration it

---

[23] Dion Gow, 'His Music Defies Analysis', *The Radio Times*, 16 March 1934, p. 791.

presents a concentrated statement of Varèse's aesthetic at its most radical. Certainly, it manifests affinities with some of the ideas we encountered in *Amériques* and *Offrandes*. But Varèse has rigorously excluded from it all the more traditional features which linked those scores to the Impressionist past. Nothing in *Hyperprism* could be mistaken for the handiwork of Debussy. A few bars might perhaps, and not inappositely, remind us of Stravinsky at his most fiercely hieratic. But the work as a whole is 'pure' Varèse in style, technique and aim.

The radical approach is already apparent in Varese's choice of ensemble, which dispenses entirely with the strings, harps, and pitched percussion of the two previous scores. Of course certain kinds of military and ceremonial music, especially those intended for performance in the open air, had long called for the mixture of wind and percussion – an obvious and famous example is the *Symphonie Funèbre et Triomphale* of Varèse's beloved Berlioz. But never before had any work called for them in the proportions specified in *Hyperprism*. Nine wind players – on flute (doubling piccolo), E♭ clarinet, 3 horns, 2 trumpets, and tenor and bass trombone – are joined by (or pitted against) an array of pitchless percussion little smaller than the complement of *Amériques*: snare drum, Indian drum, bass drum ('mammoth' again!), tambourine, large crash cymbal, a pair of cymbals, a very deep tam-tam or gong, triangle, anvil, slap stick, high and low Chinese blocks, Lion's Roar, 2 rattles (one of them large), sleighbells, and a siren. The impact of such a battery in a small hall can be overwhelming.

Equally radical is the approach to form. *Hyperprism* is the first score of Varèse which wholly justifies his statement that each of his works 'discovers its own form'. That form appears, at first hearing, as a string of dazzling and pungent sonic inspirations. Although certain *types* of music recur within it, and the recurrences are obviously intended as allusions to an earlier appearance of that type, there is little obvious repetition of any distinct musical idea. Nevertheless there is a strong sense of connexion achieved by other than thematic means, chiefly in the spheres of rhythm, timbre and harmony. And it may on first acquaintance be useful to consider *Hyperprism* as at least a potential ternary (A-B-A) form – if only because the gestures of its opening and closing portions are more like each other than they resemble the music occurring near the work's centre, where the gestures suggest a certain continuity of activity.

As previously remarked, the title is of a qualitatively different kind from *Amériques* or *Offrandes*. For most people, the strange word *Hyperprism* presumably evokes a vague sense of something 'scientific'. It's likely that Varèse had some more specific meanings in mind. But are we talking geometry or optics? In geometry, a prism is a three-dimensional polygon with at least two equal and parallel faces, a 'hyperprism' a prism extended into any number of dimensions. Thus the title may serve as a metaphor for Varèse's ideas of musical projection, with a musical idea of a few notes coming to occupy all the available dimensions just as the 'unit' – 'the smallest grouping of atoms that has the order and composition of the substance' – extends into space in the growth of a crystal. Larry Stempel, who interprets the title in roughly this sense, relates it to the work's harmonic-motivic processes: the faces of the 'prism' being 'two chromatic trichords which share the same interval shape, but not the same pitches'.[24]

As we have already seen, the question of how many 'dimensions' music may be said to occupy, as an imaginative 'object' in auditory 'space', is a very complex one. But it is by no means clear that Varèse meant his title to be understood only in terms of crystal structures. In the field of optics, the most significant properties of the prism are its transparency and its ability to refract light into its constituent colours. Quite apart from Varèse's intense concern to infuse light – ever more light (*mehr Licht*) – into his music, the prism, indeed a *hyper-prism* of superintensification, seems an apt symbol for a composer who aimed at the separating-out of every sound, every tone, as an entity itself. The action of the prism on coherent light is an ideal example of 'non-blending', and the music of *Hyperprism* is articulated in the most piercing primary colours of wind and percussion.

The 'chromatic trichords' to which Stempel refers nevertheless play a very important role – as the salient defining characteristic of *Hyperprism's* melody and harmony, they are the main means by which Varèse secures the music's strong sense of self-consistency. But it would be truer to say that most of it can be traced to a single 'seed' trichord: a figure of three adjacent semitones, at first appearance B♮-B♯-C♯, itself resembling a crystalline structure (and from now on a staple element

---

[24] Larry Stempel, 'Varèse's "Awkwardness" and the Symmetry in the "Frame of 12 Tones": an Analytic Approach', *Musical Quarterly* 65/2 (1979), p.160. Hereinafter cited as 'Stempel (1979)'.

in Varèse's musical vocabulary). Extend and project that figure into the dimensions of pitch (Figure *a*) or register (Figure *b*), and it provides a large variety of harmonic sensations, melodic curves, and spacings – and the resulting diagrams take on a prismatic appearance.

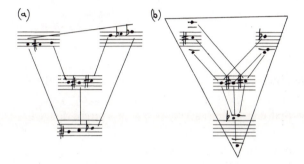

Varèse's use of this trichord is not systematic. He does not keep the pitches to a fixed order, and he does not always fill the total chromatic: the spaces between complete or incomplete trichords are as important to him as their internal structure. But as we shall see, much of *Hyperprism* is generated directly by means of them.

This applies only to the wind-instrument component of the work. The percussion sometimes co-operates with them and sometimes is a law unto itself – but it is noticeable that many of its rhythmic cells group themselves in threes, or are characterized by a triple attack.

Although the tempo-marking is an innocuous-looking *Moderato, un poco Allegro*,[25] the work begins with the force of a controlled explosion: a triple crash from cymbals, tam-tam and bass-drum, *fff*, their staggered entries already defining and subdividing the underlying pulse of the beat. *Amériques* and 'Chanson de Là-haut' had begun without percussion, 'La croix du sud' with a relatively soft, insidious percussion sonority; *Hyperprism* starts by focussing attention on the percussion from the very outset – and it is an almost continuous presence as the music unfolds. This initial blast subsides onto muted bass drum beats and the swelling growl of the Lion's Roar. Then as the rattles add their contribution to the noise, the tenor trombone proclaims the first thematic idea (Ex.1):

---

[25] *Moderato poco Allegro* in the original editions: I follow Sacks for tempo indications, which sometimes substitute Italian for the previous French directions.

Ex.1

We have observed this type of idea in the making in the two previous scores, but here it has attained its full, starkly Varèsian form: the 'melody' that consists essentially of a single pitch, doggedly stressed in irregularly changing rhythm, zeroed in upon by means of convulsive apoggiaturas (which define the seed trichord). Clearly, such writing has little in common with melody as it had come to be understood in the art-music of the preceeding centuries: and it is especially far from the wide-ranging, highly chromatic melodic idiom of the Schoenberg school, which was the latest development of that tradition. But it establishes plenty of points of reference with the melody of other musical cultures, especially oriental and Amerindian ones; as well as with recitative, chanting, cantillation, and speech-rhythm. Ultimately, therefore, it implies a vocal, not a purely instrumental archetype: if music like Ex.1 does not 'sing', it certainly 'speaks' – in an earnest, passionate, hortatory fashion that commands respect and attention.

The rhythms of Ex.1 are not duplicated by the percussion, which develop more complexly sub-divided rhythmic structures of their own along with distant moans of the siren (whose contributions become steadily louder at each appearance in the work). Ex.1's cardinal pitch, C, is resonated in various ways on the horns, and the bass trombone's low D poises it characteristically over the harmonic abyss of a major seventh (suggesting, like the tenor trombone's downward glissandos, the extension of the seed trichord through the chromatic scale). Then suddenly there is a new expression-mark of *Molto calmo*, and the musical texture begins to open out into the harmonic dimension. Against the soft wail of the siren, quiet strokes on cymbal, tam-tam and triangle reinforce a simpler rhythm as woodwind and brass spell out a still, aerated harmonic complex that swiftly and unexpectedly intensifies into a stark 'fanfare' (in Varèse's sense) with new crashes from the percussion (Ex.2):

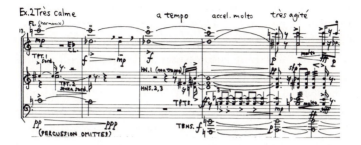

Although Ex.2 does not unfold in the shape of the seed trichord, the accumulated vertical sonority in fact amounts to three chromatic trichords spanning nine pitches (the missing three would produce a fourth trichord).

From the high-pitched C♮ to which it returns at the end of that example, the flute now launches out, over more tenuous percussion attacks, into something more resembling a conventional melodic idea (Ex.3):

While in a general way this may remind us of the original trombone statement of Ex.1, its expressive profile is entirely different – not least because it encompasses 11 of the 12 available pitches (mainly but not entirely through interlocking trichords), instead of using the trichord to emphasize merely one. Its attainment of the high E♮ brings a return of the initial tempo and a new irruption from the percussion ensemble, in a rhythmic complex that certainly incorporates elements from the work's opening, but in different and perhaps more developed relationships. The siren's wail is heard again, more stridently, while flute, clarinet and muted trumpets crescendo in a a high semitone dissonance. Immediately, there is another complete change of mood and texture.

What happens now is different from anything heard so far, and marks the beginning of the 'central section' of what I described earlier as the work's 'potential ternary form'. Horns and trombones, in a rhythmic homophony that the percussion actively underlines (and in a harmony that effectively encompasses all 12 tones, with two distinct groups of percussion to underline the two principal chords) intone a new, heavy, chant-like theme (Ex.4). As a gesture it would not seem out of place in a ritualistic work such as Stravinsky's *Symphonies of Wind Instruments*, but its hard, granitic expression marks it out as entirely Varèsian in character.

The percussion now falls completely silent for the first time in the work. A flourish from the three horns lands upon the pitch E♭, prolonged in horn 1, and a trumpet chimes in a minor ninth above, on E♮. This initiates a brief flowering of sound from the wind instruments, half polyphony, half build-up of a typically dissonant trichordial harmony, which fades away to *ppp*, leaving horn 1 again stating a new pitch, B♮. This time the clarinet strikes in, a major seventh above, on B♭.

The tempo has slowed to *Lento*, and the percussion still remains silent. The wind instruments now play a texturally complicated pattern, basically a polyrhythmic build-up with each instrument on a different pitch – save that the trumpets and clarinet each oscillate around a trichord in tones and semitones (and the piccolo around another in ninths): Ex. 5.

This builds to a climax and then cuts off, leaving the trumpets sounding their major seventh; the tempo suddenly switches to *Vivace* and the drums crash back, aided by cymbals, slap stick and Chinese blocks, in two bars of steam-hammer-like attacks. One bar of clarinet and horns on their Ex.5 pitches intervenes, then another percussion interjection. Finally Varèse re-states the whole of Ex.5 – identical in pitch, though rhythmically somewhat modified – with two punctuating percussion attacks. The second of these occurs at the climax and includes the tam-tam. Once again there is a cut-off and a complete change of texture.

Ex.5

However, the tempo reverts to *Moderato*, and there may be a sense in which the work is now returning to the character of its opening. Bass trombone (with repeated snorts on a very low pedal F♮) and two horns spell out a deep, cavernous version of the seed trichord,[26] while the percussion return to the foreground with a vengeance. Their complex rhythmic texture suddenly involves almost every player, with crashes on cymbals and tam-tam, whirring rattles, and insistent rhythms on side drum, anvil and sleigh bells. The siren's wall rises to its loudest yet; as it reaches the peak of its sonic curve the tenor trombone strikes in with a new melodic statement (Ex. 6) over a pattern of drumbeats and cymbal rolls.

Ex.6

---

[26] As F♮–E–F♯: the second horn's clef is wrong in all editions!

It was this same instrument that made the first melodic statement; and to a certain extent we are surely meant at this point to recall Ex. 1. Nevertheless important parameters have changed: though there remain similarities of texture, tone-colour and rhythm, this trombone solo centres not on a single pitch but a semitone oscillation, and eventually launches out into a phrase that encompasses eleven tones: four permutations of the seed chromatic trichord, with only one pitch lacking – the C♯ which was the focal point of Ex. 1. (Teasingly, Varèse almost but not quite allows it to appear – in the bass trombone's quarter-flattened D♮! – and there is no further occurrence of C♯ in the remainder of the work.) There are some resemblances in this latter half with the flute melody Ex. 3, so perhaps Ex. 6 could be regarded as a 'compressed recapitulation' of both ideas. The direction 'laughing' emphasizes both the vocal character of the writing, and its by no means accidental evocation of jazz-trombone style.

Piccolo and clarinet, accompanied (and perhaps imitated) by a rapid tattoo on the Chinese blocks, respond with a line of their own in piercing, high close harmony – their music relates to some extent to their activities in Ex. 5, and each instrument makes play with a trichord of its own. They climax on a high, squealing (*'hurlant'*) repeated semitone, like a band of radio noise, against a furious percussion build-up, with the siren – on this its last appearance – attaining its loudest wail of all. Suddenly all falls silent except for quiet, expectant drumbeats, marked *Vivo, molto fluido, misterioso*. Then the horns declaim a transfigured fragment of the chant-like idea, Ex. 4, and *Hyperprism* ends as abruptly as it began, with the full wind body building up a climactic nine-note harmony (Ex. 7), extended to 10 pitches by the final piccolo trill and constructed from three trichords –

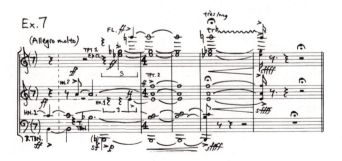

one of which is subtracted at the last moment, to be replaced by a hot shimmer of cymbals, tam-tam and triangle.

What no description of *Hyperprism* can convey – especially one which devotes space to matters such as pitch-structure, which only intermittently impinges on the listener – is the sheer *physicality* of this music, its raw power, achieved by wild fluctuations in dynamics, obsessive yet irregular rhythms and percussion impacts, and the focussed tang of the wind instruments. Like the unstable atom of uranium, this very small piece of music can unlock a truly cataclysmic power. All the conventions and decorum of musical history seem stripped away, and we are faced with the untrammelled forces of the universe.

OCTANDRE

Octandre, the immediate successor to *Hyperprism*, was composed during 1923. Varèse dedicated it to the pianist E. Robert Schmitz, organizer of the Franco-American Society, who conducted the première at the Vanderbilt Theatre in New York as part of an International Composers' Guild Concert on 13 January 1924. The work was encored – a harbinger of its relative success as one of the most accessible of Varèse's mature creations. It was published later that year by Curwen,[27] and twice peformed with considerable success in Mexico in 1925, on one occasion before a large audience of students and artists at the National Preparatory School, by Varèse's friend Carlos Chávez.

Octandre is no reversion to the post-Impressionist world of *Offrandes* and *Amériques* – in fact, it consolidates many aspects of the musical language announced in *Hyperprism*. But its manner of doing so, and its instrumental colouring, give it a superficial appearance of traditional design that has always made it one of his most approachable scores. To begin with, it dispenses entirely with the serried ranks of percussion, with their disruptive motoric and industrial rhythms. Varèse's ensemble consists merely of seven players of 'melody instruments' – flute (taking piccolo), oboe, B♭ clarinet (taking E♭

---

[27] There have been two subsequent editions – a slightly corrected Ricordi reprint in 1956, and a newly engraved score incorporating further markings by Varèse, edited by Chou Wen-Chung, issued by Colfranc in 1980: my examples follow this edition. The revisions generally concern tempi and dynamics.

clarinet), bassoon, horn, trumpet, trombone – assisted by an eighth: a double-bass who produces sounds as piercing as any wind instrument. Moreover the work, around eight minutes in length, is divided into three movements, played without a break but structurally distinct: the third of these recapitulates elements of the other two, and makes some quick bows in the direction of traditional contrapuntal associations (in the first edition it is subtitled '*en mode de Passacaille*', and it certainly contains a recognizable passage of fugato writing). In these respects – and even, at times, in sound – the work comes within hailing distance of such near contemporaries in time and timbre as Stravinsky's Octet (1922–3), Schoenberg's Wind Quintet (1923–4), or Villa-Lobos's *Chôros* Nos.4 (1926) and 7 (1924).

Varèse could have called his work *Octet* (more likely in French, *Octuor*) – for that is what it is, in the widest sense: a piece of music for eight players. Yet the title *Octandre*, though it certainly reflects the 'eight-ness' of the ensemble, is not a musical term at all, but a botanical one. 'Octandrous' flowers are those possessing eight stamens. By association, Varèse seems to want to compare his octet to an eight-pronged organism in the natural world. The connotations are sexual, and all the eight players, though often treated as individuals, have an agressively masculine music to project.

'Projection' of musical ideas against one another, by juxtaposition or superimposition, is the method by which Varèse builds up *Octandre*'s first movement. It starts with an oboe solo, like the strident cry of a bird (Ex. 1):

Perhaps we can hear in this line a distant echo of Debussy's *Syrinx*, and we should now be getting familiar with this kind of Varèsian 'opening gambit': compare the beginning of *Amériques* with its flute solo, repeating essentially a single phrase with slight rhythmic changes. But in fact the structural significance of this opening is tauter and more immediate. In its first bar, the phrase presents us with a germinal cell of four descending semitones – which with octave displacement will supply the plentiful minor ninths and major sevenths that characterize the movement's harmony – outlining a total interval of a minor third. In fact the first three tones, Gb-F-E, are equally important in themselves spanning a chromatic trichard analogous to the seed of *Hyperprism*. It is this trichord, rather than the four-note tetrachard, which provides the major links between movements.

However, when the oboe breaks free of its initial pitches in bar 4, it is first by a transposition of the four-note cell (DB compare the second tenor trombone solo in *Hyperprism*), and then by a different arrangement, missing one pitch (Gb) but spanning the minor third – which is again outlined by the next instrument to enter, the clarinet.

While the oboe holds its 'final' A, the clarinet sounds B against it, a major seventh below; and the double-bass weirdly intones a harmonic on B a major seventh below *that*, confirming the significance of the chromatic trichord. This prompts the oboe to a second strain, a new unaccompanied 'song' that summarizes most of the pitches so far touched upon but whose interest seems now to be centred upon the tritonal tension between the A♮ and the D♯ above it. (There develops throughout the work a kind of subsidiary 4-note cell, consisting of the trichord plus a tritone.) Next, via a transposition of the opening cell, the oboe makes a tritonal leap from E♮ to Bb and thence upwards in an ascending cry to a high G♮, the only pitch not yet sounded. This provokes similar ascending gestures in most of the other instruments, which leap upward to fill in a static, wide-spaced harmony (essentially a projection of the basic cell into the vertical dimension), capped by an agitated repeated-note figure from the flute (Ex. 2, over).

This new block of sound is relatively short-lived (its last component is the clarinet's strident proclamation of the ascending tritone interval, ending again on G♮): it suddenly cuts off to leave the bassoon, in an inverted parody of the oboe's precipitous ascent, plunging down to its lowest register, where it sustains a deep Bb against a pulsing, buzzing C♯ in the horn. Above, flute and oboe strike in once more with a line

apparently deriving from the end of the oboe's first solo, and stressing the tritone interval in different ways (Ex. 3). It is soon reinforced by clarinet and a trichordal crescendo in the brass.

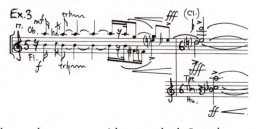

Immediately we hear a new idea, marked *Lourd et sauvage* – low, leaden, repeated brass chords with an urgent, pulsating repeated-note figure in the horn, alternating with wider-spaced chords involving woodwind (Ex. 4).

The first element of Ex. 4 starts to repeat, with a slight rhythmic shift – and then a general crescendo carries us into the climactic section of the movement. Against wide-spaced chords, some of them oscillating rapidly between high and low registers, the trumpet plays a forceful descending phrase (Ex.5*a*) which is taken up and varied by the horn (Ex.5*b*, opposite).

The faintly Spanish air of this trumpet theme should not obscure the fact that it is essentially a new statement of the movement's minor-third germinal cell; nor that three adjacent semitones and a prominent

tritone are all displayed in the flute part; nor that the clarinet's *très declamé* figure recalls the repeated-note figure of the flute in Ex.2; nor that the horn's variation of the trumpet tune ends with the figure of the clarinet's first entry in Ex.1; nor indeed that the following, very Stravinskian-sounding ostinato for bassoon against clarinet, trombone and double-bass is a transposed version – this time subsuming the minor-third cell – of Ex.4!

Naturally, all these details are not recognizable on a single hearing: but they become so with repeated listening. They amount to such a neatly comprehensive constellation of all the movement's ideas, in developing form, that it is hardly surprising that Varèse is content to bring the movement to an end without further ado. As the activity dies away in a wide-spaced harmony, *rallentando* and *decrescendo*, the oboe – which has been insisting upon its high C♮ since it first announced it in Ex.5*b* – is left exposed upon that pitch. The opening tempo returns and, '(*un peu angoissé*)' the oboe sings the movement into silence with a verbatim restatement of the first two-and-a-half bars of Ex.1 – transposed up by a tritone. Varèse marks a fermata but no stop before the next movement: this itself begins with a silent bar, so there is a just-perceptible break.

The second movement, *Très vif et nerveux*, is in effect a scherzo – though Varèse never used the term. It is a characteristic of *Octandre* that each movement is begun by a solo woodwind instrument: this time it is the piccolo, low in its register, projecting a motif (Ex.6) that is basically a single pitch, ceaselessly and irregularly repeated, broken only by the upward scoop of a semitonal appogiatura.

The pitch is the same G♭ with which the work began; the motif itself closely resembles the opening trombone entry of *Hyperprism*, and is likewise a statement of the chromatic trichord. Indeed, this sort of idea is a constant of Varèse's musical symbology. In one sense (that of the unmoving pitch) it seems completely static; yet in another (its rhythmic subdivision) Varèse immediately creates a paradoxical sense of flying momentum – which continues to be felt even when the motif is totally 'flattened out' into an immensely long-held G♮, with the E-flat clarinet (like the piccolo, making its first appearance in the work) clashing against it with a high, piercing F♮ a major seventh above. This screeching seventh gradually fades in intensity (another means by which Varèse maintains the sense of motion) and leads to a new element: two falling staccato chords, like a cadential quip. These very minimal materials immediately give rise to unexpectedly eventful and rather witty developments (Ex.7).

The trombone has taken over the repeated-note idea (thus strengthening the reminiscence of *Hyperprism*) but on a different pitch (E), while piccolo and clarinet stick to their original pitches but in fragments. The effect is to make play with the basic concepts of linear motion (a single 'horizontally' projected pitch) and vertical stasis (a held major-seventh harmony), enlivened by that of vertical motion (the staccato chords, which from their highest to lowest pitch – in the bassoon – fall a major fourteenth, i.e. a major seventh elongated by an octave).

Varèse continues this texture for some time, continually developing from the premises set up in Ex.7. The repeated E, in varied form, switches to the horn; more instruments join in; the two-chord quip (and the other higher chord marked x in Ex.7) repeat in progressively more complex rhythmic patterns. The various elements overlap and collide in continually unexpected ways (most unexpected of all being one bar of complete silence). At length the trombone resumes the repeated E, very much as in Ex.7, and then drops to D and begins a series of vertiginous major-seventh leaps to a high C♯ while the other instruments start to build up a new chord: the first shift in harmony since the movement began. The texture becomes quite densely polyphonic for a few measures as various instruments imitate the trombone's leap – either upward or downwards, and over different intervals – until the trombone settles back again around the repeated E, which it eventually holds softly while the trumpet almost imperceptibly takes over the same pitch. It swells out into a powerful crescendo and leaps up to an F♮ a ninth above, *sff,* which signals the beginning of a new section.

This is a powerful, raucous, nearly homophonic outburst for the entire ensemble. It consists (Ex.8) simply of two chords and a nagging figure in the E-flat clarinet, and harmonic content is confined to a static oscillation; but events are not quite as simple as all that.

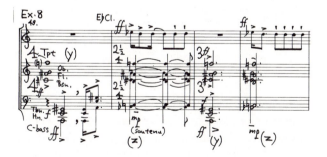

The chords are similar but not identical in pitch content (in Varèse's characteristically offhand way with the total chromatic, they include 10 different pitches, the remaining two of the 12 being supplied by the clarinet); and they are quite sharply differentiated from one another by dynamics, spacing, register, and their placing on the instruments. This latter element is further elaborated by the unusual indulgence of *octave* leaps (not sevenths or ninths) in horn, trombone, and double-bass – which however occur in the first chord only. Moreover, the chords' duration is continually varied by the changing time-signature: that has a similar effect on the clarinet's figure, which is rhythmically altered or foreshortened on each appearance. Quite literally, this music 'marks time'.

In terms of dynamic intensity, the first chord (*y* in Ex. 8) is much the more powerful, its *fortissimo* marking given only to the clarinet, which always appears against the relatively quiet background of chord z. This dynamic matching between y and the clarinet figure has the aural result of making that figure sound like the continuation from the highest note of the chord (in the trumpet): we hear a figure not of two pitches but three – F, E♭, D – outlining the minor-third cell once more, in the most forceful terms.

The elements of Ex.8 are recycled several more times with an effect of increasing tension and climax which is achieved almost entirely by the progressive rhythmic foreshortening of chord *y* and a general lengthening of chord *z*. Indeed, in emotional terms it is the movement's climax, and what occurs next has the function of coda. Chord *y* is cut off, sharp and *sec*; and a flourish on the flute leads to a little chuckling duet between oboe and clarinet (Ex.9):

While the duet continues the other instruments join in, in another of the movement's rare passages of polyphony, with a generally upward-leaping momentum. Rhythmic insistence by certain instruments on certain repeated pitches begin to remind us of the opening piccolo idea, Ex.6; and the piccolo itself returns to remind us more specifically, its low G♭ now transformed into a high F♯, just as the other instruments settle upon a final hugely wide-spaced harmony which swells out in an emphatic crescendo – a verticalization into extreme registers of the germinal cell from Ex.1. The effect is as if the movement has progressively opened out from the single middle-range pitch of Ex.6 to encompass the whole range of registral possibility

There are nine pitches in the chord, two obtained through the double bass's double-stopping. And it is one of its pitches, the B♮, which resounds on after the rest of the chord has been cut off. Without a break the third movement begins, with final quiet iterations of this B in the bass. The tempo-marking is *Grave*; a solo bassoon gives out a ruminative scrap of tune in which the germinal cell is clearly latent (Ex.11). The double bass imitates it, with different contour (perhaps achieving the hint of a 'Passacaille' that Varèse originally saw in this finale), only to light upon the four-semitone cell itself.

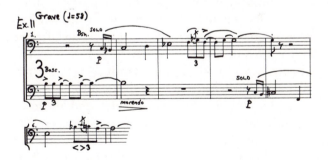

This immediately prompts bassoon and trombone to a reminiscence of the first movement: to be precise, of Ex.3. Recapitulation of past ideas in new contexts is, indeed, to be one of this finale's salient features. At once the *Grave* tempo is dropped, and the movement proper begins *Animé et Jubilatoire*.

There is a new theme on solo oboe – new, that is, except that its first half is a retrograde of the original four-semitone cell in Ex.1. Its second half, with the repeated upward leap of a major seventh, relates to several events in the second movement (Ex.12):

And Varèse, the revolutionary prophet of free form, the excoriator of academicism, presents this theme to us in what is quite recognizably a three-voice fugal exposition! The second entry, on bassoon, begins quite orthodoxly on a 'dominant' G♯; the third, on the E-flat clarinet, just misses the 'tonic' by a semitone, and starts on C♮. These three instruments eventually come together on a typically wide-spaced trichord, prompting rhythmic interjections from other instruments and a double-bass solo with some of the rhythmic characteristics of the 'fugue theme' but instead stressing the tritone interval. This possibly counts as an episode within the 'fugue' structure; at any rate Ex.12 now returns, in very varied guise, on the horn, against a high repeated-note figure in the upper woodwind.

Immediately there is another switch of texture, *Subitement très vif et nerveux*. The idea of high repeated notes gives way to a heavy, accented, pulsating chord in irregular rhythms, in middle and low registers, on seven of the eight instruments. The eighth – the trumpet – blares out a long solo line over the top (Ex.13*a*). This trumpet tune is no new idea, but a varied return of Ex.5*a* from the first movement. Seamlessly, this music flows into a second reminiscence: the chord remains in the same position, but is now sustained throughout regular 2/4 beats, with a swelling crescendo each time; and over it the trumpet, only slightly varying Ex.13*a*, produces a different figure (Ex.13*b*) that proves to be our old friend Ex.8 from the second movement.

After this neat trick of double-recapitulation,[28] Varèse continues almost exactly as he had after the original appearance of Ex.8, with the Ex.9 woodwind duet (now in oboe and bassoon) and a brief, dense polyphonic build-up – which leads, however, into the final section of the movement. It begins (Ex.14) with a brass fanfare on the ascending seventh of Ex.12's latter half, topped by a piccolo flourish which relates back immediately to Ex.6 at the start of the second movement. The E-flat clarinet joins the piccolo, and they develop the latter idea while the brass develop the former. In effect, they form two distinct rhythmic blocks, separated by register as well as material, which sometimes coincide.

---

[28] Bernard, p.142, is unwilling to acknowledge the recapitulatory function. He finds the similarity 'perhaps only mundane ... otherwise the two passages are thoroughly different'. He means, I take it, that they yield to quite different analytical explanations; but the very 'mundanity' of their clear aural connexion provides the listener with an immediate similarity which makes for a far from 'mundane' sensation of recognition and discovery.

As the music continues, the instance of rhythmic coincidence between these two fanfaring entities increases: the woodwind come more and more to agree with the brass. Finally the woodwind flatten out into a sustained chord, and then drop away into silence, while the brass carry on jubilantly. Figure *x* from Ex.12, which was embedded in their Ex.14 music from the first, now comes to the fore on the trumpet, which indulges in an elated riff with horn and trombone. With their biggest upward leap of all, the brass land upon a trichord of B, C and C♯ – and hold it in a swelling crescendo while the remaining instruments build up a version of the four-semitone cell around them and oboe and clarinet top off the texture with the start of the fugue theme Ex.12. But this is cut off, leaving the blast of the brass to bring *Octandre* to an end.

It is a short work, this pungent little octet. But is one of Varèse's most satisfying, and shows to what extent his radical new methods were capable of yielding the formal symmetries we expect of more traditional music. It also demonstrates his processes at their most obviously organic, creating many different shapes and configurations out of small germinal entities. To that extent, his choice of a title from the world of living, growing plants was absolutely justified.

INTÉGRALES

The third panel in this revolutionary triptych of pieces from the early 1920s consummates the tendencies of the other two. *Intégrales* deploys, on a much larger and perhaps grander scale, the kind of pungent, eruptive ideas that were forcibly compressed within the miniaturized dimensions of *Hyperprism*; and it extends the form-building techniques of *Octandre* to fill out its own broader design in a highly satisfying way. As a result, it has always been one of Varèse's most admired scores, and considered among his most perfectly achieved creations. It is certainly that, even though in my opinion some of the later scores considerably surpass *Intégrales* in sheer vision and imaginative scope.

The new work was composed throughout 1924, in the USA and Europe; much of it was written in Fernand Léger's studio in Paris, though the score was completed in New York in January 1925. Varèse dedicated it to Mrs Juliana Force, one of the principal benefactors of the International Composers' Guild (though the dedication does not appear on all the editions of the score). The première took place at a Guild concert in the Aeolian Theatre, New York on 1 March 1925, under the baton of Leopold Stokowski. The score was published by Curwen the following year.[29]

For the first performance, Varèse was induced or provoked into writing the programme-note quoted in full on p.137 above, with its warnings against 'sterile' analysis or looking for the expression of anything in the music except the music itself. The most he would allow was that the work 'has definite form' which (inevitably) 'may be apprehended more justly by listening to the music than by rationalizing about it'. Like *Octandre*, *Intégrales* was an immediate hit and was encored by acclamation from the audience, whose members seem to have felt free to attach plenty of local and contemporary associations to it. The painter Georgia O'Keeffe declared in a letter 'It is as good as Broadway at night and that is one of my great excitements',[30] while Varèse's critical champion Paul Rosenfeld declared that the work's

shining cubes of brass and steel set in motion ... were not merely metallic. They were the tremendous masses of American life, crowds, city piles, colossal

---

[29] Varèse introduced some revisions – mainly in dynamics, accentuation and phrase-marks, but also re-scoring two short passages – for the second edition (Ricordi, 1956), and some more for a later printing of that version. In 1980 Colfranc issued a newly-engraved critical edition by Chou Wen-Chung, based on the original manuscript and all the intervening printings; my examples follow this edition. From a careful reading of Chou's foreword he seems not to have had the manuscript itself before him, but a photocopy. Varèse in mid-1925 reported to Louise Varèse that Kenneth Curwen 'just simply mislaid' the manuscript (*LGD*, p.241), perhaps permanently. Whatever its subsequent adventures it appears to be the holograph formerly in the Moldenhauer Archives in Spokane and now with the Paul Sacher Foundation in Basle. This manuscript is illustrated and described by Olivia Mattis in *Settling New Scores: Music Manuscripts from the Paul Sacher Foundation*, edited by Felix Meyer (Basle and Mainz: Paul Sacher Foundation and Schott Musik International, 1998), pp. 174–6.

[30] *LGD*, p.230.

organizations; suddenly set moving, swinging, throbbing by the poet's dream; and glowing with a clean, daring, audacious, and majestic life.[31]

For at least one of its hearers, therefore, *Intégrales* seems to have sounded like a kind of Cubist *Amériques*. Olivia Mattis has suggested that the work could have been influenced or even sparked off by 'Vers le cristal', the artistic manifesto published in the journal *L'Esprit nouveau* by Le Corbusier and Amedée Ozenfant in 1924, which Varèse 'would have seen' in Léger's studio, and which describes Cubism as 'constructed by the interplay between internal and external forces' like the growth of a crystal.[32] Though Varèse presumably did read 'Vers le cristal' now or soon afterwards, and though he may well have found it a stimulus to composition, it is more likely that it was only a reinforcement of his existing ideas. The 'crystal' analogy had been active in his music at least since he wrote *Hyperprism*, though *Intégrales* takes it a good deal further in terms of the varied and simultaneous presentation of ideas, a central tenet of Cubism and also perhaps evoked by simultaneous reflections in the different facets of a crystal.

As to the title, Varèse had said: 'it is of no importance ... I often borrow from higher mathematics or astronomy only because those sciences stimulate my imagination and give me the impression of movement, of rhythm'. Yet *Intégrales* is one of his most suggestive and many-layered titles. The French word Intégrales is seldom found in the plural, a fact suggesting in itself that the composer wished it to be understood on more than one level of meaning. The word signifies a part of a whole, or (in mathematics) integral calculus, or (in mechanical engineering) something made out of a single piece, or a single element, just as an integer is a complete entity or a whole number. There is thus the related notion of *completeness*, as in an 'édition intégrale' – the French term for a complete edition (but also for an 'unexpurgated' one). *Intégrales* is therefore an expression of wholeness, of completion – perhaps the 'whole piece' of which *Hyperprism* and *Octandre* developed only constituent elements, while itself being, in turn, part of a larger whole.

The idea of 'wholeness' is first apparent in *Intégrales'* sense of scale.

---

[31] *Musical Impressions: Selections from Paul Rosenfeld's Criticism*, ed. Herbert A. Leibowitz (New York: Hill & Wang, 1969), p.80. Rosenfeld's review originally appeared in the May 1925 number of *The Dial*.

[32] *Settling New Scores*, pp. 174 and 176 n.8.

In sheer duration (a single movement lasting 10-and-a-half minutes) it is much the largest of the works considered in this chapter. In its instrumental requirements it resembles an enlarged *Hyperprism*. Eleven wind instruments (2 piccolos, oboe, clarinets in E♭ and B♭, horn, trumpets in D and C, tenor, bass and contrabass trombones) are joined by an even larger collection of unpitched percussion controlled by four players: cymbals (a pair, suspended, and a crash cymbal), snare drum, tenor drum, Lion's Roar (string drum), castanets, 3 Chinese bocks, sleighbells, chains, tambourine, deep gong, deep tam-tam, triangle, bass drum, twigs (Mahler's Rute again), wire brush and a slap stick. The twigs and wire brush are to be played on the shell of the bass drum. Perhaps surprisingly, there is no siren to produce *Hyperprism's* parabolas of sound. *Intégrales* is all pitch or no pitch. The figure of eleven pitch-producing instruments makes it a particularly frustrating score for those analysts determined to see Varèse as some species of 12-tone composer *manqué*: for in his characteristically dense tutti chordal complexes, one pitch of the 12-note total chromatic will always be left out! (He finds other ways of doing this, too.)[33]

The integration (no pun intended, but here perhaps is yet another shade of meaning in the title) of the wind and percussion is

---

[33] Varèse's persistent use, in this and other works, of 11-note formations, may sometimes seem his way of having fun with Schoenbergian 12-note theory and the serial analyst. But in *Intégrales*, at any rate, there is surely no deliberate attempt to tease. Schoenberg's first 12-tone compositions (opp.23–26) were certainly written between 1921–24, but few of them had yet been performed or published. It is unlikely that Varèse was aware, except in the most general way, of the Austrian's developing 'method of composition with twelve tones related only to one another'. Rather this is almost certainly a reflection of his underlying artistic philosophy. More radical than the Second Viennese School in his rejection of traditional tonal function, requiring dissonances as strong or stronger than theirs, yet like them working essentially within 12-note-equal temperament, he was as bound as they to make use of most of the pitches of the total chromatic, most of the time. But whereas Schoenberg, Berg and Webern found that to sound a majority of the 12 tones 'demanded' the sounding of the remaining ones – a gesture of closure, by which the 12-note row became the basic structural unit – Varèse deliberately resisted such demands. If it is possible to feel the absence of the unsounded tone in his 11-note complexes, it must surely be as a potential for growth. Refusing to complete the 12-note series, his harmony and melody achieve total chromaticism while still remaining, as he wished all his music to be, 'open rather than bounded'.

considerably more subtle than in *Hyperprism*. And whereas *Hyperprism* relied to a large extent on the recurrences of certain types of gesture to 'discover' its form, in *Intégrales* gestures generically similar to those in the earlier work become 'thematic' entities in their own right, and these are 'developed' exhaustively enough – mainly through varied repetition – to build up large structural periods. Moreover they are 'recalled' in forms recognizable enough to signal important turning-points in the argument. In this respect the experience of *Octandre*, too, plays an important part.

Like *Octandre*, *Intégrales* begins with an unaccompanied woodwind instrument, rather than *Hyperprism*'s crash of percussion. But the idea advanced by the crisp tones of the E clarinet is a close relation to the trombone figure quoted as Ex.1 in the discussion of *Hyperprism*. Here again is the echt-Varèsian formula of a 3-note anacrusis whose final pitch is stridently, irregularly repeated, 'projected' in a straight line, a tonal focus obstinately drilled into the listener's ears. Soft percussion entries (gong and tam-tam) prepare the way for pitched sound to accumulate around the clarinet's insistently-attacked B. Which it does, typically, in the shape of two discrete trichords on high woodwind and low brass (Ex.1):

Critical opinion seems divided as to whether *Intégrales* falls into three or four principal sections. I incline to the three-part scheme, seeing the first two 'parts' of the four-part interpretation as the distinct but intimately-related halves of the first main section of the work: the second half (after the dividing percussion writing around figure 3) being a clear genuine development (rare in Varèse) of the material in the first half. And the essential basis of that material, throughout, is

Ex.1 and more particularly the germinal trichord D-A♭-B♭, a tritone plus a tone, which is immediately expanded vertically by the woodwind's trichord. (The lower trichord in the brass is at first unrelated except as a distorted mirror of the upper one, but will assume considerable importance in due course.)

The clarinet theme is taken up alternately by muted trumpet, oboe, and E♭ clarinet, each instrument giving it a slightly different rhythmic form (and in the case of the trumpet, which puts a jazzy spin on the motif, a slightly expanded melodic content as well: the clarinet motif and the trichords having already furnished nine notes of the chromatic scale, the trumpet adds two more to make 11, but the twelfth pitch – F♮ – refuses to appear). These variants are heard against the two woodwind and brass trichords, themselves given crisp rhythmic articulation; the registers, and the pitches themselves, remain fixed as in Ex.1. So from one point of view the music is entirely static; but in fact, despite the innocent *Andantino* marking, it conveys a considerable sense of excited forward movement. Partly this is due to continuous subtle metrical variation (the time-signature is changing constantly, almost from bar to bar, sometimes by as little as half a beat); and more obviously because of the activities of the percussion. All four percussionists are continuously employed, though not in the cause of sheer noise. An intricate, delicate, finely-shaded web of sounds is being produced, some soft, some loud — ranging from pulsing rolls on tenor drum to scraps of sharply-defined march-rhythm on side-drum, castanets, or Chinese blocks; in addition to these many isolated points are marked by single attacks on chains, bass drum, sleigh bells, twigs or tambourine. By these means Varèse etches in and articulates every subdivision of his subtly irregular metrical scheme, transforming it from mere proportional changes on paper to a living, audible rhythmic organism.

A carefully-graduated *crescendo* in all instruments creates a sense of anticipation, of approach to a climax: and the percussion momentarily drop out as the E♭ clarinet, enunciating its motif much as at the beginning, suddenly reaches up from the focal B♭ pitch to a high D♭ : not a new pitch in itself (since the tenor trombone has been doggedly enunciating a C♯), but the first switch of register since the work began. Immediately all wind instruments (including the horn, silent until now) join in a great 11-note 'fanfare', a chordal build-up, finally admitting the missing F♮ and spanning the entire available register (Ex.2):

Ex.2

For the first time since the work began, the percussion is silent as the chord swells out to a climactic *sfff* on which it immediately cuts off. It is replaced by the mournful roar of the string drum as the percussion (mainly cymbals and gong) re-enter with a brief link to the second half of this opening section.

The tempo is slightly slower, *Moderato*. Whereas the 'thematic' interest has so far been confined to the high register, it now switches to the low and middle ones. The horn, practically indistinguishable as a single strand in the Ex.2 complex, now becomes a featured soloist, giving out a new version of the clarinet's Ex.1 motif against a low, grinding tritone (the horn's first two notes transposed down an octave) in bass and contrabass trombones: Ex.3*a*. The trombones' attacks are resonated by tam-tam and bass drum, while the Chinese blocks and smaller drums enunciate dry, staccato rhythmic patterns. The rest of the wind instruments answer to Ex.3*a* with Ex.3*b* – a seven-note chordal 'fanfare' dominated by a proclamatory, barking solo figure high on the tenor trombone. The high B♭ that was the work's opening focal pitch has become merely a 'passing-note' in the higher reaches of Ex.3*b*; there is now a dual focus in the horn's tenor G♮ and the trombone's B♮ a tenth above it.

Varèse develops these two entities by varied repetition, employing all the techniques he used with Ex.1, with two important differences: the motifs are not taken over by any other instrument, but remain confined to horn and tenor trombone; and they develop in close alternation, amounting to a kind of excited, argumentative dialogue. The most prominent feature of the trombone's figure is its yammering

Ex.3

quintuplet rhythm, and this in itself becomes a focus of development: the horn takes the rhythm over on one of its entries, and then the Chinese blocks – which gradually come to the fore in this passage as the main enunciator of defined rhythms among the percussion – also adopt the quintuplet figure, mimicking the trombone in the bars where it is silent (i.e., when the horn is giving out Ex.3*a*): Ex.3*c*.

Although there is some rearrangement of dynamics as the music proceeds, its sense of power, of growing climax, is (as often in Varèse) essentially cumulative — something imparted by the urgency of the repetitions, the tension between their insistence to be heard and the listener's mounting need to hear something new. When the 'new' comes, it leaps in upon the back of the final enunciation of Ex.3*a*: a wild brass flourish (Ex.4) that first imperiously stills all motion (the percussion fall silent altogether) while preparing a new *Allegro* tempo. It sparks off a dense heterophony of wind fanfares, the most complex texture we have heard yet.

Ex.4

This music, a decisive change from all that has gone before, marks the beginning of the second main portion of *Intégrales*.

While the first portion had consisted of two large spans, this one comprises several short ones, continually fluctuating in speed, timbre, and register. Due to the rapid succession of ideas, the effect is complex and fast-moving even when the tempo is officially slow; and the trumpets, which initiated the change, remain to the fore.

The 'fanfares' freeze onto a long-held *ffff* sonority (with a clear variation of Ex.1's opening figure in contrabass trombone) and the tempo changes suddenly to *Lento*. After a one-beat silent bar, a high ninth in the two piccolos chimes repeatedly against a lower one in the clarinets, while a third, similar sonority (of a minor ninth plus a semitone) is softly rhythmicized in muted trumpets and horn. The piccolo and clarinet pitches remain static, but from them the texture spreads downwards, eventually covering the whole gamut of the available register in an 11-note chord for the full wind forces, coloured by sudden shifts in dynamics and flutter-tonguing.

The percussion has contributed little since the end of the first section, but the roar of the string drum brings it back into focus as the tempo switches once more, to *Presto*. Against vigorous rhythmic figures in the percussion, the clarinets and brass continue to explore the more static chordal ideas of the preceding music; then trumpets, horn, and clarinets combine in a single chord which they enunciate in rapid proclamatory fashion, imitating the percussion rhythms. The passage is a palmary example of the familiar Varèse paradox of intense rhythmic activity coupled with absolute harmonic stasis.

Nothing capable of being dignified with the name of a melodic idea has been heard for some time, but now the Lion's Roar intervenes again, in a swelling crescendo that leads to the sudden irruption of a stamping, dance-like idea on trumpet and horn, accompanied by 'primitive' fifths in the three trombones (Ex.5).

The strong, jazzy rhythms of this unanticipated 'tune' (with its faint whiff of *Le Sacre du Printemps*) are supported and strengthened by the percussion. Its comparative simplicity of melodic line (all in conjunct motion) and harmonic content allow it perfectly to perform a very traditional function of contrast, and its effect is rather similar to that of Ex.4 in *Hyperprism*. But its dominance is short-lived; a rising shriek from the oboe brings a compressed allusion to the *Lento* music, though still in the *Presto* tempo: chiming ninths in extreme registers, on piccolos and low trombones. The trumpets and tenor trombone strike in with a new trichord, the D trumpet, bell in the air, proclaiming the topmost pitch in stammering rhythm. These three have percussion support, particularly from the gong, and alternate with the other wind instruments which respond in similar, rhythmically excited 'tuckets' (Ex.6)

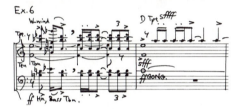

The percussion here merely reinforce some of the rhythmic attack-points; and they drop out of the picture altogether as the tempo slows, *Subito doppio più lento*, and the brass and wind break outward from their fixed pitches into a new, squealing heterophony that soon flowers in a majestic, chorale-like idea on full brass (Ex.7).

This brass music swells out to a climax that is characteristically cut short to allow a moment of utter stillness – a low, long-held D♮ on clarinet, resonated by muted horn – with only rolls on tenor drum (as heard at the very beginning of the work) to intimate that the tempo has suddenly doubled in speed. Immediately the 'primitive dance' tune Ex.5 now returns, though only briefly, in muted, sinister scoring. The three trombones, supplying its accompaniment of 'open' fifths as before, suddenly switch to a low trichord, answered by a more briefly-attacked one in high register on clarinets, oboe, and piccolos. These two alternate – low, then high, the attacks progressively briefer, more cutting, until the trichords are bouncing from low to high at only a quaver's distance, the resultant rhythm (and the intervening silences) accentuated by the percussion.

Battering rhythms in tenor drum and side-drum and the last snapping entry of the high and low trichords introduce a new trichord in middle register on horn and trumpets, which turns into a stabbing fanfare (Ex.8, closely related to Ex. 6), driving the music to a climax.

The trombones re-enter in a raucous slide, the piccolos squeal up into the high register, and the entire ensemble crashes in on a *ffff* tutti chord: another towering stack of 11 pitches, resonated by gong, tam-tam, bass drum, and cymbals.

Varèse allows this climactic chord to ebb away gently in a long diminuendo. The third and final section of *Intégrales* now begins *Lent*, very quietly, with soft resonances of tam-tam and bass drum. The Chinese blocks are heard again, in fragmentary rhythms that remind us of their important contribution towards the end of the first section. But what we hear next is, as so often, something quite new – a long, rather soulful idea sounding into silence on solo oboe (Ex.9):

This idea is probably the clearest indication in *Intégrales* that on some level the Debussian heritage continues to operate, in the shape of these curving melodic phrases that stem ultimately from *L'après-midi d'un faune* and *Syrinx*. The oboe now becomes the focus of attention, and launches into a solo in which it insists on a single pitch, F♯, in typical Varèse fashion, only to intersperse this approach with a variant of the

Ex.9 shape, which it uses to land upon a new pitch, F♮. As soon as it does so a muted trumpet elaborately echoes it (but starts by recalling the clarinet motif from Ex.1 at the very beginning of the work, a semitone higher in pitch). Woodwind, horn, and trombones join in with trichords; the tenor trombone briefly alludes, *staccatissimo*, to its contribution in Ex.3*c*, especially the barking quintuplet figure. It would seem that some much-compressed 'recapitulation' is taking place.

It continues, in an allusive kind of way. Very soft percussion attacks reintroduce the Chinese blocks with their clicking and tapping from much earlier in the work, and the D trumpet, muted, plays with two pitches a tone apart – the upper component of the original tritone-tone from the work's opening. Piccolos and oboes sound a high trichord, against which, *subitement vite*, there clash low croakings in clarinets, horn, C trumpet and contrabass trombone. A single bar's percussion break gives way to the oboe, repeatedly sounding a high A as if about to essay Ex.9 once again; instead the clarinet gives a reminder of the Ex.4 wind music, along with tucket-like writing in muted tenor trombone and Chinese blocks.

With portentous blows from tam-tam, bass drum and Lion's Roar, Ex.3*a*, the variant of the work's opening motif, reappears on tenor trombone, unmuted. Swift rhythmic foreshortenings of its initial anacrusis and a re-phrasing of the vertical complex 3*b* cut off to reveal the oboe once again a soloist, *ffff* at the top of its register on a high F♮, where it begins a brief cadenza-like solo in *Lento* tempo. This oscillates between the F♮ and the F♮ a major seventh lower, with exaggerated portamento, ending on a high, long-held A♮ while the brass and the E♭ bclarinet play with jagged, rhythmically complex scraps of fanfare – '*sèches et mordantes*' in the trumpets, '*acide*' in the clarinet, 'full-throated' in the horn. As the tempo slightly increases, the percussion ensemble takes up their rhythms, with the rapid quintuplet of Ex.3*c* prominent in side-drum. In the most complex texture in the whole work, the entire wind ensemble launches into an elaborate, multi-layered heterophony of characteristically Varèsian figures, rhythmically independent of the percussion, mostly deriving in different ways from Ex.1 or Ex.3, and underpinned by a repeated major-seventh pedal in the two lowest trombones.

This heterophony dies down and fades out; the percussion again fall silent. The solo oboe re-enters with the soulful theme Ex.9, transposed a minor third down, then rhythmically varies this idea against soft muted brass chords. Suddenly the Lion's Roar is heard and, *Presto*, the stabbing fanfare Ex.8 returns, reassigned to trumpets and tenor trombone, its dynamics even more fiercely accented than before. It provokes an excited percussion outburst that introduces in turn – as the tempo is halved – a brief fanfare of repeated notes in the brass (marked, unusually, by octave leaps in contrabass trombone and horn, which woodwind echo with more typical sevenths and ninths). A further and even shorter percussion irruption brings back an easily-recognizable variation of the 'chorale', Ex.7, in the brass. This broad, even grandiose idea provides a fitting conclusion, and it expands in short-lived glory until it 'cadences' onto a final 11-note chordal agglomeration, typically spanning the extremities of register, its resonances amplified by gongs, bass drum, tenor drum, and cymbals. It swells out slowly from *p* to *sffff* and cuts off, leaving only echoes to die away.

Like *Hyperprism*, *Intégrales* is a score that communicates a gigantic sense of physical excitement; but it is also a work of subtle and patterned architecture, shuffling and varying numerous individually recognizable elements in a design of richness and power. It is hardly surprising, therefore, that it has always been one of his most enthusiastically received works. Yet his next creation, *Arcana*, would transcend it on every level.

6 · A new star and a new heaven

[Man] is now a microcosm, or a little world, because he is an extract from all the stars and planets of the whole firmament, from the earth and the elements; and so he is their quintessence. The four elements are the universal world, and from these man is constituted. In number, therefore, he is the fifth, that is, the fifth ... beyond the four elements out of which he has been extracted as a nucleus.
PARACELSUS (TRS. A.E. WAITE)
The End of the Birth, and the Consideration of the Stars

Varèse loved nature – the mysterious nature whose secrets scientists with the patience of research doctors and alchemists are forever seeking to discover ... Nature in its most magnificent and terribly impersonal aspects moved him passionately – the sky with its speeding planets, its bursting novae, its galaxies and nebulae – the sky out of which come hurricanes as sudden and unaccountable as his own swift furies. Over his table hung a photograph of the eye of a hurricane so like a spiral nebula (spirals, symbol of the never-to-be-reached beyond ...)
LOUISE VARÈSE
Varèse: A Looking-Glass Diary (p. 228)

CHRONOLOGY 1926–27

1926 *9 April: Stokowski conducts the première of* Amèriques *in Philadelphia, repeated in New York, 13 April. ('Mr. Stokowski ... could scarcely have done anything more detrimental to the cause of modern music' – Stokowski's ex-wife Olga Samaroff in* The New York Times.*) Varèse remains in New York during the summer, working on* Arcana *for Stokowski's coming season. During the winter in New York he takes on a number of private pupils, notably the young Canadian Colin McPhee, who rents an apartment at 188 Sullivan Street for a while.*

1927 *February:* Arcana *is provisionally completed. 8 April: Stokowski conducts the première of* Arcana *in Philadelphia, repeated in New York, 12 April. ('A morass of sound which seemingly had little relation to music'*

– *Musical America; 'over Carnegie Hall there fell the shadow of Leonardo da Vinci' – Paul Rosenfeld,* The Dial.*) 17 April: the final concert of the International Composers' Guild – hereafter dissolved because of lack of finance – concludes with a repeat performance of* Intégrales, *conducted by Artur Rodzinski. Varèse becomes an American citizen. Experiments with electronic instruments with Réné Bertrand and Harvey Fletcher, Acoustical Director of Western Electric (later the Bell Telephone Laboratories). 2 June: Vladimir Golschmann conducts* Octandre *in Paris. From July to October Varèse and Louise stay in Antibes, working on the first (Indian) version of* The One All Alone.

*A*rcana, Varèse's only completely mature and characteristic work for a full symphony orchestra, was composed between 1925 and 1927, in Paris and the USA – a similar, trajectory to *Intégrales*, but taking twice as long. Leopold Stokowski and the Philadelphia Orchestra gave the first performance in 8 April 1927 and went on to present *Arcana* at the Carnegie Hall on 12 April. Stokowski – to whom *Arcana* was dedicated – was dissatisfied with the performances, telling Paul Rosenfeld that his orchestra had given him 'insufficient sonority ... The men detested the piece'. Varèse had finished the score in a hurry because of the approaching premiere, and was aware from the first that he needed to do further work on it, especially the ending. He made some revisions – nothing like as far-reaching as his revisions to *Amériques* – in 1930 and *Arcana* was published in 1931 by Eschig, Paris, with a dedication to Stokowski. But the new ending, along with further modifications and an enlargement of the orchestra, waited for 30 years until the 77-year-old Varèse got round to it, in anticipation of the work's first recording (by Robert Craft for Columbia Records). The definitive score was issued by Franco Colombo's Colfranc Edition in 1964.

The European premières, in Paris and Berlin in early 1932, were conducted by Nicolas Slonimsky. As with most of Varèse's music at the time, the critical reaction bordered on the abusive. Even so dedicated a modernist as Heinrich Strobel (later to be a guru to the post-war avant-garde of Boulez and Stockhausen) greeted the Berlin première as 'an abortion of sounding madness'. The veteran composer Florent Schmitt was more understanding: he called it 'a magnificently stylized nightmare, a nightmare of giants!'.

Although with the passage of time *Arcana* has established itself as one of the classic orchestral showpieces of the 20th century, among connoisseurs of outright modernism its reputation has remained somewhat ambiguous. One still encounters the opinion that the work is a less 'pure' or less interesting specimen of Varèse than the three highly concentrated scores that preceded it, or the percussion work *Ionisation* which followed. Some commentators regret the grand rhetoric and the elements of 'conventionality' (or at least references to more familiar orchestral styles) to be found in this big 'symphonic poem'. But it was Varèse himself who called it that, and he would not have accepted this critical disapproval. Indeed he declared in 1928: 'It is perhaps in *Arcana* that you will truly discover my thought'.[1] That rather suggests he viewed the piece as a culmination and grand synthesis of the stylistic and technical gains he had achieved on a smaller scale in *Hyperprism*, *Octandre* and *Intégrales*. His correspondence also makes clear that the relatively restricted instrumentation of those works was primarily dictated by the practicalities of performance – 'I'm fed up with the limitations of small combinations', he wrote to Louise as he began composing *Arcana* primarily for his own pleasure.[2]

The result is a score at once utterly consistent in its starkly modernistic tone, and containing the widest range of expression among Varèse's mature works. Yet compared to the earlier and more kaleidoscopic *Amériques*, *Arcana* is much more monolithic and decisive in its artistic direction. Whereas *Amériques* is relatively episodic, *Arcana* relates more creatively to the potent example of Debussy's *Jeux*, with its continual development of a network of short motifs. Yet the effect is anything but Debussian; and two elements much exploited in *Amériques* – the filigree, diaphonous orchestral textures of post-Debussian impressionism, and the 'big-city' sounds of the siren and jazz-rhythms – are rigorously excluded. From this point of view *Arcana* is indeed the 'purer' work. But it evolves its own strands of onomatopoeia.

The very large symphony orchestra employed in *Arcana* is quite close in its composition to that required for the revised *Amériques*: 3

---

[1] 'Artistes de l'avant-garde en Amerique', *Le Figaro Hebdomadaire* (Paris), 25 July 1928.

[2] *LGD*, p. 232.

piccolos, 2 flutes, 3 oboes, cor anglais, heckelphone, 4 clarinets (including 2 in E♭), bass clarinet, 3 bassoons, contrabassoon, 8 horns, 5 trumpets, 4 trombones, 2 tubas, timpani, percussion and strings. But there are some important rationalizations – one timpanist instead of two, and only six percussion players rather than *Amériques'* nine, though they wield as extensive an array of instruments. And there are notable omissions – no siren, and even more important no sign of the harps which had so largely contributed to the impressionistic, dream-like world of *Amériques*. In all its aspects, the thought of Arcana is more essentialized.

The Latin term *arcana*[3] (plural form of *arcanum*, a secret, especially a sacred secret) means knowledge that is hidden, both in a literal sense and in the sense of occult, mystical. In the terminology of alchemy the arcana were the mysteries of creation, to be uncovered and harnessed by the means of alchemical work: in a sense, physical science has continued that work, without the magico-religious mental framework. Alchemists also regarded the arcana as more or less subtle substances, such as viscous mercurial matter. Moreover, they referred to the Great Arcanum, the ultimate secret or animating power of the universe, possession of which was the goal of all alchemical and magical endeavour. This too could be understood as an actual substance: a treatise ascribed to the 13th-century scientist-monk Roger Bacon affirmed that the Great Arcanum was hidden in the four elements (fire, air, earth, water) and could only be produced by one possessing a perfect knowledge of all nature and art concerning the realm of metals. According to the 19th-century French occultist Eliphas Lévi it would make a magician 'master of gold and light', but it would never be discovered because God and Nature alike had closed it off from all forms of human science.

Very early in his career, about 1905, Varèse had become interested in the writings of one of the most brilliant and charismatic occult philosophers of the Renaissance, the Swiss physician and alchemist Paracelsus.[4] According to the standard accounts, it was his rediscovery

---

[3] Varèse's working title was the French equivalent *Arcanes*, 'mysteries'.

[4] Aureolus Philippus Theophrastus Bombastus (Baumbast) von Hohenheim (1493–1541) called himself Paracelsus (= 'greater than Celsus', the 1st-century encyclopaedist whose studies of medicine were rediscovered and translated very early in the Renaissance, earning him the sobriquet of 'the Cicero of doctors'). After studying at Ferrara Paracelsus became town physician and lecturer at the University of

in the mid-1920s of '*The Hermetic Philosophy by Paracelsus*, in the translation by Arthur Waite',[5] that provided Varèse with the initial impulse for (in some versions, just the name of) his new orchestral work. On the title-page of the published score he placed a quotation in Latin, French and English; the English version (from Waite's translation) reads as follows:

One star exists, higher than all the rest. This is the apocalyptic star. The second star is that of the ascendant. The third is that of the elements – of these there are four, so that six stars are established. Besides these there is still another star, imagination, which begets a new star and a new heaven.

This epigraph, with its air of potent mystery and occult relevation, is one of the most frequently quoted elements in popular or general accounts of Varèse. The seven stars seem to echo the seven planets of astrology; but more specifically Paracelsus's belief that the human body is analogous to the solar system, with seven principal organs connected to the seven planets. The source of the epigraph is given on the printed score of *Arcana* simply as 'Paracelsus'. On the front page of the manuscript, however, Varèse drew a grouping of seven stars and copied out all three linguistic forms of the epigraph, in three different kinds of painstaking calligraphy, styling the author 'Paracelsus the Great, monarch of Arcana'.[6] As just mentioned, commentators seem to assume that the passage derives from something they call '*The Hermetic Philosophy*'; one or two, still incorrectly but less culpably, attribute it to '*The Hermetic Astronomy* of Paracelsus'.

But Paracelsus wrote no work of either title. Waite's translations occupy two volumes, and the passage quoted by Varèse occurs towards the end of the second volume, to which Waite (not Paracelsus) gave the

---

Basel, where he rejected the previously pre-eminent authorities of Galen, Aristotle and Avicenna. During his tempestuous life he helped to transform medicine from an abstract and theoretical discipline to a science of observation and experiment. Eventually professional conflicts forced him to spend the latter part of his life as an itinerant doctor. His wide scientific, philosophical, occult and religious interests – expounded for the most part in a powerfully idiomatic German, though the original of the *Arcana* quotation is among his Latin works – made him an important and prophetic figure in the history of spiritual thought. His influence extends from Jakob Boehme to Goethe.

[5] Thus Ouellette, p.91.

[6] Varèse's title-page is reproduced as an illustration of *LGD*.

general title *Hermetic Medicine and Hermetic Philosophy*. The portion of the volume that falls under the heading 'Hermetic Philosophy' contains three works of Paracelsus: *The Philosophy Addressed to the Athenians* and, under Waite's further sub-head 'Hermetic Astronomy', a short treatise called *The Interpretation of the Stars* and a longer one entitled *The End of the Birth, and the Consideration of the Stars*. It is from the last-named 'astronomical' work – in fact, as will be seen from its title, a highly unorthodox treatise on *astrology* as a magical art – that Varèse took his epigraph.[7]

From the care the composer lavished upon lettering Paracelsus' words in his manuscript, and in placing them in the published edition, one might conclude they meant much to him. No other Varèse work has an epigraph. Yet a reported remark is sometimes quoted as a disclaimer: in 1932 Varèse said the epigraph

Is equivalent to a kind of dedication; it makes of my symphonic poem a kind of tribute to the author of those words; but they did not inspire it, and the work is not a commentary on them.[8]

---

[7] The two 'astronomical' treatises are more or less complementary, and Waite seems to regard them as a single work despite the way he has divided them. In fact the passage quoted by Varèse comes from a text headed 'Concerning the Knowledge of Stars' which Waite appends to the treatise proper among 'certain fragments and schedules on the same matter as the preceding'.

Since I have never seen a proper bibliographical citation for Varèse's famous epigraph, I give it here: Arthur Edward Waite, *The Hermetic and Alchemical Writings of Aureolus Philippus Theophrastus Bombast, of Hohenheim, called Paracelsus the Great. Now for the first time faithfully translated into English. Edited with a Biographical Preface, Elucidatory Notes, a Copious Hermetic Vocabulary, and Index* (London: Kegan Paul, 1894), Volume II, p.310. The most recent edition known to me is a paperback facsimile of the 1894 edition (Largs: The Banton Press, 1990). A. E. Waite (1857–1942), a significant figure in turn-of-the-century esoteric circles, is generally characterized as a mystic and scholar rather than a practical magician and was very much alive when Varèse composed *Arcana*; I am not aware of any contact between them, but it is even possible they could have met in Paris in the 1900s. An Initiate of the Golden Dawn in the 1890s (he seceded from it and re-founded it on more Christian lines in 1903), the American-born Waite was a dauntingly copious author whose translations include many works of Eliphas Lévi.

[8] Ouellette, p.91, citing a newspaper article by Marius Richard, 'Une partition moderne sous la signe de l'alchimie' in *La Liberté*, 24 February 1932.

In one copy of the score, though, he wrote a longer and more complex account of the music's relation – or lack of it – to alchemical ideas:

The title of my composition, Arcana, and the epigraph from Paracelsus have nothing to do with the actual composition of the work. My titles are never descriptive. There is at most a fanciful correspondence for me. I was introduced to Paracelsus, the great alchemist and physician of the sixteenth century, by his French translator, the latinist, Maurice Pelletier, when we were both young men in Paris. Years later in New York while I was working on the score (still without a title) my wife happened to come across the Arthur Waite English edition of the Hermetic Philosophy in a second hand book store and, as I glanced through it with renewed pleasure, an amusing analogy occurred to me between the transmutation of base metals into gold and the transmutation of sounds into music, and also that the process of musical composition is the discovery of the arcana – the hidden secrets in sounds and in noises. That is what gave me the idea of calling my score, Arcana.

As for the epigraph, perhaps the last lines about the stars, so rich like hermetic poetry in overtones, suggested music's need of a new heaven – my need of an expanding musical universe.[9]

Thus while rejecting any but a 'fanciful' correspondence with the music, Varèse nevertheless suggests a spiritual equivalence with the ideals of the alchemists and hermetic philosophers. In this connexion we should also remember another, undated apothegm of his:

Astronomers are searchers of the arcana of the stars; composers of the arcana of sounds.[10]

All the more important given that the Paracelsus text he associates with *Arcana* is not purely alchemical, but rather concerned with an alchemical approach to astronomy (conceived, almost inevitably in that period, largely in terms of astrology). Moreover, as mentioned above, when Varèse drew up the title-page for his manuscript he seems to have had not just Waite's edition of Paracelsus, but a French translation and the original Latin text all open before him. This implies considerably more than a passing interest in Paracelsus' writings.[11]

---

[9] *Statements by Edgard Varèse* assembled, with comments, by Louise Varèse. *Soundings 10* (published by Peter Garland, Berkeley, California, 1976), p.7.

[10] Ibid., p. 6.

[11] I presume the French version of the epigraph comes from Pelletier's edition, which I have not seen.

Perhaps Varèse merely skimmed the Waite volumes (it requires strong will to do more, given the dense and mind-bending nature of their contents), but after all Paracelsus was not a new discovery for him: he had probably imbibed enough through Pelletier to use Waite as an *aide-memoire*. Waite may have directed his attention back to the great alchemist, but this was a 'renewed pleasure': Paracelsus had been lodged in his imagination for twenty years and the 'amusing analogy' between music and alchemical transmutation had infiltrated his compositional principles long ere this. In fact, as he cannot have failed to recognize, the principle of analogy or correspondence between the inner and outer, or higher and lower worlds is the central theme of Paracelsus' 'astronomical' writings. The works of the intellect and imagination mimic, on a higher plane, the action of Nature, who 'herself is a Magus'. It is another application of 'as above, so below': once more, humanity is revealed as, in Sâr Péladan's phrase, *Le fils des étoiles*.

... man is not only flesh and blood, but there is within him the intellect which does not, like the complexion, come from the elements, but from the stars. And the condition of the stars is this, that all the wisdom, intelligence, industry of the animal, and all the arts peculiar to man are contained in them ... [Man] is divided into two parts; into an elemental body, that is, into flesh and blood, whence that body must be nourished; and into spirit, whence he is compelled to sustain his spirit from the spirit of the star. Man himself is dust and ashes of the earth. Such, then, is the condition of man, that, out of the great universe he needs both elements and stars, seeing that he himself is constituted in that way.[12]

The firmament and the new heaven are constituted by the imagination; ... Speculation produces imagination; imagination begets operation; and operation leads to judgement and opinion. Now imagination is concerned, not with flesh and blood, but with the spirit of the star which exists in every man.[13]

Man is formed in such a manner that he should derive all his knowledge in the same way as he gathers fruit from a tree. Thus originates music, the metallic art, medicine, agriculture: whatsoever the earthly body requires, that

---

[12] Paracelsus, *The End of the Birth, and the Consideration of the Stars*, Waite translation, pp. 290–91.

[13] Ibid., pp. 305–6.

he finds in the wisdom of the stars, and all wisdom, whether good or bad, is derived to him from the stars. ... In the stars then is the whole light of Nature founded. For as man seeks food from the earth in which he was born, so also does he seek it from the stars in which he is likewise born.[14]

In the light of such passages, it seems reasonable to suppose that Varèse conceived *Arcana* as an example of music as a 'star-derived' art: its transformation of its 'base' materials building, in the imagination of the hearer, an interior firmament, a 'new heaven' of the mind. It does not much matter that this merely constitutes an 'analogy' of magical working. Much magic is performed by sympathy or analogy, an element or action on one level being supposed to affect changes on another level. It is perhaps only by such analogies, 'amusing' or otherwise, that the processes which really matter are enabled to take place in their proper sphere: the imagination. One thinks again of *Amériques*, of the 'new worlds on earth, in the sky, or in the minds of men'.

None of this quite explains why Varèse should have given his work the title *Arcana*, nor why he should have described Paracelsus as 'Monarch of Arcana'. For so he was: the term 'arcana' has a special significance in Paracelsus' writings, and in the same volume from which he took his epigraph Varèse will have found a text containing Paracelsus' discussion of the nature of arcana as he understood them. This is the Fifth Book, 'Concerning Arcana', of *The Archidoxies of Theophrastus Paracelsus*, also known as the *Theophrastiana* – one of his most important and widely reprinted works of Hermetic medicine, and the first item of Waite's Volume II.

In Paracelsus' terminology the arcana are tinctures, immortal substances of amazing refinement and medicinal excellence capable of bringing the patient a 'new birth' into a new state of mental and physical health. They are 'not old things but new, not ancient but recent productions', 'nothing else than a graduated quintessence' which is 'derived from the firmament or first entity'.[15]

That is called an arcanum, then, which is incorporeal, immortal, of perpetual life, intelligible above all Nature and of knowledge more than human. Compared, indeed, with our corporeal bodies, arcana are to be considered

---

[14] Ibid., p.298.
[15] *The Archidoxies of Theophrastus Paracelsus*, Waite translation, p.47.

incorporeal and of an essence far more excellent than ours, the difference being as great as between black and white.[16]

None otherwise must it be thought of tinged bodies which have received the tincture [ie the arcanum] that they exist no more in the former life from which they were transmuted by the tincture, but far nobler, better and more healthful is the condition of the body and the form than its native origin was; and it is like natural gold made out of iron ...[17]

Once again we are talking of transformation, but transformation of the human being. The fact that in passages such as the above Paracelsus applied his alchemical talents to medicinal ends helps bring us to the root of the matter. He worked with his medical 'arcana' in order to heal, to effect a re-birth into health. Alchemy's physical operations, such as 'transmutation of base metals into gold' were always more symbolic than literally effective. Their arcane, their 'secret' purpose was to effect transformations on the inner plane, within the alchemist himself. As in Goethe's science, the ultimate function of close observation was to augment the perceptiveness of the observer. Thus in music too we experience a guided meditation upon elements of sound; following their transformations, we ourselves are transformed.

I have mentioned that Paracelsus' epigraph probably relates to the seven planets of astrology; but also that on *Arcana*'s manuscript title-page Varèse depicted seven stars. This does not look like a random configuration. At first glance it could be a constellation: the stars seem roughly arranged in the shape of a scorpion (though not of the constellation Scorpio). However I strongly suspect Varèse intended them to represent the most famous seven-starred object in the night sky, the Pleiades cluster in the constellation Taurus. This cluster is commonly shown horizontally in star maps, with the stars Taygeta and Electra at the right-hand end and Pleione on the left. If this is what Varèse has illustrated he has drawn it vertically, with Electra and Taygeta at the bottom: this has the effect of making Pleione the star 'higher than all the rest', and he has raised it higher yet by exaggerating its apparent distance from its neighbour, Atlas.

This is highly appropriate. The amount of esoteric and mythical lore surrounding the Pleiades is very considerable, and – as the only

---

[16] Ibid., p.37.
[17] Ibid, p.46.

distinct star cluster visible to the naked eye – it has been subject to observation throughout recorded history. Keats's 'Starry Seven' (*Endymion*), Tennyson's 'swarm of fire-flies tangled in a silver braid' (*Locksley Hall*), described by the 5th-century Neoplatonist Proclus as riding on the back of the Bull, are 'among the most noted objects in the history, poetry and mythology of the heavens'.[18] One of the recurrent traditions is that at certain periods only six have been visible: there are tales of a 'lost Pleiad', and the most plausible candidate for this is Pleione, the faintest of them. Thus the lines of Aratus's *Phaenomena*, a 3rd-century BC versification of an astronomical treatise by the 4th-century Eudoxus of Cnidus:

> Seven paths aloft men say they take,
> Yet six alone are viewed by mortal eyes.

Pleione is thus literally a 'hidden' or occult star, beyond the sight of 'mortal eyes', and eminently suitable for Paracelsus' star of the imagination.

* * *

It is wholly consonant with Varèse's perennial goal of a music that 'throws open the whole world of sound', and in the spirit of the Renaissance hermeticists seeking to expand human consciousness through the influence of the stars, that *Arcana* quite literally 'explodes into space' in its opening bars. They present a complex of three ideas – a pounding, athletic figure in crotchet-rhythm, shared between low bass instruments and timpani to create divergent melodic lines; a dissonant brass and woodwind fanfare, rapidly filling the middle registers and saturating a portion of the chromatic field; and a flourish on high strings, clarinets and xylophone, all in unison except for the semitonal split on its final note.

This opening motivic complex (Varèse referred to it as an *idée fixe*, and the music surely displays a truly Berliozian sense of fantasy and freedom) is to be developed in many ways. The recurrent manifestations of the pounding-crotchet idea are especially recognizable. They led the American critic Lawrence Gilman, in his programme-note for the first performance, to describe *Arcana* as 'an immense and liberal expansion of the passacaglia form – the

---

[18] Richard Hinckley Allen, *Star Names and Their Meaning* (New York: Dover Books, 1963, repr. of 1899 publication), p.392.

development of a basic idea through melodic, rhythmical and instrumentational transmutation': a description which still holds good as long as we hold to the most 'liberal' understanding of the term passacaglia.

The 'passacaglia' figure is shown below as Ex.1; the other two elements – the fanfare and woodwind flourish – as Exx.2 and 3 respectively.[19]

[19] Varèse claimed that two of the fanfares in *Arcana* occurred to him in a dream. Louise Varèse reproduces (*LGD*, opposite p.147) Varèse's letter to her of 9 October 1925 describing the dream (translated, p.238):

> I was on a boat ... In the distance I could see a light house, very high – and on the top an angel – and the angel was you – a trumpet in each hand. Alternating projectors of different colours: red, green, yellow, blue – and you were playing Fanfare no.1, trumpet in right hand ...

There follows the notation of the fanfare (identical with Ex.2 and 3 – which Varèse therefore must have considered a unity – save for some details of instrumentation). It is fascinating to note that this music was associated in his dream with changes and projections of colours, suggesting once more a colour/sound correspondence such as had inspired *Les Cycles du Nord*. The dream also recalls the central image of 'Chanson de là-haut' in *Offrandes*.

Although these three elements are strongly contrasted as to colour and gesture, they are also closely related – virtually different facets of a single idea. All three are basically built out of small segments of rising scales, and as a corollary they share a decisive rising motion, an upward striving. So the music rushes to fill the space from the depths to the heights of the orchestra, a tendency observable throughout the work.

The opening pages of *Arcana* immediately concern themselves with rapid developments and fragmentations of Exx.1–3, each idea retaining its distinct identity and instrumentation. Thus a three-note segment of Ex.1 and a drastically compressed Ex.2 lead into an expansion of Ex. 3, emphasizing by repetition its shrieking major-seventh interval. Next a lengthened version of Ex. 1 and an even more curtailed Ex.2 inaugurate processes of fragmentation: the final three-note figure of Ex. 3 juxtaposed against the initial three-note segment of Ex.1, with an interpolation of Ex. 2, itself compressed and its elements appearing in a different order. These features pass very quickly. But they imply, for Varèse, an unusual concentration of ideas, and they maintain the thrusting impetus of the opening.

Further repetitions of Ex. 1's three-note segment now introduce a slower tempo and new material, but not so new that it greatly violates the patterns of behaviour the music has already set up. There is a new, more plangent fanfare for brass and middle woodwind (Ex. 4), with a rhythmic pendant on bass instruments (Ex. 5).[20]

---

[20] This is the second of the fanfares from Varèse's dream. As notated in his letter to Louise Varèse, it is clear that he saw a precise relationship between the two, as the first (Exx. 2/3) is there marked *Allegro* and the second (Ex. 4) *Largamente* (*doppio più Lento*). This effect (of 'almost twice as slow') is achieved in the finished score merely by different metronome-markings.

Exx. 4 and 5 bear much the same relationship to each other as do Exx. 2 and 3, and are developed and juxtaposed in similar ways. (Indeed, Ex. 5 is a development of Ex. 1, with its pitches re-ordered and enlivened by octave displacement.) However, Ex.4 displays a different harmonic profile – with prominent open fifths – while Exx. 4 and 5's greater length, and the more leisurely tempo at which they unfold, allow Varèse increased scope for rhythmic variation and ornamentation, and for yet other elements to begin to make their presence felt around them.

These elements are of several different sorts. It is significant that the first appearance of Ex. 4 also marks the first entry of the unpitched percussion, notably with a stabbing quintuplet-semiquaver figure, dryly penetrating the texture on Chinese block and rattle (Ex. 6*i*). As the 'trumpet-tune' element of Ex. 4 is developed on lowing trombones, various bass instruments introduce heavy repeated-note figures (at first merely in octaves) in an alternating *p* and *sf* dynamic. The horns now take up Ex. 5, but preface it with a form of the quintuplet figure – five rapid ictuses (Ex. 6*ii*) rather than a quintuplet in fact – and this is shortly imitated by high trumpets: a stuttering tucket or fanfare strongly reminiscent of *Hyperprism* or *Intégrales*, ending in a scrap of cantillatory melody (Ex. 6*iii*).

The materials are shuffled while the heavy repeated-note figures sound out again (in increasingly thicker bass chords) against sustained harmonies in high strings and woodwind (crystalline and uninvolved). Then a new element bursts in – a rushing, agitated stream of semiquavers on strings and woodwind, unusual for its rhythmic regularity and if anything rather Stravinskian in sound, faintly recalling the characteristic string figuration of the 'Danse de la Terre' from *La Sacre*. This only lasts for three bars before it is cut off to make way for a return of the pounding opening idea, Ex. 1 – now in triplet rhythm against a thrumming tattoo of quintuplets in timpani and basses – and a scrap of trumpet melody (an extension of Ex. 4's upper line) over the same rhythm in various drums. But the semiquavers return, angrier and more forceful, leading to a compressed development of the Ex. 4 fanfare and a passage that rapidly intercuts several now increasingly familiar elements – beginning with the quintuplet figure *6i* on horns, trumpets and timpani. The heavy repeated-note idea reappears; horns develop the melodic component of Ex. *6iii*. There are extended versions of Ex.1, announcing itself as always with decisiveness and élan, and eventually returning the tempo to the crotchet = 132 of the work's opening; finally we hear another, clearly recognizable version of the fanfare Ex. 4.

The climax of this fanfare is resonated in long-held string and woodwind notes; and as these die away the percussion enter quietly, rapidly establishing a quick-march rhythm. What happens now is one of the major surprises of Varèse's entire output – surprising because so unexpected: a veritable tune. Prefacing it only with a reference to the quintuplet figure, the high woodwind (piccolos, flutes, oboes, E♭ clarinet), with glockenspiel and xylophone in octaves, launch into a cheerfully raucous little *marche militaire* with an almost conventional rhythmic support from drums, cymbals and triangle (Ex. 7).

Though possibly suggested by the trumpet development of Ex. 4 mentioned earlier (which I quote here for comparison as *7x*), this tune is highly unusual for Varèse in its length, near-diatonic plainness, rhythmic and textural simplicity (the percussion definitely plays a supporting role, and nothing else plays at all). All the same, by more orthodox composers' standards, the tune is in fact rather short, for it is soon interrupted by a soft stopped horn, introducing a passage of similar but more mysterious simplicity: quiet strings and woodwind accumulating a chord in rapid repeated-note staccato semiquavers, with scraps of tune in triplet rhythm (referring apparently to *7x*). I show this passage as Ex.8: its opposition of three against four will characterize many later passages.

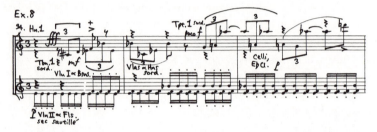

The tempo now slows to crotchet = 66, half the previous speed, with a slithery chromatic descent on bassoon and contrabassoon that could almost be a cadence.[21] Varèse marks a long fermata on its last triplet crotchet.

Arcana conforms to no formal pattern describable in conventional terms (unless we take the 'passacaglia' hint, and think of elements continually recurring in ever-developing forms and ever-changing relationships); nor does it have many clearly-marked structural divisions. But we have now arived at one of them (fig.9, p.23 of the score). In a sense, despite the many recurrences and reshufflings of material, all the music so far has been 'exposition', accumulating the various elements, many of them already interrelated, that form the subject-matter of the rest of the work. It has not taken much time (certainly less time than it took you to read this description); and it would be tedious indeed to chronicle every further development, shift of focus, or intercutting of one element with another that is yet to take

---

[21] Stempel (1974) suggests this passage is a direct reference (conscious or not) to the 'Le Tour de Passe-passe' section of Stravinsky's *Petrushka*.

place. It can, perhaps, be taken as read that the kind of processes we have already seen at work in the ensemble works of the early 1920's are in full operation throughout, on a much more extensive scale and with a correspondingly greater range of colour and physical excitement. Here I shall simply outlining the general course of the argument, and pointing out some salient events.

Throughout this whole 'expository' section the time-signature has been changing restlessly, often from bar to bar, adding to the music's effect of asymmetry and contempt for regimentation (except in areas designed to surprise by contrast, as in the metric regularity of Ex. 7's march-tune). But now the metre stabilizes into 4/4, which apart from the odd intrusive bar of 5 or 3 is held for much of the following span. The heavy, low, repeated-note idea becomes a kind of tritone pedal (on F♯ and C) in timpani and bass instruments, echoing irregularly in the depths. Together with more rhythmically active percussion it forms the background to an incantatory melody on all 8 horns (Ex. 9).

Ex. 9, whose leaping anacrusis to its principal pitch is one of the most 'typically Varèsian' melodic gestures we have yet encountered (cf.

Intégrales Ex 3*a*) is blent from several sources: Exx. 6*iii*, 7*x*, and 7 –
with which it shares a prominent reiterated tritone – among them; also
Ex. 4 in the trumpet tailpiece, while the trombones take up the
quintuplet figure. This is a good example of Varèse's developmental
techniques, so lavishly on display in *Arcana*. He brings different
elements into close but always shifting relationships (rhythmic,
melodic, harmonic, textural, positional) in order continually to create
each musical moment anew.

The complex texture and swift-swelling climax that Ex. 9 engenders
is typically cut off, to make way for a new pedal – a pianissimo tremolo
B in timpani and basses – over which muted trumpets and trombones,
very softly, give out the repeated-note figure, prefaced by a quintuplet,
with quiet percussion background. The tempo has doubled, back to
that of the work's opening. Fragmentary forms of Ex. 1 are heard, and
trumpet-calls akin to 7*x*, leading to an imposing fanfare for full brass
based on Ex. 4 and a shattering tutti in which practically the entire
orchestra joins in rhythmic unison on a fusillade of repeated-note
figures; the quintuplet motif is an important component here.
Harmonically this tutti represents an enormous expansion of the
tritone pedal with which the section began, with C at the bottom and
F♯ at the top of the texture.) This, too, cuts off and again the dynamic
drops to very quiet, with Ex. 9's opening anacrusis sounding out on
muted horns against soft percussion and a major-seventh pedal (E♭ –D)
in the bass. As more of Ex.9 is recalled in horns and bassoons, with
snaking chromatic swirls in the strings (probably a a variant of Ex.1 in
extreme rhythmic diminution) a new element intrudes on E♭ clarinet,
triangle and Chinese block (Ex. 10*a*). This swooping, spiky figure
seems much in the vein of Varèse's ensemble works of the previous few
years, but could also be seen as an inversion of Ex. 9's opening
anacrusis; and as the tempo slows (to its slowest yet, crotchet = 60) it
introduces a chant-like phrase on woodwind that looks equally to Ex.9
and back to Ex. 6*iii* (Ex. 10*b*).

Ex.10 a
(♩=132)
139. E♭ Cl

Rushing string and woodwind triplets, now very clearly a diminution of Ex. 1, lead to another tritone pedal (now with B at the bottom of the texture) which falls in irregular blows through the repeated-note idea: and over the next few pages the music consists of a series of slow waves of sound, making use of several now-familiar elements but with each wave centred around a statement of a variant or fragment of Ex. 9 in horns, clarinets, hecklephone and violas. The climax is another brief but furious repeated-note tutti, spanning the full range of the orchestra in rhythmic unison.

A single silent bar marks the transition to the next span of the music, which begins with a new use of the tritone as harmonic background (G held in the flutes against C♯ in horns) and the emergence of the percussion – guiro, Chinese block, triangle – into the foreground, developing the rhythms already associated with these instruments. Repeated-note figures sound out in various rhythms in different parts of the orchestra (the curious cry of two solo double-basses, very high in their registers, is especially prominent). Two bars of Impressionist chromatic slither in multi-divided strings perhaps refer to the Stravinskian 'cadence-figure' mentioned earlier.[22] But they also give rize to a snarling chromatic turn-figure in horns and strings which, much reiterated, drives the music into a wild heterophonic climax: an expansion of the Ex. 4 fanfare on full brass (its upper trumpet figure strongly recognizable), while all bass instruments pound away at the repeated pitch C♯ in irregularly-shifting rhythms with intermittent downward leaps to F♯, and upper strings and woodwind mirror this on a variety of different pitches and in quite different rhythm.

---

[22] Stravinsky himself ('Some Composers', *Musical America*, June 1962, p.11) thought Varèse was influenced here by *Le Sacre*; Stempel (1974) again thinks *Petrushka* a more likely ancestor.

The climax is abruptly terminated, and for the moment the percussionists have the field to themselves, in an extraordinary 'break' that strongly anticipates the approach of Varèse's next work, *Ionisation*. Starting quietly, in military march style, then leading to a passage of swiftly-alternating dynamic extremes, this produces combinations of various figures we have already heard, but reduced to their rhythmic essentials. (Not only rhythmic, in fact: the timpani's invention on the pitches A and E♭ recalls the tritone alternation that has been an important element in recent events.) We encounter the heavy repeated-note figure as the basis of the first sudden *fff* percussion tutti (supported by the two tubas, doubling timpani on the major-seventh G/F), various 'tuckets' reminiscent of Ex. 6*iii*, and indeed the quintuplet motif Ex.6i on its original Chinese block. By the time this last element has entered, the spiky E♭ clarinet figure of Ex. 10*a* has also made an appearance, so what I have just referred to as 'Ex. 6*i*' could also be viewed as a variation of 10*a*'s Chinese-block/triangle accompaniment: a good example of the way Varèse's figures meld their identities back and forth across the spectrum of the work.

The E♭ clarinet figure is developed (on both E♭ clarinets, and piccolos) as the percussion riff continues to be developed by the quintuplet figure; but then strident calls on horn, oboe and trumpet initiate another shattering tutti – shriller than the previous one but clearly developing it: full woodwind, horns, strings and some of the percussion in fierce rhythmic unison, while in the centre of the texture trumpets and trombones punch away at a repeated F♮ in irregular rhythm. The orchestral texture then starts to break up into rapidly-alternating blocks of colour and dynamics, but still fiercely rhythmic and apparently held together by a rapid, continuous quaver tattoo from one of the bass drums.[23] Hints of *Arcana*'s opening idea, the pounding Ex. 1, appear in the bass, along with developments of the repeated-note idea, spreading now in big chords across the orchestral spectrum. Horns and strings diminish Ex. 1 into a high repeating triplet figure, producing a brief fanfare deriving from Ex. 4 – and then a blatant return of a three-bar fragment of the '*marche militaire*', Ex. 7, unmistakable in its piercing scoring.

---

[23] Stravinsky (see previous footnote), attributed this passage to a further reminiscence of *Le Sacre*, and this time Stempel agrees, as would anyone – the resemblance to 'Danse de la Terre', fig. 72, is very striking.

At this point, or thereabouts, we have entered what seems the most 'recapitulatory' section of *Arcana* so far. This reappearance of Ex. 7 immediately triggers a new return of Ex. 1, in highly recognizable form, quiet and rather sinister with a three-against-four tattoo of semiquavers in side-drum against an excited triplet rhythm in the violas, triplet writing in horns,[24] and repeated-note figures in trumpets. It turns fierce and heavy, giving way to a big brass fanfare developing Ex. 4. This in turn introduces another familiar element from an earlier stage of the work – the rushing semiquaver stream on strings, now in wild heterophony against furious triplet figures in horns, trumpets, clarinets and hecklephone and a melodic line battering against the confines of a major seventh in all bass instruments. This outburst ends in a swooping downward glissando for horns, trumpets and trombones and another Ex. 4-type brass fanfare, itself culminating in a huge wide-spread chord for full orchestra (except the trumpets), starting *fff* and then dying away, its identity delineated by the vastly augmented tritone between C♯ low in the bass and G in piccolo and violin harmonics. As it dies away (to an icy wail on three muted trumpets), percussion patterns emerge, most notably the dry rattling semiquaver quintuplet figure of the Chinese blocks.

Suddenly that figure provokes something new: a quaver-quintuplet motif, heavy and solid on unison violins, violas and timpani. It is reinforced by the heavy-bass repeated-note idea, whose irregular blows now fall precisely on this new motif's accented notes. There ensues a passage of furious 'development' in which this motif (and the triplet horn writing) become two additional elements in multiple collisions and juxtapositions of already-familiar entities. Among these are Ex. 1, various rapid quintuplet figures including the Chinese block variety, fragments of fanfare, and even a brief snatch of Ex. 7's *marche militaire*, the tune now skewed about but instantly recognizable through its characteristic scoring. Trumpets seize upon the high jazzy tune evolved from Ex.4 and extend it into a long proclamatory melody, while a great

---

[24] Neither Stravinsky nor Stempel mentions that this is a direct continuation of the *Sacre* reminiscence just noted. If we compare p.57 of *Arcana* with figs. 74–75 of 'Danse de la Terre', it is very clear that Varèse's 3-against-4 rhythms and viola/horn triplet writing reflect precisely that source. What is remarkable, however, is how this near-'quotation' remains logical in *Arcana's* own terms: 3-against-4 has already been (and will be) a significant rhythmic component of Varèse's argument, and Stravinsky's ostinato bass-line is a whole-tone version of Varèse's own Ex.1!

climax builds up around it, filling out the heights and depths of the entire orchestral space with various stratified and rhythmically contrasted elements (such as a return of the rushing-semiquaver figure). The point of climax is a vast tutti chord, gradually fading away, with heavy irregular tritone chords in timpani and the rattlesnake burr of the Chinese-block figure.

Now occurs a complete change of texture: a quite sparsely-scored passage that seems designed to explore the three-against-four rhythmic element in a new way. The time-signature changes from the basic 4/4 to a steady but fast 3/4, in which flutes and cellos begin nagging at a pattern of rapid repeated crotchet quadruplets. Against this background, violas and cor anglais give out a 3-note figure (Ex.11) that can easily be understood as a distorted version of the basic cell of Ex.1.

As it unfolds the music revelas itself as a rhythmic variant of Ex. 8, bodily transposed a semitone upwards. The texture persists for some time, the pulsing quadruplets passing to trumpets and bassoons with a different 3-note figure on horns, and then to flutes, oboes, strings and 2 horns with a more piercing figure on E♭ clarinet and *sul ponticello* violins. But at length it is interrupted by a derisive woodwind flourish and a convulsive brass fanfare with thunderous percussion support. Heavy bass pounding, in the deepest registers of horns, tuba and low woodwind, rushes swiftly (via the repeated quintuplet motif) to a big tutti chord that seems literally to raise itself up in stages through the fabric of the orchestra to leave trumpets and high woodwind chattering another quintuplet at the top of their registers.

The tempo slows, leaving a single high B natural in first violins, held on glassily (Varèse directs there should be no vibrato) like a single light in a dark sky. All is quiet except for a few nervous clicks and rattles of percussion. This near-silence is broken, with almost surreal effect, only by the mockery of the trombones (Ex. 12).

Defiant laughter raised against the emptiness of the universe, or a sheer uprush of Varèse's black humour? Whatever its origin, this derisive grotesquerie has a sharply – and necessarily – humanizing effect. It reminds us that, despite all *Arcana*'s sound and fury and raw, space-age power, a very human intelligence is still in control, with a human sense of scale – and of the ridiculous.

Now Ex. 1 pounds in again, scored more or less as at the beginning of the work. If the previous section had a 'recapitulatory' feeling – albeit with the continuing introduction of new elements – this last and still extensive span might be viewed as *Arcana*'s coda, were not the whole conception of the work so open-ended. Suffice it to say that the music continues to develop in dazzling fashion, further deploying elements we have previously encountered: a form of the fanfare Ex.2, the heavy repeated-note idea, turning itself into stabbing trumpet-calls, various quintuplet tuckets, the horn motif from Ex.11. The speed doubles to minim = 132, the time-signature changes to 3/2, and the unpitched percussion set up an incisive rhythmic pattern in triplets. Medium and bass instruments soon join in on heavy repeated notes in the same rhythm, the timpani playing repeated bare-fifth chords. As other instruments overlay scraps of melody, the music takes on the character of a pounding, orgiastic dance. One is reminded of the greatly extended dance towards the end of *Amériques*, but this is shorter, more fragmentary, and less 'tune'-oriented, despite a similarly strong rhythmic pulse. It blows itself out with a stentorian figure from trombones and hecklephone, leaving the Chinese block rattling its quintuplet figures dementedly.

Suddenly the rushing-semiquaver idea and the horn triplets burst in (an almost verbatim quotation from their last combined appearance,

Ex.13

apart from transposition of pitch), followed by a full orchestral fanfare based on Ex. *6iii* – and this leads directly into what must be the most shattering climax in the entire work (Ex. 13). A huge dissonant chord spans the entire range of the orchestra, between the expanded tritone of a deep bass D♯ and a stratospheric piccolo A; meanwhile horns, trumpets, trombones and timpani (in trichords), thunderously supported by percussion, punch away repeatedly at a rapid repeated-note grouping. Previously we might have expected that to have been a quintuplet: it is now a septuplet, harbinger of the rhythmic freedom about to inform *Arcana*'s final pages. Many other things happen around this core explosion within the space of a few bars, and then the entire orchestra unites in a pile-driving rhythmic unison.

Instantly the dynamics drop away to *piano* and the texture thins for a development of the mysterious Ex.11, its 3-note melodic components on horns, trumpets, piccolos and violins (and now in triplets) against repeated quavers in *ponticello* and *col legno* strings – preserving the 3-against-4 polyrhythms within a different metrical frame. This spills over immediately into a tutti in which strings and woodwind develop the 'rushing semiquaver stream', except that this is now cast as a stream of *quintuplet* quavers. Meanwhile bass instruments, in a triplet rhythm that alludes to the orgiastic dance, proclaim a theme derived long ago from the Ex.4 fanfare. Soon this fragments into broken, two-note interjections, and the quintuplet stream itself begins to break up, gradually losing its force, as if the nova-like energy that has powered the work for so long is finally burning itself out. Abruptly, it breaks off entirely.

Divided *tremolo* basses, bassoon and contrabass clarinet sustain a low note-cluster, a clot of darkness, just at the limits of hearing. Very softly, the quintuplet figure sounds out on muted trumpets and trombones, *lontantissime*. The percussion gives off a few rattles and chitters, until even this dies away to silence: two long bars of absolute void. In this unwonted moment of calm, the music seems to turn its gaze finally on the infinitude of the night sky.

With a kind of cosmic shrug, one last fanfare blazons forth in majesty. It derives eventually from Ex.4, but Varèse's use here of comparative consonance – white-note harmony only, full of parallel fifths – makes it a new kind of sonic event, and gives it a stark, proud grandeur. Perhaps this (Ex. 14) is the star that exists higher than all the rest.

Ex.14

Like the very opening of *Arcana*, Ex.14 reaches up from the depths to the heights in a single swift, easy gesture. Piccolos and violins sustain high pitches, and the last heavy repeated blows fall against them with tremendous force, resonated by a hollow roar of percussion; but all dies away to nothing. There is a further empty bar, with the echt-Varèsian instruction: SILENCE TO BE BEATEN. Darkness falls finally as cellos and basses reintroduce the *tremolo, ponticello* cluster, underpinned by a *ppp* timpani roll. Very high violin harmonics outline a 3-note motif, ultimately going all the way back to Ex. 1, but here sounding as a desolate cry of a night-bird, or perhaps a distant train whistle. The Chinese block ticks away in a gradually slowing rhythm, including the ubiquitous quintuplet; the sound fades progressively, and merges at last into silence and night.

Arcana is over 70 years old, and has had few true successors. Rhythmically compulsive, amazingly inventive, intensely dramatic and sometimes sardonically humorous, it explores the boundaries of the sonically acceptable with a passion and strength that makes it as exciting today as it was at its first performance. But above all it creates and maintains a powerful sense of wonder, a compelling image of human aspiration etched against the backcloth of the universe.

PART 3 Microcosm and macrocosm

1938   *Collection Fernand Ouellette*

7 · Nova and Ion

CHRONOLOGY 1928–32

1928 *Founds the Pan-American Association of Composers with Henry Cowell and Carlos Chavez. 10 October: Varèse leaves the USA for Paris, where he is to live for the next five years. Initially he intends to work with René Bertrand, who has recently invented the Dynaphone. During this period he continues to correspond with Harvey Fletcher at Western Electric.*

1929 *First meeting with Alejo Carpentier, presumably through the intermediary of Villa-Lobos. 23 April: first Paris performance of* Intégrales, *under M. F. Gaillard. 30 May: première in Paris of the revised, reduced version of* Amériques, *conducted by Gaston Poulet. During this year Varèse has the first ideas for* Espace. *He also associates closely with the progressive film composer Arthur Hoérée, who is working with sound inscribed or pre-recorded on film, and discusses with him the necessity for and use of electronic equipment.*

1930 *14 March: Varèse, Villa-Lobos and Marcel Mihalovici appear together as composer-conductors in a concert at which Varèse conducts* Offrandes *and* Octandre. *Works intensively with Carpentier, Desnos and Ribemont-Dessaignes on* The One All Alone.

1931 *11 June: Nicolas Slominsky conducts* Intégrales. *14 November:* Ionisation *completed.*

1932 *6 February: Varèse makes the first of several repeated, unsuccessful applications to the Guggenheim Foundation, on Harvey Fletcher's recommendation, for a grant to enable him to work on the development of new instruments with René Bertrand. 25 February: first Paris performance of* Arcana, *conducted by Nicolas Slonimsky; repeated in Berlin, 5 March. End of collaboration with Carpentier and Desnos?*

November? (one source says May 1933): Varèse approaches Antonin Artaud for a new libretto for the One All Alone *project. 1 December: writes to Fletcher from Paris requesting access to facilities of the Bell Telephone Laboratories in return for his services to the company.*

In late 1928 Varèse returned to Paris with high hopes that he could pursue his composing career in a more stimulating and receptive cultural environment; yet the five years he was to spend there were ultimately a period of frustration and near-failure. By the end of them he had produced only one 5-minute composition – though that work, *Ionisation*, for 13 percussionists, has entered history as one of the essential achievements of 20th-century musical modernism. Yet *Ionisation* was by no means the only work,or even the principal one, on which he expended his furious creative efforts.

This is especially clear from the testimony of the Cuban writer Alejo Carpentier (1904–80). Of French and Russian parentage, Carpentier was to become a towering figure in the literature of his country and of Latin America generally; he first met Varèse in Paris early in 1929, almost certainly through their mutual friend Heitor Villa-Lobos. Of all the poets, dramatists and novelists with whom Varese collaborated, the young Carpentier may well have had the most comprehensive knowledge of music and the most profound understanding of Varèse's concepts. Having himself been trained as an architect, he was well able to appreciate Varèse's ideas of music as planes and volumes and their projection in space; as a student of anthropology and a revolutionary in politics, he could grasp the radical human implications of Varèse's musical message. His cultural and creative insights into the composer's mind probably surpassed even those of Hofmannsthal and Romain Rolland – who admittedly had known Varèse only as a young man whose ideas were still taking shape.

Carpentier had been writing musical journalism since 1922, and throughout his long life he was to produce a staggering amount of music criticism. Some of it is embodied and transfigured within the major novels of his later years such as *The Lost Steps* (1953), *Baroque Concerto* and, especially, *La consagración de la Primavera* (The Rite of Spring), in which Varèse's music – and *Ionisation* in particular – plays a significant role. Carpentier's memoir of his relations with Varèse, *Varèse Vivant*, published in French after the composer's death, is reasonably well-known to students of the music.[1] But his articles in Spanish, contemporary reports from the years he was in contact with Varèse in Paris, have remained virtually unknown, and certainly unused. They prove to add significantly to our knowledge of the composer.[2]

Carpentier was aware of Varèse's music some time before they met, and not merely by repute: he had heard *Octandre*, presumably its French première under Vladimir Golschmann in Paris in 1927. In one of his first articles about Varèse, Carpentier recalled the occasion:

I shall never forget the intense satisfaction, the joy it gave me, at the end of a concert overly laden with impressionistic phosphorescence. Here was music of extreme tensions, total plasticity, without grey areas or empty spaces earmarked for future development. This was music in movement from the first measure; music that celebrated a perennial concept of euphony, guided by a powerfully constructive force of will. After listening to drifting banks of musical fog, *Octandre* suddenly reared up with all the nervous elegance of a structure in steel.

This was the graceful conquest of space ...[3]

---

[1] *Varèse Vivant* appeared first in truncated form in *Le Nouveau Commerce*, Cahier No.10, Autumn-Winter 1967; the full text was issued in Paris – where Carpentier died – as a limited edition booklet, dated 25 February 1980; perhaps the last thing he published. My citations are from this edition, hereafter identified as *VV*.

[2] I am indebted to James Reid-Baxter for drawing this material to my attention, generously translating large tracts of Carpentier's Spanish for me, and allowing me to study the relevant parts of his unpublished thesis on the role of music in Carpentier's epic novel *La consagración de la Primavera*.

[3] 'Un revolucionario de la Musica: Edgar Varèse', published in the Havana periodical *Sócial*, Vol.14 no. 6, June 1929; reprinted in *Crónicas* Vol.I (Havana, 1976). All Spanish texts in this chapter have been specially translated for me by James Reid-Baxter.

In the same article, after a brief survey of Varèse's character, career and ideas, with especial reference to *Amériques* (shortly to receive its Paris première), Carpentier concludes with a tantalizing glimpse of works in progress as of April 1929:[4]

Edgar Varèse is currently at work on a poem for female voice and orchestra, to a text by the present writer. His next score will be a work for choir, soloists and orchestra, in both stage and concert versions, based on a poem by Tristan Tzara.

Considering the keen interest of posterity even in Varèse's unrealized projects, it seems odd that these two have not attracted more attention. The Carpentier setting 'for female voice and orchestra', was entitled *La niña enferma de fiebre* (The fever-stricken girl).[5] But this piece, whether or not it was ever completed, soon lost its independent existence. Instead it was subsumed – as may also have been the fate of whatever conception was embodied in the proposed stage or concert work on words by Tzara – into a huge composition for the stage which dominated Varèse's creative efforts during these years in Paris; and which, had it been completed, would presumably have constituted by far his largest and most ambitious work. This was a project with which Carpentier soon found himself closely involved. As early as the August number of *Le Cahier*, in another article on Varèse, the Cuban was able to write: 'He is ... working on a new piece, a miracle – *The One All Alone* – based on a text by Robert Desnos and myself.'

SIRIUS MYSTERIES

Hoc est astrum apolypticum ...
—PARACELSUS

Varèse's 'Mystery', as he termed it – presumably by analogy with the medieval mystery plays, and doubtless to avoid the conventional connotations of 'Opera' – had begun germinating in his imagination in the mid-1920s, and before it was definitively abandoned (or had

---

[4] The article was evidently written before 23 April, as it speaks in the future tense of the Paris première of *Intégrales* to be conducted by Marius Francois Gaillard, which took place on that date.

[5] It is identified thus by Araceli García-Carranza, head of the Carpentier Archive at the National Library of Cuba, in her 'Crónologia' appended to Carpentier's novel *El Siglô de las luces* (Caracas: Biblioteca Ayacucho, 1978).

metamorphosed into the separate project of *Espace*, discussed in a later chapter) – its evolution had involved, among others, Varèse himself, Louise, Carpentier, the Surrealist Robert Desnos, the Dadaist Georges Ribemont-Dessaignes, and Antonin Artaud. In view of the enormous importance that the project assumed in Varèse's imagination, and the large amount of work that he certainly expended on it, it is vital to accord it as detailed a consideration as may be possible with such materials as are now to hand. Unavoidably, this can only be attempted through direct quotations from some of Varèse's collaborators: these personal accounts of the work in progress are the nearest we can approach to it. In a sense, they are the verbal equivalent of the music examples we can draw upon in discussions of the extant works.

Among previous books on Varèse, only that by Ouellette has made a comparable attempt: and it is he who provides precious citations from the composer's own scenario. But Ouellette, writing before the appearance of Louise's *Looking-Glass Diary* and Carpentier's *Varèse Vivant*, was unable to give much account of how the project evolved. By contrast Jonathan Bernard, despite familiarity with both those texts, confines discussion of the work – under the heading *Espace* – to a brief note in one of his Appendices, commenting that 'by all accounts' (a footnote here directs us to *Varèse Vivant*), the Carpentier-Desnos collaboration 'produced ... not much of anything'.[6] Yet a vital missing link has been lying unread among Carpentier's voluminous journalistic output, a contemporary report in Spanish of the work in progress, which brings us as near as we are ever likely to get to one formative stage of Varèse's conception – and provides startling indications that 'not much of anything' is a massive under-estimate of what the collaboration had actually produced.

First a word on nomenclature. The proposed stage work is called different things by different writers: most commonly *The One All Alone*, *L'Astronome* (or *Astronomer*), and especially *Espace* – and these three titles are frequently said to refer to one and the same project. My strong impression (admittedly based on what is as yet fragmentary evidence) is of two more or less parallel projects: a 'stage' work, most intensively worked on in the Paris years, and a 'concert' work, most intensively worked on after Varèse's return to the USA in 1933. They may well have been in some respects different realizations of the same

---

[6] Bernard, p.239.

conception but, though neither was ever completed, each advanced far enough to have developed a different imaginative identity. For consistency I shall refer to the stage work as *The One All Alone*, which was indeed Varèse's original title – though he considered several others – and, significantly, the one which Alejo Carpentier always uses. Some of the alternatives, especially *L'Astronome*, may have had temporary validity; but it does seem to me misleading to use the title *Espace* in this context. *Espace* is rather the appropriate title to apply to the 'concert work' – the 'choral symphony', which Varèse may indeed have also begun during the Paris years, but which only began to assume distinct form as completion of *The One All Alone* began to seem unattainable.

According to Louise Varèse,[7] the idea of *The One All Alone* first began to take shape in 1926. Varèse had long been interested in the culture of the American Indians, and a chance remark at a lunch with the then US Postmaster General, Thomas Patton, resulted in Patton sending him 'the entire set of the Smithsonian Institution's books on American Indians that covered every aspect of their history, folklore, language, music, poetry and so on'. Louise continues:

Varèse was particularly fascinated by the legends and their laconic imagist language. He asked me to write a scenario and we chose a myth that was not only dramatic, ritualistic, and spectacular, but also philosophical. The theme: dualism: the title (Indian style): *The One-All-Alone, A Miracle*: the plot: the contest between the evil Arrow-Maker, or Sorcerer, and the mystical hero, who was, in fact, for Varèse, no other than Nietzsche's *Übermensch*. There is no point in going into that rejected project except to say that Varèse later turned the mystical man of the Indian myth into a modern astronomer who exchanges signals with Sirius and when, as in the case of his former hero, the mob turns against him, is drawn up, not into the sun, but to Sirius by what Varèse called '*radiation instantanée*'. Varese wrote his own synopsis for the *Astronomer* and spent years trying to find the right poet to write his text. More of all this later.[8]

Since the second volume of Louise's *Looking-Glass Diary* has never been published, her 'more' has never been revealed – though she has permitted publication of a brief discussion in letters, of which we will make use in due course, on the much later stage of the project which

---

[7] *LGD*, p.260.

[8] Ibid.

involved Antonin Artaud.[9] In the present citation, she concludes with the remark:

Of course the Indian idea had been an absurdity for Varèse, an aberration, a positive deflection. Varèse's music was totally unsuited to folklore, to the archaic, his conception of sound too utterly twentieth century. He realized this as soon as he began seriously to consider the music ... [10]

In view of Varèse's long-standing fascination with Amerindian culture and legend, which found further stimulation in New Mexico in the late 1930s – and in view of the fact that in 1934 he was to complete a work, *Ecuatorial*, which is a setting and striking embodiment of a Mayan Indian text – it may be doubted whether 'the Indian idea' was so much of an absurdity. It should also be remarked that Varèse was here following in the footsteps of Busoni, whose own interest in the American Indians, stimulated in the first instance by the publication in 1910 of his student Natalie Curtis's *The Indians' Book*, had led him to project a theatre work based on Indian ceremonies and actions linked 'with one of the "eternal" stories: mother, son, bride, war, peace', before he actually went on to compose his orchestral *Red Indian Fantasy* and *Song of the Spirit Dance*, and the *Red Indian Diary* for solo piano, during the period 1913–15. During the same period he actually wrote an opera libretto on an Indian legend, *The Bride of the Gods*, set to music by his American pupil Louis Gruenberg.

In the intervals between revising *Amériques* during the summer of 1927, in Antibes, Varèse made some attempt at beginning to compose his Amerindian miracle-play. Louise's memories of this are revealing.

Sometimes he sat at the piano fiddling with themes that occurred to him for his Arrow-Maker, who was to be played by an acrobat doing somersaults, cartwheels and grotesque dances and who, more than the rest, for the moment, stirred his musical imagination. He would often call downstairs to ask me to come up and tell him which one of two chords I preferred, but both being to my ears so much alike, it was impossible for me to make a choice ... That summer ... he accomplished very little. It worried him. The urge to get his stage work started was very strong in him, his imagination teemed with

---

[9] 'Varèse – Artaud (excerpts from letters from Louise Varèse to Peter Garland)', in *Soundings 10*, Berkeley, CA, 1976, unpaginated but pp.10–11.

[10] *LGD*, p.260.

images, visual and musical, but the elan was lacking – the spring that would bounce him into the middle of it.[11]

In the mention of the Arrow-Maker as a role to be taken by an acrobat, we catch the first glimpse of a circus element which was to remain part of Varèse's conception of his stage-work. For the metamorphosis of his miracle-play of the remote past into a drama of the future, and his arrow-making Indian shaman into a man of science, we must turn for testimony to Fernand Ouellette, who reproduces Varèse's first manuscript sketch for a new scenario which the composer prepared in 1928 (Illustration 7, captioned 'The first sketch of *l'Astronome*'), and transcribes it in his text (pp.115–116): though with some omissions, as comparison with the illustration will show. This fascinating document is headed with a number of jotted notes, which Ouelette has omitted from his transcription:

SIRIUS – its companion – the constellations – Legends of Sirius – what it represented for the ancients – names for it.
[indecipherable] to the conductor – Eddington – Aréunis [?] – [indecipherable]
The Year 2000 (?)

From this point Ouellette's transcription can take over.

Discovery of instantaneous radiation – speed 30,000,000 times that of light. Rapid variations in the size of Sirius (explosion) which becomes a Nova. All the astronomers examine the Companion – this is where signals are being transmitted from. (The Companion is the active agent). Unexpected reception of signals – prime numbers 1, 3, 5, 7. The governments [*replacing 'the astronomer' in Varèse's ms.*] decide they must answer 11, 12 [sic].[12] The answer to that is 17, 19. When the catastrophes occur, it is this decision which will turn the fury of the mob against the astronomer, since if he had not replied, Sirius and the Companion would not have taken any notice of Earth.

Regular messages from Sirius. Mysterious – in musical waves (supple, fluctuating). The Wise Men study them. Perhaps it is the acoustical language of Sirius. [*Crossed out by Varèse at this point and not translated by Ouellette*: Its song envelops the Earth. Haunting – yet elastic – subject to variations – according

---

[11] *LGD*, pp.266–7

[12] The '12' which stands here in Ouellette's text is clearly a typographical error: the next prime number after 11 is 13, and '13' is clear in Varèse's manuscript.

to the action – for [indecipherable] triumphant at the end – when it accompanies the luminous envelope which absorbs the Astronomer. Waves – diffusers of noise – dry – de–timbred[?]. *There follows, in the manuscript, the 'SIRIUS' music example discussed below, after which Ouellette's translation resumes.*] The brightness of Sirius is still increasing, other radiations come in from the Companion, precipitating the catastrophes. Explosions, darkness, etc.

This sketch-scenario also includes Varèse's notation of two themes – the only musical material from the project to have passed into public knowledge. These are the theme of the Astronomer – apparently for percussion alone, if it is not in fact merely a rhythmic outline – and the theme of Sirius. Ouellette states that this 'was to be scored for Ondes Martenot', but he may be misled by the reference to musical 'waves' (*ondes*) which appears immediately above it in the sketch.

Ouellette comments, apropos the scenario, that 'from a certain point of view Varèse was predicting radioastronomy and radio-sources as early as 1928'. In fact the scenario resounds with recent, much-publicized astronomical discoveries of the mid-1920s. For most of the preceding century it had been known to astronomers that the brilliant blue–white Sirius, the brightest star in the sky, was a binary star system: the trajectory of the star we can see (it is, in fact, drawing nearer to the solar system) swings from side to side, perturbed by the influence of a 'companion' so dim it is invisible to the naked eye but with a mass similar to our own sun. Theorized about by the Prussian astronomer Friedrich Bessel in the 1830s, Sirius B (the 'companion') was first detected in 1862 by the Massachusetts telescope maker Alvan Clark. Ten thousand times fainter than Sirius A, the companion was discovered to be incredibly small for a body that clearly exercises such a strong gravitational pull upon its larger neighbour. At first it was assumed – because of its dimness – to be very cool, but in 1914 Walter

Adams, at Mount Wilson Observatory, managed to measure Sirius B's surface temperature, which he estimated at an incredible 8,000° Kelvin (the actual figure is now known to be nearly four times as large). From this it followed that, to account for the dimness of Sirius B, the star must be 100 times smaller than the radius of Earth's sun; and if its mass was indeed that of the sun, this in turn meant that its density would have to be a *million* times greater.

This astonishing phenomenon attracted considerable publicity, and prompted the English astrophysicist Sir Arthur Eddington, author of popular books on astronomy (who is, of course, the 'Eddington' of Varèse's sketch), to suggest that Adams should measure the shift in spectral lines of light leaving the surface of Sirius B. According to Einstein's developing theory of general relativity – on which Eddington was well informed – the difficulty light has in escaping a strong gravitational field causes a shift of its spectral lines towards red. Adams measured the red shift in 1925, and found it in agreement with Eddington's calculations, thus proving that the 'companion' of Sirius did in fact possess an almost unbelievable density – something like a million grams per cubic centimeter.[13] Incredibly hot, dense, and dim, Sirius B was the first identified example of a White Dwarf.

The discovery fascinated Varèse. ('It's the size of a fingernail,' he once remarked to Odile Vivier, 'but its weight is beyond imagining. What Universe would achieve its disruption?') Moreover, it became the imaginative pivot of his proposed stage-work. No doubt he saw a poetic symmetry in the idea that this contemporary demonstration of the awesome forces of the universe – light, heat, gravitation – should find its echo in his own music, which strove to open up new horizons and discover principles as elemental and overwhelming in the realm of sound. Not only that: this 'Sirius-obsession' casts a revealing light on

---

[13] Eddington, as an astronomer who had also worked as a student of the Atomic physicist Ernest Rutherford, discoverer of sub-atomic particles, encompassed many of Varèse's scientific interests, and there is good evidence that the composer had read his influential study of the new physics, *The Nature of the Physical World* (Macmillan, 1928). It may even have been a catalyst for Varèse's scenario, written the same year. At one point in this book, discussing the quantum transmission of light, Eddington employs the example of light leaving Sirius and striking the eye of an observer on Earth (op.cit., p.186). For Varèse and Eddington see John D. Anderson, 'Varèse and the Lyricism of the New Physics', *The Musical Quarterly* Spring 1991, Volume 75 Number 1.

Varèse's much-quoted disclaimers about *Arcana* and the Paracelsus quotation he had placed on its title-page. For, soon after completing that work, he was now embarked upon a music-drama centred, literally, upon the activities of an 'Apocalyptic Star'.

As the jotted notes at the beginning of his scenario show, he was well aware – and perhaps intended to make use of – the fact that Sirius had occupied an important position in the cosmological thinking of ancient cultures. The very name comes from the Greek word for sparkling or scorching, and was also used in adjectival form, according to Eratosthenes, to denote stars with a 'tremulous' light. It is identified in Babylonian cuneiform texts dating back to 1000 b.c., under the name Kak.Si.Di., and in ancient Chinese astronomy as T'ien-lang, the 'celestial jackal' – curiously so, as in Western tradition Sirius is part of the constellation Canis Major, the Great Dog. Sirius was especially prominent in ancient Egyptian culture. Under the name Sept (in Greek, Sothis), it was one of the strongest influences on scientific, agricultural and religious life, and was worshipped as the star whose first heliacal rising (its first annual rising on the eastern horizon just ahead of the sun) inaugurated the growing cycle of each year, since it immediately preceded the annual flooding of the Nile. Represented by the hieroglyph of the Dog, Sirius was associated with Anubis, but also the divinities Thoth, Osiris and Isis-Hathor; several temples have been found to incorporate alignments with Sirius's rising; and it has long been theorized that the Egyptian calendar was regulated by a 'Sothic' dating from the rising of Sirius and the Sun together on New Year's Day, an astronomical event which occurs every 1460 years.

In Classical Antiquity the rising of Sirius at midnight was celebrated at the Eleusinian mysteries. But in early astrology its influence was generally believed to be malefic. Homer called it 'a sign to mortal man of evil augury'. Hippocrates believed it controlled the weather, with resulting effect on human health. Its rising with the Sun in late summer was routinely associated by the poets with dry, unhealthy weather: 'the terrible scorching Dog-Days' (Horace, *Odes* Book III, 13); 'The Dog-star, that burning constellation, when he brings drought and diseases on sickly mortals, rises and saddens the sky with inauspicious light' (Virgil, *Aeneid*). Manilius, in his *Astronomica* written probably in the early years of the reign of Tiberius, describes its progress through the skies thus (in the 1697 translation of Thomas Creech):

Next barks the *Dog*, and from his Nature flow
The most afflicting Powers that rule below.
Heat burns his *Rise*, *Frost* chills his setting Beams,
And vex the World with opposite extremes.

There are, moreover, Sirian traditions in the New World: the star played a role in the astronomy of the Maya of Central America, and the street layout of the ancient city of Teotihuacan in Mexico includes alignments to it. In North America, Sirius is one of the principal stars (the others are Aldebaran and Rigel) on which the mysterious Bighorn Medicine Wheel in Wyoming – probably a sacred calendrical device of the Cheyenne Indians – is sighted, as is the probably much older Moose Mountain wheel in southern Saskatchewan. Finally, in the legends of the Hopi Indians of Arizona Sirius features as the Blue Star Katzina, from which beings visited earth in the very remote past.[14] This last example is significant insofar as Varèse might have gleaned it from his readings in American Indian folklore, and his futuristic astronomical drama may thus retain roots in Indian myth (indeed, his attention could well have been directed towards the Hopi by the fact that Busoni had used several of their folk-melodies in his 'Red Indian' compositions). In any case, as the other examples illustrate, Sirius has exercised a powerful effect on the human imagination since earliest times: so in centering his scenario upon it Varèse was – quite consciously – tapping into a theme of archetypal, mythic power as well as of modern science.

Varèse proceeded to elaborate his initial sketch into a much more detailed scenario, 'of several pages' according to Ouellette, who unfortunately only quotes its beginning and end. Most of what he does

---

[14] The Hopi word 'Katzina' means a spirit who conveys prayers to the gods. This is not the place to raise the controversial issue of the Dogon tribespeople of Mali, West Africa, who not only have a religion centred on Sirius but appear to possess a detailed and reasonably accurate knowledge of the workings of the Sirius star-system which could never have been gleaned by naked-eye observation (and which, in fact, they attribute to direct teachings from Sirian visitors of long ago). The issues raised by this curiosity have been fully – perhaps too fully – aired by Robert K. G. Temple in his book *The Sirius Mystery* (London: Sidgwick & Jackson, 1976). Since the Dogon beliefs were only published by French anthropologists in 1950 they have no relevance to Varèse's project, except as a supporting example of a Sirius cult in a sophisticated but non-technological society.

quote I shall leave uncited, as we derive a much more coherent account from Alejo Carpentier's writings. But it needs reiterating that the basic ideas of the scenario were always Varèse's own, and it is worth quoting the opening lines (in Ouellette's transliteration),[15] both for their own evocative and visionary effect and to stress how central Sirius – for Carpentier never calls 'the Star' by its name – was to Varèse's whole conception.

> The sky. A summer's night. All the constellations will grow pale as Sirius grows more and more intense. Milky Ways.
> The height of the tower can be sensed. Low down in the distance, the city. Chorus, voices, astronomer.
> A voice: The point, the point, it's getting bigger.
>
> Shouts, circle, horizon, Equator, light of a world.
>
> Eye! Dizziness! Red! Aldebaran!
> Exploding altogether – Sirius!
>
> Dizzying space
>
> One light alone on everything that exists!
>
> *Distant voices* – We know. We know.
> Sirius and his Companion glow.
> And the Companion is the master now.
> And Sirius obeys ...

This then was the scenario that Varèse brought with him to Paris: in fact, his principal creative goal in coming to Paris was probably precisely the composition of this stage-work. He had called his scenario *l'Astronome*, but according to Louise he had not yet (and still had not several years later, when collaborating with Artaud) fixed the title: he 'considered *The Astronomer*, perhaps, or *The Miracle*, or *Sirius*'.[16] It is odd that she does not mention the original title, *The One All Alone*: not only because this is what Alejo Carpentier always calls it, but also in the light of the fact, recently revealed in an important article by Olivia Mattis,[17] that the Indian myth form of the stage work was still under

---

[15] Ouellette, p.116.

[16] 'Varèse – Artaud', p.10.

[17] 'Varèse's Multimedia Conception of *Déserts*' (*Musical Quarterly*, Volume 76, No.4, Winter 1992), especially pp. 570–572. (I cite this article hereafter as Mattis 1992.)

consideration as late as 1930, i.e. two years after Varèse had outlined the 'Sirius' scenario and a year after he had given it to Carpentier, Desnos and Ribemont-Dessaignes to flesh out.

In a letter of 15 July 1930, Varèse asked Louise to prepare a draft scenario which he could turn over to them for polishing. He demanded 'apocalyptic unity' and told her not to forget 'the aspect of returning to the primitive: pounding dance of fear, almost voodooistic prophetic cries, shaking, twitching, and the ending as grand as the heavens. Apocalypse. Apocalypse.' The central character of Louise's typescript scenario,[18] which is in the style of an Indian fable, is called The-One-All-Alone, and the figure of the Arrow-Maker remains the embodiment of the negative forces opposing him. It is difficult to see why two such radically different scenarios should still have been under discussion at this point: but it may well be that Varèse felt the original 'Indian' form contained essential features which Carpentier and his colleagues had not so far managed to bring out in their work on the 'Sirius' form.

As already noted, in 1929 (at the latest) Varèse had entrusted his *l'Astronome* scenario to a trio of poets: Carpentier, Desnos and Ribemont-Dessaignes; they worked on it with him for more than two years, though it hardly occupied all their attention.[19]

Early in 1931, for the Havana *Sócial*, Carpentier wrote an account of the collaboration which is so detailed (and has, apparently, so completely escaped the attention of Varèse scholars) as to be worth quoting *in extenso*. Not only is this article, 'Edgar Varèse Composing For The Stage',[20] far fuller than the account he gives in *Varèse Vivant*, but it differs from it in several important respects, which I shall note as we come to them. It seems certain that aspects of the work went through many different stages of formulation, and that in *Varèse Vivant*, written 36 years later than the *Sócial* report, Carpentier may be

---

[18] According to Mattis 1992, a copy of this is in the Sophia Smith Women's History Archive of Smith College, Northampton, Massachussetts.

[19] Desnos' famous break with André Breton and the other Surrealists took place in 1930. Ribemont-Dessaignes had already made his own exit, in 1925, in the direction of the 'Grand Jeu' group. In early 1930 he collaborated with Varèse on an article entitled 'La Mécanisation de la Musique' (published in April 1930 in the magazine *Bifur*).

[20] 'Edgar Varèse Escribe Para El Teatro', *Sócial*, Vol.16 no.4, April 1931. Reprinted in *Crónicas* Volume I (Havana, 1976).

talking about the final stages, not yet reached in early 1931; or indeed about stages that had already been rejected by this date.

Almost at the beginning of the *Social* article, Carpentier gives some precious particulars about Varèse's intentions for scoring the stage-work, and its performance prospects:

... Shut away in his study on the outskirts of Paris, surrounded by his tam-tams, Chinese blocks, whips, drums, and wave-producing apparatus,[21] the composer is preparing to confront the Berlin public – Kleiber is to conduct[22] – with one of the most tremendous musical and choreographic events of modern times. The action is divided into seven *movements* performed by vocal soloists, massed choirs, dancers, acrobats and mimes, while the orchestra accompanying them calls for the largest brass section ever used (including several saxophones), quadruple and quintuple woodwind, organ, several ondes Martenot, and a full percussion section, extended to include spiral-shaped rails, a guiro and several maracas. Virtually no strings, just an ensemble of double-basses and a few cellos ...

The one all alone will be a sort of summa of Varèse's aesthetic: synthetic decor, built by engineers, not painters, exploiting every possibility offered by the use of electricity on stage, with superimposed planes, various parts of the action taking place simultaneously, and heavy velvet curtains as backcloth.

Carpentier then produces a detailed description of the scenario, with a few quotations from the text he has supplied to Varèse. This vivid account seems to be the only complete and coherent report of the action, as it was envisaged by Varèse in 1931.

In the Prologue, groups of voices placed all over the theatre launch into a song of alarm, of dread at the appearance of a huge new star which has begun communicating with the earth:

> *The cities are full of questions*
> *Never has there been so much weeping!*
> *Never has there been so much laughter!*
> *The wild beasts*
> *are emigrating in the night.*

---

[21] '*aparatos productores de ondas*'.

[22] Erich Kleiber was currently Director of the Berlin Stadtheater. Though Carpentier's statement may reflect hope rather than fact, it suggests that some negotiation, at least, had taken place between Kleiber and Varèse.

> *In the forest, the augurs*
> *believe they can read the flight of the birds.*

The windows of the city remain open; mankind anxiously scans the sky. Only five characters remain unaffected, or lost in their dreams: an astronomer who gesticulates on the top of his tower (on stage, this is done by the means of a huge automaton), two lovers singing to each other at a garret window, and two chess-players (an aristocrat and an artist) who have chosen to ignore the life of the city. A visionary [*iluminado*] gathers the choirs at the foot of the astronomer's tower, claiming that the star-gazer is 'in love with the stars, a provoker of disasters', a sort of Antichrist, a caller-down of curses:

> *And seven mountains of fire*
> *shall burn along the horizons of cities,*
> *And horses that rise from the sea*
> *shall neigh over your dead bodies ...*

The astronomer, completely caught up in his gesticulations, does not respond to the crowd's frightened questioning.

The hour of dawn arrives, and the sun does not appear. Loudspeakers situated on different parts of the stage, and in the auditorium, announce that 'the sun has not been seen anywhere on the planet' ...

This idea of the sun failing to rise does not feature in Varèse's preliminary scenarios, but Carpentier makes much of it, and in *Varèse Vivant* he asserts that it in fact goes back to the original conception of the work in Indian myth:

... the original germ of the idea for this 'mystery' came from a tradition of the Pueblo Indians of New Mexico, which had attracted the attention of the composer's wife Louise ... on the day when it no longer had any worshippers, the sun would cease to show itself and the world would henceforth be plunged in deepest night. This belief had already aroused the curiosity of C.G. Jung who speaks about it in his memoirs (Chapter IX). In our opera, the Astronomer was guilty of having made mankind forget the existence of the sun by diverting their spiritual attention to a star which had just appeared, to which he attributed higher powers (one can see the relationship of this myth with that of the ancient Aztec one of the 'four suns' ...[23]

---

[23] *VV*, pp.11–12. Carpentier's reference to Jung is to Section II 'America: The Pueblo Indians' in Chapter IX of *Memories, Dreams and Reflections* (English Edition, Collins and Routledge, 1963; Fontana, 1967). Jung quotes the chief of the Taos

Louise Varèse makes no mention of this aspect of the story in her account quoted above, but that need not mean it was not already present in some form.[24] Carpentier's 1931 article continues:

The terror rises. And the transmitters continue to announce disasters all over the earth: Lindbergh's plane has vanished from the sky;[25] a fleet has sunk without trace in the ocean; the bars of the prisons have gone soft, and all those condemned to death have escaped; the stock-markets are crashing – *Anaconda, Rio Tinto, Parana!* – in all the capital cities of the world ...

(In *Varèse Vivant*, Carpentier slightly expands on this last detail: 'Varèse asked us to have the choir chant out the names of various shares quoted on the stockmarket – Anaconda, Rio-Tinto, Parana – whose attractiveness was enhanced by the power of the words.')

Pueblo – in the area of New Mexico which Varèse was also to visit in the late 1930s – as telling him 'We are the sons of Father Sun, and with our religion daily we help our father to go across the sky. We do this not only for ourselves, but for the whole world. It we were to cease practising our religion, in ten years the sun would no longer rise. Then it would be night for ever.' (Fontana ed., p.280). The Aztec myth of 'the Four Suns' – in fact quite widespread among the early Amerindian cultures – is a cyclic creation/destruction myth of four worlds, standing for successive ages of the Earth, each illuminated by a different sun related to one of the four elements, and each ending in global catastrophe. We now live under the fifth sun ...

[24] On the other hand the idea, so important in Varèse's scenarios, of signals exchanged between Sirius and Earth, is absent from Carpentier's 1931 article. It is just barely suggested in a section of his much briefer description of the action in *Varèse Vivant*, which also indicates a different order of events (and an explanation of the working title): '... a public square somewhere in a city that resembled, no question about it, New York. Day refuses to dawn. Everything stems from this non-daybreak. The opera begins in darkness. Those on their way to work stop walking. they remain on stage, awaiting orders, information. It's up to the audience to say what has to be said. Soon the actors form a huge crowd, jammed together, looking at the audience ... Finally a Herald [*Annonciateur*] gets up in front of the crowd. Perhaps, up there, on the top of his tower, he-who-is-all-alone, *The One All Alone*, can explain what is going on. ... No answer is forthcoming; at best, telegraphic signals from the orchestra (which in this case has the role of mediator between the audience and what is taking place on stage). Unable to answer the questions put to him, the Herald is stoned ...'

[25] The American aviator Charles Lindbergh, whose historic solo flight of the Atlantic had taken place in 1927, remained an international celebrity well into the 1930s.

Here a hint of political content now enters the 1931 narrative. We should recall that Varèse was evolving his 'miracle' in the Depression, in the aftermath of the Wall Street Crash:

Labourers on their way to work wonder if they should bother going to their factories, since day has failed to break. A politician and a businessman get up on their respective podiums:

> *Comrades, do not be alarmed*
> *whatever happens,*
> *work until you collapse.*
> *We shall take care of Peace,*
> *Equality, Fraternity,*
> *Justice, Religion ...*

But their speeches are interrupted by a racket of sarcastic protests. The words 'Peace', 'Justice', 'Fraternity', 'Religion', provoke menacing howls of laughter. A hunchback, a black and a prostitute try to climb onto the orators' podium. A huge policeman arrests them. The crowd hurls itself at him, but stops suddenly as newspaper vendors mount the stage, after running in through the auditorium, shouting news of fresh cataclysms. Simultaneously, all the death-penalty escapees burst onto the stage, pursued by the police firing guns ...

And the star, the enormous star, which is responsible for all these misfortunes, begins to move slowly in the sky. Its light floods the stage with a twilight that turns red. We see the astronomer capturing one of its brilliant rays. Beggars, workmen, tuxedo-clad nightwalkers, policemen, newspaper vendors, terrified women all question the astronomer anew. He remains absorbed in his experiments. Then the Visionary from the prologue, and the black man, begin singing two psalms, which the crowd soon joins in. The Visionary announces the end of the world in long, slow, heavy phrases, while the choir, directed by the negro, howls voodoo monosyllables mixed with *naniga*[26] and Indian words and magic incantations – a verbal counterpoint, created by the present writer. Suddenly the choirs fall silent, and the whole mass of performers, in a frenzy of terror – terror of the milennium – launches into an almost hysterical dance, hammering on the stage with their feet like music-hall eccentrics. A kind of thunderous pealing of bells, from the full orchestral forces, interrupts the dance. The chants of the magician and the

---

[26] Afro-Cuban black religion. (Carpentier's footnote.) We recall Varèse's requirement for 'almost voodooistic prophetic cries'; and with Carpentier's next sentence his idea of a 'primitive pounding dance of fear'.

visionary spread through the choirs again. And suddenly, in near silence, the dance recommences, more and more tragic, accompanied by no more than a distant rumbling of electric hammers.[27]

Meanwhile, the light from the star has changed from blue to violet, from violet to red, from red to white. Searchlights, hitherto hidden, start to sweep the auditorium with their piercing beams ... The crowd, crazy with terror, starts to climb up the tower. The orchestra and the vocal forces are at maximum power ... But here, the miracle takes place.

The beam of light from the star starts to revolve furiously, boring into the astronomer's body. He disintegrates gradually, becomes incandescent,[28] and vanishes without trace into the atmosphere. The crowd falls back to the rear of the stage, where it remains as if turned to stone by fear. There is a brusque silence. The star disappears from the heavens. Normal light floods the streets of the city once more ... But now all that is left on stage are a few wax dummies, staring at the audience with their absurd, fixed gaze. And the curtain falls slowly, to the crackle of static in the highest register the human ear can hear.

Carpentier's delineation of the drama's apocalyptic climax may be supplemented here by a report of the film-maker and photographer Brassai, to whom Varèse described his conception of it, at presumably the same period:[29]

... the stars ... end up by absorbing him completely ... But, in the final scene, when the astronomer is volatilized into interstellar space, factory sirens and airplane propellors were supposed to come into action. The 'music' was to be as strident and unbearable as possible, so as to terrify the audience and render it *groggy*, as he put it. At that moment, he told me, the powerful spotlights

[27] Carpentier was later to note (*VV*, p. 11) that 'Varèse was particularly keen' on the idea of 'electric hammers'. Possibly these unusual – and probably unrealized – instruments corresponded to 'the noise of the *Drill*' in Varèse's second scenario, quoted by Ouellette.

[28] This conception was already central to the 'Indian myth' form of *The One All Alone*. In Louise Varèse's scenario the hero's body is pierced by the arrows of the arrow-maker, which then turn into rays of light which begin to radiate in all directions. Olivia Mattis (1992, p.572) convincingly sees this as an essentially alchemical conception of the transmutation of man into Godhead.

[29] Brassai [pseudonym of Gyüla Halász], 'Edgard Varèse où la musique sidèrale', article in the Paris weekly *Arts-Spectacles*, issue of 8–14 December 1954; quoted here from Ouelette pp.118–9.

supposedly raking the sky up on stage would be turned abruptly down into the auditorium, blinding the audience and filling them with such panic that they wouldn't even be able to run away·

The idea of the work's ending which Carpentier conveys in *Varèse Vivant* is different from – and apparently more affirmative than – the stark, dehumanized apocalypse here described. As it hinges more satisfactorily on the return of the light of the sun, it may have been a later, improved conception – and it was apparently to have made use of the previously-projected Carpentier setting of 1929:

... Suddenly, a great silence falls like an imploration, a prayer for the dawn to break. The world will not be destroyed this night, this too long night. [...] On the stage – that is, the levels – sunrise. It is already the universe of *Déserts*. [...] In the end, the sunrise is due to the pleas of a little girl ('*la niña enferma de fiebres*', the character of a poem Varèse had asked me to write in Spanish for setting to music) who, sick and delirious, called on the sun to help her drive away the phantasms of a night that was too long and peopled by frightful visions.[30]

The next two sentences of *Varèse Vivant* then seem to write a definitive finis to the project:

The score of *The One All Alone* was never written, for Varèse's return to America interrupted our collaboration. But Louise Varèse was good enough to tell me that the composer, haunted by the subject (which he himself had given us) liked our text.

Note that Carpentier says the 'score' (*partition*) was not written; not that the music, or at least some of it, was not composed. And if we turn again to his 1931 *Sócial* article we receive a very different impression:

Every week, Varèse tells Ribemont-Dessaignes, Desnos and myself of the progress he is making on his score. Of the seven *movements* that comprise *The One All Alone*, four are already orchestrated. In the isolation of his Villa des Camélias, the powerful fingers of the President of the International Composers' League pound out the sombre chords of the prologue, over which there rises the piercing shriek of a baritone saxophone. The song of the two lovers follows, then the voices of the stock market, the howls that accompany the disintegration of the city's neon advertisments, the percussion that punctuates the paragraphs enunciated by the politician and the businessman.

---

[30] *VV*, pp.11–12.

I cannot believe that the author of *Arcanes*, of *Intégrales*, of *Hyperprism*, has ever created effects of such intensity, such energy, such deep-felt expressiveness. And, most important of all, such pure lyricism, a lyricism utterly free of scholastic tricks and so close to true poetry ...

Thanks to the labours of its composer, *The One All Alone* will, I do not doubt for a single instant, be one of the most total works of our age, inhabiting a sound-world of incomparable richness.

These are perhaps the two most frustrating paragraphs in the entire Varèse literature. Four movements orchestrated, indeed! This apparently substantial musical component the composer had created for *The One All Alone* by the date of Carpentier's *Social* article has never seen the light of day, nor is likely to: either it was destroyed or thrown away or, equally likely, parts of it may exist but in inchoate or unrecognizable form as sketches or drafts. Moreover the collaboration with Carpentier, Desnos and Ribemont-Dessaignes itself collapsed at some point after the article was written. We do not know the reasons. Carpentier's explanation in *Varèse Vivant*, quoted above, that Varèse's departure for America was to blame, looks like a charitable fiction: it was in 1932, with at least a year's further sojourn in Paris ahead of him, that Varèse decided to solicit an entirely new scenario from Antonin Artaud.

It is easy enough to imagine arguments and differences arising between three volatile poets and aestheticians and the volcanic, intemperate composer. And Carpentier in *Varèse Vivant* gives a brief glimpse of him in peremptory and demanding mode:

Every week we would bring Varèse the scenes we had finished. And every week work began all over again. 'That's not quite it yet.' 'More condensed, the text.' 'The star that's appeared in the sky is a Nova.' 'I must have dwarfs, and a hunchback, for the final scene.' We worked away. We worked away ... The text was written out like a musical score, on several lines, on staves ...

(We recall the 'Orphic' poetry of Varèse's friend Henri Barzun.) Probably Varèse's own conception of the piece was in a continuous state of flux, the very power of the basic idea overwhelming all conventional ideas of writing for the theatre. Indeed, Carpentier states that as early as 1929 the composer 'was dreaming of a circus ... inspired by Barnum & Bailey' as his preferred means of staging his 'mystery':

... a huge striped tent, complete with poles and ropes, with a special train and a convoy of waggons, a circus whose actors, mimes, singers, choristers and freaks were signed up to perform, coast to coast, from the Atlantic to the Pacific of the USA, a vast 'mystery', in one gigantic act ... It required different levels, spaces, acting areas. Varèse conceived of his enormous opera much as a circus impresario might dream up a simultaneous spectacle on several different levels. Here you would have the characters of the prologue; a bit further back, the characters of the first tableau; on the three levels – plus the stage – those of the dénoument ... for this monster opera ... Varèse had substituted for the temple of Bayreuth heaven knows how many waggons criss-crossing an entire continent.[31]

The strange mixture of the practical and impractical in this 'circus' project – Carpentier has left out the gigantic orchestra that would inevitably have had to form part of the travelling company – may also have helped to doom the collaboration.

Though he may have been 'inspired by Barnum & Bailey', Varèse's idea of a circus presentation also strongly recalls the still-born *Un songe d'un nuit d'été* project he had discussed so enthusiastically with Cocteau, Satie and Picasso in 1914–15, in which Shakespeare would have been enacted by actual circus performers. Here in *The One All Alone* the Parisian fascination with the circus, already given classic expression in Satie's *Parade*, would have found a fantastic futuristic apotheosis.

In fact, the more we look at this elusive 'Mystery', the more it comes indeed to resemble, as Carpentier noted, 'a summa of Varèse's aesthetic' – but a 'summa' that has roots in the early, lost works of the pre-War period. We might ponder the links between Sirius and the Aurora Borealis as depicted in Varèse's lost *Les cycles du nord*, which was apparently intended to express his 'unbelievable exaltation' at watching 'pulsating incandescent streamers of light' in the sky (above, p.24). Maybe the attraction for him of Sâr Péladan's *Le Fils des Étoiles*, which he had planned to turn into an opera, was precisely its 'stellar' connexions with Sumero-Akkadian astrology, and the transfiguration of its hero, the 'son of the stars' into a magus not, perhaps, unlike the *Astronomer* of *The One All Alone*. Even more striking are the parallels with the myth of *Oedipus and the Sphinx*; here too a lone hero, resolved and condemned to find out the truth, confronts a terrible prodigy and mediates between it and the population of a city. Despite its futuristic transformation, the dramatic image is essentially the same.

---

[31] *VV*, pp.9–10.

Louise Varèse has commented that 'Varèse's idea ... was *Mob versus Übermensch*',[32] but if the Astronomer was to be embodied by a huge automaton, as Carpentier states, and the crowd to metamorphose into wax dummies, one wonders if the guiding idea was not, rather, of the man of destiny as *Übermarionette*, a concept adumbrated by Edward Gordon Craig and enthusiastically developed by Busoni in his one-act operas *Arlecchino* and *Turandot*, both originally designed for puppet-theatre presentation. Like Oedipus, the *Übermensch* is an heroic figure who strives to master his fate by discovering his true identity, and thus controlling his inner nature. But also a tragic figure, because his discoveries reveal to him that he is in the grip of a higher level of fate, which in turn continues to control him (as *Übermarionette*). Varèse's repeated approaches to this theme suggests he felt in it a distinct autobiographical force. Indeed his famous depressions seem to have stemmed from feelings of helplessness to be truly free – free of the weight of tradition, or the burden of his past. The wish for an 'apocalypse' that would sweep everything away, as at the end of *The One All Alone*, must at times have been very strong.

* * *

In 1932[33] Varèse approached the most notorious contemporary figure in French avant-garde drama: the playwright, producer, actor and theorist Antonin Artaud. Like Desnos and Ribemont, he had been allied with Surrealism, but had broken with André Breton even earlier than they. In many ways Artaud – whom Varèse liked personally and whose ideas he greatly admired – must have seemed the ideal collaborator. It was at this very period that Artaud was engaged in elaborating his ideas for his Theatre of Cruelty, protesting against the artificial values of the predominant culture. He was arguing instead for a revival of the drama as an elemental rite: violently physical, cathartic, paroxysmic, laying bare the implacable cosmic forces of fate, communicating basic human needs and emotions and involving the metaphysical side of human nature. To this end he was advocating the fullest use of spectacle and theatrical devices including sounds, lights, colours and rhythmic movement.

---

[32] 'Varèse – Artaud', p.10.

[33] November 1932 seems to be the accepted date at least from the Artaud side. Olivia Mattis (1992, p.572) states that it was Varèse's attendance at one of Artaud's lectures on The Theatre of Cruelty in May 1933 that sparked the collaboration, but this seems uncomfortably late.

Like Varèse, Artaud was strongly in favour of the use of puppets, as a means of introducing metaphysical fear in stage production. Music and dance, also, were much in Artaud's thoughts at this time: his experience of the Balinese dancers at the 1931 Colonial Exhibition had struck him with the force of a revelation. It is in fact a moot point to what extent Artaud might have derived some of his own theatrical ideas of the Thirties from his consequent discussions with Varèse about music. (Or, indeed, whether Varèse had seen and been influenced by any of Artaud's productions for the Alfred Jarry Theatre in its 1928–1930 seasons.) Certainly Artaud's famous 1935 production of Shelley's *The Cenci*, with loudspeakers subjecting the audience to sounds relayed from various parts of the theatre, seems to have picked up resonances of the Varèsian aesthetic.[34]

Artaud, for his part – and strikingly unlike Carpentier – appears not have known any of Varèse's own works at first hand. Yet the collaboration got under way regardless, on the strength of apparent temperamental and intellectual affinity: what Louise Varèse has acknowledged as 'their remarkable, their total agreement on ideas for the stage, as well as their warm personal sympathy for each other'.[35] In 1934, sending Varèse a copy of his play *Héliogabale où l'anarchiste couronné*, Artaud wrote that he loved Varèse's music

without having heard it. Both because hearing you talk about music has enabled me to dream of it, and because I know that with your music in revolt we shall be able to look forward again to a new state of the world.[36]

By this time composer and librettist had at least sketched an 'outline' of the text. But progress was slow, and once Varèse had returned to New York he was unable to prod Artaud – who in any case was always in poor health – into sustained action. Ouellette quotes a letter Varèse wrote in December 1935, showing that he had heard nothing from Artaud since then. He speaks of wanting to apply himself seriously to the work 'in the late spring, during my stay in Mexico', and claims 'it will be possible to have the instruments I envisage built'. Some time

---

[34] Cf. Varèse and Ribemont-Dessaignes' *Bifur* article of 1930, which in a typically Varèseian passage speaks of the elements of sound as a group which may be split up along different volumes and planes by means of loudspeakers arranged throughout the auditorium to give the sense of movement through space.

[35] 'Varèse – Artaud', p.10.

[36] Quoted in Ouellette, p.117.

after this Artaud eventually sent Varèse a libretto – or rather, a 'Stage Scenario': the form he now favoured in place of fully worked-out dialogue – entitled *Il n'y a plus de firmament* (There is no more firmament). A version of this was eventually published in Volume 2 of the posthumous Artaud *Oeuvres complètes*,[37] apparently without any awareness on the part of the editor that the text had any connexion with Varèse, whose name appears nowhere in the book!

Il n'y a plus de firmament belongs to the genre of 'subjective manifestos', with elements of political polemic, aimed at the individual rather than the mass, in which the details and movements were to be worked out in the course of production with the active collaboration of the actors. Artaud's scenario was planned in five 'movements' (one recalls at once Carpentier's remark that in 1931 *The One All Alone* was envisaged in 'seven movements'), but in fact Artaud only succeeded in completing the first four of these.

Comparisons of *Il n'y a plus de firmament* with Varèse's original manuscript scenario, and with Carpentier's account of the project, reveal manifold differences of style, approach, and orientation. For one thing, Artaud's text is considerably less coherent. Nevertheless several of the primary ideas of Varèse's conception can still be glimpsed, some of them now strangely distorted into Artaudesque fantasmata. Once again the world is in the grip of a cosmic catastrophe, interpreted by some members of the crowd as the Moon falling into the Earth, or as 'two worlds ramming one another. As if the earth had blown up in the sky'. But the identity of the communicating star is again revealed to be Sirius, and Artaud's idea of the 'great discovery' that there is no more firmament (and also, for some reason, no more Pyrenees!) seems to have been prompted by Varèse's original ideas of the 'discovery of

---

[37] Paris: Gallimard, 1961, edited by Paul Thevenin. The English translation by Victor Corti – from which I have quoted below – was published by Calder & Boyars in 1971: *Antonin Artaud Collected Works Volume Two*, pp. 79–93, with textual notes pp. 228–232. According to Ouellette this published text (called a 'Stage Synopsis' in the English edition) is a later draft – although Thevenin, presumably incorrectly, dates it to 'about 1931 or 1932' – which differs in some particulars from the scenario Varèse had received (in 1935). Nevertheless it seems to form a substantial enough basis for a discussion of Artaud's conception of the work. The Editor's comments on the manuscript and typescript sources for Artaud's text (English edition, pp.228–9) show that he was unaware of the draft Artaud had sent to Varèse, which is now in Ouellette's possession.

instantaneous radiation' and the consequent exchange of signals. Thus there are repeated announcements on a public-address system:

STUPENDOUS DISCOVERY. SKY PHYSICALLY ABOLISHED. EARTH ONLY A MINUTE AWAY FROM SIRIUS. NO MORE FIRM-AMENT. CELESTIAL TELEGRAPHY BORN. INTERPLANETARY LANGUAGE ESTABLISHED.

And later: 'The word Sirius is heard in every tone of voice and on every pitch in the scale, getting louder as they go up'.

Half-familiar characters appear. Artaud's 'Great Pointer' echoes to some extent the 'Visionary' of Carpentier's account; and the revolutionary mob of beggars, convicts, tramps and other underworld denizens whom he leads recalls the escaped prisoners of the earlier libretto. Even the reference to the stock-markets can be found, though reduced now to a single vague phrase ('Wheat's going up, gold's going down') among many miscellaneous voices in the crowd. Above all, the image of the Astronomer in his tower is still present, though in Artaud's text the character does not appear until 'Movement IV' and has now become 'the Scientist' (to be freely re-designated 'the Inventor' when other, lesser scientists are in dialogue with him), who occupies 'a gigantic metal bridge, overhanging the stage'. The concluding argument among the scientists (between 'intellectual castrati and scientific basses') makes considerable play with the idea of 'instantaneous radiation' and whether the looming disaster is the result of 'Science [coming] before everything else'. The final words of the Scientist on the Bridge, and the directions for the end of 'Movement IV', seem to connect back to Brassaï's description of Varèse's ideas for the end of the piece as a whole.

THE SCIENTIST: The Molecular grouping in Sirius is everything. These two forces, ours and theirs, had to be put in touch with one another. I have already begun signalling. There you are.

He rushes over to his apparatus.

Night comes on as the curtain falls.
The rumble of air savagely thrust back begins to well up. Sounds rush forward, made up of the blasts of several sirens at their highest point. Violent percussions intermingled.
Cold light reigns everywhere.
Everything stops.

Artaud's indications as to the use of music and instruments, though of course extremely impressionistic, must surely derive in part from Varèse's instructions, as well as from his own ideas. It should therefore be noted that tom-toms and other drum sounds are specified in 'Movement III', as are the 'Aeroplane motors' reported by Brassai. (But then, so is the playing of the *Internationale*: Artaud's text seems on the whole more overtly and bluntly 'politicized' then Carpentier's account). There are practically no musical indications in 'Movement II', but Artaud's description of the music at the opening of the whole work, in 'Movement I', is interesting for all its poeticization, and seems thoroughly imbued with the Varèsian vision of sounds moving freely in space:

... Harmonies cut short. Raw sounds. Sound blurring.

The music gives the impression of a far-off cataclysm; it envelops the theatre, falling as if from a vertiginous height. Chords are struck in the sky; they dissipate, going from one extreme to the other. Sounds fall as if from a great height, stop short and spread out in arcs, forming vaults and parasols. Tiered sounds.

These are synchronized with changing colours which become steadily more complex, 'agonizingly multi-shaded'.

The sounds and lights break up into fits and starts, jerkily, like magnified Morse, but this will be to Morse code what the music of the spheres heard by Bach is to Massenet's [sic] *Clair de Lune*.

Artaud, as noted above, seems never to have written the final 'movement' of *Il n'y a plus de firmament*; the principal manuscript ends with some notes beginning 'Suggested act in street', from which it seems possible that he contemplated the Scenario being acted in the open air. The notes also mention that 'One can act in a public square if the weather is fine, as one needs room, / or else in a hangar, a factory, a garage ...'[38] There may be some connexion here with Varèse's ideas of *The One All Alone* being presented by a travelling circus.

We simply do not know why Varèse eventually abandoned his Sirian stage-work. Possibly in one sense it was never definitively abandoned, simply laid aside while his interest was engrossed by other projects, notably the comparably ambitious (and also unachieved) *Espace*. But the lack of a libretto that was either complete or corresponded exactly

---

[38] English edition, p.93

to his grandiose yet shifting conceptions was clearly a major stumbling-block. Since Carpentier reports that a large part of the work had already been composed in 1931, it may be that Varese had hoped to adapt much of this pre-existing material to the replacement text that Artaud was to write for him – only to find, when he finally received the incomplete 'Stage Scenario', that it was too incompatible in content and style. It is, moreover, difficult to see how Artaud's aesthetic of the scenario, in which the text hardly exists before a performance and is essentially to be developed by the actors as 'moving hieroglyphs', could be reconciled to the demands of a fixed musical score. (None of Varèse's works make use of improvisation.) Such thoughts are, of course, pure conjecture. Yet compared to the vivid apocalyptic drama outlined in Carpentier's article of 1931, Artaud's scenario appears (to this writer at least) at best a sketchy and self-indulgent gloss on Varèse's original vision.

It may *not*, of course, have appeared like that to Varèse: indeed its 'modernity' and violence of language may have been more to his liking than the somewhat more traditional concepts of poetry and stagecraft that we glimpse, through the medium of Carpentier's writings, in the Carpentier-Desnos-Dessaignes collaboration. But he clearly found himself in the end unable to make use of Artaud's scenario; and after the composer's death, Louise Varèse told Carpentier that he had remained haunted by the subject – and by the 1931 libretto in which Carpentier had taken a major hand.[39]

Apparently another reason for Varèse's dissatisfaction with *Il n'y a plus de firmament* was that both the character of the astronomer and the multi-media aspects of his ideas were missing (in fact both are suggested, but only in a very vestigial form). Louise herself has written that:

... Artaud's scenario did not ... 'flesh' Varèse's idea, which, simplified, was *Mob versus Übermensch* – the kernel of thought to be hidden – metamorphosized into a new musical–theatrical art form to replace obsolete opera – a theatre spectacle of music, including chorus and movement, including his hypnotically rhythmical fear-dance, of voices, cries, exclamations, etc. Not words as commonly used like most of Artaud's dialogue. An apocalyptic drama of hate and terror ending in an apotheosis of light – a blinding blaze of light. Varèse used to say he wanted to make an

---

[39] *VV*, p.12.

audience feel the 'powerful joy' of an intense, terrifying, salutary emotion that would annihilate, at least momentarily, the personal ego ...[40]

The non-achievement of *The One All Alone* – and the subsequent disappearance of all identifiable musical materials for it (so that, as noted above, it had until recently been believed that almost nothing of the work had in fact been composed) – must rank among the greatest creative tragedies of Varèse's career. For through the various scenarios we are certainly afforded glimpses of an extraordinary vision, which might well have given birth to one of the definitive musico-theatrical works of the 20th century. That vision continued to haunt the composer, as he attempted to bring it to birth in a different form: *Espace*.

IONISATION

During 1930–31 – at the same time, therefore, as he was deep in the throes of creation of *The One All Alone* – Varèse composed *Ionisation*, for an ensemble of 13 percussionists. Indeed, given the dramatic role that percussion, and percussion-dominated dances, were intended to have in the latter stages of that huge theatre-piece, one might spare a passing thought for their possible interrelationship: was the 5-minute *Ionisation*, apparently so complete in itself, partly intended as a study for the larger work?

The 22-year-old André Jolivet, studying with Varèse during that period, was a regular witness to its creation. As he recalled in a radio interview after Varèse's death, it was mapped out bar by bar on huge sheets of music-paper of Varèse's own design. The first edition of the score bears on its final page the date 'Paris, November 14, 1931'. *Ionisation* was not, in fact, destined to be heard in Varèse's native land for many years: but it was to prove very important in the maintenance and consolidation of what little European reputation he had. He dedicated it to Nicolas Slonimsky, who conducted the first performance at Carnegie Hall, New York, on 6 March 1933. Soon afterwards Henry Cowell conducted it in San Francisco, and published the score in his New Music Orchestra Series in 1934. In that year Slonimsky, at a chaotic recording session in New York, succeeded in making a 78 rpm disc of the piece: the first work of Varèse ever to be

---

[40] 'Varèse – Artaud', p.10.

recorded. An obscure item, poorly distributed, the record nevertheless garnered significant admirers in France, notably Jean-Louis Barrault and, even more important, Jolivet's friend and contemporary Olivier Messiaen – who, after the war, made a point of analysing *Ionisation* in his master-classes for the benefit of students such as Pierre Boulez, Iannis Xenakis and Karlheinz Stockhausen. Nevertheless, the European première did not take place until the 1951 Darmstadt Festival, when it was conducted by Hermann Scherchen. A revised edition of the score was published by Ricordi in 1957.

Ionisation remains one of Varèse's most extreme statements of a conception of music only tangentially related to the past. Written almost throughout for instruments of indeterminate pitch (plus two sirens whose pitch is constantly changing in an indivisible continuum), its most patent concerns are rhythm and timbre; and, less immediately apparent but overridingly important, form. As a corollary *Ionisation* seems to renounce melody and harmony, as those terms have traditionally been understood; and – for all but a fraction of its length – specific pitch. Nevertheless one might maintain (as have Slonimsky and others) that it simply deals in wider conceptions of melody and harmony than are recognized by the Western traditions. Certainly *register* continues to be important: the 'melodic' possibilities of writing for gongs, drums or anvils of different sizes, high, medium, or low, are thoroughly exploited. And thematicism as such – the development of specific motivic entities, here primarily identifiable by their rhythmic profiles – is still very much in operation as a principal form-building agent.

The ensemble of *Ionisation* is extraordinary for its range of colour and timbre – a true 'percussion orchestra'. Yet most of its constituent instruments had featured in Varèse's earlier scores, and the ensemble is a veritable but logical summation of the composer's fascination with the possibilities afforded by this previously neglected musical resource. Altogether, the 13 players dispose of: a crash cymbal; 2 bass drums (medium and low) laid flat, plus one (very deep) upright one on which is mounted a cencerro (a cow-bell without clapper, muffled and struck with a drum-stick); 3 tam-tams (high, low and very low); gongs (medium and low), bongos (high and low); 2 tenor drums; 4 side-drums of two slightly different sizes (one of the smaller with snares relaxed); string drum (Lion's Roar); 2 slap-sticks; 2 guiros; 3 Chinese blocks (high, middle and low); claves; 2 triangles; 2 maracas (high and low); *tarole* (a very shallow, high-pitched military snare drum); suspended cymbal; hand cymbals; castanets; tambourine; 2 anvils (one higher than the other); 2 groups of sleigh bells; 2 sirens (high and low, operated by a thumb brake); and also tubular bells, a keyboard glockenspiel with resonators (commonly replaced in performance by the more familiar celesta) and a piano. Around 40 instruments: it is difficult to arrive at a logical total of sound-producing entities (are claves or maracas one instrument or two?).[41] The score comes complete with a chart provided by Morris Goldberg, percussion instructor at the Juilliard School of Music, suggesting an effective disposition for the ensemble and specifying the appearance and dimensions of the various instruments.[42]

The extraordinary variety of timbre in this ensemble is produced by the selective groupings of instruments that have reverberating membranes (the various drums); which produce wooden resonance (claves, Chinese blocks) or friction (Lion's Roar, guiros) or shaking (maracas, tambourines); also metallic sounds (triangle, cymbals, anvils, tubular bells, glockenspiel). Glissando effects ('parabolas of sound', in Varèse's own phrase) are available from the two sirens; and towards the end the piano's chords engender a tone-cluster effect, the aggregatation of the harmonics producing a bell-like sonority.

---

[41] The distinguished percussion group Les Percussions de Strasbourg have, with Varèse's sanction, often performed *Ionisation* in their own version for six players, employing all the specified instruments, with electric sirens operated by a foot pedal. The composer also authorized the substitution of Ondes Martenots, placed 'at opposite ends of the hall, if possible diagonally', for the sirens.

[42] There is nonetheless room for confusion, especially in the French nomenclature Varèse used for his various drums. In addition to the idiosyncratic *Tarole* he specifies a *Tambour Militaire*, two *Caisses roulantes* (which he translates as 'side-drum'), and two *Caisses claires* (which he calls 'snare-drum'; it is one of these that has its snares relaxed). Above, and throughout, I have translated both *Tambour militaire* and *Caisse claire* as side-drum, since these are both, generically speaking, military field or parade drums with adjustable snares, the *Caisse claire* slightly the smaller of the two. The *Caisse roulante* I translate (following Goldenberg's chart and more orthodox usage) as the tenor drum – larger than the side-drums, and without snares, resembling a small bass drum. We should also note that Varèse's *Blocs Chinois* or Chinese Blocks are rectangular wood blocks of three different pitches, not the round wood bells which are today normally called Chinese or Temple blocks, and are lower in pitch than Varèse requires.

Because of its instrumentation, *Ionisation* occupies a unique position in Varèse's output. Yet to some extent this uniqueness is more apparent than real. There is no doubt that the work grew out of the compositional approach he had been pursuing for at least the previous decade, and it points forward towards his later music – especially the electronic works, which in 1930 he was still physically unable to realize. It has also often been claimed that *Ionisation* constitutes the first, or first significant, attempt in Western music to compose a piece entirely for percussion. This is rather wide of the mark. Arguably the most important such attempt, it was by no means the first, and Varèse would have known some of the previous examples.

Percussion orchestras of various kinds are a staple feature of many non-European musical cultures: one thinks of African tribal drums, and perhaps especially the Gamelans of Bali, Java and Sumatra. According to Vivier (p.92), at the time he composed *Ionisation* Varèse knew little about these ensembles. Nevertheless one should not forget that there remained a residual French tradition of lively interest in gamelan music, traceable back to the first visit of Javanese musicians to Paris as part of the Dutch pavilion at the International Exposition of Summer 1889 – an event which famously influenced Debussy. A Balinese solo gamelan attracted much attention at the 1900 Exposition, which Varèse visited as a teenager. And in the Spring of 1931 – while Varèse was composing *Ionisation*, therefore – a large gamelan, played by a full troupe of Balinese musicians, was featured at that year's Paris Colonial Exposition. Varèse would surely have taken the opportunity to hear it – just as his erstwhile pupil Colin McPhee did, actually *en route* from New York to Bali, where he was to live for several years and begin publishing his authoritative studies of gamelan music.

Whatever possible substratum of gamelan may lie beneath *Ionisation*, the work's entire expressive stance has little or nothing to do with Oriental conceptions of music. Rather, it openly displays much more obvious connexions with aspects of South and Central American popular music: especially the extensive body of native percussion, with which Varèse had much closer and more immediate experience. During his Paris sojourn of 1929–33 Varèse was much in the company of Heitor Villa-Lobos, who kept open house on Sundays in the Boulevard Saint-Michel, and he participated with the Brazilian composer in improvisation sessions on Latin-American instruments. The guiro, cencerro, maracas, bongos and claves – all featured in

Ionisation – are South American in origin, staples of the *batucadas*, popular Brazilian dances with heavy percussion accompaniment. Alejo Carpentier, a friend and admirer of Villa-Lobos since the early 1920s, was a frequent witness to their discussions.

Villa-Lobos had 'fixed' the folk-techniques of the 'batucadas' in several of his works (the *Chôros* in particular). The ritual goes as follows: around a wooden table, under a tree, twenty or thirty folk-musicians are gathered. Each has brought along three, four, six, eight percussion instruments. They all lay them on the table. We wait. A sort of general, a Kappelmeister, turns up, armed with a whistle. Wait. Everyone expectant, tense. The whistle goes. Everyone starts. In mid-stream the players change instruments. *Muta, Da Capo, Ad libitum* ... This goes on for twenty minutes, half an hour. Suddenly, silence falls. A sudden, unbearable silence. The players look at each other, lift their instruments above their heads defiantly. The silence gets longer, becomes interminable. the whistle goes again. Off they all go. And this goes on for nights on end. [...]

What attracted Varèse to Villa-Lobos's music was the intense liveliness infused into certain of the *Chôros* by a percussion section which, in addition to the traditional western elements, had been enriched with instruments already classical in Brazil and Cuba: claves, maracas, hand drums – played with the palm, knuckles, fingertips – Indian whistles, little bells, and curious mandolins made out of armadillo hide.[43]

Varèse also consorted with many jazz musicians, making a close study of their instruments and performance techniques – though he did not share Carpentier's and Desnos's addiction at that time 'to fat Brick-Top (in the rue Fontaine), or playing records of Sophie Tucker and Vaughan de Leath'. Nor should we forget the erstwhile Futurist, Luigi Russolo, whom Varèse saw on a regular basis at this time, still perfecting various noise-producing instruments, the latest being the 'Intonarumori', which Varèse introduced at a public lecture in 1929.

Carpentier's reminiscences also report a remark Varèse made after a discussion with Villa-Lobos about rhythm. Rehearsing of one of his early string quartets, the Brazilian had told its players 'The rhythm *is* the piece'.

---

[43] VV, pp.21–3. In fact, in *Ionisation* only the bongos, claves, and maracas are new to Varèse's scores. Carpentier's 'little bells' (*grélots*) had appeared with the translation 'sleigh bells' as early as *Amériques*, and the guiro is prominent in *Arcana*.

'He's right', Varèse pointed out a little later. 'But it's not enough to speak about rhythm. Rhythm is just the constant of a given beat. We need something else. The percussion needs to speak, it needs to have its own pulsations, its own circulatory system. It has to breathe its energy into the whole orchestra – as happens in the *batucadas*'.[44]

In the Western European tradition a few examples of music for percussion alone can be discovered from as far back as the 17th century, like the elaborate *Marche pour le Carrousel de Monseigneur à Versailles* (1685) composed for two pairs of timpani by the brothers Philidor. In the first half of the 19th century Berlioz had vastly enlarged the role of the percussion in the orchestra, on the basis of practical experiment, often having instruments manufactured to his specifications, with results which are familiar in works such as the *Symphonie Fantastique*, *Grande Messe des Morts*, and *Roméo et Juliette*. Several later French composers, including Debussy, had written boldly and poetically for orchestral percussion. Stravinsky, too, had considerably enhanced its prestige: not just in *Le Sacre du Printemps* but, most notably, in *Les Noces* (composed 1914–17) – which in its final form, after several different instrumentations, emerged in 1923 as a vocal work with an accompaniment of pitched and unpitched percussion (4 pianos, xylophone, timpani, crotales, bell, various drums, tambourine, cymbals and triangle).[45]

More or less simultaneously with Stravinsky the burgeoning school of South American composers had begun making use of the rich store of native percussion instruments on their continent. Villa-Lobos's lavish employment of percussion in his early orchestral scores such as *Amazonas* and *Uiraipurú* (both 1917) is an early example.[46] By the 1920s the Mexicans Chavez and Revueltas had followed suit, and in 1930, as Varèse was composing *Ionisation*, the Cuban composer Amadeo Roldán produced his *Rítmicas* Nos.5 and 6, studies in Cuban folk rhythms for a small ensemble of percussion alone.[47] Ouellette (p.108) tends to dismiss the significance of the Roldán works. But there is a direct link between Roldán (1900–39) and Varèse, and it is

---

[44] Ibid, p.23

[45] It is worth mentioning also Stravinsky's unfinished 1919 version of *Les Noces*, with its accompaniment of pianola, 2 cimbaloms, harmonium, 3 side drums (small, medium and large), tambourine, bass drum, triangle, and 2 small suspended cymbals.

[46] In some respects these works adumbrate characteristics of *Amériques*.

to be found in the person of Alejo Carpentier – a close friend and collaborator with the Cuban composer. Carpentier recalled:

Varèse had a weakness for Latin American composers, in particular for the Cuban Amadeo Roldán, two of whose orchestral scores I possessed: *El Milagro de Anaquille* and *La Rebambaramba*, both to scenarios of my own. Did Varèse really like Roldán's music, inspired by Cuban folklore? I doubt it. [...] The only thing that interested him was the way the percussion was used – with a whole arsenal of drums (different from those of the traditional orchestra), guiros, claves, maracas and bongos, all instruments whose percussive potential filled him with wonder [...] Varèse studied the way Roldán had notated them – right hand maracas, left hand maracas, different ways of using the drums, etc.[48]

Carpentier himself, to judge by his History of Music in Cuba, attaches greater significance to Roldán's percussion *Rítmicas* than does Ouellette: partly because of the significance for him of Afro-Cuban drumming, which was the inspiration of Roldán's pieces. In such *bata* drum performances, he notes that the basic beat often

takes on the dimension of a *rhythmic mode* [...] a genuine phrase, made up of note-values and groups of values, which cover several bars when notated, prior to their acquiring a rhythmic function by dint of repetition [...] So just think of the disconcerting effect of movement, of inner palpitation, that is created by the simultaneous playing of several rhythmic modes, which end up establishing mysterious relations with each other, while still retaining a certain independence of 'plane' – and you will have some faint idea of the magic worked by certain *bata* drum performances![49]

With this folk-archetype in mind, we are perhaps better able to judge the significance of Roldán's *Rítmicas* – however modest their pretensions – as Carpentier estimated them:

In these works ... Roldán frees himself from 'documentary folklorism' and discovers, within himself, motives of genuine Afrocuban physiognomy. The

---

[47] The first four of the works Roldán called *Rítmicas* are for piano and wind instruments.

[48] VV, p.21. Carpentier's account of the interest Varèse showed in the Roldán scores is reminiscent of Henry Cowell's remark in his 1928 *Modern Music* article: 'I have frequently noticed that when Varèse examines a new score, he is more interested in the instrumentation than in the musical content, although no amount of brilliant scoring will interest him in a work in old-fashioned style.'

[49] *La musíca en Cuba* (Mexico City, 1946), pp.299–300 [translation here by James Reid-Baxter].

rhythms have ceased to be literal quotations; they are now personal visions of the traditional cells. In the two final *Rítmicas* he executes, with the self-awareness of the trained artist, a feat parallel to that of the *bata* drummers, moved purely by instinct. Rather than rhythms, he here creates rhythmic modes – whole phrases which mingle and complement each other, giving rise to periods and sequences.[50]

Perhaps Carpentier discussed the *Rítmicas* with Varèse. In any case Roldán's *La Rebambaramba* – one of the two scores which Varèse studied, presumably in 1929 or 1930 – received its première in Paris on 6 June 1931, in the first of Nicolas Slonimsky's famous 'Pan-American Concerts': the same concert that included the European première of Ives's *Three Places in New England*. The second concert, on 11 June, featured Varèse's *Intégrales*.

Other composers could easily be drawn into this discussion. It was in 1930, precisely, and in Paris, that Darius Milhaud composed his Concerto for Percussion and Orchestra. It is, moreover, highly likely that Varèse had observed the use of a large body of percussion (again, in an orchestral context) in the few scores by Charles Ives that had so far been published. Of these by far the most radical was the 'Comedy' second movement of Ives's Fourth Symphony, published as Vol.2, No.2 of Henry Cowell's New Music Edition in January 1929 (and performed two years earlier in New York under Eugene Goossens). This polyrhythmic fantasmagoria makes use of, *inter alia*, piano, celesta, triangle, high and low bells, high and low timpani, Indian drum, small and large gongs, snare drum and bass drum with cymbal. Unpublished and unperformed at that time, however, was the Symphony's finale, in which the percussion ensemble functions as a rhythmically separate entity throughout.

Nevertheless there had already been some suggestive examples of the use of a percussion ensemble on its own, as an entire musical organism. Alexander Tcherepnin's Symphony No.1, premièred in Paris in October 1927, attracted considerable attention on account of its scherzo, scored for unpitched percussion supported only by *col legno* strings. In its own terms this movement is something of a *tour de force*, reducing the thematic materials of the symphony's first movement to purely rhythmic entities. Another example, slightly earlier still, would

---

[50] Ibid., p.315.

surely have been familiar to Varèse, little though he may have thought
of it as music: the then-notorious *Ballet Mécanique* (1924) by George
Antheil. Premièred in Paris in 1926 and repeated in New York in 1927
(three months after Ives's 'Comedy' and just before the Carnegie Hall
performance of Varese's *Arcana*), this work was poorly received by the
critics, yet its *succès de scandale* solidified the young American's
reputation (however short-lived in the event) as an iconoclast and
experimenter. *Ballet Mécanique* tends to be regarded nowadays as at
best a historical curiosity; Antheil was not, perhaps, a very good
composer, but he was neither talentless nor unimaginative. His work is
strongly reliant on instruments of definite pitch, and its 'barbaric'
rhythmic ostinati and 'machine rhythms' (pretty clearly parasitic on *Les
Noces*) have nothing of Varèse's refinement and complex intricacy. Yet
in some respects it could be a significant precursor. Antheil's ensemble
– of pianolas, xylophones, glockenspiel, timpani, side-drum, tenor and
bass drums, gong, triangle, cymbal, wood-block, large and small
airplane propellors and large and small electric bells – has certain
points of contact with Varèse's: such as the use of piano clusters and,
most strikingly, the way the airplane propellors supply the glissando
element of constantly wavering pitch which Varèse required from his
sirens. (And remember that according to Brassai, Varèse was planning
to use airplane propellors in *The One All Alone*.) In Antheil's own
explanation of *Ballet Mécanique* as evoking 'the barbaric and mystic
splendour of modern civilization – mathematics of the universe in
which the abstraction of "the human soul" lives', it seems possible to
detect a not-so-distant echo of Varèse's pronouncements about his own
music.

American composers were to prove particularly adept at taking up
and developing the idea of works for percussion alone. In 1934, the
year he published *Ionisation* in his New Music Orchestral Series, Henry
Cowell completed his own *Ostinato Pianissimo* for percussion – a work,
admittedly, of a far more quietistic, Oriental cast of mind – and within
a few years was able to publish an entire volume devoted to percussion
music by American composers. This included a set of *Three Dance
Movements* for percussion and piano by William Russell, clearly
influenced by *Ionisation* even though much simpler in rhythmic
structure. Cowell's pupil John Cage employed various percussion
ensembles in many of his early works of the 1930s, culminating (if that
is the word) in 1939 with his *First Construction* (*In Metal*) for a large

percussion ensemble and the *Imaginary Landscape No.1*, which uses gramophone turntables revolving at constantly-varying speeds to obtain glissando effects not dissimilar to Varèse's sirens. More significant perhaps is the work of the Minnesota-based radical composer John J. Becker, a close associate of both Cowell and Ives and a champion for Varèse, whom he first met in 1933. Becker's *The Abongo* for dancers and 29 percussion instruments (including a large contingent of timpani) dates from that year, and he produced a further percussion-based ballet, *Vigilante*, in 1938. And reverting to Central America, one should remember the inspiring and irrepressible figure of Silvestre Revueltas – yet another mutual friend of Varèse and Carpentier – whose most spectacular employment of Amerindian percussion occurs in the dionysiac 'breaks' for four competing percussion groups, in this case combined with full orchestra, of his *La Noche de los Mayas* (1937). However, none of these earlier (or later) percussion works diminishes Varèse's originality – for, unquestionably, *Ionisation*'s origins are principally to be found in his own compositions of the previous decade.

Most obviously, Varèse's work extends the percussion writing (which had already often treated that instrumental department as a collective soloist) to be found in *Hyperprism*, *Intégrales* and, especially, *Arcana*. (It can hardly be denied that the several episodes in the latter work for the percussion ensemble alone points directly towards the general conception of *Ionisation*.) Thus, although folklore associations, which the Amerindian instruments perhaps inevitably import, do play some part in *Ionisation*'s rhythmic structure, they do not dominate it – as for instance they undoubtedly do, through dance-patterns and ostinato repetitions, in the finale of Revueltas's *La Noche de los Mayas*. But the efforts of these other composers do suggest that the artistic climate into which *Ionisation* burst was not wholly hostile or unprepared. As Varèse himself would have said, he was not essentially ahead of his time. He simply expressed his time in a far more radical and thorough-going way. What distinguished *Ionisation* from these previous attempts were (1) the much greater size and scope of Varèse's chosen ensemble, which allowed him to exploit (2) a much greater intricacy and complexity of rhythm and colour – quite as rich as in his compositions for other instrumental forces. But, as this suggests, the wide rhythmic and colouristic spectrum are not intended to balance, or compensate for, the renunciation of specific pitch: rather (3) the piece is as highly developed – and founded on much the same compositional assumptions – as Varèse's other works. Despite its unique instrumentation, *Ionisation* is very much of a piece with the rest of his output.

* * *

Thus Nicolas Slonimsky was able to discuss *Ionisation* in terms of a dialectic of two contrasted subjects – not only in the brief bar-by-bar analysis which prefaces the 1957 republication of the score, but also in a longer typescript essay only published (to the best of my knowledge) in a French version in Odile Vivier's book.[51] In the latter he goes so far as to aver that the form 'is that of a sonata-overture': a classicizing terminology which is questionable to say the least (the 'second subject' does not make its appearance until the work is half finished), and which one might have expected Varèse to reject outright – had he not himself shown some measure of approval for the essay by revising and annotating it and himself communicating it to Vivier. Vivier, however, justifiably sceptical of Slonimsky's appeal to Classical archetypes, preferred to recall Varèse's off-repeated statement that each of his works discovers its own proper form, and quoted him from another context:

There is an idea, the basis of an internal structure, expanded and split into different shapes or groups of sound constantly changing in shape, direction, and speed, attracted and repulsed by the diverse forces. The form of the work is the consequence of this interaction.[52]

Such a conception of form seems in any case far more appropriate for a work whose title derives from the realm of atomic physics. 'Ionisation' is the term for the dissociation of electrons from the nucleus of the atom and their transformation into negative or positive ions – a process involving the operation of immense natural forces within infinitesimal space. Varèse's percussion piece evokes these forces, with its propulsive currents sweeping through – and articulated

---

[51] Vivier, pp.98–100.

[52] ibid., p.97. Vivier's source for this quotation is Varèse's Notes in the catalogue of the Exposition Cadoret (New York, Galèrie Norval, November 1960); but it had already appeared in the text of the composer's 1959 lecture on 'Rhythm, Form and Content' at Princeton University, and found its way subsequently into his *Perspectives of New Music* article (Fall-Winter 1966) 'The Liberation of Sound', from which it is quoted on p.148 above. In lecture and article, the next sentence reads: 'Possible musical forms are as limitless as the exterior forms of crystals'.

by – myriad individual points of sound. The various groupings, associations, agglomerations and interrelationships which are built up from these (so to speak) sub-atomic sonic particles, produce the work's overall form – a complex form ultimately derived from extremely simple basic materials. And the first stage in the formal process is, precisely, Varèse's choice of instrumentation: for these 'particles' are the raw sounds produced by each percussion instrument, its unique characteristics, its individual timbre and modes of attack, its various appropriate beaters. These special characteristics, being fixed, cannot be renounced, and they are not: the Central American instruments retain their folklore associations, the military drums play march rhythms. But each of these given elements takes its place as a fragment in a mosaic of such over-arching scale and intricacy that their identities are subordinated to the overall design. To resume the atomic metaphor, the music's process of 'ionisation' transforms what should be untransformable – the sonic 'ions' – into something very different from the state in which we first heard them.

At one level, therefore, the music enacts the play of natural energies, pursued to their furthest level of abstraction. Yet since these minute particles in their 'mineral inanimacy'[53] are, simultaneously, the ultimate basis of life itself, the music Varèse has composed from the sound-objects supplied by *Ionisation*'s percussion ensemble seems to have for its real subject the mind and spirit of 20th-century man, able by means of his reason to impose form and structure on these innermost mysteries of the physical universe, yet still in thrall to the drives of his own unconscious. As often in Varèse's compositions, the score seems to be mediating between the wonders of the cosmos, the primal elements of creation, and the violent emotions of urban alienation, perhaps specifically on the streets of New York: the modern city as the ultimate 20th-century structure composed from individual human 'ions'.

The work's opening bars seem indeed to present a phantasmagorical cityscape or industrial landscape, a world of night and shadow. A rhythmic kick, distributed by player 3 between tenor drum and two bass drums (in itself an important motif: Ex.1), reveals a penumbra of soft metallic sounds from gongs, cymbals and snareless side-drum.

---

[53] The phrase is James Reid Baxter's, applied to *Ionisation* in his thesis on Carpentier and music.

Above this background shimmer, the voices of the sirens rise and fall in a kind of ghostly canon, while the rhythmic figure is repeated, and repeatedly transformed.

Ex.1

More instruments enter, and a snarling crescendo from the Lion's Roar brings a sudden, brusque *ff* outburst from gongs, cymbals, triangle and the deepest bass drum. Immediately a clearly-defined rhythmic theme or pattern (Slonimsky's 'first subject') strikes in on side-drum (player 4) and bongos (player 3), with subsidiary reinforcement from maracas (Ex.2).

Ex.2

In the comparative regularity of its rhythmic structure Ex.2 bears more than a passing similarity to what I called the '*marche militaire*' music in *Arcana*. As noted above, Varèse makes no attempt to deny the nature and derivation of his *tambour militaire*. The two principal elements of Ex.2, divided between side-drum (2*a*) and bongos (2*b*), go together as subject and counter-subject but are perfectly recognizable separately: each is often developed as a motif in its own right. In fact rather than pursue Slonimsky's misleading sonata terminology it would be better to consider Ex.1 and Ex.2 as two more or less equipollent 'subjects' or sound-complexes which Varèse juxtaposes, alternates, and to some extent combines as the piece proceeds. They are eventually to be joined by a third complex (Slonimsky's 'second subject'), which enables the form-building processes to be pursued with greater intricacy – but not for some time yet.

The first statement of Ex.2 is immediately followed by a brief résumé of what has taken place so far: a compressed version of the elements of the introduction (Ex.1), followed by the up-beat and opening bar of Ex.2. This now leads into an episode, with the tarole (player 9) and Chinese blocks (player 7) presenting fragmentary variants of 2*a* and *b* respectively against other percussion (such as castanets, player 11) in a predominantly triplet rhythm. A point to note here is that though the contributions of tarole and Chinese blocks (given as Ex.3) are indeed 'variants' of Ex.2 elements in the sense that their rhythms are similar and the instruments are operating in something of the same relationship, the correspondence is by no means exact – they establish their own forms of the motivic rhythms. Indeed practically every instrument in the ensemble develops its own 'rhythmic signature' through which it proclaims its identity – though as we shall see, such characteristics may quickly be exchanged with or appropriated by other instruments. These 'signatures' tend to involve smaller note-values (more rapid attacks) the higher the pitch of the instrument, and longer ones (slower attacks) the lower: thus in Ex.3 the rhythms are to some extent diminutions of the Ex.2 forms, the tarole and Chinese blocks coming higher in the pitch spectrum than the side-drum and bongos. The combinations side-drum/bongos (plus maracas) and tarole/blocks (plus castanets) are examples of instrumental and timbral relationships which, once established, remain fairly constant throughout *Ionisation* but which progressively ramify to establish connexions and associations with yet other instrumental groupings, eventually involving the entire ensemble.

Ex.3

Ex.2 itself now returns, with some added emphasis from the whip, and the texture enlarges to take in an increasing number of instruments – the tarole and Chinese blocks, the guiro (player 6) and maracas (player 8), sharing another rhythmic variant of 2*b*, and others playing softly in both duple and triple rhythms. Meanwhile the most prominent players swap functions: player 3's bongos now imitate the rhythmic profile of 2*a*, while player 4, playing side-drum and tenor drum together (to obtain 'high' and 'low' pitches), imitates that of 2*b*.

An intrusive bar of 2/4+3/8, concentrated in tarole, sleigh bells and castanets suddenly breaks up the prevailing 4/4 time and concludes with player 7 giving a dactylic rhythmic flick across the three Chinese blocks from high to low. A further variant of Ex.2, its rhythms becoming steadily more simplified on bongos, side-drums and maracas, has for tail-piece a variant of the blocks' three-impact figure, on claves and maracas; and this leads to further rhythmic-textural development which the Chinese blocks (heard against guiro, bongos and suspended cymbal) conclude by supplying a rhythmic tattoo that swiftly becomes a stream of rapid quintuplets (a foretaste of the third sound-complex). There is, at this point – Fig.6, 32 bars into the work – a clear sense of a structural division. In its basic elements, the uncanny and startling sound-world of *Ionisation* has now been fully evoked: from wood, metal and skin, from dance and march, from jazz and machine, from stars and concrete. Now it is to be briefly but thoroughly explored.

What occurs next is an episode of free development which is also an intensification of the music's sense of suppressed violence and directed rhythmic power. It starts off with a variety of 'military' rhythms (all of which could be regarded as variants from Ex.2) in the various side-drums and bass drums, with maracas and loud rim-shots on the tarole much to the fore. Simultaneously the high siren adds its minatory whine and the rasp of the guiro, like the wing-case of some enormous exotic insect, dryly pierces the accumulated textures. Elements of the opening sound-complex Ex.1 are thus being infiltrated into material deriving from Ex. 2. This leads swiftly to the loudest music we have yet heard – an explosive *ff* outburst, in rhythmic unison throughout the ensemble, combining wood and metal instruments in an extremely hard sonority and developing the triplet figures which have been encountered at various points so far (Ex. 4). Here again one senses the presence of subject and countersubject: the battering triplets are a development of 2*b*, and the more complex tattoo of the tarole and castanets a form of 2*b* – but mediated through their 'rhythmic signatures' established in Ex. 3.

Ex. 4

(Slonimsky's analysis in the published score merely refers to Ex.4 as 'a sudden outburst of sonority'. In his longer essay as communicated by Odile Vivier, he remarks that this 'climax of sonority is attained at the middle of the work, 37 bars after the beginning, and concluding 41 bars before the end.'[54] The structural position of this sudden climax is even more intriguingly central than Slonimsky suggests. Leaving aside *Ionisation*'s 17-bar coda – which because of its instrumentation and the use of fixed pitch is clearly distinct from the rest – the principal, 'unpitched' portion of the work is 74 bars long; and as Slonimsky notes Ex.3 breaks out precisely in the middle of that span, at the beginning

---

[54] Vivier, p.99.

of bar 38. The music before and after that point is not, however, barred in exactly the same way; there are some compound bars and the second group of 37 sees more frequent changes of time-signature. Yet if we regard the crotchet of the opening 4/4 bar as *Ionisation's* basic unit of pulse, bars 1–37 contain a total of 146 crotchets, and bars 38–71 also 146 crotchets; the first impact of Ex.3, falling on the 147th crotchet beat, thus appears *exactly* at the mid-point of the work's principal span.)

The dynamics of this climactic passage rise in a crescendo effected by military rhythms in side-drums, tenor drum and tarole, leading to a 5/8 bar in which these drums and the Chinese blocks recall in their loudest terms what I called the 'rhythmic flick' motif, which is assuming an important role as a punctuator of events. This is followed immediately, and at the same intense dynamic level, by the introduction of a new element in a massive unison statement, dominated by complex quintuplet rhythms: Ex.5. This is the third of *Ionisation's* main sound-complexes, starkly delivered by five players in unison on bongos, side-drums, Chinese blocks, maracas and tarole: in Slonimsky's terms the 'second subject'.

Ex.5

This rhythmic theme is punctuated both by continuing triplet figures in cencerros (players 1 and 2) and tenor and bass drums (player 3 – the latter clearly a form of his motif in Ex.1), and by the growls of the Lion's Roar (player 5) – always coinciding with player 3's Ex. 1 variant, and reinforced by castanets, cymbals, tambourine and the deepest Chinese block). The cumulative texture is at once shattering and grotesque, a superb example of Varèse's sonic imagination at its boldest and wierdest.

From now on the myriad elements from which the music has been woven are brought into multiple, and ever more abrupt, collisions and juxtapositions. In another clear structural turning-point, the 'second subject' – and with it the whole 'central climax' – is broken off as unexpectedly as it erupted. The air is suddenly filled with metallic sonorities, and specifically those of instruments that were not involved in the climax at all. A rhythmic tapping on the anvils from player 12 (their first entry in the work, and surely a sly reference to the dwarfs of Nibelheim in *The Ring*!) counterpoints syncopated attacks on gong, tam-tams, cymbals and triangle, with the two sirens in a kind of wailing counterpoint of dynamics: the high siren managing two crescendo-diminuendo parabolas to the low siren's one.[55] The whole passage can be considered a variation on the opening sound-complex Ex.1, but with the omission of player 3's rhythmic drum figure.

Ex. 6

---

[55] The sirens are always louder the higher they rise in pitch.

There now ensues a violent and dynamic development, principally of varied forms of the different elements of the second complex, Ex.2, and involving the entire percussion ensemble. Side drums, bass drums, maracas and Chinese blocks are much to the fore, but the syncopated 'background noise' of gongs and cymbals continues, and so do the eerie sonic curvatures of the sirens and the rhythmic interjections of the anvils (see Ex.6).

Here we can see new relationships being formed between instruments of skin, wood and metal, the 'military' rhythms of the side-drum and tarole being imitated – but with an individual rhythmic augmentation – by the anvils, while the 'countersubject' takes on three simultaneous rhythmically related forms in bongos, maracas and triangle, and the staggered attacks of the gongs and tam-tams (player 2) are mimicked by the group of tarole, caisse claire and suspended cymbal (player 9).

The whole passage forms a general crescendo, leading to a single climactic *fortissimo* attack on the metal instruments. This is immediately followed by the irruption of Ex.7 – a heavy, pounding figure on the membranes of all the bass drums, with support from tambourines and castanets: and a clear development of the work's introductory motif from Ex.1.

Ex.7

A brief snatch of *pianissimo* textures from other instruments leads to an immediate repetition of the pulverising Ex.7 and then, carried through on the voice of the Lion's Roar, a resumption of development of Ex.2 offshoots. If we were following Slonimsky's 'sonata' model, the next few bars could be interpreted as an extremely concise recapitulation, for what happens after them has to be considered the work's coda. Thus for three bars the 'first subject' *2a* reappears on side-drum, but with its 'countersubject' *2b* turned into a elaborate heterophony of rhythmic variations in bongos, Chinese blocks, anvils, castanets and maracas. (In fact, if we think of these bars more as a further development of Ex.2 as 'sound-complex', we are more likely to be impressed by the heterophony as such, with seven independent rhythmic lines being heard simultaneously.) And at the same time this passage is clearly a continuation of the previous development, for the sycopated gong and cymbal attacks continue, and the sirens return, finally attaining unanimity and swelling out to an urgent *ff*, suddenly cut short.

As the echoes fade the heterophony is suddenly replaced by an instrumental solo from player 9: the tarole strikes in, still urgent but *pianissimo*, with its 'personal' variant of 2*a* as seen in Ex.3. We might expect the Chinese blocks to follow, as in Ex.3, but the tarole, with support from player 12's snare drum, takes over the blocks' figure itself. A further *ff* outburst now combines forms of Ex.7 with the characteristic quintuplet rhythms of the 'second subject' Ex.5. The low siren takes off on an ascending curve while loud but unanimous attacks, in a suddenly slower tempo (crotchet=52; up till this point the work has been at a uniform crotchet=69), break out in gong, tam-tams and bass drum.

It takes a moment or so for the slower tempo to register on the listener's consciousness, and the realization to dawn on ears and mind that the work's crucial event has been reached: we are hearing sounds of definite pitch. The piano (player 13) has joined in, first with a huge forearm cluster and then with articulated pitches, doubled by players 10 and 11 on the tubular bells and keyboard glockespiel. Together they produce a repeating pattern of harmonies, typically Varèsian in their wide span and intervallic content (Ex.8).

Ex.8

A transformation has taken place in the way that we hear music. We have become so acclimatized to the indefinite pitch of the percussion ensemble that these tolling, bell-like sounds, saturating a large portion of the chromatic spectrum, have a stunning effect.[56] They fall upon the ear almost with the force of a revelation, as a rebirth of defined tone. So dramatic is this stroke that it is easy to read into it a hint of almost religious solemnity (and Slonimsky has likened this concluding section of the work to a final chorale). Yet the revelation is ambiguous. Whereas before *Ionisation* seemed to be taking place in a free, 'unbounded' space, there is suddenly once more an up and down, a horizontal and vertical.

As the chordal complexes of Ex.8 sound over and over again, syncopated against rapidly-changing time-signatures, fragments of the previous music continue to make themselves heard – Ex.1's background of gongs and cymbals, short variants of Ex.2 in side drum, tarole and bongos, rhythmic flicks from the Chinese blocks, the rise and fall of the sirens. Unlike these fragments – all in their way dynamic, rhythmically active, capable of fissile interaction, combination or metamorphosis – the harmonies of Ex.8 remain static, deliberately witholding harmony's own mode of movement, which is modulation. On one hand the effect is of a calming-down of the riotous energies we have previously experienced. On the other, the percussion music seems to be diminished and subordinated as if to a gravitational force: no longer able to be experienced on its own but only in relation to a chordal complex that functions like a multi-layered pedal-point. That may indeed be the intended effect – just as the particles dispersed by the process of ionisation are reintegrated by the gravity operating within the nucleus of the atom itself. And indeed in relative rather than specific pitch terms the chordal complex opens up a wider pitch spectrum than anything we have hitherto experienced from the unpitched percussion alone – from the deepest gong and lowest piano bass to the highest register of the glockenspiel.

---

[56] The pitched instruments are not the only new arrivals. We are also hearing for the first time the 'Grand Tam-tam *très profond*', the deepest of all the gong family, which adds an extra, chasmic resonance to the ensemble. Its attacks (by player 12) are co-ordinated with the two smaller tam-tams, the gong and bass drum (from players 1 and 2). The predominant gongs/bells sonority makes these closing bars perhaps the only portion of *Ionisation* which might claim a direct influence from Gamelan music.

The integration of the fragments of Ex.1 and Ex.2 – that is, of the work's two main 'sound-complexes' – into the harmonic context provided by Ex.8's chordal pedal-point seems to give notice that the cycle is complete. And the music starts to ebb away, energy draining out of it. The dynamics fade; the sirens tail off in a final decrescendo; player 4's side-drum beats its way irregularly into silence, accompanied as ever by the bongos of player 3; the bell-like chords of Ex.8 leave their overtones hanging in the air. Swiftly, the whole ensemble dissolves into silence. The last 'thematic' elements we hear are disconnected splinters of Ex.2 (and one tiny allusion from player 4 to the quintuplet rhythms of the third sound-complex, Ex.5). The very last sounds are the upper components of Ex.8, *pp*, then a *ppp* attack on player 12's very low tam-tam, and finally a *pppp* touch from player 9 on a suspended cymbal – the whole under a long fermata which allows everything to dissolve into nothingness, back into its nocturnal mystery. The lights go out; the city sleeps.

8 · Path of the lightning

Do not abandon us,
Spirit of the Sky,
Spirit of the Earth.
Give Life, Give Life!
– from the text of *Ecuatorial*

CHRONOLOGY 1933–34

1933 *6 March: Slonimsky conducts the première of* Ionisation *in New York. In April he performs it in Havana, Cuba, where the work is so well received it has to be immediately encored. Varèse begins composing* Ecuatorial. *3 August: he abandons Paris, frustrated and disappointed. With Jolivet he visits Catalonia; in Barcelona he meets, among others, Joan Miró and Roberto Gerhard. He then travels via Madrid to Vigo, where he joins Louise aboard the liner* De Grasse. *27 September: they arrive back in New York and decide to settle there again after considering and declining Diego Rivera's offer of a house in Mexico. (The offer is taken up instead by Leon Trotsky, who is murdered in that house by Stalin's agents in 1940.) Varèse has several meetings with Harvey Fletcher, but without concrete results.*

1934 *15 April: Slonimsky conducts the première of* Ecuatorial *at a Pan-American Association concert in New York. Varèse unable to wrest a libretto out of Artaud.*

E*cuatorial*, for a bass voice (in its later version, a unison chorus of basses), 4 trumpets, 4 trombones, piano, organ, 2 Theremins (later, Ondes Martenots) and percussion, was composed during 1933–1934. The work – dedicated 'To L. V.' (Louise Varèse) – is a setting of an invocation from the *Popul Vuh* (The Book of Counsel), the most notable of the surviving sacred texts of the now-vanished civilization of the Maya Quiché of Central America: often referred to as the Maya 'Bible'. The original codex of the *Popul Vuh* in the Quiché language has in fact long been lost, and the text is extant only in a transcription and Spanish translation made at the beginning of the 18th century by the priest named in the preface to Varèse's score as 'Father Jimines'.[1] However, Varèse presumably first discovered the supplicatory prayer in *Leyendas de Guatemala* – a collection of poetic reworkings of his country's legends, from both the Indian and Spanish traditions, by the Guatemalan poet, novelist and essayist Miguel Ángel Asturias (1899–1974).

Asturias (who was eventually to win the 1967 Nobel Prize for Literature) was a half-Indian *mestizo*, and as a student had taken part in the overthrow of one right-wing dictatorship in Guatemala, only to have to flee his native country with the arrival of the next one. During a decade in Paris he had studied the mythology and culture of the American Indians at the Sorbonne under the leading Maya scholar Georges Reynaud, himself the author of a French translation of the *Popul Vuh*. Asturias became one of Varèse's circle of friends in Paris during 1928–33. Probably Varèse knew his searing political novel *El Señor Presidente*, an almost hallucinatory evocation of the horrors of the Guatemalan dictatorship, which at that time circulated in typescript, unable to be published until 1946.

However, in view of the substratum of Amerindian myth underlying the conception of *The One All Alone*, there could well be wider ramifications to Varèse's association with Asturias – who was coming to see himself as a literary spokesman for his Mayan ancestors and for their mythic modes of thought as expressions of the subconscious, opposed to the limitations of European rationalism. It was in Surrealism, with its emphasis on the analysis and exploitation of

---

[1] The Dominican Friar Francisco Ximénez carried out this work in 1701–3 while priest of the parish of Chichicastenango. His manuscript transcription and translation is preserved in the Newberry Library in Chicago.

dream material (enthusiastically promulgated by Varèse's collaborator Robert Desnos) that Asturias was discovering the techniques which would enable him to explore the Amerindian mind. His later works would include the novel *Hombres de maiz* (Men of Maize, 1949), an epic tale of the rebellion of an Indian tribe against the desecration of their mountain home by Europeans (remember Varèse's childhood opera *Martín Paz* and, indeed, *Ecuatorial* itself!), while his posthumously-published literary testament *Tres de cuatro soles* is a reinterpretation of the Maya-Aztec creation myth of the Four Suns (which Carpentier had seen as an important element in *The One All Alone*, cf. p.228 above).

In 1932 – the year that Asturias gave public expression to his admiration for *Arcana*, in an article written after that work's Paris première – he presented Varèse with the French translation of his *Leyendas de Guatemala*, equipped with a preface by Paul Valéry, and a handwritten dedication in Spanish 'to Edgar Varèse, master magus[2] of sounds'. This clearly supplied the spark from which *Ecuatorial* took fire; and Varèse's knowledge of Spanish was sufficient for him to use Fr. Ximénez's original text, making some slight cuts and elisions.[3]

As he worked on the score Varèse came to conceive the vocal part in terms of an artist he knew personally and immensely admired: the renowned Russian bass Fyodor Chaliapin with his immensely powerful voice. Chaliapin even agreed to take part in the first performance, but in the event this proved impossible and the singer at world première – given on 15 April 1934 at a Pan-American Association of Composers Concert in New York Town Hall under the baton of Nicolas Slonimsky – was Chase Boromeo, whose voice had to be amplified by means of a hand-held megaphone. This solution was not a success, and *Ecuatorial* then languished unperformed for 25 years. When the second performance finally took place in New York in 1961, Varèse substituted a chorus of basses for the single voice, and Ondes Martenots for the Theremins. The work has since sometimes been performed with a single (electronically amplified) bass soloist, while keyboard synthesizers are occasionally substituted for the Ondes

---

[2] In Spanish, *maestro mago* – the term recurs in the text of *Ecuatorial*: 'Maestros magos, dominatores, poderosos del Cielo'.

[3] In 1937, completing the circle, Asturias published his own Spanish version of the *Popul Vuh*, based not on Ximénez but on Georges Raynaud's French translation.

Martenot. It was also in 1961 that *Ecuatorial* (in the version for chorus and Ondes) was eventually published by Ricordi in New York.[4]

In a note prefixed to the published score of *Ecuatorial*, Varèse stated that the text he had chosen from the *Popul Vuh*

... is part of the invocation of the tribe lost in the mountains, having left the 'City of Abundance'.[5] The title is merely suggestive of the regions where pre-Colombian art flourished. I conceived the music as having something of the same elemental rude intensity of those strange, primitive works. The execution should be dramatic and incantatory, guided by the imploring fervour of the text ...

Apropos the title, Varèse also wrote to Odile Vivier that '*Ecuatorial* was a title that had a fairly geographical connotation ...'. It ought perhaps to be remarked that the title was not original to Varèse. As he must certainly have been aware, his Chilean friend Vicente Huidobro had published a volume of poetry entitled *Ecuatorial* in 1918.

One aspect of the text, however, is especially significant in view of our discussion of *The One All Alone* in the preceding chapter, and of the fact that Ecuatorial was the first major work to emerge after the dissolution of Varèse's collaboration on that project with Carpentier and Desnos. For what he has chosen to set is an invocation to Dawn, an imploration for the Sun to rise. Thematically linked as this is to one of the principal images in *The One All Alone* – the sun's failure to appear anywhere over the earth – it suggests that *Ecuatorial* has its roots in the same creative idea, and perhaps even makes use of musical material that Varèse had originally intended for his visionary stage-work. To Vivier he gave a slightly different gloss on the notes for performance: 'It should be performed as a drama and an incantation'.

The ritualistic and hieratic dimension of *Ecuatorial* is implicit in the austerity of its instrumentation. The music is rooted in the ceremonious

---

[4] The version for solo voice was recorded in 1972 for Nonesuch records, with the bass Thomas Paul as soloist, under the direction of Arthur Weisberg. Kent Nagano, for Erato and Riccardo Chailly, for Decca, have more recently recorded it thus, so this form appears finally to be establishing itself.

[5] The Quiché nation, though part of the great Mayan civilization of Mesoamerica, did not inhabit the lowlands of the Yucatan peninsula but lived further to the south, in the mountainous regions of what is now Guatemala. Their capital Utatlán (now Santa Cruz del Quiché) was the most powerful city in the Maya highlands before its destruction by the Spanish conquistadors in 1524.

brass of trumpets[6] and trombones, and a percussion ensemble whose constitution – even though it requires six players – is unexpectedly limited for a work composed in the wake of *Ionisation*. Surprisingly, no Amerindian instruments are used at all, and Varèse employs instead an essentially 'European' body of timpani, 2 snare drums, 2 tenor drums, 3 bass drums of various sizes, 2 tam-tams, gong, suspended cymbal, tambourine and temple blocks.[7] There is no attempt, therefore, to annexe *Ionisation*'s kaleidoscopic range and subtle gradations of timbre. *Ecuatorial*'s sonorities are craggy, hewn from bold primary colours, and though the percussion has an important role to play, the main interest is often centred elsewhere. Much of the work's special character is owed to the way Varèse handles the three different varieties of keyboard instrument – the piano, the organ, and the Theremins or Ondes. It is these which give the work its special flavour of exotic, incantatory fantasy: not only on their own account but in the way they mediate between the other elements of the ensemble.

Apart from its brief appearance in *Ionisation*, the piano had not featured in a published work of Varèse since *Un grand sommeil noir* in 1906. Though it often sounds in *Ecuatorial* as a kind of anti-harp, or a hard-toned kithara, much of the piano writing is essentially percussive, and indeed it often operates in close collaboration with the percussion – most of all with the timpani, whose role is frequently melodic. To some extent this piano/timpani axis foreshadows aspects of the instrumentation of a much later score, namely *Déserts*.

The organ, which appears here for the one and only time in Varèse's printed works (it features briefly, more or less transformed, in his electronic ones), also performs a multiple function. To some extent, as other commentators have noted, it substitutes for the body of woodwind we might normally expect in a Varèse ensemble work. But it is also used in consort with the Theremins, which extend its upper range. And it is, moreover, important in its own right. The organ was an instrument Varèse knew well, above all from his choral conducting, and he admired the work of several modern organ-builders. According to Odile Vivier, Varèse shunned the idea of performing *Ecuatorial* with

---

[6] Varèse actually calls for three different kinds of trumpet – a high D trumper, one in C and two in B flat – though this is not specified in the published score, and all four are written at sounding pitch.

[7] These are the round wood blocks which are today often called 'Chinese blocks', rather than the rectangular 'Chinese blocks' specified in *Ionisation*.

an ordinary concert-hall organ or an electric organ: his ideal was a good church organ. That notion presupposes a certain kind of acoustic for the work (and suggests that Varèse was not unhappy to see it invested with religious associations in its place of performance). And the acoustic consequences do not stop there, for the instrument itself imposes another condition. It is significant that Varèse, while specifying in a note to the score that effects such as the *vox celesta* and *vox humana* 'should never be used' (no doubt because of their cheap associations), leaves the general choice of stops to the organist and conductor. In the nature of the instrument, many of these choices will involve octave doublings – which up to now have generally been foreign to Varèse's mature harmonic idiom. In fact, although much of the material of *Ecuatorial* is woven from close-knit chromatic cells, such basic, 'primitive' intervals of the octave and the fifth begin to assume importance once more, emphasizing the work's roots in an ancient culture.

With the Theremins, Varèse was finally composing for an actual electronic instrument of the kind he had long dreamed about, with capabilities which differed considerably from the traditional constituents of the orchestra. Like many other musicians Varèse had become fascinated by the possibilities of the Theremin, or Thereminvox, which possessed a pure soprano-like tone yet had a range of about six octaves, and was operated by the movement of the player's hands in the air in proximity to two antennae, one vertical and one horizontal. Created and developed in Petrograd during the Russian Civil War by the musician-inventor Leon Theremin (1896–1993), this revolutionary new device was first demonstrated by him in the early Soviet period. He first came to America in 1928, and gave a demonstration at the Metropolitan Opera House in New York. Although Theremin's recital repertory largely consisted of arrangements of classical and popular works, both Soviet and American composers were inspired to write for his instrument. Joseph Schillinger's *First Airphonic Suite* for Theremin and orchestra was premièred in 1929, and Henry Cowell's *Rhythmicana* Concerto (for another of Theremin's inventions, the Rhythmicon) was well under way before Varèse – whose history of interest in prototype electronic instruments now extended over 20 years – began work on *Ecuatorial*.[8] For the first performance of his new work, he commissioned Theremin to build two instruments to his personal specifications in order to extend

---

[8] For more details of Theremin's carer and the operating principle of his instrument see Stephen Montague, 'Rediscovering Leon Theremin' in *Tempo No.177*, June 1991.

the available range, especially in the higher registers. Unlike the standard Theremin – whose player never actually touched the instrument – the model constructed for Varèse possessed a keyboard, with a range extending an octave and a fifth above the highest C of the piano, capable of producing sounds up to 11,500 cycles per second. The fate of these instruments after the première seems to be unrecorded. Late in life Varèse still regarded the substitution of the Ondes Martenot, a more widespread and convenient instrument, as a somewhat unfortunate compromise: its timbre, he felt, lacked the raw power and freshness he desired for *Ecuatorial*'s sound-world. Another of the Theremin's attractions must have been the way it afforded him an unbroken continuum of sound: and the swooping glissandi he composed for it are in one sense a logical development of his writing for sirens in *Ionisation*.

But the Theremin, unlike the siren, was capable of true and complex melodic lines – as is the Ondes Martenot. In the ensuing description of *Ecuatorial* I shall refer for consistency only to 'the Ondes', since they are the instruments that stand in the published score. But the original conception with Theremins should not be forgotten. These instruments (whether Theremins, Ondes, or indeed in some recent performances keyboard synthesizers) play a very significant role in *Ecuatorial*, both singly and together. Their intermittent co-operation with the organ, to form a single sound-entity with a vastly extended upper register, has already been

mentioned; but they mediate in several different directions, depending on the many different kinds of music they are given – towards the trumpets, towards the voices (a 'soprano' tone to balance the basses), and sometimes, in their lower registers, towards the percussion. Though they are essentially melody instruments Varèse is able, by using a pair, to write harmony for them, and contrapuntal lines; and he seems acutely conscious of the 'vocal' qualities that can be wrung from them. It is in *Ecuatorial* that we first encounter the high, agonized cries which, by human or electronic means, will resound so disturbingly in *Etude pour Espace*, *Déserts*, *Poème Électronique* and *Nocturnal*. But whereas in *Nocturnal* the soprano solo sounds as a voice of individual consciousness against the collective of the chorus of basses, in Ecuatorial, whose bass chorus part was originally for a solo voice, the 'electronic sopranos' of the Ondes are rather an element in the encircling cosmology of sound, like fantastic bird- or monkey-spirits of the tropical forest of the Guatemalan highlands.[9]

Ecuatorial opens with a very substantial instrumental introduction, occupying about a fifth of the entire work. The first sound we hear is a high octave C♯ from the piano, bestowing additional, bell-like resonance upon the initial tone of a shard of descending chromatic scale. This opening (Ex.1) is mysterious, fragmented, and also as yet inchoate, an untapped potentiality. Essentially it is a single chromatically-descending line, its semitonal decline enlivened by tritone intervals, then thirds, to encompass 11 tones of the chromatic scale – but split up, between piano and trumpets, in a species of *Klangfarbenmelodie*, into an exchange of discrete, cellular solos that sound like independent motifs. Soon the piano reshapes its initial entry into a close-knit 3-note bass figure, a kernel for future growth.

With the first scattering of soft rhythmic sounds among the percussion, the rest of the ensemble begins to stir to life, and the music (so far confined, in Ex.1, to a fairly narrow band of middle register) begins to expand, to define and fill the potentially enormous acoustic space available to *Ecuatorial*'s specialized instrumentation. About half the trumpets and trombones essay a muted fanfare-anacrusis to a held G♯ which the piano resonates in rapid repeated notes (mimicked by

---

[9] In which context we might recall the song of the enchanted bird of the Amazon forest, the *Uirapuru*, impersonated in Villa-Lobos's symphonic poem of that name by the primitively amplified 'violinophone' – a violin with a resonating horn attached.

flutter-tongue in trumpet 4). Quiet tritone chords in trombones and timpani introduce a subterranean organ entry, harmonizing the descending chromatic cell from Ex.1 in parallel tritones (see Ex.1*b*). From these low-lying sounds the hammered G♯ resumes, and a sudden convulsion – G♯'s leaping up and down the octaves in piano, trumpets and organ – brings the first, dramatic entry of the Ondes: sounding from on high, at full volume, Ondes 1 with the swooping glissando that is one of these instruments' trademarks. At this first appearance they associate with the trumpets; their mingled voices sustain the resulting dissonant harmony in a long diminuendo while the percussion body increases in number and rhythmic definition.

As the sound of the Ondes dies away the organ initiates an immediate dive back into the depths for a further glimpse of Ex.1*b*. At once, however, trombones and trumpets rear up in a fanfare that climbs towards a re-entry of the Ondes. They swoon dramatically down from the top of their register (the interval spanned, a glissando of a minor ninth, is one of their characteristic signatures) and merge with the higher sonorities of the organ, which itself rapidly precipitates the melos downward again to its lowest pedals – the entire dizzying plunge spanning a vast gamut of seven and a half octaves. This touches off an angry exclamation in bare octave doubling on the organ manuals, which extends into another brass fanfare (now in octaves like the organ) on trumpets and trombones. The whole swift vertiginous process is shown in Ex.2.

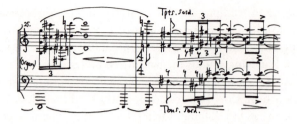

The music begins to assume shape and scale through the abrupt juxtaposition of colouristic blocks – trumpets, trombones, percussion, ondes, organ, piano – each with characteristic motivic forms of its own, and defining a different level of the musical space, from very high to very low, often with dramatic oppositions of loud and soft dynamics also. As the tempo suddenly doubles (from ♩= 60 to ♩= 120) the mood becomes more excited and momentary associations begin to form between the discrete instrumental elements. Ex.3 shows some of them: piano with timpani, trombones with organ, then piano and organ, their harmonies echoed by the brass. Each doubling accentuates a motif while modifying its timbre. Among the most important figures are the bass figure *x* of fourths and tritones, and the insistent brass fanfare on a single pitch approached by a snarling chromatic anacrusis. These motifs, and ones very similar to them, will recur and vary themselves throughout the work.

As these materials are developed, the music accumulates both tension and momentum, and the textures fill out as more of the instrumental elements come together to extend the range of gesture. At bar 46 a development of the fanfare seen at the start of Ex.2 builds up on piano, organ, and full brass, the percussion joining in two bars later (as the tempo suddenly broadens again) in an angry tutti, with Ex.1*b* developed in trombones and piano. Only the Ondes are absent from this tutti, and even as it dies away they re-enter in a lyrical contrapuntal duet, tinged with exotic fantasy. Partly supported by some piano doublings and underpinned by soft triplet rhythms in percussion, this is by far the longest melodic statement we have yet heard from any instrument (Ex.4).

The Ondes' mysterious song raises the tension further. As the tempo increases once more (to ♩=80), the organ slams in with a development of its octave exclamation from Ex.2, touching off – with piano and full brass – the biggest fanfare yet. As shown in Ex.5, below, the trombones rise and fall majestically; then as the snare drum and bass drum press forward urgently, and the fanfare-figure from Ex.3 returns on a solo trombone, a *staccatissimo* muted trumpet whips up the excitement and suddenly, with the blazing grandeur of an equatorial sunrise, the bass voices enter as part of a massive tutti that is (literally) rooted in the powerfully archaic sonority of bare octaves and fifths (Ex.5, p.274).

The effect – even without the first trumpet's sensational ascent to a screaming high D – is almost as shocking as it is impressive: the rhythmic and harmonic unanimity, spread over such a vast space and given such a powerful gravitational pull by means of the intervals themselves, creates a wholly unanticipated effect of cadence, of sudden

Ex.5

immovable tonal certitudes. This vibrant harmony of fifths is, as it were, the very earth out of which the music has arisen, from which it has been able to grow into its multifarious chromatic shapes; and from that earth the the great Mayan 'Invocation from the *Popul Vuh*' now lifts its voice to the skies.

Although, as previously noted, the original conception of *Ecuatorial* as a work for solo voice seems never entirely to have been set aside, the version for massed chorus of basses has always seemed to me more appropriate to both music and text. The 'Invocation' is a collective prayer, by or on behalf of the whole tribe. Varèse's setting, both in its drama and its ritualistic and hieratic character, enhances that sense, which is further inherent in the solidity of tone and sonority a large choir can bring to bear on an already weighty passage like its entrance in Ex.5. But as the work proceeds we will find that he treats the single austere melodic line of his unison chorus of bass voices with exceptional variety and inventive power, spanning a huge tessitura (from E♮ below the bass stave to the F♯ above the stave); specifies many different kinds of tone-colour and attack; requires the execution of large glissandi, of quarter-tones, of spoken or half-spoken rhythmicized passages; and intersperses the text with sonorous vocables of his own devising. This range of musical means corresponds to the kaleidoscopic range of emotions evoked by the text, the terrors and exaltations of a corporate soul bound up with the elemental forces of the natural world.

As already mentioned, *Ecuatorial* was first composed with the deeply expressive and versatile voice of Chaliapin in mind, and in transferring his solo line to a chorus Varèse retained strong feelings about the quality and characterization of the voices. '... Above all, not church choristers,' he wrote to Odile Vivier on 13 September 1961, stressing the 'incantatory declamation which the text demands (Calvinist choirs please abstain) ... as singers, one ought to have Spaniards, or even blacks – peoples who have a good sense of drama and who devote themselves, or Russians!'[10]

Oh, constructores, oh formadores,	O Builders, o Moulders!
vosostros veis, vosostros estuchais,	You see. You hear.
no nos abandonais,	Do not abandon us,
espiritu del cielo,	Spirit of the Sky,
espiritu de la tierra.	Spirit of the Earth.
Dadnos nuestra descendencia,	Give us our descendants,
nuestra posteridad	our posterity,
mientras hai dias	as long as there are days,
mientras hai albas	as long as there are dawns
que numerosos sean los verdes caminas,	May green roads be many,
las verdes sendas	the green paths
que vosotros nos dias.	you give us.

Almost throughout, the vocal line is doubled at the unison by some element of the ensemble; and these doublings serve not merely for support and maintenance of pitch but as a dynamic reinforcement against the clamorous, barbaric intrumental surroundings and, most important of all, a further means of varying and transforming the tone-colour. The doubling of the grandiose first entry, 'Oh constructores', is shared between the organ and Ondes 1 in its lowest register, so that the voices literally pulse with an electric tension. They continue with similarly broad and sustained music, against insistent drum-rhythms, until they reach 'No nos abandonais'. Here they

---

[10] Vivier, p.107.

divide: the words are delivered rapidly and urgently by one half of the chorus, sung *quasi parlato* to a descending chromatic motif traceable back to Ex.1, while the other half, in rhythmic unison, actually do speak the words, giving them a 'raucous' tone. For 'Espiritu del cielo' and the following phrase the choir reverts to a broadly melodic idiom, doubled in Ondes 2 and first trombone, with sonorous trombone harmony (Ex.6). Variants of this theme will appear several times.

'Dadnos nuestra descendencia ...' then follows immediately as a high, rapid syllabic setting, marked 'percussive declamation' and feverish in character, doubled by Ondes 2 and the bass trombone (marked at one point '*quasi pizz.*'!), against pounding piano chords rhythmically shadowed by gongs and tam-tam. As the phrase about 'verdes caminas' (green roads) comes up all the drums, with cymbals and tambourine, quietly suggest a striding march-rhythm, and the piano's left-hand takes over the doubling of the voices, *staccatissimo*, while Ondes 1 begins a chromatic ascent into the stratosphere. At this point, the voices cease, the brass fanfare from the start of Ex.2 reappears (bodily transposed down a fifth), and a varied form of Ex.2's ensuing plunge from high Ondes to low organ pedals precipitates the next section.

Que tranquilas muy tranquilas   Peaceful, very peaceful
estén las tribus   may the tribes be.

Que perfectas muy perfectas   Perfect, very perfect
sean las tribus.   may the tribes be.[11]
Que perfecta sea la vida   Perfect may life be,
la existencia que nos dias.   the existence you give us.

The first two sentences are sung sonorously but with appropriate calm to melodies which are rhythmic variants of the one in Ex.6, but with the intervals opened out to tritones and perfect fifths (thus recalling figure *x* from Ex.2). The organ doubles the first sentence in octaves, against quiet thrumming march-rhythms in timpani. The second is doubled by trombone 3, in harmony with trombone 4, and set against simpler rhythms in the three bass drums. Between these statements comes a swift brass and organ fanfare, its tessitura extended upwards by the Ondes, and a clanguorous eruption from the piano in battering repeated chords, supported by the timpani, developing figure *x*. This element overlaps with the voices in their second sentence, and only breaks off as they start the third, 'Que perfecta sea la vida ...', again doubled by trombones. (Ex.7, below, includes the end of this piano/timpani figure.)

Ex.7

Appropriately – or perhaps punningly – the harmony which now forms around the vocal line is just as thoroughly dominated by 'perfect' fourths and fifths as is the melody itself, with quiet chordal textures in piano, timpani and trumpets and a peacefully decorative, 'hardly audible' right-hand ostinato of fourths and fifths in the organ, itself derived from the vocal melody. But while all the instruments gradually

[11] This is omitted from the English translation printed at the beginning of the published score.

fade in volume, the voices retain their *forte* dynamic, and ascend to an agonized, imploratory yelp of a high E♭, at the word 'dias', echoed by gong, tam-tam, cymbals and *fff* bass drum. The tribe clearly has no automatic expectation of answer to their prayer: it is a matter of life or death.

Their rising shout brings a kind of lightning-flash: on organ and piano, a further development of the organ's octave figure from Ex.2. This closely resembles the form which immediately preceded Ex.5, and is followed by a compressed form of the ensuing brass fanfare, and a variant of the massive trombone motif seen in that example. The tempo increases to ♩=100, and the percussion ensemble breaks in with a strongly rhythmic ostinato on drums and cybals, while the Ondes wheel and swoop like hawks in glissandi on high. The trombones re-enter, holding the tone F♯ in octaves – to aid the choir, doubled by Ondes 2, in finding this high pitch for the starting-point of their next extry. It proves to be their most agitated and feverish contribution yet.

Oh, maestros gigantes	O Master Giant,[12]
huella del relampago	Path of the Lightning,[13]
esplendor del relampago	Splendour of the Lightning,
gavilam maestros magos	Falcon! Master-magi,
dominadores poderosos del cielo,	Powers of the Sky,
procreadores, engendradores.	Procreators, Begetters!
Antiguo segreto,	Ancient Mystery,
antigua ocultadora,	Ancient Sorceress,
abuela dia,	Ancestress of the Day,
abuela del alba.	Ancestress of the Dawn!
Que la germination se haga,	Let there be germination,
que alba se haga.	Let there be Dawn.

So far the chorus has invoked the spirits of Sky and Earth in general, but now they call on them imploringly as individuals in a frenzied entreaty that brings back, as accompaniment, several important ideas from the introduction and subsequent passages, working them together in close juxtaposition and variation that it is surely permissible to describe as 'development'.

---

[12] Thus in the official English translation, though the Spanish has the plural form, 'Master Giants'.

[13] This line is omitted from the English translation.

A variant of the piano-and-timpani music and trombone anacruses from Ex.2 accompanies the appeal to 'maestros gigantes', while the lines about lightning follow immediately, doubled by trombones, against the drums-and-cymbal ostinato heard just previously with a new fanfare figure for three muted trumpets (in parallel fourths, and ascending by perfect fourths and tritones), while the ondes stab away at a high repeated seventh. The Falcon ('gavilam') then ascends *fortissimo* in broad note-values, doubled by Ondes 1, to another E♭ shout, against full brass and organ harmony. The pulse of a rapidly-reiterated low B♮ in Ondes 2 then drills its way insistently through the organ harmony, to introduce the most elaborate percussion ostinato yet heard, a veritable native march-music for all six players, aided by the piano (Ex.8).

The piano drops out, but the percussion continues as, with the effect of a massive eruption, the climactic events of Ex.5 return in splendour – the trombone fanfare-figure, the *staccato* first trumpet, and the massive fifths-dominated harmony in organ and brass, from which the voices launch *fff* into 'procreadores, engendradores' to almost the same music as 'Oh, constructores ...'. The textures are somewhat simplified, but the music is bodily raised by a semitone, increasing the intensity of its majestic fervour (and sending the first trumpet up to a stratospheric D♯). The Ondes do not take part this time, but the percussion march continues throughout, creating one of *Ecuatorial*'s biggest dynamic climaxes so far.

Almost immediately, these massive sounds disappear, to be replaced by very quiet ones. 'Antiguo segreto ...' is sung softly, against the lightest percussion noises, to a low descending chromatic line (recalling the chromaticism of Ex.1). A calm development of Ex.7 supervenes for 'abuela del dia ...', the original vocal melody broadened and doubled by Ondes 2 and the harmony restricted to organ and soft repeated piano chords (with the organ's peaceful figuration of fourths and fifths still important). This time there is no agonized end shout: the music slows to ♩=60 (the opening tempo of the introduction) and variants of Ex.1's chromatic cells are heard split up between Ondes, piano and trombones. The percussion figures previously seen at the start of Ex.3 reappear, and a high, dissonant harmony builds up in Ondes, organ and muted trumpets. This dies away as the voices (marked '*très nasal – percutant*') rapidly mutter 'Que la germination ...': the effect is like a cowed congregational response.

The Ondes fade into silence on an altitudinous minor ninth and, with only a few quiet drum-attacks, the voices are suddenly raised in weird vocables (Ex.9):

Everything about this figure, its manner of production, its quarter-tone inflections, seems calculated to bring into the music a further element of stangeness, of exotic ritual. The invented phonemes (an effect Varèse was to use in later vocal works), with their expressive timbre, have an quality of alien inscrutability, suggesting the actual tribal chanting of the Mayan peoples. (Remember the 'verbal counterpoint' of 'voodoo monosyllables mixed with naniga and Indian words and magic incantations' which Alejo Carpentier had created for the libretto of *The One All Alone*.) From here on Varèse employs them occasionally to break up and contrast with the coherent words of the text; and at this point Ex.9 signals the division between the first half and last half of the invocation.

Selve belleza del dia	Hail Beauties of the Day,
dadores del amarillo	Givers of Yellow,
del verde.	of Green![14]
(Ho o ha)	
dadores de hijas, de hijos	Givers of Daughters, of Sons!
(Hóngh! Hengh Whoo Héngh)	
Dad la vida existencia	Give life, existence,
a mis hijos, a mi prole,	to my children, to my descendants!
que no haga ni su desgracia	Let not your power,
ni su infortunio	let not your sorcery,
vuestro potentia,	be their evil
vuestro hechicheria.	and their misfortune.

The whole of this section, the incantatory vocables apart, is delivered in a rapid choral mutter (actually marked 'sombre – Mumbled'). The principal direction is '(Half sung – Half spoken) but pitch must be observed', and the only movement of pitch is by the conjunct semitones first adumbrated in Ex.1, usually descending to an off-repeated lowest tone. This mode of vocal delivery is contrasted with the loud, nasal 'ritualistic' vocalizations in the manner of Ex.9, complete with quarter-tones, and final exclamatory downward glissando. The instrumental contribution throughout is quiet and restrained: limited at first to quiet high melodic fragments on the Ondes, isolated touches on drums and cymbals, and equally isolated dissonant dyads (minor seconds and major sevenths) in timpani and piano. After the second nasal vocalization, however, on the *fff* syllable 'Héngh!', the percussion ensemble (all the drums plus cymbal and tambourine, accompanied by soft chords in the piano), presses forward in a softly insistent march-music characterized by repeated triplet rhythms, which accompanies the remainder of the rapid 'mumbled' chanting from 'Dad la vida la existencia' to 'vuestro hechicheria' – during which last word it falls silent.

---

[14] The reference is to the staples of life, the principal foods of the tribe: the yellow of ripe corn, the green of the maize leaf. Cf. Asturias's novel about the Maya, *Men of Maize*.

Now ensues an instrumental interlude, beginning with a quiet, mysterious organ solo which contrasts a melodic use of perfect fifths, octaves and tritones with dissonant harmony in tritones and ninths. Continued in trombones, the music rises to a C♯ pitch, held by trumpet 4 and rapidly repeated in the piano and in trumpet 1, fluttertongue. (This recalls the similarly repeated G♯ near the start of the Introduction.) Over this hammered pitch the organ and the Ondes re-enter, and dissonant harmonies build up in full brass and organ to fill the space beneath. Once again the Ondes do their downward swoon from Ex.2, *vibratissimo* – only to rise again in brief duet as the percussion ensemble strikes in with the heavy march-music of Ex.8. Excited fanfare-figures for trombones and muted trumpets (the latter harking back to Ex.1) unfold above the tribal march, which builds to a climax for the return of the voices.

Que buena sea la vida	May it be happy, the life
de vuestros sostenes,	of your upholders,
de vuestros nutridores,	your providers
antes vuestros bocas,	before your mouths,
ante vuestros rostros,	before your faces,
espiritus del cielo,	Spirit of the Sky,
espiritus de la tierra,	Spirit of the Earth.
(Hoo oh ah	Whoo hé oh ha)
Dad la vida, dad la vida.	Give Life! Give Life!

The voices resume, however, in their calmest and most sustained melodic character, developing the melody originally used for 'Que tranquillas ... esten ias tribus', doubled first in organ and then trombones over quiet drum figures. At 'Antes vuestras bocas ...' we encounter another vocal effect (Ex.10) against jagged piano chords and the tolling sound of gongs and suspended cymbal: a chromatic descent, related to Ex.1, through three different vocal colours, from half-inarticulate glissando to speech-song.

After this the sustained melodic style is resumed, the voices straining upwards gradually in an effortful chromatic ascent, once more supported by the organ. The word 'tierra' (Earth) fades away in a whisper, and suddenly the inarticulate vocalizations break out *ff subito*, threatening and imploratory, as a kind of florid shake in voices and organ, and soon calling on the full instrumental ensemble for what is perhaps the climactic section of the entire work.

As in several of his compositions, Varèse's strategy in building a crowning climax is to bring highly contrasted elements – contrasted in colour, timbre, rhythm and pitch-span – into ever closer and more violent juxtaposition. Brass and percussion, piano and organ, high trumpet, Ondes; trumpet fanfares, trombone slides, bursts of piano-and-timpani ostinati: they are all here, articulating in their different ways the most dissonant aspects of *Ecuatorial*'s basic materials, its semitonal chromaticism and its tritonal melodic intervals. In the midst of it all, the chorus lifts up its voice in desperate appeal, giving tongue to those inarticulate phonemes which appear to stand at one and the same time for ritual responses and cries of human distress. The music seems to embody, here most powerfully of all, the experience and world-view of a 'tribe lost in the mountains', exposed to a world so elemental that thunder, lightning, volcano and the wild beasts are all to be feared and propitiated. 'Dad la vida, dad la vida!', they chant in frenzied prayer.

Trombones and organ, developing the opening chromatic cell of Ex.1, bring a sudden stillness and quietness. A development of the latter instrument's rapid octave figure from Ex.2, in trombones, organ and piano, leads to a chromatically dissonant, but quiet, fanfare on muted trumpets and trombones. The percussion ensemble returns with a quieter version of a section of the Ex.8 'tribal march', against a rhythmic pulsation on Ondes 2, introducing the voices once again.

(Ho hé whoo)	
Dad la vida,	Give Life,
oh fuerza envuelta en la cielo,	O All-Enveloping Force in the Sky,
en la tierra,	on the earth,
en los cuatros angulos,	at the four corners,
en las cuatro extremidades,	at the four extremities,
entanto exista el alba,	as long as dawn exists,
entanto exista la tribú.	As long as the tribe exists.

The introductory ritualistic vocables are heard not only against elements of the Ex.8 percussion march but a much-compressed version of the Ondes' duet, Ex.4; and they pass straight into the first few lines of text, delivered '*crié*' in an urgent, fanfare-like rhythmic variant of the vocal melody seen in Ex.7, massively doubled by trombones and muted trumpets, while the piano – marked 'Quasi timpani' – angrily develops figure *x*. Against quiet reminders in the organ of Ex.1's opening phrases, the chorus then sings 'en los quatros angulos ...' to a sweeping, sustained phrase that really does push them to their extremities – spanning the widest tessitura required of them anywhere in the work and ending in a dramatically precipitous glissando (Ex.11).

Swelling brass harmony builds up during the latter bars, only to be cut short and replaced by a third and final version of the Ex.7 music, its harmonic interrelations unchanged but transposed by a tritone from the original appearance, complete with the organ's right-hand figuration, and the vocal melody doubled in one of the Ondes. The piano's contribution is limited to soft chords, while the gongs, tambourine and cymbals add soft pulsations of sound. Into this momentary island of calm bursts the angry piano-and-timpani music from Ex.3. This provokes Ex.12: the final, and most intense climax of

all. The choir delivers the last line of text, 'as long as the tribe exists', as a fervent appeal sung to another wide-spanned line, supported by Ondes and trombones, underpinned by organ, rounded off by a final shattering explosion of the Ex.8 march and two *fortissimo* statements of Ex.1's descending-semitone cell on full brass and organ.

These ferocious sounds are abruptly sheared off, and replaced by the unearthly voices of the Ondes, in another shortened version of their duet from Ex.4, swooping up to a long-held major-seventh harmony against very light drum and cymbal rhythms. This is the start of an instrumental coda, mostly quiet, balancing the work's introduction but much shorter. The prayer, the ritual, the display of human awe and terror is over. We are left, it seems, with the empty sky and forest, where the natural forces themselves are still active, but in passionless tranquillity.

The organ follows the Ondes, with a near-exact repetition of the solo with which it began the instrumental interlude after 'vuestra hechicheria'. Briefly it touches the lowest regions of the pitch spectrum, resonated by soft attacks on tam-tam, gong and timpani. A chromatic fragment on muted trumpet leads us upward to the Ondes, whose voices sound together in the empyrean: drawing the ear upward, as the flight of two eagles might draw the eye upward into the vast spaces of the sky. As a side-drum taps away softly (played with knitting-needles to produce a very small staccato sound) – still bound to the earth, it seems – these exotic electronic birds join in a final variation of their Ex.4 duet, sliding up at the end to a long-held final harmony in the uppermost reaches of register. Ondes 2 holds an E two octaves above the treble stave, and Ondes 1 a G, a minor third above that. This is the last sound we hear: a plangent, piercing minor third that swells, with the pitiless ease of electronics, to such a fierce dynamic level it is almost painful, only to fade away into utter, ringing silence.[15]

It is *Ecuatorial*'s sound-world – the Ondes, the organ, the male voice or voices – which render it apparently unique among Varèse's surviving works, although elements of that sound-world are of course carried over into the late electronic works and *Nocturnal*. It would seem less unique had he achieved *The One-All-Alone*, or its successor project, *Espace*. But they remained unrealized, while in Ecuatorial the sonic

---

[15] One might recall here Varèse's plan to have *The One All Alone* conclude with 'the crackle of static in the highest register the human ear can hear' (above, p.231).

apparatus was integrated with conspicuous success. One hesitates to call any single work of Varèse his greatest, but *Ecuatorial* certainly comes near that distinction. Arnold Whittall (who does not share my hesitation) has justly described it as:

that enigmatic prelude to the long silence, a passionate, primitive prayer for survival, which in its simplicity and seriousness is utterly remote from the kind of radical experimentation that was shortly to gain ground in America.[16]

It is with 'the long silence' that we must now concern ourselves. Though *Ecuatorial* shows Varèse, now 50, at the height of his powers, this magnificent work did not presage a period of success and productivity. Quite the reverse. After its première in 1934, as far as the musical world was concerned, a great silence descended. There would be no further major Varèse première for 20 years. In all that time, despite long bouts of desperate, Herculean effort, he completed no large works at all, and nothing of lasting importance save a single page for flute. Mystery, almost as deep as that which enshrouds his lost early music, consumed his creative path: lacking (as he felt) the technical means to achieve his most desired goals, he descended into the abyss of frustration. The sounds were sent forth into space, but they did not return.

---

[16] Arnold Whittall, *Music Since the First World War* (London: JM Dent, 1977), p.274.

9 · Lost in space

*From a nearby house were issuing piercing, prolonged, wailing, strange sounds
which suddenly – following a rapid downward glissando – turned into
something that sounded like the panting, spasmodic roaring of some huge,
unidentifiable animal.*

'It's Edgar Varèse, working with his electronic equipment', said Gian-Carlo.
'And that's supposed to be music?' asked Teresa ...

ALEJO CARPENTIER,
La consagración de la primavera

CHRONOLOGY 1935–1949

1935 *Beginning of Varèse's deepest artistic crisis. Attempts to create an
acoustic laboratory. About the end of the year Artaud sends him a draft of*
Il n'y a plus d'une firmament.

1936 *16 February: Georges Barrère gives the première of* Density 21.5
*(composed the previous month) in New York. From 15 June to the end of
November Varèse is in Santa Fe, New Mexico, where he lectures and makes
contact with the Indian tribes of New Mexico and Arizona. During the
winter works on* Espace.

1937 *3 March: André Malraux and Varèse announce they are to
collaborate on* Espace. *17 April: Varèse begins a further visit to Santa Fe,
where he teaches an orchestration course at the Arsuna School of Fine Arts
and founds a Schola Cantorum, abandoned after only a few rehearsals.
November: Varèse moves to San Francisco, taking a house on Washington
Street.* Trend, *a ballet by Hanya Holm to the music of* Octandre, *receives
the* New York Times *award as the year's best dance production.*

1938 *15 February:* Offrandes *performed in San Francisco. Shortly* *afterwards Varèse falls ill and requires an operation and two months' convalescence. May: he and Louise move to Los Angeles, where they will stay until 1940. Varèse looks for work and research possibilities in Hollywood, where he approaches cinema sound studios for the use of their facilities. Probably at this time he first meets John Cage.*

1939 *Lectures at the University of Southern California. With the aid of an electrical engineer, attempts the recording of sounds at different pitches, achieved by varying the speed of a turntable.*

1940 *Walter Anderson, editor of* The Commonweal, *publishes Varèse's article 'Organized Sound for the Sound Film' – originally a proposal made by letter (22 April) to the Hollywood producer André Dumont. October: Varèse returns to New York, taking up residence once again at 188 Sullivan Street. During the next decade his music is very little performed. He continues to work on* Espace, *'but I would tear up at night what I had written during the day or vice versa'. From this year onwards he makes unavailing attempts to contact Theremin in the USSR.*

1941 *Varèse founds the New Chorus (from 1942 called the Greater New York Chorus), with which he performs vocal works from the 12th to early 18th centuries. He is trying to acquire several Theremins for use in* Espace.

1942 *From this year until 1945 Varèse selects extracts from* Hyperprism, Octandre, Intégrales *and* Ionisation *for the soundtrack of Thomas Bouchard's film* Fernand Léger in America *(first screened Paris, 5 April 1946).*

1943 *24 April: First concert of the Greater New York Chorus, as a benefit for the Co-ordinating Council of French Relief Societies.*

1944 *Refuses an offer of the* Legion d'honneur, *obtained for him by Paul Claudel.*

1946 *Boris Morros, who is directing the film* Carnegie Hall, *persuades Varèse to compose a work to feature in it, parodying an orchestra tuning up before a concert. Varèse sketches* Tuning Up, *but this work is neither used nor definitively completed and remains unknown until 1998.* Étude pour Espace *is perhaps mainly assembled this year (the exact date of composition is unknown).*

1947 *20 April: première (and so far only performance) of* Étude pour Espace *at a New Music Society concert in the New School for Social*

Research, West 12th Street, New York. Varèse is displeased with the performance and becomes uncertain about the whole Espace *project.*

1948 *Summer: At the invitation of Otto Luening, Varèse gives a seminar in composition and lectures on 20th-century music at Columbia University, New York.*

1949 *23 January: a performance of* Hyperprism *in a memorial concert for the critic Paul Rosenfeld brings Varèse's music back to the attention of the New York public. This year or next he arranges Baroque music for Bouchard's film* Kurt Seligmann: La Naissance d'un tableau. *The Chinese composer and musicologist Chou Wen-Chung becomes a pupil of Varèse on the recommendation of Colin McPhee, and studies with him until 1953. By June at latest Varèse is making the first sketches of what will become* Déserts; *the music is conceived as the sound-track for the film which, in March, he had proposed as a collaborative project to the actor-director Burgess Meredith. Meredith in turn persuades Varèse to write a piece for a new musical he is directing and acting in,* Happy as Larry. *This becomes the* Dance for Burgess, *completed on 9 December in time for the Boston preview on 27 December.*

The entire period covered by this chronology is dominated by a single, ultimately unrealized and perhaps unrealizable project – the 'choral symphony' *Espace*. At the very beginning of this time-span Varèse composed one other short work – a single page of music – in the shape of *Density 21.5*. Just as his immense labours on *The One All Alone* went unsalvaged, while the brief independent *Ionisation* became one of his most successful works and a cornerstone of the percussion repertoire, so while *Espace* could never be realized, this tiny flute work became his representative to the musical world at large, and entered the repertoire of flautists everywhere. He did, eventually, present some of *Espace*'s material in a performable guise as the choral work *Étude pour Espace*, only to withdraw it for revision and leave those revisions in such a state of uncertainty that *Étude pour Espace* has remained unheard and unavailable for study for over half a century. And in 1946 he sketched, without bringing to any definitive form, the parodic *Tuning Up*, unheard during his lifetime and only edited into performable shape by Chou Wen-Chung in 1998.

Inevitably, therefore, this chapter is largely devoted to *Espace*. But we should begin with a consideration of *Density 21.5*, which forms a kind of bridge between *Ecuatorial* and Varèse's 'cosmic choral symphony'.

DENSITY 21.5

The only 'canonical' score to emerge from the 20 years of silence was Varèse's smallest, physically if not in duration. In January 1936, in response to a commission from the flautist Georges Barrère, Varèse wrote a short work for solo flute. Barrère specifically desired something with which to inaugurate a flute made of platinum which he had had specially constructed (it was valued in a contemporary issue of *The New York Times* at $3,000). Varèse accordingly entitled his offering *Density 21.5*, referring to the specific gravity of the element platinum.[1] Wilfrid Mellers remarks that 'the title presumably means that this music is the "aural reality" of the metal: the sound-experience that can be revealed through it'.[2]

Barrère first played his new flute, and Varèse's piece, in public at a Benefit Concert for the New York Lycée Français in Carnegie Hall on 16 February 1936. Varèse subsequently revised *Density 21.5* prior to its first publication, a decade after this première, in the July 1946 issue of *New Music Quarterly*; a further decade passed before the piece was issued by Ricordi. Despite its small dimensions, it is an important addition to the exiguous solo flute repertoire, and one of immediately recognizable distinction. As a result (and with its brevity as a positive aid) *Density 21.5* has become perhaps the most frequently-heard of all Varèse's creations.

In *Ionisation* we saw Varèse dispensing altogether with melody instruments. *Density 21.5* forms the antipodes to that conception: a melodic solo without percussion or accompaniment of any kind. But the flute is an instrument he had always written for with instinctive sympathy and effectiveness – witness the opening of *Amériques*. Moreover, it is an instrument strongly associated with the Impressionist repertoire upon which so much of Varèse's own musical language is ultimately founded. Its master is Debussy, and the *loci classici* two works which I have already mentioned on several occasions,

---

[1] This is now generally considered to be 21.45.

[2] *Music in a New Found Land* (London: Barrie & Rockliff, 1964), p.160.

and which I have suggested as profound influences on Varèse: *L'après-midi d'un faune* and *Syrinx*. The latter especially – Debussy's evocation of Pan's death-song, his only work for unaccompanied flute – cannot fail to have been at the forefront of Varèse's mind, whether as a partial model, a competitor, or an influence to be avoided at all costs.

Density 21.5's small scale (not so much its length, for it lasts about 4 minutes in performance, slightly longer than the usual duration of *Hyperprism*, but the sparseness of the notes, which fill merely one or two pages of music, depending on the edition) has made it the most amenable of Varèse's works to analysis of the most exhaustive kind – pitch-analysis, naturally enough, as by its nature the piece is concerned with the linear projection of individual pitches.[3] Yet there is much still to be learned from an approach that takes in its possibly unconscious connexions, and more probably conscious divergences, from the Debussian model.

Mellers (*loc. cit.*) has described the melodic language of *Density 21.5* as one of 'melismatic arabesques oscillating around nodal points, and of incantatory repetitions that change very slowly'; he draws the obvious comparison with *Syrinx*. 'Melismatic arabesques' conjures up something more florid and fluid than Varèse's rather severely swooping anacruses, and he had by this time made 'incantatory' repetition such an essential part of his personal melodic language that its links to Debussy are no longer in themselves of much significance.

Rather more significant, perhaps, are the echoes of the 'incantatory' musics of the peoples of Central and South America. There are moments when *Density 21.5* seems to anticipate Varèse's discovery, later in 1936, of the music of the Navajo and Hopi peoples of the South-western USA. Moreover, this upward-soaring flute music immediately follows, in his output, the vertiginous Theremin duet that concludes *Ecuatorial*. Although no flute, whether platinum, wood or bone, can boast the dizzy compass of those electronic instruments, nevertheless *Density 21.5* could well be seen as an appendix to the Mayan prayer, a lone human song in response to the wheeling birds of desert, forest or mountain-top.

---

[3] The major studies include Bernard pp.217–232; Gumbel (*Zeitschrift für Musiktheorie 1/1*, pp.31–8); Nattiez (*Music Analysis 1*, pp.243–340); Tenney and Polansky (*Journal of Music Theory 24*, pp.221–30); Wilkinson (*The Score 19*).

It is not inappropriate to call this a song: repetitions and nodal points notwithstanding, *Density 21.5* is by far the longest sustained melodic line in Varèse's surviving output. The main point of contrast with *Syrinx* is the direction of that line. Debussy's soulful masterpiece is a blank, despairing outcry, its trend always downward, in weeping, sighing phrases. Varèse's line seeks from the first to rise (if only by a semitone), to walk, to fly. Compare their opening phrases, Ex.1*a* and *b*: different forms of the selfsame chromatic cell.

While both phrases result from immense compositional craft, Debussy's is designed to communicate naked emotion; Varèse's to suggest *suppressed* emotion, mystery, and a process of thought.

The single line that comprises *Density 21.5* divides, of course, into several contrasting sections, some of them quite short. But the overall impression is of organic and purposeful – if sometimes painful – growth, opening out from an initial, low-lying, tight-closed group of three pitches to traverse in due course practically the entire available register of the flute. This area represents only about half of the musical space available to Varèse in the works for ensemble. Writing for a single instrument, he is unable to employ two of the essential features of his other compositions – the simultaneous use of high treble and low bass registers, and the use of block chords. But that should not be taken to mean that the work is devoid of harmony. The successive, horizontal presentation of pitches leaves a vertical resonance in the mind: in *Density 21.5*, harmony is as thoroughly implied as in a Bach solo violin or cello suite. (Nor, as we shall see, is it devoid of another Varèse characteristic – percussion – even though that is secured only by a fleeting 'effect'.) Varèse further eschews metrical variety – except for two bars, the entire 61-bar piece is disposed into common time, although the bar-lines are fluidly composed across where necessary. He avoids extremes of tempo, too – there are only two, moderate, and closely related tempi (crotchet=72 and crotchet=60), although Varèse is insistent that they should be strictly observed. Everything conspires, therefore, to direct our attention to the work's purely melodic aspects.

Though any examination of the microstructure of *Density 21.5* will tend to break it into short sections (Jonathan Bernard finds no less than 12 of these[4]), it seems truer to the piece's nature to stress its melodic continuity. We can think of it in three large paragraphs of roughly equal length: in fact of 23, 17 and 21 bars, or 92+68+84 beats including silences. If this outline suggests a possibly ternary shape with longer outer sections flanking a slightly shorter central one, we find the suggestion amplified by the music itself, since the central section contrasts with the other two on various levels, and the third section contains returns to, or reprises of, features of the first.

These long spans arise from a very small seed or crystal which Varèse then 'projects' in various ways and directions. Examples 2 and 3 show the whole first section of *Density 21.5*, and also how this large paragraph articulates and modifies the 3-note chromatic cell, F-E-F♯, with which the work begins. In itself, in the most restricted manner possible, this shape (marked *x* in the example) suggests potential for movement upward or downward, through progressive widening of

Ex. 2

---

[4] Bernard, pp.218–228.

intervals: this is what happens in bar 2, as the line moves first down to C♯ and up to G, spanning a tritone. That interval is the second crucial element in *Density 21.5*. Shape *x*, in its essence, describes a curve from an initial pitch down to a lower pitch, and then up to a pitch a semitone higher than the first. The constituent intervals can be widened: the minor third in bars 7–8, for instance, will prove almost as significant as the tritone. The shape can be inverted, retrograded, or the order of its three tones changed. Displacement by one octave (bars 11–12) and then two (16–17) projects the cell onto a wide sector of the sound-spectrum. But it exerts its force over the whole melodic paragraph. That Varèse wished to impose severe restraints of pitch and shape on his evolving monodic line cannot be doubted; yet pitch-analysis can lose itself in detail when perhaps the most important element is general shape and gesture rather than the precise function of pitch in any predetermined scheme.

The music's character is at first tentative, groping, yet gradually gaining in confidence and assertiveness. Slowly it rises, first to the G, with the tritone leap C♯-G a kind of repeated jumping-up motion eventually rewarded by clearing A and making an effortful climb through B♭ to C♮ – marked by a comma pause, the line so far having spanned a major seventh – before continuing through D♭ to the climactic D♮ at bar 11. In fact bar 9 sounds as if it is about to re-present the original 3-note cell, but the shape is vastly extended by the oscillation of its first two tones D♭-C, making the appearance of the expected D♮ in all senses climactic, in time, register and dynamic. The line has climbed a minor ninth, and the D become the base for new tritone leaps, both up and down this time, a minor ninth above the original C♯-G configuration. The climactic phrase in bar 13 broadens and expands the tritone idea while carrying the music for the first time into the flute's high register, and ends in a long-drawn-out crescendo, on E, followed by the longest measured silence so far.

The flute begins again, quietly, on the E an octave below – a new statement of the three-note 'seed' motif, transposed a major seventh above its initial appearance. This time it grows a segment of ascending chromatic scale as tailpiece, though this is disguised at first by the angular octave displacements. In bar 17 these force the music up to the highest pitch yet heard: Ex.3. The next phrase, beginning on B, also uses a chromatic scale segment – but this time a descending one. It is followed by a leap of a ninth from that same B to a high C♯ and a trill

– but this phrase too is essentially a scale segment (incorporating the seed *x*) and the final phrase (bars 21–23) sums up the trend by showing the segment in its simplest form, as a slow chromatic ascent and descent – followed by another dizzying leap to an abrupt rhythmic figure, like a bird-cry. It presages something new (in fact, the beginning of the next main section of the piece) but is itself an extension of the scale-segment. The whole process is very simply shown in Ex.3:

Ex.3

We could describe this whole first section of *Density 21.5*, then, as itself consisting of three parts, each beginning from the three-note cell *x* presented in the opening bar. The first (of eight bars) manifests gradual growth and upward expansion of intervals; the second (of six) concentrates first on the figure's initial semitone, then on the tritone so prominently arrived at in bar 2; the third (of nine) takes the semitone interval and extends it by means of segments of a chromatic scale.

The second section of the work, by contrast, juxtaposes a comparatively large number of ostensibly distinct ideas, moving from one to another in a much shorter musical space. This imminent change of character had been signalled by the sudden rhythmic outcry followed by a half-bar's silence in bar 23; and the section itself begins in a lower register with short rhythmic figures separated by rests: Ex.4.

Ex.4

Notes marked + to be played softly, hitting the keys at the same time to produce a percussive effect

The much more rhythmically defined character of this music, as against that of the first section, is reinforced by Varèse's performance direction '(sharply articulated)' and by the 'percussion' effect which he reserves for these bars. The notes marked + in the example, he specifies, must 'be played softly, hitting the keys at the same time to produce a percussive effect'. The result can be heard with various degrees of convincingness on the existing recordings, but there is no doubt that the outcome is a dry metallic timbre which sharply differentiates these bars from all that has gone before. A distant echo of modern industry – or perhaps a steel band? – has penetrated the post-Debussian Arcadia.

The initial stress on the minor third, E-C♯, harks back to bars 7–8; but that same low C♯ was heard with almost equal insistence near the beginning of the work – the 'base' from which it attempted its leaps. The D♮ a minor ninth above was the sharply emphasized (*fff*) goal of those flights, leading on to an elaboration of the tritone interval; and sure enough the appearance of that same pitch here leads on to a brief exploration of the tritone D♮-G♯. These few abrupt, almost pointillist bars, therefore, present an extreme compression of the first 14 bars of the whole work.

So it is no surprise that the music now moves on to the highest pitch previously attained to launch a new vertiginously descending figure – new, and yet a transposition of the original 'seed' *x* (Ex. 5).

This is repeated partially and then completely. The new, slower tempo is not immediately apprehensible, since the downward anacrusis of Ex.5 has brought the shortest note-values so far; but it becomes so as the flute descends to a low G♮ to project a slow ascending line that contains within it new references to the seed-motif, to a fragment of chromatic scale, and to the rising tritone interval. This line reaches A♮, a tone higher than the G♮ of Ex.5, which now defines a new 'ceiling' for the music as the original slightly faster tempo returns and we hear the bright rhythms and varied repetitions of what one is almost tempted to call a tune (Ex.6):

The static, repetitive quality of this idea is one of the 'tuneful' things about it. Its clear rhythmic definition and confinement to a small number of pitches recalls, perhaps, the folk-flute music of South America, and Varèse may well have had some such association in mind. But for all its liveliness the tune has in fact brought a cessation of harmonic movement within the evolving line that is *Density 21.5*: it bounces within the confines of a seventh, continually hitting its head against the high A♮, and presently this induces a sense of tension requiring release. The result is a descent that lands on C♮ above the stave, a pitch not touched upon for a long time, and never before heard in the work at this octave. The slower tempo returns, accentuated by a change to much broader note-values, and the line drops a sixth to E♭. Here, with several rhythmic variations, the flute mulls over combinations of the adjacent pitches E♭-D♮-D♭: new variations of the 3-note 'seed', *x*. The mood is weary. The work's central section then ends with a major-third drop from E♭ to B♭ – perhaps recalling the minor-third drop with which Ex.4 opened, and bringing the music to its lowest point in the register for some time.

A further drop, to the lowest available F♯, brings a restoration of the original tempo, and a quiet, specific statement of the 'seed', rhythmically identical to the opening of Ex.1. So the third and final section of *Density 21.5* begins with a clear gesture of recapitulation, the work's initial idea recalled at a semitone above its original pitch. As in several of Varèse's other approximately 'ternary' works, this last section seems to recapitulate elements from the two preceeding ones, but it also therefore contains the biggest contrasts, and produces something new to create an effective coda.

The first 'recapitulatory' statement of the seed motif is followed by further rhythmic variants of it, the line presently ascending to a C♯ above the stave by way of prominent tritone intervals, while the dynamic level rises from *p* to *ff*. As at the beginning of the second section, the effect is of a rapid résumé of the ground covered in the opening bars of the first, but now in a much more recognizable form, harking back to the music of Ex.1 in character as well as interval structure. With the arrival at the C♯, however, there comes a complete change. The flute leaps upward a further minor ninth, to the highest pitch yet attained in the whole work, a D♮: and in these stratospheric regions it performs, for five bars, a nagging oscillation in rapidly-changing rhythms between the high D♮ and the B♮ a minor third below.

I think this is a 'recapitulatory' gesture towards the work's second section: the effect is distinctly, and doubtless deliberately, reminiscent of the 'folk tune', Ex.6 – but since the oscillation is now confined to a mere two pitches, and the rhythm is less clearly defined, the quality of 'tune' has practically disappeared. What it shares with Ex.6, and indeed intensifies, is the sense of a sudden interruption, a static rocking back and forth within narrow confines, a freezing of harmonic motion. With its high register and dynamic level it is also the work's climax: or rather, the climax is the extravagant gesture with which it ends in bar 50, the repetitions having created the requisite amount of tension (Ex.7):

Ex.7

The vertiginous 2½-octave downward leap to the A, sensationally reinforced by repetition, accent, *fff* dynamic, and the re-adoption of the slower tempo (which persists now until the end) is the most dramatic outcome of the music's obsession with the tritone interval (which has been most commonly expressed in terms of the two pitches D♮ and A♭ or G♯). As we see in the continuation of Ex.7, it leads on to an inverted transposition of the 3-note 'seed' motif, and then a repeated high, bird-like cry that may well remind us of Ex.5 (it uses two of the same pitches) but is a further exploitation of the tritone interval and – like Ex.6 and the passage partially represented at the beginning of Ex.7 – a further example of confinement to two or three pitches in the upper register.

The way out of this is another steep descent – from the C♮ to a *ff* E an octave and a sixth below, from which the flute easily moves to its bottom C♯. From this base it essays two long upward flights, which provide the coda to the entire work and also finally break free of the x cell, whose influence recedes as the flute sculpts new contours of ascent. The first, moving mainly in conjunct intervals but finally interpreting these as an upward leap of a ninth to A♮ above the stave, is mainly quiet and lyrical. The descent from the A♮ is quickly achieved by means of a tritone figure, landing the music – for the first time – *ff* on the bottom note of the flute's register, C♮: opening out the available register yet further, at a very late stage in the piece. From this pitch the final ascent arches upward, twice, as far to D♮ a ninth above, twice back to the bottom C♭, and then finally with increasing confidence and a growing crescendo, climbs higher and higher. The last interval we hear is a tritone, as the flute soars to an E♯ (=F♮) above the stave, and then on to the B♮ above that.

Ouellette has called *Density 21.5* 'one long cry', and spoken of its 'tragic intensity'. But that description seems to me to fit *Syrinx* better. Varèse's work speaks at times of frustration and constriction – and certainly of solitude: that is a necessary implication of its medium. Yet compared to Debussy's piece he has created a dynamo of constructive activity, an examination of restrictions in order to transcend them – and the whole movement of this coda, taking the music upward and outward, proclaims at least a temporary liberation, out into that 'silent' interplanetary space which is alive with messages, for those with ears to hear.

ESPACE

It is difficult to pin down the moment when Varèse finally abandoned work on *The One All Alone* to concentrate his energies on *Espace*. Artaud's draft libretto for the former work (which Artaud called *Il n'y a plus d'un firmament*) had arrived towards the end of 1935, before the composition of *Density 21.5*. After the flute piece there seems no further mention of the former project, and *Espace* was certainly under way later in 1936. Perhaps it would be a mistake to regard the two projects as separate in *Espace*'s beginnings, and some writers have certainly regarded the two as part of a single continuum: different expressions, the first for the stage, the second for the concert-hall (even though those terms would have to be redefined to accommodate Varèse's vision) of a single idea at different stages of its development. However the first stirrings of *Espace* seem to have begun to crystallize in Varèse's mind in Paris in 1929 – as a conception parallel to but fairly distinct from *The One All Alone*. If the latter was his 'opera', *Espace* would be his 'choral symphony' for the times. All his titles are significant, and none more so than *Espace*: literally 'Space' – which in its cosmic, three-dimensional, geographical and musical senses, sums up so much of his essential vision: sounds moving in space, from the depths to the heights, from the Earth to the furthest stars.

As with *The One All Alone*, Varèse began with a sketch scenario which, in revised form, has since been published by several writers.[5] This document is as quintessential a statement of the composer's heroic modernism – in its humanistic and political, as well as artistic and scientific aspects – as anything he ever wrote.

Theme: TODAY. The world awake! Humanity on the march. Nothing can stop it. A conscious humanity, neither exploitable nor pitiable. Marching! Going! There is only going.[6] Millions of feet endlessly tramping, treading, pounding, striding, leaping.

Rhythms change: quick, slow, staccato, dragging, racing, smooth. Go. The final crescendo giving the impression that confidently, pitilessly the going will never stop ... projecting itself into space ...

Voices in the sky, as though magic, invisible hands were turning on and off the knobs of fantastic radios, filling all space, criss-crossing, overlapping, penetrating each other, splitting up, superimposing, repulsing each other, colliding, crashing. Phrases, slogans, utterances, chants, proclamations. China, Russia, Spain, the Fascist states and opposing Democracies all breaking their paralyzing crusts.

What should be avoided: tone of propaganda as well as any journalistic

---

[5] Dorothy Norman, 'Ionisation – Espace', in *Twice a Year*, VII (Autumn-Winter 1941), pp.259–260; Henry Miller, *The Air-Conditioned Nightmare* (New York: New Directions, 1945), pp.163–4; Ouellette, pp.131–132; also in a French version, beginning 'Que le monde s'éveille ...', in *Le Poème électronique Le Corbusier* (Paris, 1958) and *Liberté* 5 (1959) – the latter printing is erroneously titled *Déserts*. I quote here from Ouellette, with a couple of corrections of spelling or typographical errors, and some slight modifications in the light of the version given by Henry Miller.

[6] This sentence, not in Ouellette but in Miller, who indeed draws attention to it, curiously echoes the medieval inscription from Toledo which profoundly influenced the last works of Luigi Nono: *Caminantes, no hay camino, hay que caminar* (Travellers, there is no road, there is only going). It is not impossible that Varèse knew of the inscription.

speculation on timely events and doctrines. I want the epic impact of our epoch, stripped of its mannerisms and snobbisms.

I suggest using here and there snatches of phrases of American, French, Russian, Chinese, Spanish, German revolutions: like shooting stars, also words recurring like pounding hammer blows, or throbbing in an underground ostinato, stubborn and ritualistic.

I should like an exultant, even prophetic tone – incantatory, the writing, however, lean and bare, active, almost like the account of a prizefight, blow for blow, the audience kept keyed-up, tense and unconscious of the style of the announcer.

Also some phrases out of folklore, for the sake of their human, near-the-earth quality. I want to encompass everything that is human, from the most primitive to the farthest reaches of science.

With its references to march-music and to the treatment of 'phrases out of folklore', this scenario strongly suggests that something of the general musical language of *Espace*, at least as Varèse originally conceived it, may be reflected in *Ionisation* and *Ecuatorial*. But it is clear that *Espace* was intended to be on an altogether vaster scale. It was to be a 'symphony' for chorus and a large orchestra, which Varèse originally hoped would include the participation of electronic instruments. It is difficult to avoid the impression that Beethoven's Ninth was to some extent a conscious model; but, like *The One All Alone*, Varèse's 'symphony' went through several metamorphoses, much more difficult to separate and chronicle than in the case of the stage work. The years 1936–7, part of which Varèse spent in New Mexico, seem (as related later in this chapter) to have been especially fruitful, in imaginative if not in practical terms, for the advancement of this amorphous *magnum opus*. We seem also to glimpse a transition from one form to another. A report in the *New York Times* of 6 December 1936 speaks of a single-movement work lasting about 15 minutes, which Varèse hoped would be completed by the following Spring, 'without the bizarre electronic appliances he foresees, but he hopes it will suggest the possibilities of the space element ...'.

As with *The One All Alone*, it was a problem to find a suitable text for the appropriate portion of his 'choral symphony'. In early 1937 André Malraux, whom Varèse had known in Paris, entered the picture as a possible collaborator. The leading anti-fascist and future Gaullist minister came fresh from his experiences fighting on the Republican side in the Spanish Civil War, and hard on the heels of the publication of *Days of Wrath*, the American edition of his *Le Temps du mépris*. He had with him the manuscript of *L'espoir* (*Days of Hope*), which he read one night to the Varèses in their Sullivan Street apartment. On 3 March, at a press conference at the Hotel Mayflower arranged by Malraux's publishers, the novelist and the composer announced that they would work together on *Espace* – a project which the New York papers, in view of Malraux's communist tendencies, were quick to dub Varèse's 'Red Symphony'. The projected text, according to a report in the *New York Times* for 4 March, would be a poetic rewriting of

lyric passages of 'Days of Wrath', reflecting what goes on in a communist's mind in the face of death for the cause. These will be the words for the chorus in the third and closing movement of the symphony.

To convey the natural aspirations of the hero for the good things in life, the terror of death and the final exaltation of consecration to the cause, Mr. Varèse will call upon new electrical instruments, he said, and will have sections of the orchestra and chorus wired to amplifiers in different sections of the auditorium so that the music will sometimes hit the hearer on the back of his neck.

This report also outlines some ideas about the nature of the chorus:

Since the choir is to take part in a revolutionary symphony, Mr. Varèse said it would include Negroes. Mr. Malraux added that it would also include Russians, and that he had no doubt the symphony might be performed immediately anywhere they might wish in Russia ...

The idea of a Russian performance shows a touching naïvety on the part of composer and author, given the nature of the music that Varèse was surely intending to write: it was now over a year since Shostakovich's opera *Lady Macbeth of the Mtsensk District* had been condemned in *Pravda* (in the notorious editorial entitled 'Muddle Instead of Music') and withdrawn from the stage for its crime of dissonant modernism.

It will be noted that the work for which Malraux was to provide the text – and, as far as we know, this text was never written – was now a symphony in three movements. Ouellette reproduces some brief notes jotted down by Varèse at about this time, outlining a 3-movement work of about 40 minutes, the movements to be played without pause:

a full-orchestral first movement, a short lyrical slow movement for strings alone,[7] and a finale deploying the full forces including a large chorus 'to be used to the full extent of its possibilities: singing, humming, yelling, chanting, mumbling, hammered declamation, etc'.

These notes make no mention of electronic instruments, and the importance for *Espace* of an electronic component seems to have come and gone with the composer's changing conceptions. The *New York Times* report of 1936, like that of 1937, mentions the placing of loudspeakers in the auditorium to direct the movement of sounds in space (a fundamental Varèsian idea, later realized in *Déserts* and *Poème Électronique*) and it also alludes to the microtonal division of the chromatic scale 'with the aid of electricity'. This may be a reference to instruments such as the Theremin: Varèse demonstrated a Theremin at one of his lectures in Santa Fe in 1936 and certainly some years later he attempted to re-establish communication with Leon Theremin with a view to acquiring 'several' of his instruments for use in the performance of *Espace*.

Varèse's evolving ideas for the work's presentation were perhaps its single most revolutionary aspect. As mentioned, he was at first thinking only of the projection of sound around a single auditorium and, typically, within the score itself: his outline for the three-movement version of the symphony states that the first movement

... is built on the shifting play of planes, volumes, masses in space; very dynamic, abrupt in its statements, devoid of all rhetorical and pedantic developments.[8]

In one of his 1936 lectures delivered at Santa Fe he also talked of the sound-projection in visual terms, saying that it aroused

... a feeling akin to that aroused by beams of light sent forth by a powerful searchlight – for the ear as for the eye, that sense of projection, of a journey into space.[9]

---

[7] One perhaps regrets the fact that this movement especially was never written, as it would have been unique in Varese's output: an 'Adagio for strings'!

[8] Ouellette, p.134.

[9] Varèse, 'Music and the Times', lecture at Mary Austin House, Santa Fe, 23 August 1936. This is the much-anthologized lecture usually published under the title 'New Instruments and New Music'.

Varèse eventually – Ouellette believes sometime between 1937 and 1939 – came to envisage *Espace* as being performed in all the world's capitals, from where it would be heard around the globe in a simultaneous broadcast. Thus the 'voices in the sky' and the invisible hands turning 'the knobs of fantastic radios' of his original conception ceased to be metaphorical, but the essential ingredients of a global radiophonic event. Each choir would sing in its own language, and the work would be timed precisely in seconds[10] so that choral entries in Paris, Moscow, Peking or New York could be exactly synchronized, creating a vast song of liberation for all the peoples of the world. In this global hymn of brotherhood and freedom, we see even more clearly the desire to create a 20th-century equivalent to Beethoven's Choral Symphony – the work which seems to have been constantly in his thoughts in 1936, and which he described to an interviewer in Santa Fe as 'the greatest choral work'. But for all its idealistic ambition, Varèse's intended contemporary equivalent was clearly an idea of appalling complication. It was not much simplified when the composer later dreamed of having his work presented in the context of a vast multi-media festival (Barcelona was his favoured site), with rapid sequences of projected visual images to coincide with the music.[11]

Varèse was to go on wrestling with *Espace*, in varying forms, for a further decade at least. Certainly one endemic drawback was that the work as he saw it came increasingly to depend on electronic means of performance and transmission which simply did not yet exist. His imagination, as usual, had taken flight far in advance of technology, and this time disastrously so.

Nevertheless, the reason for the non-completion of *Espace* cannot merely have been technical. At least as important were personal, psychological factors. The later 1930s, and the whole of the 1940s, were a prolonged period of frustration, illness and depression for Varèse, which came near to breaking his spirit. And the unremitting sequence of mass tragedies thrown up by the Spanish Civil War, the Sino-Japanese War, the Second World War with its concentration

---

[10] Anticipating the compositional techniques of electronic music, notably Varèse's own *Poème électronique*.

[11] Another anticipation of *Poème électronique*. Barcelona, seat until the beginning of 1939 of the increasingly Communist and decreasingly Anarchist Catalan government, ceased to be a practicable venue with its conquest by Franco's armies and the final defeat of the Spanish Republican cause.

camps and the detonation of the atom bomb (Varèse's beloved atomic science employed for mass destruction), followed with hardly a break by the continuation of the civil war in China and then the Korean War, must have seemed to make a mockery of *Espace*'s intended message of brotherhood, of the idea that there could ever be 'a conscious humanity neither exploitable nor pitiable'.

Many years later, Varèse's erstwhile collaborator Alejo Carpentier, in his novel *La consagración de la primavera*, created an imaginative evocation of the composer's isolation during this period, struggling to bring his ideas to birth. It is 1943, in New York, and two of the novel's protagonists are dining with an Italian musician at a restaurant which must be very near 188 Sullivan Street.

From a nearby house were issuing piercing, prolonged, wailing, strange sounds which suddenly – following a rapid downward glissando – turned into something that sounded like the panting, spasmodic roaring of some huge, unidentifiable animal. – 'It's Edgar Varèse, working with his electronic equipment', said Gian-Carlo. – 'And that's supposed to be music?' asked Teresa, whose musical outlook was rather conventionally traditional. '*Chi lo sa?*' answered the Italian, evasively.[12]

It was presumably around the same time as the dramatic date of the passage just quoted from Carpentier's novel that Henry Miller began writing the essay 'With Edgar Varèse in the Gobi Desert', eventually published in 1945 as part of his *The Air-Conditioned Nightmare*. Throughout Miller's polemical chapter – which tells us, perhaps, rather more about its author than about Varèse – it is clear that *Espace*, though never mentioned by that title, remained Varèse's 'coming opus'; indeed the chapter opens with a version of the Scenario text ('Theme: TODAY. The world awake! ...) quoted on p.299. But Miller's essay, though it has little concrete to tell us about the work, is one avenue of approach to the question of what eventually happened to *Espace*. Indeed, his title furnishes a clue: part of it, at least, slowly metamorphosed into his first work to use electronic tape: *Déserts*. Varèse made no secret of the fact that *Déserts* made use of elements

12 Carpentier, op.cit., p.277. (Translation here by James Reid Baxter, who points out that the same passage contains references to John Cage and Anaïs Nin.) It is poetic license to suppose Varèse had 'electronic equipment' to work with in his studio in early 1943. He did, on the other hand, have sirens, and Carpentier's characters may be assumed to have overheard these.

taken from *Espace*, but the gradual change in the conception from one work to the other was evidently a long and complex process.

Paradoxically, the transformation must have begun in 1936–37 during his two long sojourns in New Mexico, which he undertook without Louise in order to teach and lecture in Santa Fe and Albuquerque. During this time *Espace* as originally conceived was occupying him deeply. The published examples of his correspondence from those years, to Louise, to André Jolivet and others, eloquently testify to the profound impact which the experience of the Southwestern desert had upon Varèse's imagination.

Certainly that region must rank among the world's true magical landscapes. In the words of the American novelist Willa Cather, 'Elsewhere the sky is the roof of the world; but here the earth was the floor of the sky'. Under that enormous sky the irresistible forces of tectonic upheaval, wind and water have sculptured this ancient-seeming but geologically young land into a dramatic topography of desert canyons, rugged mountains, huge table-mountain mesas, dry river courses and barren scrubland. Just as its cultural landscape was shaped by diverse Native American peoples and later by Spanish and Anglo-American colonization, the adobe buildings of Indian pueblos and early colonial architecture blend in organic unity with the natural shapes of the desert. Its barren beauty, vast sense of scale, vivid colour, isolation and atmosphere of the elemental must have answered perfectly to Varèse's creative needs and aims. On 14 November 1936, when he seems actually to have been at work on *Espace*, he wrote to Louise:

More and more I love the strength and the desolation of this land – its violence – its very clear sky ... and the stars that sparkle as in legends. I'm tired of schools, of styles, of modernisms. More than ever only the epic interests me – and the great cries into space. For no one – or only for those capable of understanding the signal.[13]

Some of the phraseology here is strongly reminiscent of *The One All Alone* – and in the deserts of New Mexico Varèse finally made personal contact with the Native American tribes whose mythologies had stimulated his imagination to conceive his Sirius stage-work. Indeed meeting Indians at first hand seems to have been one of his uppermost concerns as soon as he arrived in the Southwest. Starting with visits to

---

[13] Quoted in Mattis (1992), p.574.

the Santo Domingo pueblo immediately to the south-west of Santa Fe, where he befriended one of the tribal elders, he later made contacts among at least four of the Indian nations which occupy reservations in the area: the Apache, Zuni, and Navajo, whose vast reservation, straddling New Mexico and Arizona, surrounds the lands of the Hopi. Varèse visited pueblos, obtained permission to view traditional ceremonies and dances, and later apparently went camping in the open with bands of Indians. Probably he saw some of the impressive and haunting ruined cliff-dwellings of the vanished civilization of the Anasazi. He declared himself especially interested in the nomadic, warrior tribes, the Navajo and Apache. This is not surprising given the beliefs of the Navajo Dinee (people), who build their hogans to face the rising sun, and whose cosmology depicts starry constellations, placed in the sky by the First Man and First Woman. He must have heard among the Navajo the characteristic music of the Native American flute, some aspects of which he had already, wittingly or unwittingly, evoked in his own *Density 21.5*, but he wrote to Jolivet that he

wouldn't dream of touching their music. Magnificent, when it forms part of their rites; outside of that context it is meaningless. As for their rites, no white man knows, ever knew, nor will ever know anything.[14]

There can be no doubt that Varèse's months in the Southwest continued to exercise an influence over his developing conceptions in the following years, when he stayed in Los Angeles and tried unavailingly to interest the Hollywood film studios in the production of films with 'organized sound': films no doubt like that which he conceived a decade later in connexion with *Déserts* (below, p.339). In a recent article, Olivia Mattis has sensitively suggested how the desert opened out the conception of *Espace* in a new direction:

... we can suppose that the title *Espace* represents not only astronomical space ... but also the unbroken terrestrial expanse of the south-west, as well as the spaces, what Varèse called the 'deserts' of the mind. One understands from his descriptions that each concept, 'desert' and 'space', is at once a literal representation and a psychological symbol, and that the two words were for him interchangeable terms. They both represent a frontier to be crossed ...[15]

---

[14] Mattis, op.cit., p.575.

[15] Ibid., p.576.

After his return to New York in late 1940s, the overwhelming image of
the desert still remained with Varèse. It was at this time, beginning
probably in the winter of 1940–41, that Henry Miller, who had first
come to know the composer in Paris in the late 1920s, now took up
with him again. Varèse was still wrestling with the problem of a text for
his choral symphony; the projected Malraux collaboration had long
ago expired, and it seems that in the interim he had also approached
e.e. cummings, without success. At some point in the early 1940s,
Varèse turned to Miller to request a text, in a conversation from which
Miller has transmitted two telling phrases.

> ... talking to Varèse about his new work, asked if I would care to contribute
> some phrases for the chorus – 'magical phrases', said Varèse – all that I had
> previously heard [of his music] came back to me with redoubled force and
> significance. 'I want something of the feeling of the Gobi Desert', said Varèse.
>
> The Gobi Desert! My head began to spin. He couldn't have used an image
> more accurate than this to describe the ultimate effect which his organized
> sound music produced in my mind.[16]

Varèse had never seen the Gobi Desert, apart perhaps from
photographs. No doubt he used the name to evoke a natural space so
far away as to be almost other-worldly. The desert he knew best was
that of the American Southwest. His call for 'magical phrases', too, is
revealing. From the beginning, the *Espace* scenario had envisaged a text
which would at least partly have been constructed of disjointed
phrases, including 'phrases out of folklore'. It is perhaps possible to
discern, over the years, a move away from a structured text towards one
more concerned with 'the vocal and evocative qualities of individual
words and phrases' – as Chou Wen-Chung has written of *Nocturnal*, a
later work whose development, at least as far as its text was concerned,
seems to have followed a not dissimilar progression to that of *Espace*.
Certainly this seems to have been the verbal end-product in the only
portion of *Espace* ever put into performable shape, the *Étude pour
Espace* (below, p.311).

The extent to which Miller responded to Varèse's request is
ambiguous. Towards the end of his essay 'With Edgar Varèse in the
Gobi Desert' he asks rhetorically: 'what am I to offer Varèse for that
Gobi Desert stretch of his sonorous score?' and then prints a kind of

---

[16] Miller, op. cit., pp. 172–3.

scenario, meant to 'append a footnote to [his] new opus'. He does not directly offer this text for setting, and it is clearly less designed to give Varèse the 'magical phrases' he was looking for than to be a personal expression of what the 'Gobi Desert' image conjures up in Miller.

What is remarkable about Miller's untitled scenario – enacted by post-holocaust survivors in the Gobi Desert, which has become 'a place of refuge' – is the fact that it establishes no point of contact with Varèse's 'The World Awake' manifesto (which Miller himself had used to begin his essay), but contains close reminiscences of the earlier 'Sirius' stage work, *The One All Alone*. It is possible – probable, even – that Varèse may have discussed that project with Miller (and possibly in Paris in the Twenties rather than New York in the Forties). At any rate, Miller certainly seems to have thought he was writing something that might appeal to Varèse, or at least interpret to Miller's readers what Miller felt Varèse was about.

One paragraph brings the 'Sirius' parallels especially close:

A dervish springs up and begins to whirl like a top. The sky turns white. The air grows chill. Suddenly a knife flashes and in the sky a gleam of light appears. A blue star coming nearer and nearer – a dazzling, blinding star.[17]

Elsewhere the scenario has more of the improvisatory, ejaculatory quality of Artaud's *Il n'y a plus de firmament*, with its vivid but somewhat jejeune 'musical directions' ('A huge gong resounds, drowning everything. Again, and again, and again. The a shattering silence. When it has become almost insupportable a flute is heard – the flute of a shepherd invisible ...'[18]). But at least Miller is convinced of the power of Varèse's music to produce from such indications a powerful emotional effect. And his scenario contains one individual character, 'The Magician', whose air of esoteric authority resonates with that of Varèse's Astronomer, and who announces 'A new world is about to be born ... What is magic? The knowledge that you are free.'[19] At the end of his article Miller provides, in advance, an answer to the query of Carpentier's character Teresa:

What a sound [Varèse 'blowing his horn'] makes in a world lying cold and dead! *Is it music*? I don't know. I don't need to know ... All's quiet now along

---

[17] Ibid., p.176; compare p.230 above.

[18] Ibid., p.177.

[19] Ibid., p.177.

the Western, the Eastern, the Southern and the Northern Front. We're in the Gobi at last. Only the chorus is left. And the elements: helium, oxygen, nitrogen, sulphur et cetera. Time rolls away. Space folds up. What is left of man is pure MAN ... [20]

Though he may have approved of the sentiments behind Miller's scenario, Varèse did not make use of it. Despite a decade of work, no doubt intermittent but surely at intervals tremendously intensive, he never managed to bring his 'choral symphony' to satisfactory realization. Apart from the partial exception of the short and, in a sense, instrumentally compromised *Etude pour Espace*, the grand conception – *Espace* itself – seems not to have advanced beyond the stage of sketches. But apparently there were eventually very many sketches, which Varèse kept with him and which he was able to use later as a quarry for the material of his works of the 1950s. Chou Wen-Chung has testified to the existence of this large body of sketch material:

For many years there was a tremendous collection of sketches that I saw constantly because they were hanging there in his studio. He had them on a long line – on the wall in front of his desk – that he called his 'laundry line'. At that time he was composing *Déserts*. ... And the laundry-line sketches did not change very much, other than those in front of his working space. Of course, I should have had the foresight at that time to really look at them more closely. It is my opinion those were the sketches he worked on during the period when he did not finish any particular work. In looking at the material in *Déserts*, *Poème électronique*, *Nocturnal*, and certain sketches, I find that the material for all these is related to the sketches that he was working on in the 1940s. Now, what happened to that enormous amount of sketches? Apparently at some stage, close to his death, he decided to throw them out. I think he told Mrs. Varèse at one stage, suddenly, that they were getting in his way. He was writing new works, and yet he was examining the old materials. Mrs. Varèse managed to salvage quite a bit of this material, but we lost a great deal. ... [These sketches] probably were for *Espace* (in fact, 'probably', here, is a very cautious word: I think they no doubt were for *Espace*).[21]

---

[20] Ibid., p.178.

[21] *The New Worlds of Edgard Varèse: A Symposium* edited by Sherman Van Solkema (New York: I.S.A.M. Monographs Number 11, 1979), pp. 88–89.

ETUDE POUR ESPACE

Only fragments of *Espace* got as far as a public hearing, and those only as they were incorporated in the *Etude pour Espace*, performed just once and never subsequently released either for performance or (save one page) publication. As its title suggests, this work was a 'study' for *Espace* – an 'étude hors d'oeuvre', as Varèse termed it. His intention seems to have been a presentation of as much of the material as could be brought within the capabilities of a vocal group, such as his own Greater New York Chorus, and such supporting instruments as might be available. So the Etude was perhaps born more out of his need and desire to hear some of *Espace*, after ten years' labour, in actual performance, than from a strong creative urge to produce a 'finished' work with its own expressive profile. However, after the disbanding of the Greater New York Chorus it fell to the New Music Society, which had a small chorus of 22 voices, to mount the one and only performance of *Etude pour Espace* on 20 April 1947,[22] conducted by Varèse.

The work is scored for chorus, two pianos and percussion. According to Chou Wen-Chung, the pianos were a substitute, and perhaps a rather despairing one, for the wind ensemble that Varèse had actually envisaged for the piece. It appears the chorus was too small, even so, to hold its own against the instrumental line-up; they were perhaps also too unfamiliar with Varèse's idioms, and the special demands he seems to have placed on the voices in *Etude pour Espace*. Varèse's estate contains an archive recording of the performance on three 78 rpm discs. From this recording Varèse would later select the few brief passages which reappear, in entirely transmuted form, in *Poème électronique*. But the only generally-available account of the

---

[22] Ouellette's much-quoted date of 23 February is incorrect. It is therefore unclear how much credence can be placed on his date of 'February 1947' for the *Etude*'s completion, especially since the published facsimile of the final page (see below) bears no visible date and Chou Wen-Chung has stated that the precise date of composition is unknown. But completion a couple of months in advance of the première, if the performance was already scheduled, would seem plausible enough. Chou (*The New Worlds of Edgard Varèse*, loc. cit.) has described the *Etude* as 'written for a particular occasion in 1947 to try out his ideas'.

work is Ouellette's description, based on the basis of an audition of the discs.[23]

This is not exactly detailed, but some salient points emerge from his comments, especially as to the use of the chorus and the percussion writing.

Perhaps for the first time in the history of music,[24] Varèse dispensed with a coherent text having a meaning of its own and instead selected various phrases from different languages, none having any meaning in relation to the others, and perhaps not even in itself. ... Varèse began from the principle ... that a chorus must have concrete words to bite into, that consonants are necessary, and that it cannot therefore be given only vowels or diphthongs to sing. The chorus speaks, declaims, and becomes, so various are the sonorities of its words, a sort of percussion section. In addition, the chorus also performs a melodic function, since Varèse employs it, in certain sections, in its full polyphonic capacity.

After commenting that the use of the chorus is very different from that encountered in *Ecuatorial* and much closer to *Nocturnal*, though in that later work 'the semantic dimension has not been suppressed ... as it was in *Etude*', Ouellette continues:

The use of the percussion is also very solid, with some unique inventions. ... The aggression in [*Etude's*] percussion attack hits one in the pit of the stomach. And the search for infinity, expressed by the chorus, is very clear in certain sections. ... Later, Varèse used two or three excerpts from *Etude* in his *Poème électronique*, though they were so transposed and filtered as to become unrecognizable. He also used the soprano's cry in *Nocturnal*, though 'skewering' it with a piccolo.

This is Ouellette's only reference to a solo voice (as shown below, there are at least two). His reference to the 'very solid' use of the percussion is impressionistic rather than specific, but I take him to mean that percussion attacks are perhaps more rhythmically unanimous, calculated for weight and impact of sonority, than in other Varèse compositions.

As for his description of the role of the chorus, and its multilingual

---

[23] Ouellette, pp. 163–164.

[24] Certainly not so. The meaningless invented language of Arthur Bliss's *Rout* (1920) comes immediately to mind, and there must be other examples.

text, this element in the *Etude* clearly derives from one of the fundamental aspects of the *Espace* project: the 'phrases of American, French, Russian, Chinese, Spanish, German revolutions ... phrases out of folklore' mentioned in Varèse's 'Humanity on the march' scenario (above, p. 299). It is, however, remarkable that Ouellette, a poet, chose to concentrate on the 'a-semantic' nature of this text. Doubtless much of the choral writing is of this nature, the phrases chosen for their purely musical effect, like the nasal or groaning vocables in *Ecuatorial*. Yet there is evidence that some sections, at least, are semantically coherent, as at the work's ending.

To date, all that has been published of *Etude pour Espace* is a single page: the last, which appeared in facsimile of Varèse's manuscript in the magazine *Possibilities*.[25] The page only indicates the presence of one piano, and in fact the caption describes the work as 'Etude, for percussion, piano, and chorus'. Six percussionists are shown, playing (as far as can be made out) high and low gongs, cymbals, bass drum, tambour de basque, side drum, guiro and triangle. The vocal forces are divided between SATB chorus, humming, and soprano and tenor solos, who sing the same Spanish text, one after the other: '*noche oscura de fuego amoroso*'.

'Dark night of the fire of love ...': this is a line from the *Dark Night of the Soul* of St. John of the Cross. In the early 1950s Varèse was marking passages from this book, 'which never left his bedside table', in the search for a text for the vocal work that ultimately became *Nocturnal* (below, p.384). But its earlier role in *Etude pour Espace*, and perhaps therefore in *Espace* itself, seems so far to have remained almost unnoticed. Though Varèse was not in any conventional sense religious, it is entirely understandable that this classic expression of spiritual

---

[25] *Possibilities 1* (Problems of Contemporary Art), Winter 1947/8, p.98 (NY: Wittenborn, Schultz, Inc.). The facsimile accompanies the feature 'Edgard Varèse: Answers to 8 Composers (Robert Palmer, Adolph Weiss, Milton Babbitt, Henry Cowell, Harold Shapero, Kurt List, Jacques de Menasce, John Cage).' Cage is credited on the title page as the editor (music) of *Possibilities*, which describes itself as 'an occasional review'. It should further be noted that on p.109 of this issue is a list of Varèse's works which gives a duration of 10 minutes for *Etude* – as might have been deduced from its filling three 78 rpm discs – and which, fascinatingly for this late date, lists among the orchestral works *Trois Pièces, La Chanson des Jeunes Hommes, Rhapsodie Romane, Prélude à la fin d'un jour, Bourgogne, Mehr Licht, Gargantua* and *Les cycles du nord*: in that order and without any indication of their being lost or destroyed.

struggle and mastery of despair should have obsessed him in the 1940s, the period which, for him, was truly a 'dark night of the soul'. It appears – and Ouellette seems to sense this when he describes *Etude pour Espace* as 'a work in which the composer's suffering abruptly explodes after his long silence and struggles in the desert'[26] – that the great communal proclamation of *Espace* had eventually issued, in *Etude*, in an entirely personal appeal: a cry, if not for help, then at least to be heard, and for the creative fire of love. That seems to be the burden of the anguished, rising tenor-soprano line, soaring to a stratospheric E♭ and then fading out in the last echoes of percussion and piano.[27]

As of early 2002, *Etude pour Espace* is now the only completed work of Varèse that remains unavailable for scrutiny or performance.[28] The epithet 'completed' needs some qualification, of course: Varèse was certainly dissatisfied with the work as it stood, and according to Chou Wen-Chung three copies of the score exist among Varèse's papers, each one carrying a different – and presumably conflicting – set of revisions. (Apparently a further, incomplete copy exists in the Philips archives in Holland.) Even so: whatever the difficulties involved in bringing it to a publishable and re-performable state; whatever its status as a 'makeshift' sample of Varèse's ideas around 1947 – one can only concur with Ouellette that *Etude pour Espace* should be made available. Even from the little that can be known about it, it is clearly unique in his oeuvre, a vital piece in the jigsaw of his life's work; and almost certainly of more significance than the two short works, its near-contemporaries, which have recently emerged into the light.

---

[26] Ouellette, loc. cit.

[27] This is not the 'skewered' soprano line which Ouellette mentions as being quoted in *Nocturnal*.

[28] Professor Chou – who in 1979 went on record as considering the existence of three divergent copies made the work impossible to perform (*The New Worlds of Edgard Varèse*, loc.cit.) – has apparently agreed to undertake an edition of *Etude pour Espace* for Ricordi, but there is as yet no precise schedule for its completion.

TUNING UP

Varèse's pronouncements in the later 1940s were often tinged with bitterness and frustration, and contempt for the domination of American musical life by 'middlemen' – producers and impresarios. It was becoming clear to him that his more ambitious projects would, for the present, be unlikely to secure a hearing in his adopted country, even if he managed to complete them. The case of *Tuning Up*, not a major project but a mere *jeu d'esprit*, no doubt gave him positive proof of this state of affairs.

He had met the film producer Boris Moross in the 1930s through their mutual friend Walter Anderson, who had published Varèse's essay 'Organized Sound for the Sound Film' in his magazine *The Commonweal* in 1940. Although Moross was unable (or unwilling) to help Varèse to gain access to the Hollywood sound studios in order to pursue his acoustic researches, he did remember the composer, and in 1946 used Anderson as an intermediary to ask Varèse to compose a short piece for the feature film *Carnegie Hall*, which Moross was producing.

Though it includes cameos of many musicians including Fritz Reiner, Leopold Stokowski and Bruno Walter, *Carnegie Hall* is a romantic comedy with a large element of fantasy, summed up by perhaps its most famous sequence, in which the cellist Piatigorsky is seen performing Saint-Saëns's *Le Cygne* to an accompaniment of multiple harps. It was therefore very much in the nature of the film that Moross should have approached Varèse to compose a parody of an orchestra tuning up before a concert. Varèse saw possibilities in this idea far beyond anything that the producer imagined – partly, no doubt, because he knew the piece would be played by the New York Philharmonic under Stokowski. Without discussing a fee, he began sketching the music, only to find that Moross in time became disenchanted with the idea and dropped it before Varèse could bring his work to a conclusion.

From the surviving materials it is clear that he had conceived the idea of a kind of playful fantasy on his own (and other) music, with quotations from some of his scores emerging from the sound-continuum of an orchestra improvising on the pitch A, along with a few phrases from the standard repertoire. It is possible that work on *Tuning Up*, as the piece was logically titled, largely or wholly preceded the composition of *Etude pour Espace*. Perhaps its collage-like nature may even have suggested the nature of the *Etude* as an arrangement of a number of pre-existing ideas.

Varèse preserved some drafts of *Tuning Up*; but with no incentive to proceed further the score was never completed and remained entirely unknown. Only at the end of 1995, when Riccardo Chailly proposed to make new and authoritative recordings of Varèse's entire output, did Chou Wen-chung happen to show the record producer Andrew Cornall the sketch material for the piece. As a result, a performing version was jointly commissioned by the Royal Concertgebouw Orchestra, the publishers Ricordi, and the Decca Record Company. Thus *Tuning Up*, 'reconstructed and edited' by Professor Chou,[29] was first performed under Chailly in a studio recording in the Grote Zaal of the Concertgebouw, Amsterdam during May 1998, and premièred in a public concert in the same hall as part of the opening concert of the Concertgebouw's 1998–99 season on 24 August.

Chou's report on the manuscript materials[30] and how he has dealt with them makes clear that Varèse had left two short drafts – neither of them a first draft, as they have the appearance of revisions of a yet earlier version, incorporating pasted-in fragments of manuscript pages and photocopies. From his description it would seem than these drafts are distinct elaborations of the same basic idea, rather than two parts of a single piece, as they have virtually identical beginnings and only gradually diverge to entirely different conclusions. Nevertheless, as both offered possibilities for performance, Professor Chou decided to combine them sequentially into a single piece with a two-part design. (In the score, this gives a total of 100 bars, the first 40 corresponding to one draft and the latter 60 to the other.) This conception is aided by the fact that both drafts are woven around the 'tuning-up' pitch A; and whereas one draft ends softly, with 'open' and isolated sounds that Chou has likened to the ending of *Déserts*, the other ends decisively, with open A's on the full orchestra through six octaves. It was therefore possible to treat the drafts as respectively the opening and closing portions of a piece lasting five minutes in performance.

---

[29] This is the wording on the Decca recording. The Ricordi score describes *Tuning Up* as 'completed from sketches' by Chou.

[30] Decca 460 208–2, 'Varèse: The Complete Works'. Much of this paragraph, and the next, derives directly from these notes.

Tuning Up is scored for a large standard symphony orchestra with quadruple wind, two harps and a typically Varèsian array of percussion requiring six players – a large enough body, all told, to handle the quotations from *Amériques*, *Arcana*, *Ionisation* and *Intégrales*. Some of the instrumentation – the inclusion of two sirens, for instance – is clearly due to Chou's inference from Varèse's sketchy indications. He has explained that the most 'enigmatic' aspect of the drafts was the many large *crescendo-diminuendo* hairpins, extended over many bars yet unsynchronized with, and indeed often contradicting, the dynamic marks of the instruments which had been assigned music. Chou rejects the possibility that these hairpins represent some electronic instrument. Recalling instead that Varèse's two sirens, high and low, were constantly with him in his studio and could easily be taken to Carnegie Hall for the projected performance, he has interpreted the hairpins as referring both to the sirens, and to the other instruments of the orchestra – those not involved in the notated music – going through the routine of tuning up. He has also expanded and elaborated the percussion parts to highlight or contrast with the melodic and rhythmic aspects of the pitched materials, and to correlate with the rise and fall of the sirens' whine.

While Chou was surely correct in his interpretation of these notations, there are bound to be reservations about his decision to combine two different drafts to create a single two-part piece. No doubt this was the most practical course in order to make *Tuning Up* long enough to be worth programming. Yet the two drafts do seem to be alternative workings-out of one short work, half the length of Chou's edition. Had Varèse brought it to a conclusion he might have made a definitive decision in favour of one draft rather than the other, and worked it up to a finished state (possibly incorporating aspects of the rejected draft which he found valuable). Realistic in programming terms or not – and certainly welcome in the way it allows us to hear Varèse playing in different ways with his diverting idea – Chou's edition brings into being a piece which, in its still-small space, contains far more verbatim 'recapitulation' than occurs in any other existing Varèse work: inevitably so, as the two drafts begin almost identically and take some time to diverge. It is – to put it mildly – highly unlikely that Varèse intended such an effect of large-scale repetition. This reservation aside, it could well be argued that the repetitions make the music easier to grasp for audiences unfamiliar with Varèse. One can only agree with Chou that *Tuning Up* is 'a perfect overture to Varèse's music, and an equally fascinating opening for any symphonic concert'.

In one respect *Tuning Up* sounds totally unlike any other Varèse work, for it is dominated by the sound of open strings. The pitch A, around which orchestras tune, is omnipresent, though contrasted with and often drowned out by completely non-tonal music; and Varèse frequently builds up structures of open fifths on this foundation. In fact he had a lifelong fondness for this most resonant of intervals, often used to dramatic and evocative effect in his other scores – but never, as here, within the deliberate evocation of a tonal context.

The solo oboe sounding A – giving the orchestra the pitch, as before any typical symphony concert – is the first sound we hear in *Tuning Up*, followed by the swelling wave of woodwind and brass doing just what the title says. Against this background the orchestra leader tries out a scrap of tune: the only extant violin solo in Varèse (Ex.1).

This sounds like, but perhaps is not, a quotation: it suggests, if anything, the Stravinsky of *L'Histoire du Soldat*. And it is followed immediately by a typical 'fanfare-complex' in brass and woodwind, with some support from strings (Ex.2).

This appears to be built from allusions to two elements from different Varèse works – the horn-trumpet call is a version of Ex.3 from *Intégrales* (which will emerge more explicitly later), and the spiky woodwind flourish from Ex.6 of *Amériques*. Low gong and cymbal sounds introduce the solo oboe again, now as if improvising with its A as a base pitch, leaping up an octave or a fifth and playing with other pitches, eventually landing on the E♭ a tritone above the initial A. The tritone interval, always significant in Varèse's work, has much to do in

Tuning Up to counteract the 'open' tuning sounds. As a horn resonates
the E♭ two octaves below, strings and woodwind continue their tuning
noises, and the timpani launches into an aggressive solo mimicking the
oboe's line. This brings in its wake a rhythmic tattoo from the
percussion ensemble, and a solo for trumpet playing with the tritone
(now G-D♭) in a wild, rather jazzy solo. At the end a second trumpet
joins in, and they sweep up in unison to a high sustained A. Around
this gathers a full-scale quotation of the wild tutti from *Amériques*
shown as Example 8 on p.118 – the passage which Varèse had already
reproduced in reduced form in the second song of *Offrandes*. Virtually
exact for woodwind, strings, horns and trombones, but minus the
original trumpet parts (since the trumpets continue to sustain their A)
and with simplified tuba writing, this quotation is embellished with
more complex percussion writing than it received in *Amériques*, and
with a crescendo on the high siren. This reaches its dynamic peak in an
otherwise empty bar, after the quotation has been suddenly cut off.

Percussion patterns from *Ionisation* mingle with snapping staccato
brass rhythms from *Intégrales* while woodwind and strings go on 'tuning
up' and the low siren moans away in the background. This issues in a
two-bar fanfare from *Intégrales*, varied and rescored for the full
orchestra. Strings and horns then restate the 'tonic' A and woodwind
and brass flick the pitch up and down in octave leaps, uniting on a full-
orchestral tutti A six octaves deep. This lasts for a single bar; then it
dissipates in small sounds and resonances for xylophone, bass clarinet,
harps, low strings, low clarinet, tuba and finally muted trumpet, which
reiterates a B a seventh below the oboe's opening A. Here the music
seems to pause slightly: in fact this was the 'open' ending of the first of
Varèse's two drafts, but in Chou's realization of *Tuning Up* it becomes a
near-to-central point of relaxation before the fun begins anew.

Exactly as at the beginning, we hear again the oboe's A, the violin's
Ex.1, the 'fanfare complex' Ex.2. This time it picks up the low siren,
whose crescendo-diminuendo leads straight into a different quotation
from *Amériques*: the swirling impressionist chromatics, with multiple
glissandi in strings and harps, which followed the first appearance of
the chant-like string melody Ex.13 in that work. Once again the
percussion writing is more elaborate than in *Amériques* itself, and the
high siren is added, sounding into an otherwise silent half-bar. More
'literal recapitulation' of the previous draft follows: the oboe's playing
with A, landing on E; the timpani's aggressive rejoinder; the jagged

trumpet solo, rising to the high A and bringing the (first) *Amériques* quotation back again. This time that formidable tutti is extended into a kind of fantasia on short motives from the final section of *Amériques*, with 'tuning up' sounds continuing in those instruments not playing notated music in any specific bar.

In what must be the most Ivesian passage in Varèse's output, foreign bodies begin to infiltrate this melange, though they pass so swiftly not every hearer will immediately recognize them. Two muted trumpets, in thirds, enunciate a phrase from Pierné's *March of the Little Tin Soldiers* (marked 'crisp'). In the next bar flute and horn introduce a figure from the *Marseillaise* – the same figure Varèse had quoted in trumpet and voice in the first song of *Offrandes*. The tutti is cut off to reveal the two sirens at different stages of their dynamic parabola: and in the percussion, a famous rhythm: the tapping anvils of the Nibelungs from Wagner's *Das Rheingold* (Ex.3a). This is simultaneously a reference to *Ionisation*. In one of the wittiest instantaneous transformations in his output, Varèse allows the 'Nibelung' rhythm to suggest two other pieces which make use of it: Beethoven's Seventh Symphony (a phrase from the first movement's first subject swiftly and elegantly introduced on the flute, to the irresistibly incongruous accompaniment of Chinese blocks: Ex.3*b*) and then his own *Amériques*. This third and last *Amériques* quotation paraphrases the pounding, rhythmic tutti shortly before that work's final section.

Ex.3 (a)

More 'tuning up', with two-siren accompaniment, and a snatch of *Yankee Doodle* on trumpet and high woodwind, now introduces an entire fanfare-complex from *Arcana*, extended and then suddenly cut short. In a duplication of the start of the 'coda' of the first half of *Tuning Up* horns and strings, *fff*, enunciate the 'tonic' A, which is solemnly echoed by full brass and timpani over three octaves. Woodwind and brass flicker up and down the A's in octaves, once again arriving at a massive unison spanning six octaves A from the heights to the depths. Embellished by rolls on timpani and full percussion, it swells to a grandiose *sffff* close.

Although, as noted above, *Tuning Up* as edited by Chou Wen-Chung probably little resembles the piece that Varèse might have completed in its overall form, by combining both his extant drafts in a single span Chou has maximized the realization of Varèse's basic concept, and in the process presented a highly diverting and unexpected addition to Varèse's catalogue of works. So much of Varèse's music is concerned with struggle and agonized revelation we tend to forget his explosive humour, which is celebrated in *Tuning Up*, and is also dangerously evident in his next work, *Dance for Burgess*.

DANCE FOR BURGESS

During 1949 Varèse approached the actor-director Burgess Meredith to propose collaboration on a film to be called *Le Désert* with music by Varèse – the project which became *Déserts*. Meredith in his turn asked Varèse to compose something for him. He was about to act and dance in, as well as direct, an unconventional – indeed 'avant garde' – kind of musical comedy called *Happy as Larry*, to be choreographed by Anna Sokolow and featuring mobiles by the sculptor Alexander Calder. He suggested Varèse contribute a short dance to the show, and Varèse, whose relations with Meredith were much warmer than with Moross, agreed. The result was called simply *Dance for Burgess*.

The performance score, dated 9 December 1949, was copied directly from Varèse's draft by Chou Wen-Chung, who had become Varèse's pupil earlier in the year. He had to work in haste, leaving no time for the composer to correct or revise, so that the dance would be ready for the show's preview in Boston. It was first performed at the preview on 27 December and again on the show's opening night in New York on 6 January 1950 – after which *Happy as Larry* folded, a critical disaster, and nothing more was heard of *Dance for Burgess* in Varèse's lifetime.

In fact he seems to have viewed it as merely an occasional work, as he made no subsequent effort to have it published or performed – though he did, apparently, make some revisions to the score. After his death *Dance for Burgess* remained unpublished and not generally available, though its existence was known to *cognoscenti*.[31] A copy of the score was eventually placed in the Library of Congress, and at least one performance took place with Chou Wen-Chung's approval when the London Sinfonietta, conducted by David Atherton, included the piece as part of their 'complete Varèse' concert series at London's Queen Elizabeth Hall on 21 January 1984. Neverless, it appears that at that time Professor Chou was of the opinion that it was 'not a real Varèse work'.[32] It was only in the late 1990s that – as a result of the Riccardo Chailly / Decca project already mentioned in connexion with *Tuning Up* – Chou produced a final, authorized edition of *Dance for Burgess* for performance and publication, jointly commissioned by the Concertgebouw, Decca and Ricordi.[33]

With a duration of less than two minutes *Dance for Burgess* is Varèse's shortest work, about the length of the middle movement of *Octandre*. Compared to his other scores it is certainly 'simplified' in some respects – Varèse was willing to go some way to accommodate the sensibilities of Broadway musicians, if not their audiences – but it is still genuine Varèse. Even 'characteristic', if we view it as the only achieved work in a line of projected dance pieces going back through *Danse du Robinet froid* to the circus *Songe d'une nuit d'été*. Chou has stated that the original scoring was for

... a conventional Broadway ensemble and Varèse, pressed for time, did not

---

[31] Larry Stempel quotes the trombone 'cadenza' in the course of his 1979 *Musical Quarterly* article (Stempel, 1979, p. 159).

[32] Bernard, p.238, quoting a phone-conversation of 1983 with Chou. However Bernard's query in his annotated list of Varèse's works whether someone 'other than Varèse had a hand in determining the final form of this work' (loc. cit.) must apparently be answered in the negative. Bernard further states that the reproduction of the manuscript in the Library of Congress is dated 30 December 1949 – perhaps the date of revisions following the Boston preview.

[33] The Decca record set describes this as a 'completed edition'; the Ricordi score as 'corrected and completed by Chou Wen-Chung'.

use some of the instruments for more than a couple of notes – the string bass, for example, was assigned only one note![34]

As edited by Chou the *Dance* is scored for piccolo, E♭ clarinet, B♭ clarinet, bass clarinet, horn, 2 trumpets, trombone, tuba, percussion, piano and string quintet. He suggests, however, that multiple strings may be used, or none at all, *ad libitum*, and in fact all of the strings' material is doubled in the wind instruments. It is probably preferable, therefore, to regard *Dance for Burgess* as a piece for wind instruments and percussion, and this is how it appears in the Decca recording (and how it was performed by the London Sinfonietta). Three percussionists are required, to handle a typical (if slightly undersized) Varèsian body of 3 Chinese Blocks, mounted tambourine, snare drum, tenor drum, bass drum, sleigh bells, cowbell, high suspended cymbal, Chinese crash cymbal, a gong, timpani (only two drums: one tuned to C below middle C, the other 'tuned beyond its lowest register to produce a strong yet pitchless tone'), guiro, claves, a second set of Chinese blocks, and a string drum (Lion's roar).

There seems to be no record of Anna Sokolow's choreography, and the music itself – which is in 4/4 or 2/4 time with only a few single bars in more irrational metres (3/8, 5/8, 5/4) – suggests a rather abstract 'modern dance', though with suggestions perhaps of a Cubist ragtime. It begins with the percussion alone – a spattering of sounds loud and soft from drums, blocks and guiro in comparatively simple texture for a Varèse work, with a repeated quintuplet figure emerging on claves. Meanwhile the only melodic material is a 4-note segment of chromatic scale on clarinets (pointed up by sleigh bells), which is then

---

[34] Chou Wen-Chung, liner notes to Decca 460 208–2.

vertically expanded by trumpets. These preliminaries over, the main 'dance' element struts forth on the full ensemble (Ex.1). The piano part, doubling the trombone with its louche glissando, puts one faintly in mind of some of Charles Ives's theatre-orchestra pieces, such as *In the Inn*. Brass, clarinets and percussion fragment the elements of this 'tune' and pass to a tutti in ragtime rhythm with static, repeated chords high and low in the ensemble. A percussion 'break' led by side-drum sees the quintuplet figure taken up by brass as a tiny fanfare.

A rhythmically unanimous tutti with repeated crowing 'Scotch snap' figures (Ex.2*a*) is interrupted by a florid, declamatory trombone solo marked 'quasi cadenza' (Ex.2*b*), accompanied only by side-drum:

This idea – all two bars of it, which may be considered the climax of *Dance for Burgess* – is directly comparable to the characteristic trombone solos in *Hyperprism* and *Intégrales*, yet more extravagant in its huge leaps. (These perhaps were meant to encourage similarly daring leaps, or at least flamboyant gesture, from the dancer on stage.) In a brief encapsulation of previous events, the trumpets' quintuplet fanfare is heard, then a single bar of the 'Scotch snap' Ex.2*a*, and two bars of percussion solo, similar to the work's opening. Finally a raucous high woodwind cry and a tumultuous sextuplet descent precipitate a final cadence, of sorts (Ex.3).

Chou Wen-Chung has described *Dance for Burgess* as 'a wildflower swaying in the waste of a desert storm', which is perhaps altogether too fragrant a characterization. The music's derisive grotesquerie – certainly a typical aspect of Varèse's humour, and plainly related to similarly grotesque moments in, for instance, *Amériques* and *Arcana* – is surely more redolent of the dance-hall: though the imagined location would seem to be a smoky dive rather than any Broadway theatre. If little more than a squib, the piece at least packs enough explosive to make it worth hearing from time to time. But the fact that Varèse managed (however provisionally) to complete it in a short time seems to bespeak a returning compositional confidence which would soon bear altogether richer fruit in his other Burgess Meredith-related project. Although the film on which they were to collaborate never happened, the music Varèse was writing for it would soon become *Déserts*.

PART 4 All alone in the night

1960s (photograph by Thomas Bouchard)   *G. Ricordi & Co Ltd*

Deserts of the mind

You cannot understand how much I love the desert.
VARÈSE TO ODILE VIVIER

CHRONOLOGY 1950–1954

1950 Happy as Larry *opens in New York on 6 January and closes immediately. Jack Skurnik, owner of the Elaine Music Shop on 44th Street, proposes recording Varèse's complete works on LP on his own EMS label. May-June: the first LP –* Ionisation, Octandre, Intégrales *and* Density 21.5 *– is recorded by the Juilliard Percussion and New York Wind Ensembles conducted by Frederick Waldman, under the composer's supervision, and issued in October as EMS401. Varèse visits Germany to teach at the Kränichsteiner Musikinstitut's Darmstadt Summer School for New Music, at the invitation of Wolfgang Steinnecke, where his students include Luigi Nono; he also attends conferences elsewhere in Germany.*

1951 *EMS401 is voted Best Recording of the Year at the New York Audio Fair. Varèse meets Dallapiccola at the Berkshire Music Center. Harold Burris-Meyer writes to Magnecord Inc., providing specifications for equipment to be adapted for Varèse (the equipment is not produced).*

1952 *22 March: tape-recording equipment is finally installed in Varèse's studio. He begins taping factory sounds for the Interpolations for* Déserts *(this continues through 1953). 4 July: sends Merle Armitage an elaborate proposal for a film version for* Déserts. *Jack Skurnik dies before he can record a second Varèse LP. Winter: Elliott Carter introduces Varèse to the young Pierre Boulez, who is conducting* musique concrète *at Columbia University, and who later reports on the* Déserts *project to Pierre Schaeffer in Paris.*

1953 *Meets Ann Macmillan, who becomes his studio assistant for work on* Déserts.

1954 *Between January and October Varèse completes the first tape Interpolation and part of the second. 5 October: he returns to Paris after an absence of more than 20 years to complete the electronic tapes for* Déserts *at the studios of RTF. 2 December: Hermann Scherchen conducts the première of* Déserts *at the Théâtre des Champs-Elysées, in a concert which is broadcast live on French Radio, provoking a near-riot in the audience. 8 December: Bruno Maderna conducts the first German performance of* Déserts *in Hamburg (repeated in Stockholm on 13 December).*

NEW MUSIC, NEW ART

Apart from the sole and hardly-noticed performances of *Étude pour Espace* and *Dance for Burgess*, the world had heard no new music from Varèse for nearly 20 years when *Déserts* – a work in seven sections, four for wind and percussion instruments punctuated by three 'Interpolations' on pre-recorded magnetic tape – received its riotous première in Paris in 1954. The landscape of modern music had changed radically since the 1930s, and the position which Varèse occupied in it was at once more precarious and in some ways more hopeful.

After its long suppression by the totalitarian dictatorships, the most adventurous music of the 1920s and 30s could be revived, performed, studied, discussed by a new generation who had the most powerful ethical reasons to reject the bourgeois traditionalism that had attempted to silence it for ever. The spirit of extreme radicalism in music once more occupied the theatre of Europe rather than the USA – at first, indeed, in Paris, where Réné Leibowitz, a disciple of the Second Viennese School, had started teaching according to Schoenberg's precepts. Meanwhile at the Conservatoire, Olivier

Messiaen, close friend of Varèse's pupil Jolivet and a passionate admirer of Varèse's work, introduced a coterie of remarkable young pupils – Pierre Boulez, Karel Goeyvaerts, Karlheinz Stockhausen, Jean Barraqué and later Iannis Xenakis – to the mainstream of European musical modernism, and to conceptions which they immediately began to take in directions their elders had hardly dared to contemplate. The intellectual ferment took root in Germany, at the annual Summer Schools for New Music in Darmstadt and the New Music Festivals in Donaueschingen, where other figures, such as Luciano Berio, Luigi Nono and Henri Pousseur made their first international appearance. Varèse himself came to teach and lecture at Darmstadt, a legend in his lifetime to his eager audience.

All the young composers of the European avant-garde were touched, to a greater or lesser degree, by the force of his personality and the power of his vision; yet in the works they were producing, none of them remotely resembled him in style or aesthetic orientation. Goeyvaerts, Boulez and Stockhausen – prompted by, among other examples, Messiaen's experimentally 'serial' organization of note-lengths and dynamics in his piano Etude *Mode de valeurs et d'intensités* – promulgated what they saw as a 'logical' development from 12-note serialism: particularly from the intricately and ascetically motivic form of it that had been practised by Webern. Pitch was not the only element that could be structured in a fixed, twelvefold serial ordering: so too could metrics, register, durations of individual notes, dynamics, types of attack, instrumental colour and indeed every parameter that made up the individual identity of a sound. By relating these nested parameters to each other and to the overall structure of a work through the various applications of a controlling twelvefold series, they arrived at the concept of 'total serialism' in which every aspect of every moment of the piece was a result of the composer's control: a music of complete intentionality, in which nothing was left to chance. This, at any rate, was the theory; and by treating each sound as an object whose every characteristic could be mathematically expressed these composers naturally began to look to electronics as a method of 'pure' composition that allowed them total control and a complete absence of human error.

Through the years that Varèse had been fretting in despair of ever obtaining the means to realize his ideas, significant advances had been made in means of sound-reproduction. By the end of the 1940s true electronic composition was beginning to become a reality, spurred on above all by the introduction of the tape-recorder. Captured on electronic tape, sounds could be subjected to physical manipulation, to dissection, segmentation, rearrangement and reversal. Sound became, in the title of Pierre Schaeffer's influential 1952 article, 'L'Objet Musical'.[1] In Paris, Schaeffer had begun to analyse acoustic phenomena and, closely associated with French Radio, to explore the resources of *musique concrète* – taking mechanical, human and other everyday noises and then varying, distorting and otherwise transforming them to produce new sonorities and build these into large-scale musical designs and sound-collages through tape editing, cutting and splicing, signal filtering, superposition of sounds, varying tape speeds and other physical operations. Several tape-recorders could be used as simultaneous sound-sources, and sounds could be distributed via loudspeakers so that they would, indeed, appear to 'move in space'.

In one sense the work of Schaeffer and his colleagues – notably Pierre Henry, with whom he produced the electronic *Symphonie pour un homme seul* (1949) and the 'opéra concrète' *Orphée* (1953) – was a revival, with better technology, of the Futurists' attempts to bring noise within the realm of music. Meanwhile a studio of electronic music was established by Cologne Radio. Work at this second centre pursued a divergent course, perhaps typified by Stockhausen's two *Elektronische Studien* (1953–4): compositions were to use only electro-acoustic material – not pre-recorded sounds but sounds generated by the electronic equipment itself (usually by sine-wave generators). Whereas the spirit behind Schaeffer's experiments seemed more poetic and anecdotal, the Cologne enterprise – closely linked from the first with the Darmstadt Ferienkurse – aimed at something like a 'pure' electronic music whose theoretical premises were a kind of technological extension of serialism.

Within a few years the distinction, at first so important, between *musique concrète* and 'true' electronic music would be eroded as composers began to integrate both approaches and the technology continued to develop – and from the beginning, the new avant-garde shuttled between both centres. Schaeffer demonstrated his work at Darmstadt and Donaueschingen; Stockhausen composed his first

---

[1] *La Revue Musicale*, No. 212 (April 1952).

electronic piece, *Konkrete Etude* (1952) at Schaeffer's Paris studio. Messiaen had already produced an electronic essay, *Timbres-Durées*, with technical assistance from Pierre Henry; Boulez had created his *Etude sur un son* (1951); Barraqué too had composed an *Etude* for 3-track tape. Goeyvaerts, who began his electronic piece *Nr.4, with dead tones* in Paris (1952), followed Stockhausen to Cologne to produce *Nr.5, with pure* (i.e., sine) *tones* and *Nr.7, with convergent and divergent sound layers*.

Even in the USA, events were moving. John Cage, long interested in electronic possibilities, had been galvanized by Boulez's reports of Schaeffer's work and produced a collage of recorded sounds for his fifth *Imaginary Landscape* (1951–2). On 28 October 1952 the first concert of electronic music created in America was presented in New York at the Museum of Modern Art by Vladimir Ussachevsky, who taught at Columbia University, and Otto Luening – a former pupil of Busoni. The latter offered a *Fantasy in Space* based on transformed flute sounds.

The electronic ventures of the European avant-garde were indebted to the technical resources of radio corporations; Luening and Ussachevsky, initiating an American trend, benefited from university support. Varèse, by this time engaged on *Déserts*, had still not succeeded in gaining access to any such resources and was forced to work on his own. The new sound-sources he had longed for were becoming a reality; yet their practitioners, on the whole, were using them in very different ways from those he had foreseen for his own music. To simplify to the point of caricature: Schaeffer and his followers seemed driven by taxonomic curiosity and a sense of fun, the Cologne group by a severely 'abstract', analytical impulse that sought to free their work from all merely human associations.

Ironically, Varèse's thought was moving in a different direction. Having spent much of his career studiously avoiding the constraints of Schoenberg's 12-note method, he was not about to submit to total serialization. He wanted, he told Schuller, to 'initiate [the sound], and then to let it take its own course'. As ever, with Varèse, the 'voyage into space' was the paramount impulse. In this he was already ahead of the younger generation, who were all to retreat from such extreme systematization by the end of the decade in order to reintroduce the elements of chance.

Throughout his career Varèse had associated with painters and other visual artists, more receptive to his ideas than most professional musicians. The years after World War 2 found him in close rapport with the emerging 'New York School' of Abstract Expressionists. These included his friend Alcopley (*nomme de guerre* of the Dresden-born painter and scientist Albert L. Copley) and such now more celebrated figures as Franz Kline, William De Kooning, Robert Motherwell, Jackson Pollock and Mark Rothko. Their art aspired to imitate the condition of music, which they viewed as not imitative of anything but 'absolute', intimately involved in the manipulation of its own physical medium. Concentrating on the act of applying the paint in itself, Pollock and others developed the dynamic and spontaneous methods of 'action painting'. They found much to admire in Varèse. *Possibilities*, edited among others by Motherwell and John Cage, was the journal of their membership, The Group; as we have seen, its first number devoted space to Varèse, and in 1950 The Group invited Varèse to lecture on his music and ideas.

It has been speculated that Varèse was influenced in turn by the New York painters – as his younger contemporaries, John Cage, Earle Brown and Morton Feldman certainly were – in the direction of a new view of musical freedom, especially freedom for the performer to make his own decisions. The editorial Statement which opens the first issue of *Possibilities*, signed by Harold Rosenberg and Robert Motherwell, proclaims among other things: 'The question of what will emerge is left open. One functions in an attitude of expectancy. As Juan Gris said: you are lost the instant you know what the result will be'. Although these sentiments run counter to Varèse's repeated affirmations that his works were in no sense experiments – all his experimenting had been done *before* he began composing – he certainly became more interested in improvisation, and even made some experiments with jazz.

At the same time he seems to have been devoting more energy to his own paintings and drawings. As he told Alcopley,

I have always drawn and painted a little, but I am not a painter. Playing with colors and lines gives me great pleasure and is a diversion – a relaxation from composing ... I did a good deal of mechanical drawing at school – an excellent manual discipline – so that I am a pretty good doodler.[2]

---

[2] 'Edgard Varèse on Music and Art', p. 187. In the realm of 'doodling' would seem to be the 'Spiral Drawing' reproduced courtesy of Chou Wen-Chung in the box inlay of Decca 460 208–2, even as it reminds us of Varèse's fascination with spiral forms.

Nevertheless, though Varèse may not hold a position in art history as of right, in the way that minor Expressionist Arnold Schoenberg clearly does, such of his artworks as have been reproduced tend to refute the statement that he was 'not a painter'. They are professionally done and have a haunting intensity; though predominantly abstract, their imagery echoes or reflects obsessive aspects of his music. One gets the impression that painting offered him, as to Schoenberg, an alternative channel of expression when music became too difficult.

The five paintings used as illustration to his posthumously-published conversation with Alcopley were all drawn from the years 1951–53, within the time-period of *Déserts*. As no colour photographs seem to be available it is impossible to comment on his palette, but the monochrome reproductions suggest a predominantly dark, sombre, oppressive colour-sense. An ink and crayon abstract of 1952, *Epure*, has an almost Edvard Münch-like sense of black despair. A *Toto* of 1953, in the same medium, is perhaps reminiscent of Jackson Pollock in its sense of wild yet dense-packed movement. An untitled painting from 1951 has a mandala-like circular shape. Towards the foot of the picture is a sinister tangle of curtain and curtain-rod-like tubes: one of these has mutated into a broad-bladed spear, its shape echoing the forms which snake, upon another tube, diagonally across the picture: perhaps lamps, more likely suspended cymbals. A contrary diagonal appears as a jagged, glowing line, as if of electric current or the wave-form in an oscilloscope; above these, more flexible lines, perhaps electric cables, snake into the gloom. More nearly representational still is *Portes* (1952), done in crayon and ink on wood: here doorways, gateways, bridges are reflected in a Cubist prism, endlessly reproducing themselves in a jammed perspective. There seem to be echoes here of Boccioni's triptych *States of Mind*, especially its first panel *Those Who Go*, with its rhythmic and repetitive articulation. The wish to pass through, implicit in the whole idea of a door, seems frustrated as the doors cram themselves into the available space like an impenetrable wall. The most distinct bridge, in the lower centre of the picture, appears to pass over a gulf yet, like a creation of M.C. Escher, ineluctably returns the eye to the plane from which it began.

It seems, moreover, as if Varèse introduced a visual aspect into his compositional routine. Certainly some of his 'curiously shaped and variously colored and textured work sketch collages', as Alcopley terms them,[3] have been reproduced since his death as quasi-art-works, though it remains unclear if the composer himself considered them to be such. As Louise informed Alcopley:

Varèse always preferred making things to buying things readymade. For his work paper he used to open up the envelopes that came in his mail and paste them on pieces of yellow copy paper, brown wrapping paper, anything at hand, making long strips, often of two or three feet, on which he would draw his staffs and write down his musical ideas, often with coloured inks.

Art-works or not, these sketches are among the most eloquent visual signs of Varèse's creativity. Tiny atomic processes, extremely precise rhythmic figures for percussion, interlocking and related to one another by their spatial layout on the page, sometimes free-floating without any staves or pitch-reference: violently scribbled instructions, arrows and parabolas lead off in different directions. Jonathan Bernard has pointed to evidence that, in at least some of his works, Varèse may have composed the percussion parts after the pitched instruments had been fully scored. These sketches seem to suggest that, in others, percussive rhythm was the germinating seed from which the whole conception sprang. They enshrine, as it were, revelatory instants of kinetic activity: fragmentary, floating in space, yet with the potential to fill the universe.

DÉSERTS

... a magical word, suggesting correspondences with infinity.

VARÈSE

If we regard the whole 'silent' period as the necessary prelude to *Déserts*, probably no work of Varèse had as long and painful a gestation; and as the last really extensive work which he lived to complete it assumes a special importance within his oeuvre. But in any case its importance is immense for the simple reason that it incorporates his first essays in 'electronic music' proper: it is one of the first works in musical history – and the first of prime artistic significance – to combine taped sounds with conventional instruments. In comparison to it *Tuning Up* and *Dance for Burgess* were

---

[3] Ibid., p. 192.

indeed 'minor works'; *Déserts* is a major statement, simultaneously grim and inspiring.

Déserts emerged gradually out of *Espace*. There was perhaps no single obvious demarcating moment when the one conception crossed over into the other; but it may not be entirely fanciful to see the music for electronic tape as the 'chorus' in a new incarnation of Varèse's idea for a 'choral symphony'. This impression is reinforced by the fact that the work also grew from the various ideas for films with music – and that music to include a chorus – which he had entertained in the early 1940s. The 'cinematic' aspect was reinforced by his arranging activities for Thomas Bouchard's films later in that decade. *Tuning Up*'s abortive relationship to the film *Carnegie Hall* is part of this movement: and indeed the chiming 'coda' of the first of its two versions in Chou Wen-Chung's realization is one passage which seems prophetic of the new idiom fully unveiled in *Déserts*. Varèse's original scheme was to combine auditory and visual aspects, the music to be performed in conjunction with a film (which would be shot after the score was composed) whose images would synchronize with or contradict the sounds as a kind of counterpoint of media. But the component was never realized, despite the proposed collaboration with Burgess Meredith in 1949 on a film to be called *Le Désert*. As far as we know this advanced no further than discussion.

Presumably Varèse was not thinking of the ultra-Romantic 'descriptive symphony' *Le Désert* by Berlioz's contemporary Félicien David. As in *Amériques* and *Espace*, his eventual title conjures up another immense space, a virgin territory or void, which might provide a spiritual habitation for humanity's most elemental impulses: 'I chose the title *Déserts* because for me it is a magical word, suggesting correspondences with infinity'. Despite his mention of the Gobi Desert to Henry Miller, the deserts he must had most vividly in mind were those of the Four Corners region of the American Southwest, particularly those of western New Mexico. But to Odile Vivier he wrote that the 'deserts' he intended to evoke were

not only physical deserts of sand, sea, mountains and snow, outer space, deserted city streets, not only those destructive aspects of nature which evoke sterility, remoteness, timelessness – but also this distant inner space which no telescope can reach, where man is alone in a world of mystery and essential solitude. I do not expect that the music will transmit anything of that to the listener ... though such ideas can be the genesis of a work during the course of composition, the music is obliged to absorb everything that is not purely musical.[4]

Varèse composed the instrumental portions of *Déserts* between Summer 1950 (though sketching certainly began the previous year) and late 1952 – that is, essentially before he began work on the tape component. One obvious consequence is that the overall structure was probably fixed in his mind before he came to introduce 'organized sound' on tape; this idea is confirmed by the fact that he designated the taped sections 'Interpolations'. Thus the pre-existing instrumental music may to some extent have determined the nature and organization of the taped sounds, or at least the kind of relationship between instrumental and electronic music which Varèse had to create. But there was also a purely circumstantial reason for composing the instrumental music first: he still lacked even the most rudimentary equipment with which to realize the electronic sections. It was only in late 1952 that Varèse was approached, through Alcopley, by an 'anonymous benefactor' who proposed to donate the necessary equipment. In fact the 'benefactor' was Louise Varèse and Alcopley himself, who jointly purchased, as a gift, an Ampex model 401A tape-recorder and accessories for the composer.

The tape Interpolations are thus his first essays in *musique concrète*. Ultimately they derive from a wide range of sounds which Varèse recorded from percussion instruments and at various industrial sites – ironworks, sawmills, and factories – around Philadelphia at Westinghouse, Diston and Budd Manufacturers during 1952 and 1953. But he still required the resources of a properly-equipped sound studio to proceed further. During 1953 the composer Ann Macmillan, who worked as a music editor for RCA Victor, met Varèse and subsequently became a pupil and assistant. In early 1954 she helped him record the sounds of the organ at the Church of St. Mary the Virgin in New York, and also enabled him to begin transforming his raw recordings into 'organized sound'.

During this 'post-instrumental' period (if not from the work's inception), Varèse was prepared to countenance the performance of *Déserts'* instrumental portions on their own, and a première was mooted for June 1953, to be conducted by Frederik Prausnitz, though

---

[4] Vivier, pp. 147–8.

the idea fell through. He was also pursuing the possibilities of a realization of his work on film, and in July 1952 sent the impresario Merle Armitage a detailed proposal for a film version which he hoped might interest Walt Disney. (Apparently he was attracted to the idea of involving Disney because of the latter's association with Stokowski in *Fantasia*, a film Varèse in fact disliked.) Passages from this text are of great interest for the composer's conception of *Déserts* as finally completed, not least because it makes crystal clear that his thinking was not confined to earthly deserts but continued to range the infinitudes of outer and inner space.

By deserts must be understood all deserts: deserts of earth (sand, snow, mountain), deserts of sea, deserts of sky (nebulae, galaxies, etc), and deserts in the mind of man.

For this multiple conception of deserts, visual image and sound will be used each in its unique way to communicate the beauty and the mystery of that solitude which finds such an intense, though perhaps not consciously understood, response in every human heart ...

... the score will be written first, rehearsed and recorded on the sound track. Duration, 20 to 30 minutes, approximately. The score will be a complete unit in itself. The dynamic, tensions, rhythms (or better RHYTHM, element of stability) will naturally be calculated with the film as a whole in mind

... The views of earth, sky, water will be filmed in parts of the American deserts: California (Death Valley), New Mexico, Arizona, Utah, Alaska: sand deserts, lonely stretches of water anywhere, solitudes of snow, steep deserted gorges, abandoned roads, ghost towns etc. For star galaxies, nebulae, mountains of the moon, existing photographs could be used ... The whole must give a sense of timelessness, legend, Dantesque apocalyptic phantasmagoria.

I have chosen deserts because I feel them and love them, and because in the United States this subject offers unlimited possibility of images which are the very essence of a poetry and magic ...

I plan to use an instrumental ensemble of about twenty men, and a small chorus of the same number ... [5]

Although Varèse talks in the future tense ('the score will be written

---

[5] Extracts from the more extensive quotation in Mattis, 1992, pp. 561–2. The first sentence's close correspondence with Varèse's description of *Amériques* (above, p. 104) is very striking.

first') there can be little doubt that he had in mind the instrumental music of *Déserts* which by this time was already largely composed. As Olivia Mattis has pointed out, his proposed duration and size of ensemble closely resemble those of the published score. She has also noted that 'the presence of a chorus links *Déserts* concretely with *Espace*, his unfinished choral magnum opus'.[6] Yet in the end *Déserts* was completed without any choral component. It may well be that the electronic interpolations, still unrealized when Varèse wrote this film proposal, came to supplant them entirely. Nevertheless even after the first performance of the complete *Déserts* he continued to speak of possible film applications for the music, apparently with the addition of a vocal element.[7]

Varèse's compositional activities during 1953, while he was engaged in collecting material for and resolving his difficulties with the Interpolations, remain cause for speculation. He was certainly not inactive. In January 1954 the *New York Herald Tribune* reported that, on the contrary, he was 'far advanced' on a quite different composition, an orchestral work commissioned by the Louisville Orchestra of Louisville, Kentucky.[8] As is well known, from 1948 to the present day this fairly small regional orchestra, then conducted by Robert Whitney, has maintained a highly enlightened policy of commissioning a contemporary composer to write a new work for première performance on each of its subscription concerts. In 1954, with the aid of a grant from the Rockefeller Foundation, it began to issue each season's new works on LPs that would be available in record stores and on subscription: the celebrated 'First Edition Records' series. It rather looks as if Varèse was among the composers commissioned – as were such contemporaries as Villa-Lobos, Halsey Stevens, Henry Cowell, Wallingford Riegger and Peggy Glanville-Hicks – for the first batch of LP releases.[9]

---

[6] Ibid., p. 562.

[7] Varèse's idea for a film version of *Déserts* was only realized 30 years after his death, in an interpretation, first screened in 1995, by the video artist Bill Viola. Although this has several times been shown in conjunction with the music in live performance, Viola's visual conception differs profoundly from that set out in Varèse's proposal to Armitage.

[8] Abraham Skulsky, 'Varèse Set to Launch Electronic Music Age', *New York Herald Tribune*, 24 January 1954, section 4 p.5.

[9] These even included a primitive work for electronics and standard instruments, the *Rhapsodic Variations for Tape Recorder and Orchestra* (1954) jointly composed by Otto Luening and Vladimir Ussachevsky.

The *Herald Tribune* article, based on conversations with Varèse, reported that the new piece was entitled *Trinum*. This Latin adjective means threefold or triple. Apparently the principle of 'threefoldness' was built into the fabric and structure of Varèse's entire conception. In three movements or sections, played without a break, it was concerned with three basic elements, 'tension, intensity, and rhythm'. The last-named was to be treated, according to Varèse's customary definition, as an element of stability, 'not as meter'. As for 'tension' and 'intensity', these are the terms he was also to use in connexion with *Déserts*, referring to size of intervals and 'acoustical result' (below, p.347). The musical texture was to be characterized by intervals occurring predominantly in groups of three – presumably recalling the trichordal formations of the instrumental works of the 1920s. The title *Trinum*, however, actually tells us that a fourth dimension was involved: time. The Latin adjective is ordinarily found in the plural, *trina* – the singular form is used to connote the passage of time (as in the phrase *trinum nundinum*, a period including three market-days).

Varèse also said that although he was writing *Trinum* for orchestra, he intended, after the first performance, to free it from the limitations of the tempered scale by working upon it a transformation into 'organized sounds on tape'. Ouellette has declared, rather remarkably, that 'there is no doubt that the three sections of this work became the three taped interpolations in *Déserts*'.[10] He advances no evidence for this statement, admitting two sentences later that 'the matter still remains in doubt'; it seems to me highly improbable. By the time of the *Herald Tribune* article Varèse had amassed all or nearly all the tape recordings of external sounds which would become the raw materials of the Interpolations – which do not appear to be based on even the most notional instrumental framework. What Varèse said about *Trinum* should probably be viewed in the light of his later statement that he would like to make an electronic version of *Intégrales*: i.e. a transcription into electronically-generated sound of a pre-existing instrumental score. There also remains the possibility that he viewed the prospective first performance of *Trinum* as part of its compositional process: that he was writing it for orchestra *in order to obtain a recording* which he would subsequently transform by means of electronics, as several later composers have done. On the other hand,

---

[10] Ouellette, p.180.

it seems rather likely that the music of *Trinum* bore a family resemblance to the *instrumental* portions of *Déserts*, with its rich abundance of sonorous trichords.

Whatever the truth of these speculations, *Trinum* did not emerge. It may be that Varèse's demands, both in playing and scoring, were beyond the somewhat modest capacities of the Louisville Orchestra, which acted as a restraint on several of their contributing composers. It may also be that he was less 'far advanced' with the composition than the *Herald Tribune* article suggested, or that its general concepts were fully worked out but not yet transferred to paper. In any case, his attention had already been diverted back to the completion of *Déserts* by an offer from an unexpected quarter. Alerted by Pierre Boulez, in January 1954 Pierre Schaeffer extended an invitation to Varèse to come to Paris to complete work on the Interpolations at the studios of the Groupe de Musique Concrète, Club d'Essai, at French Radio (RTF) in Paris.[11] Here technology – though by no means ideal or advanced technology, even for its time – was available for him to electronically transform and organize his collection of recordings into the sonic patterns and configurations he required.

Nevertheless, prior commitments (possibly including further work on *Trinum*) intervened, and it was only on 5 October 1954 that Varèse landed at Le Havre and proceeded to Paris with his tapes and structural diagrams. By this time he had, in fact, already created a preliminary version of the first Interpolation and part of the second. At the RTF studios Varèse completed the second and produced the third. His assistant, and occasionally his adversary, in this final creative act was Pierre Henry.

The world première of *Déserts* followed soon after, on 2 December 1954 at the Théâtre des Champs-Elysées (where Stravinsky's *Le Sacre du Printemps* had received its baptism by riot over 40 years before), with a long-time champion of new music, Hermann Scherchen, conducting members of the ORTF orchestra. (Even before the *Sacre* première, Scherchen had assisted Schoenberg with the rehearsals and first performances of *Pierrot Lunaire*.) Pierre Henry operated the tape sound-system. All the omens seemed favourable; in fact they were too good to be true.

---

[11] Later the Groupe de Récherche Musicales (GRM), Institut National de l'Audiovisuel, Paris.

For a composer who had become almost totally unknown in his native country, it seemed that Varèse was being offered the most prestigious possible platform. He had been very satisfied with the rehearsals, and delighted with a huge oriental gong which the ORTF had secured for the performance from the Musée de l'Homme. The tape Interpolations were to issue from two loudspeakers, placed either side of the orchestra. The concert – for which no admission was charged – took place before a large audience that included fellow-composers like André Jolivet and such cultural luminaries as André Malraux and Henri Michaux. Moreover, it was given a simultaneous stereophonic broadcast. This was only the second experiment with stereo that French Radio had made, and for that very reason the programme was assured of a huge listening public. To hear the concert in stereo, listeners were required to have two radios, one tuned to the station France-Inter and the other to Chaine National, both of which were carrying the programme live and broadcasting complementary halves of the signal. Varèse's new score was prefaced by an explanatory lecture from the young Pierre Boulez (who had met Varèse for the first time in New York the previous year).

To Varèse's surprise, however, *Déserts* was sandwiched between a Mozart Overture and Tchaikovsky's *Pathétique* Symphony: a bizarre piece of programming that certainly allowed it to achieve maximum impact – and maximum incomprehension. From the start of the first 'Interpolation of organized sound' protests and disturbances arose in the audience – which rapidly, in true Parisian fashion, divided into two camps. From one faction came vocal expressions of outrage, whistling, and more scatalogical obbligato additions to the music; the other faction began protesting at the actions of the first, trying to shout them down and applauding enthusiastically. Pierre Henry turned the volume of the tape to maximum to drown out the turmoil, but when the instrumental music began once more it could hardly be heard against the continuing pandemonium. Those who remembered the première of *Le Sacre du Printemps* have testified that the tumult during the first performance of *Déserts* was even more intense. The disputes and faction-fighting spilled out onto the streets after the concert. Most of the press criticism after the event ranged from the abusive ('a work written by a madman, including a great deal of saucepan banging and solos for flushing toilets with fanfares for stock cars ... what our "electrosymphonist" needs is a trip to the electric chair') to the condescending, although Antoine Goléa, Claude Rostand and Jean Roy stood up for Varèse.

The young Greek architect-composer Iannis Xenakis had attended the rehearsals of *Déserts*, but had stayed at home on 2 December to tape-record it from the radio. After the concert Varèse visited Xenakis and his wife in their small flat, listened to the tape of the broadcast, and wept. 'They don't understand anything,' he said. 'They don't even want to listen.' But he went on to the studios, indomitable, to start refining the Interpolations.

Not even a full-blown Parisian *scandale* could halt the progress of *Déserts*, however. A sufficient number of people sensed that a classic expression of musical modernism had been born. Further performances followed rapidly – in Hamburg on 8 December and in Stockholm on 13 December, both conducted by Bruno Maderna and both riot-free. The US première of *Déserts* took place on 17 May 1955 at the National Guard Armoury, Bennington, Vermont under the direction of Frederic Waldman; and it was first given in New York on 30 November of the same year, in one of the Camera Concerts at the Town Hall, conducted by Jacques Monod. The score (of the instrumental portions only) was published by Ricordi in 1959.

Varèse continued to refine the tape Interpolations, as progressively superior technology became available to him. He seems to have prepared two subsequent versions before, in November 1961, at the invitation of Vladimir Ussachevsky and with the technical assistance of the sound-engineer Max Mathews and the Turkish composer Bulent Arel, he was enabled to carry out an extensive and final revision of the tape Interpolations at the Columbia-Princeton Music Center in New York. From then on the revised version (very different from the original) has been used in all complete concert performances of *Déserts*. Yet it appears that he did not in fact disown the first version. Some months before his death he gave his own tape of the original Interpolations – probably the only stereo version in existence – to the electronic composer Ilhan Mimaroglu.[12] He also told Mimaroglu that, just as the instrumental sections of *Déserts* could be performed without

---

[12] Mimaroglu published this tape on 'The Varèse Record' issued by Finnadar Records, New York (SR 9018) in 1977. The master tape held by the Groupe de Récherches Musicales is in mono only. The revised master is held by the Columbia University Computer Music Center.

the tape, so either version of the Interpolations could be given in concerts, if necessary without the instrumental sections (and thus as a pure tape composition). It is clear that Varèse also subjected the instrumental music to considerable revision before publication. A copy of the original conducting score, prepared for Varèse by Chou Wen-Chung, which is now in the collection of O.W. Neighbour, contains a number of insertions and rewritings in Varèse's own hand.

Déserts calls for 2 flutes (doubling piccolos), 2 clarinets (doubling Eb and bass clarinets), 2 horns, 3 trumpets (one of them a high D-trumpet), 3 trombones, 2 tubas, piano, and five percussionists playing a daunting array of pitched and unpitched instruments comprising 16 different kinds of membrane drum, 17 wooden instruments and 13 metal ones. These are scored not only for rhythmic ictus of immense force but also with the utmost refinement, to yield extremely fine and subtle gradations in timbre. If this indicates, to some extent, a new approach, most of the instruments themselves are individually familiar from previous Varèse scores. One unfamiliar one is the vibraphone: and both this and the piano (enlarging on its role from *Ecuatorial*) are primarily used to double and amplify many of the figures and harmonies produced by the other instruments, helping to create *Déserts*'s peculiarly plangent and sonorous individual sound-world.[13] There is no string section, but most important of all is the role demanded of '2 Magnetic Tapes of electronically organized sounds transmitted on 2 channels by means of a stereophonic system', controlled by an operator who is cued in by the conductor. The second, fourth and sixth of the work's seven sections consist of these 'Interpolations of organized sound'. The electronic and instrumental musics are never heard simultaneously: Varèse himself wrote of the work's form as developing 'antiphonally' between instruments and tape. As previously mentioned, he authorized the performance of the instrumental portions alone should the tapes not be available, and this practice has occasionally been followed up to the present day – though the effect, as has justly been remarked, is tantamount to performing Beethoven's Ninth Symphony without the chorus![14]

---

[13] Odile Vivier has justly (and poetically) described the piano's role in *Déserts* as 'comme une cithare de résonance' (op.cit., p,149).

[14] Pierre Boulez, for one, has frequently programmed *Déserts* as a purely instrumental work, and has twice commercially recorded it in this form.

Given the 'choric' function of the tape, this is no idle comparison. If the new electronic music of Paris and Cologne, whether *concrète* or purely generated, lacked anything, it was the spiritual dimension. The young avant-garde were witnessing every day a ruined Europe emerging from a war that had been nourished on tribal fantasies and irrationality cloaked as rationalism. In a new permutation of the age-old and equally irrational conflict between 'objective' science and 'subjective' metaphysics, they were trying to renounce all the polluting traits and aspirations of Romanticism, from which Modernism itself had evolved. Schoenberg himself was seen as irredeemably corrupted by late-19th-century mysticism and habits of musical thought; their ikon was Webern, with his 'pure', pellucid constructions. (They knew little as yet of Webern's own mystical leanings.) Their new electronic music was inward-turned: a social music composed, in a sense, for a small group, for the ears and dialectical attentions of colleagues and rivals, fellow researchers into the nature and application of sound.

Déserts, on the other hand, looks outward, to nature: it carries electronics, as they had not been carried before, into the desert places of the world and of the soul. It conveys intense emotion, arising out of a mystical topography. This was what made it so shocking, and what makes it still, unlike its European contemporaries, an overwhelming musical experience nearly half a century after it was written. Varèse had no reason to reject the spiritual aspirations of early-20th-century Modernism: he was of its generation, its surviving representative. He had not, like Marinetti or Ezra Pound, been seduced by Fascism: he remained stubbornly proclaiming what he had always proclaimed. But in the aftermath of war and chaos the utterance is both more refined and immeasurably more tragic in its resonance.

The total duration of *Déserts* is a little over 25 minutes. The Interpolations last a few seconds under nine minutes; the instrumental music between 15 and 16.[15] Varèse himself described the instrumental portions as follows:

The music played by the ensemble could be considered as evolving in

---

[15] This is the consensus from recorded performances. The original Interpolations were slightly longer – 9'22" in total – but even this does not account for the precise timings suggested in the published score (Colfranc, 1959), which specified 13'20" for the instrumental portions and 10' 08" for the Interpolations. The latter duration may refer to one of the intermediate versions.

opposing planes and volumes, producing the impression of movement in space. But the intervals between the notes, determining the ever-changing and contrasted volumes and planes, are not founded on any fixed assembly of intervals, like a scale or series ... They are determined by the demands of this particular work. The work progresses in opposing planes and volumes. Movement is created by intensities and tensions, exactly calculated and functioning in opposition to one another; the term 'intensity' referring to the desired acoustical result; the word 'tension' to the size of the interval employed.

He had spoken of his music in similar terms before the war, but there are notable refinements here. Even as he denied using 'any fixed assembly of intervals, like a scale or series' – a clear reference to the new hegemony of serialism in European music – he laid a new stress on the importance of different intervals to create his characteristic 'tensions, volumes and planes'. And to a new extent these entities *are* the music of *Déserts*.

For though Varèse's underlying methods remain basically the same as they were in the 1920s and '30s, the musical fabric of *Déserts'* instrumental portions is very different from the works of those decades. With instrumental attacks calculated to a nicety, in fantastic detail, on every subdivision of every beat,[16] it nevertheless communicates a kind of epic featurelessness, appropriate indeed to the topography of its title. Themes, motifs, salient melodic cells – the earlier music had been rich in these. Here they are few. Instead there are two-note figures which seem in their components to split the functions of attack and decay; and otherwise there are instrumental entries on single pitches, solo, unison or staggered, verticalized into chords and extremities, endowed with brief life by rhythm, ictus, timbre, dynamic swelling and decay, instrumental colour of great refinement varying the tone-quality of sustained pitches. Sonorous, plangent, every instrument or group of instruments becomes a species of bell, a tolling, resonating, chiming voice. In no work of Varèse is his conception of colliding and overlapping planes more obvious to the ear.

The result is to throw the Interpolations into strong relief. By

---

[16] In a few cases these multiple divisions are indicated on the page by a veritable lions' cage of vertical dotted lines, lending the score an appearance quite unlike any of his others.

refraining from doing so many things that a large ensemble might do
– instead, pursuing a limited and limiting range of unorthodox
objectives – the composer creates the most effective setting to show off
the huge variety and eventfulness of his taped sounds, and also
establishes many subtle relationships between the instrumental music
and the different bell-tones that are merely one feature of the
Interpolations. The paradox is that the most human, dramatic music
in *Déserts* is the music on tape.

The work begins as a plangent bell-scape, a kind of Cubist evocation
of the bells of Paris, perhaps, heard across a desert of city roofs, that
freezes conceptually into a parched, dry, metallically resounding
wasteland. A tolling minor ninth (F–G) on tubular bells, xylophone,
low piccolo and clarinet is resonated on the piano and muted
trumpets. Soon another major ninth (D–E) sounds in the bass, on
horns and piano (Ex.1).

This grave, poised, hieratic music – two 'planes' proceeding at first in
parallel – has many long-range stuctural consequences. The grouping
of instrumental attack predominantly in twos, for instance, presages
the many important two-note figures throughout the work. But on its
own terms this passage, deliberate and almost marmoreal in its gestures
(distantly reminiscent, indeed, of Stravinsky's *Symphonies of Wind
Instruments*) seems to be something new in Varèse. Certainly the stress
on the comparatively 'soft' interval of the major ninth appears to signal
a new concern with less harsh, almost consonant material. Yet the

evolving sound-complex is of two major ninths a dissonant *minor* ninth (E–F) apart; and as clarinet, bell and bassoon start to divide the ninths into equal segments, sounding treble C and bass A, the harmonic construction begins to reveal ladders of superimposed perfect fifths: that consonant interval whose systematic extension can undermine tonality and embrace all 12 pitches of the chromatic scale.

For several more bars these two fifths-complexes (reading upwards F–C–G in treble, D–A–E in bass) continue to be the only pitches sounded. But the *unpitched* percussion, which Varèse uses here in a very restrained manner, plays a subtle supporting role: a 'high' group (two suspended cymbals of different sizes) and a 'low' group (three different sizes of gong) shadow and imitate the high and low fifth-complexes, with simultaneous and then divided attacks.

The downward extension of the treble fifths-complex would be B♮; the upward extension of the bass one, B♭. At bar 14 Varèse suddenly introduces both of these pitches simultaneously – but in the bass, the B♭ on muted tuba a minor ninth above a trombone's pedal B♮. Soon these are joined by C♯, a *major* ninth above the B♮ – preserving the structure of major and minor ninths but also, with the pitches of the opening still sounding, dividing the sound-spectrum into superimposed fifths and tritones. This expansion and subdivision of the harmonic premises of Ex.1 soon manifests itself in a characteristically Varèsian fanfare-gesture for brass and wind (Ex.2).

Ex.2

The concluding harmony is quietly sustained while the percussion – so far very discreetly used – comes into prominence with military-style rhythms on snare drum and field drum and an angry melodicization of tritone and minor ninth in the timpani. This leads immediately to a development and aggrandisement of the fanfare-complex Ex.2, with vibraphone and xylophone helping the piano to resonate the pitches of the wind. As its concluding harmony is sustained, new intervallic elements emerge – a repeated major seventh in the two tubas, C–B (inversion of the minor ninth), and an oscillating minor third on the flute (written as an augmented second, E♭–F♯: see Ex.3*a*).

Thus from its opening premises of ninths and perfect fifths, the harmonic and melodic cells of the music have begun to grow, in a highly organic way, into other and more complex intervallic configurations. The process continues in the succeeding bars, where two sets of perfect fourths (fifths inverted) – G–C high on the piccolos, C♯–F♯ low on the tubas, both of them echoed in the piano – symmetrically interact with one another. The high pair acquires a B a minor sixth below the G (which, with octave displacement, could be regarded as the next link in an ascending chain of fourths from C♯–F♯); the low pair acquires a D a minor sixth above the F♯ (which, with octave displacement, could be regarded as the next link in an descending chain of fourths from C and G). The other brass, muted, with clarinet and E♭ clarinet, build up a soft harmony of fifths and tritones. These intervallic transmutations seem to proceed as inversions of each other (fifths becoming fourths) or semitonal augmentations or diminutions (fourths, tritones, fifths, minor sixths, building up across spans of minor or major ninths or sevenths). We have seen such processes at work in many of Varèse's earlier scores. But to detail these intervallic complexities is totally to ignore the most striking characteristic of the passage, which is the way each wind instrument enunciates its tones in a different dynamic curve, each swelling and diminishing independent of the others. Here is 'projection' along many simultaneous planes, and the result is, in fact, uncannily prophetic of some of the electronic music we shall shortly be hearing.

The comparatively deliberate pace of this opening portion of *Déserts*, and its sparse, clear textures, make it especially easy to appreciate Varèse's favourite analogy with crystalline structures, every facet a different aspect of the same basic elements. But the 'electronic' wind harmony is now interrupted by new features, highly anomalous by the standards of Varèse's pre-War music (Ex.3*b*).

A solo horn gives out a new, almost arpeggio-like figure, dividing the span of a fifth into a sequence of two minor thirds (cumulatively a tritone) plus a semitone. Then the horn essays the leap of an *octave*, F♯ to F♯ – a pure consonance practically unparalleled in earlier Varèse; and though the tubas and piano seek to undermine it immediately with their shadowing minor ninth, they themselves are starting out from an F♯ two octaves below the horn. No sooner have we experienced this sonic surprise than the tubas, doubled now by the timpani, deliver another: a repeated, insistent *major* third, D♭–F. Although this is soon overlaid by a rapid quintuplet semiquaver trumpet-call on a high A, and more wind-instrument harmony emphasizes ninths and tritones, the tubas' thirds persist, and so do the octave leaps in the horns. Indeed, these consonant intervals are immediately developed further, and surely not without a tinge of mockery (Ex.4).

The octave becomes a tolling 2-note downward leap, E to E, brightly and ringingly repeated on flute, piano, glockenspiel and trumpet, above a very low major third A–C♯ in tubas and piano, and a horn B♭ which forms a tritone with the E but also a major sixth (the major third inverted) with the C♯. Here again the bell-like conception of the music is very clear (it would hardly sound out of place within Stravinsky's *Les Noces*); one also has a distinct impression of a Varèsian chuckle at the raised eyebrows such consonance will cause. Piano, glockenspiel, xylophone, flute and piccolo then 'decorate' – or form crystals around – the E–E octave, in triplet patterns that insert an F for semitone inflection.

The brass and other wind now break in angrily in a series of passages reflecting the harmonic structures of the 'fanfare' Ex.2. The rapid quintuplet tucket, previously heard in the trumpet, is taken up and developed in trombone and horn. Tritones and ninths abound, first as harmony and then as abrupt falling intervals in trumpets, horns, piano and timpani. The passage reaches a kind of climax on high trumpets, trombones, flute and piccolo, and leaves the horns musing on a new fan-shaped figure (related to the horn solo at the start of Ex.3*b*) that opens out from a third, via a fourth, to a tritone (shown as Ex.3*c*). The trumpets take up a form of it, *pianissimo* (Ex.3*d*), still sounding as the first 'Interpolation of organized sound' breaks in upon the proceedings through the speaker-system.[17]

This opening instrumental section of *Déserts* can be viewed as a kind of exposition, organically generating the materials for the remaining sections. Though not devoid of Varèse's characteristic volatility and elements of violence, on the whole it possesses a sculptured poise and sense of inevitability that places it among his most humane and immediately approachable music. No barren desert this, one might think: though the fibre of the music is sparse, cut to the bone, bare to the point of asceticism, its sounds are wonderfully rich and evocative. But as we shall rapidly discover, the tape Interpolations, in their 'antiphony', are the emotional antithesis of the instrumental music.

In his programme-note for the first performance of *Déserts* Varèse spoke of the tape component in these terms:

The Interpolations of organized sound are based on what one might call 'raw' sounds (friction, percussion, whistling, 'swishing', or sonorities of lashing,

---

[17]   On the fourth beat of bar 82. Varese was very concerned to prevent any breaks between the instrumental and taped sections, and so carefully specified the exact entry-points.

crushing, breath) which – thanks to electronics – have been filtered, transposed, transmuted, combined and composed so as to adapt them to the pre-established plan of the work. Combined with the electronic sounds, as elements of structure and stability, there occur some brief citations of the instrumental section.

The first Interpolation is largely derived from industrial sounds of friction and percussion, with an element of instrumental percussion – and these origins remain palpable even in Varèse's final version of 1961, though they are much more obvious in the original version heard in 1954.

Here Varèse had finally arrived at – or at least, produced the first preliminary sketch of – the ideal he had pursued all his creative life: a musical space, 'open rather than bounded', within which sound-masses moved. Here at last his composition was freed from the restrictions interposed by conventional instruments, instrumentalists, or forms of notation, and a stereophonic sound-system was available to project the sounds where he willed. Listening to the result, we descry its musical direction – and any expressive meaning it conveys – through the sense of the motion of sound-masses, defined by timbre, pitch and (sometimes) attack rather than melody, harmony and rhythm. This makes it difficult to describe the course of the Interpolations in terms of 'musical' detail, because their elements are so thoroughly in flux and provide so few fixed points of reference.

Yet it is highly revealing of Varèse's expressive intentions to compare and contrast the general characteristics of the original First Interpolation, as used in 1954 at the Paris première, and the final, 1961 version familiar from later recordings and performances. Though some of the basic sound-material is common to both versions, these are indeed so different as to constitute independent tape compositions. And there is no question – though one should not read any pejorative implications into the term – that the 1954 version is much more 'primitive' in its techniques. In it, the 'raw' sounds are often relatively untransformed, and although a sizable component clearly derives from Varèse's industrial samplings he seems, still, to be relying heavily on the sounds of actual percussion instruments – among which timpani, snare-drum, claves, woodblocks and gong remain plainly recognizable. There is also a 'church-organ' effect (largely absent from the 1961 tape) which was surely obtained from an actual instrument rather than any electronic construct. The other striking feature of the 1954 tape is how comparatively one-dimensional the 'musical argument' seems: the various elements are seldom mingled to any extent but presented as a linear succession of sounds, often separated by actual gaps and silences. Within these limitations – clearly imposed by the limitations of the equipment available to him – Varèse has in fact composed an impressively lively train of ideas, but (to these ears at least) a rather coolly abstract one.

The 1961 version (coming, let us remember, after at least two intermediate forms, and the experience of composing *Poème Électronique*) shows a truly enormous technical advance, which gives birth to a far more gripping and indeed visionary musical experience. Like the 1954 version it begins with a vigorous 'percussion' attack, but this metamorphoses almost immediately into a furious continuum of metallic beatings, hissings and drilling sonorities well-nigh impossible for the ear to trace back to actual physical instruments. As far as one can tell, the industrial samplings make up a far larger proportion of the basis of this version, but Varèse continually transmutes them away from their origins, to function purely 'as sound'.

Paradoxically, this absence of clearly identifiable sound-sources seems to stimulate the brain to invent onomatopoeic analogues. The early critics' likening of various elements of the tape to automobile chases, buzz-saws, flushing toilets and the like, though ill-intentioned, may strike a certain chord in all but the most humourless listeners: and Varèse, though intense, was hardly humourless (remember the mockery of the laughing trombones in *Arcana*!). But these incidental resemblances are not the point– it is the total musical experience being built up by a myriad sonic manipulations, of which those resemblances are a very fleeting part.

In contrast to 1954, the tape is many-layered, the sounds intricately interwoven, and not only moving in space but changing in character (through envelope and wave-form) as they do so. Moreover, there are now no gaps in the sound. The Interpolation is a seamless continuum. Its dominating sonorities are metallic, fricative, drill-like, saw-like – sometimes producing high trumpet-like overtones. Glissandi, practically unknown to the 1954 tape, help to link events and change pitch-areas. The Interpolation seems to fall into two halves, the second introduced by low swooping glissandi which may remind listeners in the late 20th century of the song of the Humpbacked Whale: an entirely fortuitous resemblance to a natural sound that had never been recorded in Varèse's lifetime.

The overall effect of the multi-layered stream of sound is hallucinatory, dreamlike – or rather, nightmarish. Anecdotal resemblances to the noises we encounter in real life are continually subverted by the continuing processes of transmutation, carrying them out of the conscious focus of our minds. What, in fact, Varèse seems to be seeking to do is to give auditory reality to the *unconscious*, to the vast unacknowledged mental/emotional hinterland of being, which deals not in facts and figures but in images, symbols and metaphysical realities. As sound succeeds sound with gathering volume and momentum, we seem caught up in a manic, surreal, invigorating and yet nightmarish evocation of the 'deserted city streets'; the chaos and sound-thronged loneliness of the contemporary machine-dominated world. It is not perhaps too fanciful to hear, in *Déserts'* 'antiphony' of instruments and tape, an antiphony of the conscious, rational, scientifically creative mind with the unconscious, irrational, raw (indeed ravening) and inarticulate emotional life that underlies it.

While the 1954 version of the First Interpolation, less viscerally gripping, ended with a repeated 'percussion' pattern, it is a relief to find the 1961 form emerging into sudden stillness from a manic chattering effect, and dying away with the threefold repetition (from different directions) of a fading bell-like tone. The instrumental music now resumes with the start of the second and longest orchestral section, seamlessly answering the tape with three soft sustained wind tones: a middle C♯ on horn I, a B♮ on contrabass tuba an octave plus major ninth below, and a C♮ on horn II, an octave plus semitone below horn I, precisely bisecting the distance between horn I and tuba into two minor ninths.

This may serve as a brief reminder of the bell-like ninths with which the whole work opened; and indeed the succeeding music clearly stems from Ex.1, in that Varèse now presents a very high major ninth, F♯–G♯, in flute and piccolo, moving against its interval-inversion, a minor seventh D–C in middling-low register on trombone and horn. The distance separating these two complexes is two octaves plus a tritone. The entries of the instruments are staggered, not simultaneous, and their dynamics are staggered too, so that each sustained pitch is marked by its own 'electronic' pattern of *crescendo* and *decrescendo*. Once again the idiom is spare and still: with a few variations in scoring (the low D shared between muted and unmuted trombones and then horn II, the C doubled in horn I and trumpet) this is for a while the only pitched material we hear.

This time, though, the percussion is immediately active. It contributes a kind of tensile rhythmic skeleton on cymbals, tambourine, snare drum, blocks and wood drums – the attacks often matching and shadowing those of the wind instruments, but also exploring much smaller subdivisions within the comparatively long beats. Throughout this second instrumental section, in fact, the percussion plays much more as an ensemble and has a far more prominent rôle than in the first, both as a sound-stream proceeding in parallel with the wind and in actual solo passages. This is an index of the changed character of the music, which in contrast to the calm and monumental first section is far more nervous, troubled, and kaleidoscopic. It seems as if aroused, and profoundly disturbed, by the electronic nightmare of the first Interpolation.

Nevertheless the actual intervallic and motivic elements out of which this music is constructed are, as its opening passage suggests, direct derivations and developments of the materials and processes laid out in the 'expository' first section. As a result these processes need not be expounded in quite so detailed a fashion. The music soon gathers way in a succession of fanfare-like outbursts that relate back to Ex.2. A typical passage (Ex.5, opposite) shows several important features in close concatenation.

Here the timpani once more provides a forceful melodization of tritones and minor ninths, and a locally-significant (because much-repeated) fanfare-anacrusis that stacks up superimpositions of perfect fifths and tritones. The trumpet's high repeated A's (shadowed here by the horn's repeated E♭'s an octave plus tritone below) refer back to the quintuplet trumpet-call of the previous instrumental section, which always appeared at the same high A pitch: it is continuing to develop in different rhythms, and is taken over by the piccolo and E♭ clarinet (in 2-octave unison) and B♭ clarinet in the next two bars. These unisons seem to prepare the octave B♭'s in piano, piccolo and flute, a very angry transformation of the tolling-octave idea we saw in Ex.4!

The percussion suddenly drops out while the wind give tongue to the biggest and loudest Ex.2-type fanfare, so far, forming the climax of the section. This is followed immediately by music of a very contrasting kind (Ex.6a).

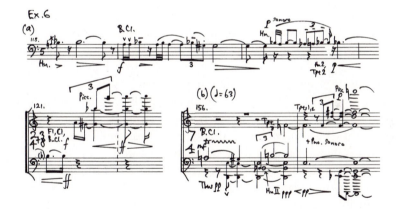

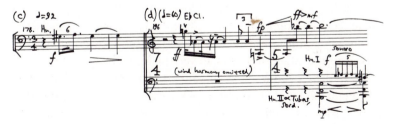

These wavering figures of minor and major seconds – almost like scraps of folk-music in the incantatory effect imparted by their conjunct motion – seem ultimately to stem from the complex of Ex.3; though they are subject without warning to typical Varèsian octave expansion, as in the woodwind flourish in the example's last two bars. Their appearance here, though instantly noticeable, is comparatively brief. They will become important later on, and some of their later derivations are shown here as Exx.6*b* to *f*.

For the moment Ex.6*a* introduces a lengthy passage of 'development', in the sense that the materials exposed during the opening instrumental section continue to reform, 'crystallize' and interpenetrate in ways unnecessary to describe in aggressive detail. The tempo is faster again and the effect kaleidoscopic; new sonic patterns come to the fore as local centres of attention, each swiftly receding to make way for the next. Nevertheless, several distinct episodes can be delineated. The first is marked by the quintuplet flourish, in trombones and tubas, confined again to the repeated pitches A and E♭. Next high woodwind sustain an F *in alt* as background to intricate percussion rhythms which, once more, seem to subdivide the long note-values of the wind into their smallest component particles. This detailed, delicate, toccata-like ensemble work for the percussion persists against more broken material in the wind, such as a series of reiterated B♭'s which horn, trombones, tubas and bass clarinet, approach by way of upward-swooping *portamenti*.

This tendency for the wind instruments to zero in upon a single pitch, 'frozen' against percussion activity, is soon carried to a remarkable extreme. The tempo slows, and wind instruments temporarily drop out as Chinese blocks and tom-toms continue to explore rapid quintuplet rhythms. Then the bass clarinet, with Ex.6*b*, introduces a flourish on wind and piano that softly covers almost the entire gamut of sound from low to very high, the highest pitch of all being C♮, three octaves above middle C♯. This pitch the xylophone seizes upon in rapid septuplet attacks, almost like a rhythmicized tremolo. Meanwhile the brass instruments sustain and resonate in overlapping entries upon the single pitch of C, a semitone above middle C. These two contrasting planes persist in a harmonic stasis which generates considerable tension, until their hold is broken by a faster fanfare that once more sounds a large gamut of pitches in a short space of time. This develops into a more spread-out succession of wind pitches, underpinned by even crotchets tolling a repeated G♯ on the timpani.

Now a jerky little ostinato of major sevenths and tritones starts up on clarinets, supported by vibraphone and xylophone. The repeated two-note rhythm seems a distorted reflection of the tolling octave bell-sounds from earlier in the work. Then a solo horn tremolo (Ex.6*c*, which contrives to remind us of the folk-like Ex.6*a*), is taken up by bass clarinet, and brings spikier writing for high woodwind and percussion. The piccolos and E flat clarinet insist repeatedly, in brief, piercing fanfares, on a high band of sonority spanning a minor third, B♮–D♮, this span emphasized and resonated in repeated chords on piano and xylophone.

Poised brass harmony, stressing sevenths and (in the tubas) low thirds, now serves as background to development of Ex.6*a*'s semitonal motion, through an octave augmentation on E♭ clarinet and a chromatic expansion of the horn trill which sounds even more like a scrap of folk-melody (Ex.6*d*). Immediately, there follows a single slow 11/4 bar that – in most un-Varèsian fashion – presents a succession of single pitches, each one differently scored, with a rapt, mysterious fragility that suggests Webernian *Klangfarbenmelodie*. Varèse marks the passage very carefully: *As pp as possible – no vibrato – steady – all the instruments exactly on the same level of loudness.* Counting the high B♭ that hangs on directly from Ex.6*d*, and counting the high trilled piccolo A as two pitches, A–A♭, this bar spells out a complete 12-note series: (B♭)–C♯–D–F–F♯–B–C–A (A♭)–G–E–E♭.

Déserts is not in any orthodox sense a 12-note work, and is not 'founded' on any such series. But this bar, in its enigmatic fashion, seems to be telling us something about the nature of the pitch-material from which the work is crafted – or rather, of the changes that have been wrought on that material. *Déserts* opened with its attention fixed on major ninths, fifths, and tritones; as Varèse spells out this note-row for us (Ex.7), it seems now to be concerned with minor ninths separated by octave augmentations of thirds (or sixths).

This gnomic concentration on a pitch-succession immediately gives

way to music without fixed pitch at all: a soft rhythmic toccata for percussion, marked *sempre pp – but crisp – with utmost precision*. This leads in turn to a sudden angry *Marcatissimo* fanfare, harking back to Ex.2, for the full wind body plus piano, and a brief review of elements that are becoming familiar – the folk-like horn phrase from Ex.6*d*, varied on bass clarinet (see Ex.6*e*); tolling crotchets in the timpani, now on F♯; brief fanfares defining a high B–D band (now however stretched from a third to a tenth, and pierced by a dissonant E♭); timpani, with hard sticks, melodicizing fifths and ninths and tritones in rapid triplet figures. Once again the percussion ensemble enters on its own, but this time not with its usual highly intricate rhythms. Instead, with a jaunty ostinato which both in rhythmic profile and instrumentation (tom-toms, cencerro, guiro and slap-stick are prominent) conjures up a hint of a Latin-American dance-band. The swing of these bars serves to 'play out' the second instrumental section; the second tape Interpolation takes over seamlessly, as if we were simply hearing another sort of percussion.

Unlike the complex and lengthy events of the First Interpolation and the succeeding second instrumental section, the Second Interpolation (shortest of the three) and succeeding third instrumental section (shortest of the four) are comparatively simple in their elements, perhaps constituting a kind of intermezzo, an episode, within the overall span of *Déserts* as a whole. In this case the Interpolation is substantially the same in its 1954 and 1961 versions: common elements are heard in identical order and relation to one another. But by 1961 Varèse had got rid of the original dry, one-dimensional acoustic and, as with the other Interpolations, had situated the 'organized sound' in an aural continuum suggesting far greater depth and imaginative layering.

The taped sounds take over directly from the percussion ensemble with a series of attacks that are somewhat lower in pitch, suggesting bass drum or low timpani. Presently we hear a buzzing sonority which rises in intensity to a drilling sound, surrounded by silvery, chittering bursts of white noise. A melancholy tolling – midway between a gong or deep bell – then leads into what proves to be the main body of the Interpolation. Several different sonic elements are heard here, but the dominant one is an isolated, hollow percussion, sounding at first like a falling drop of water but soon coming to resemble a distant hammer-stroke. There is also a high tapping, perhaps produced by a xylophone or other wooden source, and scattered drum sounds; and an actual melodic figure of more obviously 'electronic' provenance, repeated several times, dropping apparently by a major third and then a tritone. These water-drops, hammerings or tappings are at first isolated and spread out in time, but they accumulate in frequency and density, creating an effect of mysterious, unseen activity in the gloom of a deserted mineshaft. Eventually the hammering increases in intensity until the point where the third instrumental section resumes the musical argument with an initial timpani and brass attack (Ex.8).

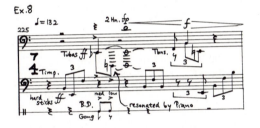

These triplet figures are hardly new: they are a feature that has occured several times since near the very outset of the work – what I have termed the timpani's 'melodicization' of the salient fifth and tritone intervals. And the beginning of this third instrumental section swiftly reviews some now-familiar elements. The brass zero in upon a single pitch (D above middle C); then, against sustained wind harmony, the xylophone gives out a high tapping on C♯ – immediately recognizable as the tapping figure from the tape Interpolation. The 'Latin-American' percussion combo from the end of the second instrumental section is now heard, followed by further hard-stick timpani writing plus brass in the manner of Ex.8.

Another 'Ex.2-type' brass fanfare follows, but this is interrupted by a new element – a piercing figure of three descending semitones on E-flat clarinet, with a supporting pitch on B-flat clarinet that re-admits the possibility of octaves to the harmony: Ex.9*a*. Immediately this is repeated in the form of a decisive tutti – prefaced with the basic intervals of ascending fifth and tritone – reinforced by octaves on the piano and a hint of 'contrary motion' (Ex.9*b*).

After this outburst the tempo slows; the texture suddenly grows very sparse and quiet. For a time the interest centres merely on softly sustained F♯s, taken up in turn by several instruments, with a dissonant 3-note chord – a minor ninth over a minor third – irregularly spaced beneath it. The clarinet tries to give this alternation of pitches a melodic shape, falling from the F♯ to the B, the top note of the chord. But the F♯ remains, freezing all movement, eventually dying away on trumpet, muted trombone and vibraphone in unison. This 'open', echoing music makes way for the Third (and last) Interpolation.

At last, Varèse unleashes the full power of the electronic forces available to him. Interpolation III forms the climax (or catharsis) of *Déserts* as a whole. If Interpolation II appeared a kind of shadowy, subterranean episode, we now emerge into the searing neon light of the urban desert, full of the noise and activity that so exacerbate existential solitude. The sense of nightmare, of auditory surrealism, is even more pervasive than in Interpolation I. So is the air of violence; and the temptation to relate the sounds to anecdotal auditory images of war and rapine and torture is hard to resist. Here, too, the advances of the final 1961 tape over the original version are most patent, though the same general remarks apply as in the comparison of the first and last versions of Interpolation I. Quite apart from the vast improvement in the sound-continuum itself, many of the constituent materials remain recognizable but have undergone a complete 're-composition' in terms of order and internal relationships. (For example, one element that plays a large role in the original version, especially its opening stages, are the 'church-organ' outbursts. These are whittled down in the 1961 tape to a single example, almost at the centre of the Interpolation.)

The 1961 tape begins with a variety of swooping glissandi (only perfunctorily achieved in 1954) and then develops for a while as a series of abrupt, staccato juxtapositions of high-pitched and low-pitched sounds, with the glissandi still in evidence. Before long the music is invaded by an enraged fusillade of surreally distorted 'industrial' sounds, suggestive of percussion, drilling, sirens, Very high, sustained or swooping sonorities begin to emerge – *almost* human, almost articulate, trembling on the edge of vocalization: and if human, clearly in pain or distress. At this point the 'church-organ' blasts in – wrathful, maybe patriarchal in effect, with thudding drum-sounds and further electronic glissandi surrounding it. The high, voice-like tones rise to a scream, then become less human, more metallic. Slow, dull blows fall, infinitely heavy: one thinks of industrial hammers, a giant's footsteps; perhaps the distant detonation of bombs. Then drilling sounds (or machine-guns). These two sonorities, bass and treble, begin to cluster in denser and denser complexes, along with keening or whistling bands of high-pitched sound which rise steadily, pitilessly, to a deafening, ear-skewering climax. At its very peak the lower-pitched sounds suddenly cut off, leaving the high-pitched one – the electronic scream – resounding alone for several seconds.[18] A scream of terror, or of protest? In the aftermath of this sonic assault, the fourth and final instrumental section of *Déserts* sets in, on quietly sinister, martially determined percussion.

This final section of the work does not even attempt to rival the emotional impact of Interpolation III. It is not a climax but a kind of epilogue and summing-up, at first agitated and impulsive, but becoming quiet, meditative, elegiac. Almost throughout, the wind instruments and the percussion ensemble play alternately, in 'antiphonal' exchanges. At first these exchanges are agitated, even angry; but even they are measured, giving each gesture a space and solidity that is a positive relief after the crowded, unstable dream-continuum of the tape music. Brief bursts of fanfare interrupt percussion activity which – including as it does three bars filled only

---

[18] This same general gesture is found at the end of the 1954 tape, but in far less effective form. The 'scream' only hangs on for a split-second after the dropping-out of the low (and much more obviously percussive) sounds.

with the rolls of the field-drum – has a distinctly military aspect, perhaps a military funeral. There are indeed moments, and this is one of them, where *Déserts* – assisted of course by its instrumentation – brings to mind Berlioz's *Symphonie Funèbre et Triomphale*.

The immediate climax is an 'Ex.2-type' gesture; then a lapse into quietness as the vibraphone reintroduces the folk-like turn from Ex.6*d*, above a bass harmony of tritone and fifth in the piano. There follow timpani figures distantly echoing Ex.8, high xylophone tappings reminiscent of Interpolation II. Other forms of Ex.6 are heard – as a low trill on bass clarinet; then as in Ex.6*d*, *sonoro* on solo horn; and finally *dolce* on solo tuba high in its register (Ex.6*f*). Brass instruments presently hone in, as on previous occasions, on a single pitch – D a ninth above middle C – in a crescendo that swells to *fff*.

Percussion take over (claves against suspended cymbal roll; then very *sharp*, *pesante*, *secco* timpani outlining major-seventh intervals against minor ninths in a *sharp*, *marcatissimo* xylophone). This builds into a toccata-like *incalzando* fusillade: timpani, xylophone, bass drums and piano finally agreeing on the hard-edged triplet rhythms we saw in Ex.8 (which go back to nearly the opening of the work). The brass, resonated by the piano, respond with a majestic 'Ex.2-type' gesture that affirms, for the last time, the basic harmonic structure of stacked fifths and tritones. A partial repetition and then a silent bar bring, in opposition to these 'open' intervals, a quiet unveiling of a segment of chromatic scale, its constituent minor second sounding at different octaves. Exx.10*a* and *b* show these contrasting entities.

The final horn E♭ in Ex.10*b*, appearing at first to be the next semitonal extension of the chromatic segment, in fact inaugurates the ending of the whole work: a passage that closely mimics the ending of the third instrumental section. Here again a single pitch (now E♭) is quietly passed from instrument to instrument, with a three-note chord tolling beneath it. In fact, the harmonic structure is precisely that of the end of the previous instrumental section, simply transposed down a third – a quiet, elegiac chiming on solo wind and piano, punctuated by short silences, with the softest of percussion support. Thus *Déserts*, after all its sonic surprises, takes a gentle farewell, gradually renewing our acquaintance with silence. The final E♭, in flute, piano, and vibraphone, just hangs over into the last bar, a long 7/4. Varèse directs the conductor: *beat the silence*. As so often in his works, the music seems finally to have exhausted what it can do on the physical, acoustical plane, yet nonetheless is felt to be continuing, at some other level of being, as it vanishes in the parched, ambient air.

11 · Inquisition

CHRONOLOGY 1955–58

1955 *Late January: Varèse returns to New York. Works on a short electronic score,* La Procession de Verges, *for Thomas Bouchard's film* Around and About Joan Miró. *17 May: first US performance of* Déserts *at the National Guard Armoury, Bennington College, Vermont, conducted by Frederic Waldman, who plays the work twice. (The New York première is at Town Hall on 30 November, conducted by Jacques Monod). 7 December:* Around and About Joan Miró *given its first showing (Fogg Museum of Art, Cambridge, Mass.).*

1956 *Ricordi, New York begins the publication of Varèse's complete works. The Philips Company issues commissions to Le Corbusier and Varèse for the company's Pavilion at the 1958 Brussels World Fair. December: makes a brief visit to Paris.*

1957 *February: further short European visit to confer with Philips. 26–28 April:* Around and About Joan Miró *presented at the New York Metropolitan Museum of Art (Third International Film Festival). July: Varèse encourages the young Frank Zappa, who approaches him unsuccessfully for composition lessons. 2 September: arrives in Holland and moves to Eindhoven to prepare* Poème électronique *in the Philips Laboratories.*

1958 *2 May-October:* Poème électronique *for three magnetic tapes is transmitted many times each day at the Corbusier-Xenakis Pavilion of the Brussels International Exhibition. June: Varèse in Paris, where he plays* Poème électronique *to, among other, Pierre Schaeffer, Jolivet, Henri Michaux, Alexander Calder and André Malraux. Malraux proposes that Varèse should return to Paris and take over the whole premises of a reorganized Club d'Essai to pursue his work with organized sound. The scheme remains unrealized although Varèse counts on it, with fading hopes, for the next two years. July: he leaves Paris for the last time and returns to New York. 9 November:* Poème électronique *is presented at the Village Gate Theater, Greenwich Village. Bogen-Presto, a division of the Siegler Corporation, offers to provide Varèse with a studio to continue his work, but later withdraws the offer.*

Although Varèse's plans to combine *Déserts* with a film element never came to fruition, his next work, as well as being his first essay for tape alone, was his only original film score.[1] In fact it exists only as a film soundtrack, and this fact has put it, for many years, outside the public domain. During the 1940s, in New York, Varèse had been introduced to the film-maker Thomas Bouchard by their mutual friend Fernand Léger, and at Bouchard's request he had provided extracts from several of his works as the accompaniment to parts of the film Bouchard was making about the artist, first shown in 1946. Varèse subsequently selected and arranged some Baroque music for Bouchard's film about Kurt Seligmann, *La Naissance d'un tableau*. However he was most creatively involved in the film about Miró which Bouchard made in the early 1950s, *Around and About Joan Miró*. The subject was highly congenial to Varèse, who had known Miró since the 1920s and indeed owned some of his paintings.

For one sequence in Bouchard's film, depicting the Good Friday procession in the Catalan village of Verges, he agreed to contribute an electronic score: *La Procession de Verges*. This tape composition – 'a combination of four different tapes', according to Ouellette – is apparently another essay in *musique concrète*, prepared by Varèse on

---

[1] The August-November number of the Paris journal *l'Age du cinéma* included an announcement that Varèse was to compose music (presumably electronic) for *le Minotaure*, a film directed by Hans Richter, but nothing more is known of this project.

primitive equipment in his New York home, in a similar manner to the first *Déserts* Interpolation. Ouellette (p. 174) indeed states that *Verges* was composed while Varèse was still carrying out 'research into the sounds he would require' for the Interpolations, which would imply a date of 1952–3 and make it his first electronic composition altogether, preceding the Interpolations themselves. But in this he seems to be mistaken: *Around and About Joan Miró* was not shown until December 1955 and it seems unlikely Varèse's score was created long before. The fact that Chou Wen-Chung has (also incorrectly) listed *Verges* as belonging to 1956 probably also indicates a late 1955 parturition.[2]

Unfortunately Bouchard's film has not been seen in public for over 30 years, and so Varèse's composition remains unheard.[3] It is reported by both Ouellette and Bernard as lasting 2 minutes 47 seconds, comparable therefore to one of the *Déserts* Interpolations in length. In the absence of the film itself we are thrown back on Ouellette's brief account of the *Verges* sequence (we should note that Ouellette himself had not seen the film and was relying on a description given him by Bouchard). This was the only portion of Bouchard's 55-minute film – otherwise a vibrantly coloured celebration of Miró – that was shot in black and white. Verges is some 60 miles from Barcelona, and like many Catalan towns celebrates its own distinct annual festival, combining pagan and Christian origins in unique traditional imagery. The Good Friday procession begins at midnight.

In the narrow streets – lighted solely by the flickering glow emanating from shells stuck to the walls of the houses – we see boys and men walking towards us, dressed in blue and white tights, with their faces hidden behind death's

---

[2] See Bernard p. 256, n. 3 on the dating question.

[3] It was unavailable to Jonathan Bernard when he was researching his book; he could only report (p. 238) that 'at least one copy of the film is still presumed to exist, but its whereabouts are unknown'. More recently, the heirs of Thomas Bouchard were initially persuaded to release the soundtrack of *Verges* for the Decca 2-disc set of Varèse's 'complete' works issued in 1998. The title even appeared on Decca's early publicity for the CD release. However I understand that, for reasons unknown, permission was withdrawn just before the CDs went into manufacture – making Verges the other unfortunate omission, along with *Etude pour Espace*, from 'Varèse: The Complete Works'. A copy of the film is believed to be held in the archive of Spanish Public Television, RTVE.

head masks. They dance and dance, as though bewitched by the Gregorian melodies sung by tall, cowled figures. Following them are the young girls, gliding slowly through the shadows, and grief-stricken penitents, all chained together and accompanied by a statue of the Virgin Mary wearing a crown of lighted candles. Lastly, come soldiers in Roman-style armour surrounding a fourteen-foot-high wooden figure of Christ.

Ouellette comments 'such a sequence of images was bound to fascinate Varèse, who had once lived in a Romanesque house',[4] but there are more cogent reasons why these images would have struck a powerful chord in him. This thriving Christian/pagan religious folk art, full of theatre and purgatorial emotion, recalls the folk traditions of Central and South America: religious terror and the shadow of the Inquisition are evoked. Whether or not *La Procession de Verges* uses 'Gregorian melodies', it must certainly incorporate bell-sounds, such as Varèse had used in *Déserts*, and one wonders if he adapted any of *Etude pour Espace*, with its associations with St. John of the Cross.

But there is a further aspect, unmentioned here by Ouellette or Bouchard. It is possible that Varèse visited Verges when he was in Catalonia in 1933. In any case, he will have known that the Festival for which Verges is famous throughout the region does not take place on Good Friday but on the preceding evening, Holy Thursday, when the Dance of Death is enacted through its streets. These 'boys and men ... in blue and white tights' and 'death's head masks' are, precisely, the death-dancers who may be seen in Verges to this day: the 'white' on their costumes is a painted skeleton. Thus the Good Friday procession is in some sense an extension of the Dance of Death. The elemental grimness of this conception must have appealed strongly to him, and suggests that *La Procession de Verges* is the true forerunner – perhaps even the first sketch – of the major electronic composition to which Varèse would shortly turn his attention.

POÈME ÉLECTRONIQUE

> *... I wanted it to express tragedy, and inquisition.*

It was not only in France, Germany and the USA that the tape revolution was leading to the establishment of electronic music

---

[4] Ouellette, p. 174.

studios. In Holland, from 1952 onwards, the Dutch composer Henk Badings had begun experimenting with tape compositions at Nederlandsche Radio Unie (NRU) at Hilversum, at first with quite limited facilities; and it was primarily due to his advocacy that in 1957 a permanent – and for the time quite lavishly equipped – electronic music studio was set up as a subdivision of the Philips Gloeil-amperafabrieken at Eindhoven.

The timing of this development was very fortunate, as the Philips Radio Corporation and its associated electronics firms had already begun to consider plans for their contribution to the World Fair to be held at Brussels in 1958. It had been decided to construct a special Philips Pavilion for a spectacular display of the contemporary possibilities of electronics, and in January 1956 the artistic director of the Eindhoven plant, M. Kalff, was despatched to invite the distinguished architect Le Corbusier (Charles-Edouard Jeanneret) to prepare the design for it. Le Corbusier immediately seized upon the idea of combining technology and the arts by creating a building which would be the 'vessel' or 'bottle' containing a total art-work. He envisaged an integrated experience in sound, space, vision, colour and structure – a 'multi-media event', as we would now say – addressing the creative potential of electronics and associated sciences in contemporary society. And he immediately thought of Varèse – whom he had known in Paris in the 1920s and 30s but with whom he had had no contact for 25 years – as the one composer who could create a musical component worthy of the conception.

To the grudging agreement of the Philips management – who would clearly have preferred to have music in familiar style from a composer whom they had already worked with, such as Badings – Le Corbusier absolutely insisted on Varèse's participation, and on their awarding him a very generous commission fee. He himself, in June 1956, issued the invitation to Varèse, suggesting that he provide the music in the form of a prepared tape, but leaving him otherwise entirely free to create a world of sound in whatever manner he wished. The total event, in Le Corbusier's conception, would be an 'Electronic Poem' (*Poème électronique*), though in the event that title has attached itself to the tape-composition which Varèse provided for it.

Varèse made a short trip to Europe in early 1957 to negotiate with Philips, who nevertheless fought a strong rearguard action to have him replaced by someone more famous and less radical (Copland, Walton, and Marcel Landowski were mentioned as alternatives). It was only due to the strongest insistence from Le Corbusier and his assistant Iannis Xenakis – now a passionate partisan for Varèse and his music – that Varèse's appointment was finally confirmed. He returned to Holland on 2 September and immediately established himself at Eindhoven, to commence work in the new Philips laboratories.

After his decades of struggle, Varèse's most cherished desires had suddenly been rewarded. At last – at the age of 74 – he found himself provided with the technical means, and the opportunity of presentation, which would allow him to compose a work absolutely unfettered by the limitations of conventional instruments, and whose sounds were to be projected into space: the dream he had only been able to realize to a very limited extent in *Déserts*. At Eindhoven he enjoyed a range of facilities which were without precedent at that time: an elaborate studio system had been assembled for his work on the composition, backed by a team of skilled sound engineers and technicians. It was almost as if fate was allowing him one chance to prove what he could do in optimum conditions.

Not that conditions were entirely to his satisfaction, even so. Eager to proceed as fast as possible, and used to the enthusiasm of American and French technicians, Varèse soon found himself frustrated by the attitude of some of the Dutch engineers. The equipment, also, while good for the 1950s, still fell short of the reach of his imagination. Le Corbusier had stipulated the creation of 480 seconds' worth of music, and Varèse had to compose it second by second. The project proceeded with what seemed exasperating slowness, and it continued to be viewed with mistrust by the Philips management. When, in December, a fragment of the work in progress was presented to them, the music was condemned for its lack of melody and harmony. Le Corbusier – then working in India – had once again to exert his influence, even threatening to withdraw from the project entirely if Varèse's commission should be revoked. Nevertheless, despite these obstacles, Varèse was able, between September 1957 and April 1958, to achieve a result which reflected a unique style of electronic composition, one utterly independent of any established studio conventions.

As in the tape music of *Déserts*, Varèse combined electronic and concrete sounds, though he was now able to use a much bigger range of each. The essential difference, however, was that he now had access to a vastly larger arsenal of modifying devices, including tape manipulation, filters, generators, oscillators and reverberation units. The sounds were recorded on a 3-channel tape, of which two channels were reserved for reverberation and stereo effects; for their public performance each track had its own playback head, linked to amplifiers and loudspeakers.

Although the initial idea of the Pavilion was Le Corbusier's – with an interior (to use his own analogy) in the shape of a cow's stomach, through which the public would pass as 'nutrients' to be 'digested' by the effects of sound and vision – most of his time was spent in India during 1957–8, working on the city of Chandigarh. It was in fact Xenakis who prepared the mathematical and three-dimensional models for the building, evolved its final shape, chose its materials and supervised its construction. (He also composed a short piece of his own for electronic tape at the Philips studios in Paris, *Concrèt PH*, based on the sounds of burning charcoal, for performance in the intermissions between Varèse's work.) Xenakis had designed the pavilion's exterior in the shape of a three-peaked circus tent, and for its interior surfaces he provided a series of hyperbolic and parabolic curves along which Varèse's music could be projected. The projection was achieved by feeding the 3-channel tape system, via 20 amplifiers and telephone relays, to elaborate arrays of loudspeakers: some positioned along these curves, some buried within the walls and ceiling alcoves during the building's construction. Out of these '400 mouths', as Le Corbusier called them, the *Poème* issued and swept the vaulted interior in continuous arcs of sound.

Different sources give different totals for the number of speakers employed. 400 is most frequently mentioned, but 425 and 350 are also quoted, and Le Corbusier himself sometimes spoke of 150: doubtless some of the arrays were counted as single units. Whatever the total, they were divided into groups positioned above the entrance and exit and in the three peaks of the pavilion, joined by 'sound paths' of single speakers leading along the ribs of the roof; and there were also large speakers, positioned low down, to handle the deep bass and other special sounds. Adding to the complexity of the wiring layout, the way the sounds were projected along the 'paths' was determined by a 15-channel control tape, each track of which contained 12 separate signals. Thus a total of 180 (=15 × 12) control signals was available to route the sounds in the desired directions, in association (or rather counterpoint) with visual effects.

These latter were created and projected by means of a comprehensive system of light sources – also regulated by the control tape – that included slide and film projectors, spotlights, bulbs, ultra-violet lamps and flourescent lights of various colours, to produce the changing patterns of coloured images which Le Corbusier had selected. These images were of different sizes, sometimes combining into vast evanescent murals on the inner surfaces of the pavilion. Among them were photographs of birds and wild animals, masks, ritual objects from many cultures and tribes, skeletons, cityscapes, atomic explosions; there were also paintings, montages, handwritten or printed texts. But there was no attempt at synchronization between image and music. Rather, a deliberate dissociation or disjunction between aural and visual impressions was part of the desired effect – as was the reverse, on the quite numerous occasions where they achieved an essentially random concordance. Le Corbusier had, in fact, originally suggested that right in the middle of the presentation there should be 'an abrupt and total silence, and white light at the same moment – something to twist the audience's guts inside them' (an idea which, consciously or not, rather recalled the vision Varèse had had for the ending of *The One All Alone*). But Varèse – if he ever tried to do so – found it impossible to incorporate Le Corbusier's silence within the piece as he conceived it, arguing that it was exactly at this mid-point that he needed to have the most noise.[5]

The Philips Pavilion was officially opened on 17 April 1958, but the sound-system, much to Varèse's dismay, was not ready. The Pavilion then closed until 2 May, when the *Poème électronique* was finally presented to the public. It was then repeated there throughout the Exposition, for six months. The figure of 15–16,000 visitors per day is often quoted: as the capacity of the Pavilion was for 500, this suggests a daily schedule of between 30 and 32 presentations – perfectly possible, of course, with an 8-minute piece. At a conservative estimate, perhaps two million people experienced Varèse's music: a number approaching in some measure the worldwide audience he had once envisaged for *Espace*. The reactions of individual members of this immense public, drawn from all over the world, were quite as varied as

---

[5] This was not literally true. In fact, at the exact centre of the work, around four minutes in, there *is* a short silence of a couple of seconds dividing the phrases of a quiet crooning voice.

one might expect: terror, anger, stunned awe, amusement, outrage, wild enthusiasm. But there is no doubt that the work had an enormous impact.

That precise impact is one that cannot be recreated, for Le Corbusier's pavilion, the unique aural and visual environment for which the *Poème* was composed, was demolished soon after the end of the Exposition. But the tape exists, and may be played in concert conditions; it is also available on record in a two-channel reduction specifically made for issuing on a Columbia Records stereo LP in 1958. Thus Varèse's contribution to the event can still be appreciated as music – possibly the most powerful piece of electronic music ever composed. Since the movement of sounds in space was so essential a part of the original conception, at the very least an effective stereophonic image is necessary for the work to make its proper impact: and this impact seems to be heightened the more speakers are available, and the larger the acoustic space in which the music is able to resound. This lesson was learned early, when the US première of *Poème électronique* – given on a primitive stereo system in the small Village Gate Theater in Greenwich village in November 1958, shortly after Varèse's return from Europe – turned out to be only a pale reflection of the Brussels experience (even though the work was well received, and immediately repeated).

As noted above, Varèse was able to use a much more extensive range of raw sounds in *Poème électronique* than was possible in *Déserts*. Pure sinusoidal tones, bell-sounds (he had a rich choice in the churches of Holland and Belgium), solo and choral voices, piano, organ, percussion, machine noise, the sound of aircraft: all these appears, occasionally without electronic modifications but almost always subjected to elaborate processes of pitch transformation, filtering, and alteration of their characteristics of attack and decay. Indeed, the really important feature of the *Poème* is the vastly increased means by which he could shape and work upon these elements. After recording, the multifarious 'sound-images' presented by the raw materials were juxtaposed, combined and synchronized, by means of precise editing, onto the 3-track tape. Through loops, filters and other devices, the sounds were re-created, re-shaped, acquiring new frequencies, shedding their customary associations and taking on fresh ones. *Poème électronique* is therefore not so much *musique concrète* (though it may start out from the same aural bases) as a prime example of 'Organized

'Sound', to use the term Varèse favoured and had already used in connexion with the tape interpolations in *Déserts*.

As in the case of the *Déserts* Interpolations, there exists no readable 'score' of *Poème électronique*, or even the sort of integrated graphic representation that has been published for such electronic works as Stockhausen's *Elektronische Studien*. In the course of composition Varèse did indeed produce visual, diagrammatic analogues of the music that was to be created on tape, drawn as multicoloured curves and parabolas on large sheets of graph-paper, mapping out the musical events second by second. These he freely displayed to composers, technicians and other enthusiasts for his work. From those which have been reproduced,[6] it is possible to see that Varèse was concerned with the precise correlation of time, dynamics, intensity, higher or lower relative pitch, and the 'contrapuntal' combination of separate bands of sound. Certain elements – those of a more percussive nature, or percussion-derived – are precisely notated, at least as regards their rhythm and variations of tempo. Such indications confirm that *Poème électronique* was as precisely and scrupulously 'composed' as any work for more conventional forces. Among those who examined Varèse's diagrams was Odile Vivier, who transcribes a note written on one page in red ink:

There is no difference between sound and noise, noise being a sound in the course of creation. Noise is due to an aperiodic vibration, or a vibration which is too complex in structure, or of too short a duration to be analysed and understood by the ear.[7]

The absence of any conventional score, or indeed of present access to Varèse's charts, severely limits any discussion of *Poème électronique* in its compositional aspects, since there is no material that may easily be reproduced for reference or musical examples. Commentators are forced to fall back on generalized descriptions of the sounds and the associations they evoke. A merely anecdotal, personal description of the music as it appears to one listener may not be considered to be of much use. But it is clear from Varèse's various comments on the piece (for instance, of the female voice near the end: 'I wanted it to express

---

[6] See, for example, illustration 17 in Vivier's book, and (in colour) the box inlay to the 1998 Decca 'complete Varèse' CDs.

[7] Vivier, p. 166.

tragedy – and inquisition') that he did intend specific associations to be invoked in the audience's mind. Indeed the music's power to evoke inner visions by aural means – to evoke them all the more easily because of the absence of the conventional barriers caused by instrumental timbres – would seem to be one of the *Poème*'s prime functions, and the secret of its powerful impact upon a mass audience.

Moreover the succession of events, and to some extent their expressive nature, can be objectively established and agreed; and they manifest many of the characteristics now familiar from Varèse's earlier instrumental and vocal music. Though new in its medium, and the handling of it, the musical differences between *Poème électronique* and his previous output are differences of degree rather than of essential nature; indeed, the tape composition has its roots in, and makes some more or less explicit references to, its instrumental forebears. Finally, the temporal dimension – the tape's unalterable second-by-second progress – provides a time-frame as fixed and precise as the numbering of bars, within which we can pinpoint the sonic events as they take place. Thus some account of the music as the ear experiences it still has value. Electronic the work most certainly is: but it remains the 'poem' that the title proclaims it.

Poème électronique is born from bell-sounds: huge, deep ecclesiastical bells whose sombre tolling starts to measure time and whose overtones resound to fill and define a very large acoustic space. The effect establishes a number of parallels with the instrumental opening of *Déserts*, but here the realistic bell-tone imports certain imaginative associations. The apparent acoustic ambience has, from the outset, a cathedral-like quality, and the illusion of a cathedral will be exploited later on, though at various times the music also evokes other vaulted spaces – a factory, a mine-shaft, the stellar heavens. About 15" in, a low electronic hum takes over from the bells: it emerges from under them to introduce a series of percussive sounds, echoing taps and pulsations both metallic and wooden in their timbres; miniature glissandi like mosquitos or tiny sirens; a pulsed electronic buzz. The ear is drawn generally upward, plane by plane, into a band of very high-pitched whistling sound, which swells in a crescendo of piercing, hissing intensity only to be abruptly cut off (a faint foreshadowing of the work's end).

A percussive interlude supervenes – as an episode of real percussion might do in one of Varèse's instrumental works. Three elements can be distinguished: a 'wooden' tapping vaguely reminiscent of bongos, short bursts of a fiercer 'electro-metallic' noise, and a squeaking/croaking sound, the voice perhaps of some extraterrestial frog, hopping freely between high and low registers.

Very soon, however, the attention is rivetted by a genuine melodic element: a plangent three-note call in the middle register, rising approximately by conjunct semitones. In its construction, therefore, this figure reflects a characteristic Varèse motif – one we find as early as the opening trombone solo of *Hyperprism*, though there the first two pitches are merely grace-notes, whereas here all three are of approximately equal length (the second is slightly shorter than the other two). But the idea of the upward chromatic slide is essential to both the instrumental and the electronic work – and though the three pitches remain aurally distinct, the electronic medium affords Varèse more of the sense of a continuous glissando, the final pitch continuing to slide a little towards the sharp side. The figure is repeated three times. Almost articulate – not quite a voice, not quite a clarinet – it conveys a sense of inexpressible melancholy and solitude, like the swinging of a door in a long-abandoned building.

Next, about 77" into the work, a vigorous 'development section' ensues with a return of some of the earlier percussive sounds – drilling and hissing on sustained pitches which rapidly become more mobile through glissandi, and the reappearance of the frog-like croaking, whose detached notes move jerkily across an ever wider and more abrupt spectrum. In the midst of this the sad 3-note figure sounds out again, more distant. The glissandi spawn more rapid echoes, ascending like the multiple cries of a flock of gulls, startled from the earth and continuing to rise higher and higher into insect-like voices, which seem finally to vanish at the upper limit of hearing.

A more 'industrialized' clamour now strikes in, with a more various repertoire of sounds than heard hitherto. A number of drum sounds are prominent; indeed, this passage begins with resemblances to timpani, and side-drum attacks are distinguishable at various places. There are also drillings and hammerings, and an urgent, distant siren which is soon imitated and vastly enlarged by the rise and fall of a strident electronic glissando. This gives way to a resonant wooden tapping, and then (approximately 150" into the work) a reminiscence of the deep bells with which *Poème électronique* opened.

The return of the bells, like a structural punctuation, is the signal for a different kind of event: sustained electronic tones on particular pitches, building up two dissonant chordal complexes similar to those encountered throughout Varèse's instrumental output. Harmonic homogeneity is characteristically avoided, since the constituent tones are just as strongly differentiated as the instrumental timbres in his orchestral tuttis: a palmary example of 'the sensation of non-blending'. The second of these chordal complexes swells in a great crescendo, leading to a further 'percussion break' in gradually accelerating rhythms until (about 215 seconds in) we suddenly hear something which is unmistakably a human voice.

Whether choral voices, or a single enormously expanded female voice, is not at first clear. The sounds seem to be emitted by mouths without lips or tongue, and no consonant is clearly distinguishable; yet the breathily imploring words which we hear half-sung, half-wailed seem to be: '*O God ...*' This is the voice which Varèse wanted 'to express tragedy and inquisition'. Already semi-disembodied, it is caught up into the distance, into a ghostly glissando never produced by any throat, becoming an eerie yet still almost-human presence, a fluctuating song like the voice of the wind, sometimes breaking into indistinguishable words, and once almost imitating the sad 3-note call. Meanwhile scattered electronic percussion holds the foreground, and then, as the female ghost-voice continues to rise and fall in the distance, a much more realistic percussion body enters to one side, with characteristic Varèsian march-rhythms and a suggestion of male voices, almost like some half-remembered passage from *Ecuatorial*. (It is, in fact, almost certainly a snatch of *Etude pour Espace*.) The percussion rhythms continue for some time, gradually becoming less 'acoustic' and more 'electronic' in effect, an echoing wave of sound that seems to evoke a crowd of shuffling feet. The incorporeal masculine voices meanwhile return – under complex acoustical manipulation – to suggest now chanting, now radiophonically distorted communication in which no actual words may be distinguished.

Gradually this passage fades, about 330" after the beginning of the work, into a moment of silence. Its effect is very different from the sudden, intensely dramatic silence Le Corbusier had suggested Varèse should put at the mid-point of his work. We are considerably further than the mid-point, and the feeling is rather of a point of repose, perhaps of exhaustion: at any rate, a relaxation of concentration before what proves to be the climactic portion of *Poème électronique*.

We hear a harsh electro-metallic buzz, swelling out in a crescendo and then fading again to be replaced by subterranean rhythmic poundings. The various percussive sounds heard earlier in the piece, along with sustained electronic pitches, are deployed in a fresh developmental passage along with industrial-type noises and bell-sounds of a new, higher-pitched kind. Just before 400" in we hear a single wordless female voice, somewhere in the distance, giving tongue to vast melismas, an elaborate, wide-spanned arioso, at once ecstatic and imploring. It soars up to an inhuman level, beyond the capacity of any Queen of the Night, and begins to fade: at which point male voices strike in urgently, in a passage that evokes tribal chanting within the cathedral acoustic of the opening. Fricative, crackling percussion sounds assail this choir, and then jagged, imperiously-repeated outbursts from a great organ. Amid all the clamour the melancholic 3-note cry reappears for the last time.

A deep booming, as of thunder, and an arc of sound which might be a tornado wind, or a swooping aircraft, initiate the final assault on the ear. As always, Varèse seeks to draw that organ of hearing upward, as a huge parabolic electric glissando sounds out with greater force than any siren he ever employed in his more orthodox works. While the thunder continues to roll, the arc reaches its highest point in a clot of sustained white noise, painful in its intensity, which is still growing in volume in the extreme upper register when it, and the *Poème électronique*, is suddenly extinguished. The really shocking, dramatic silence is the one to which the listener's ears must become accustomed now that the work is over.

Vivier has claimed – perhaps on the basis of personal communication from the composer – that these final seconds 'evoke the storm-winds at Villars'.[8] Certainly there is throughout *Poème électronique* a deep dichotomy, an imaginative tension, between its comparatively scientific means of sound-production and the suggestion it undoubtedly contains of the voices of nature, of audible human activity, and of the purely internal sounds of dream and nightmare. In this work, freed from the constraints of tempered notation, of instrumental tessitura, Varèse was never more essentially himself: a poet of the wild, ungovernable natural forces beyond all the accumulated decorum of artistic tradition – an invoker of the raw

---

[8] Vivier, p. 167.

sonic materials of myth and ritual. Yet, as we have seen, his expression of these forces is disciplined, often by very similar techniques of juxtaposition, of tone colour, of horizontal and vertical sonority, as had governed all his works in non-electronic media. With its eight minutes' duration, *Poème électronique* is in some senses still only a sketch towards the possibilities of the new medium. Yet it is also a long-meditated and fully-achieved work of art, a shattering emotional experience, the one electronic score which remains as contemporary today as when it was first heard: a perpetual 'music of the future'.

12 · Beyond the night

I kissed his shadow.
ANAÏS NIN
The House of Incest

CHRONOLOGY 1959–65

1959 *The Koussevitsky Foundation commissions a work from Varèse (eventually to emerge as* Nocturnal*). 4 September: Varèse lectures at Princeton University. 27–30 November: Leonard Bernstein conducts four performances of* Arcana *at Carnegie Hall. During the winter Varèse revises the tape* Interpolations *of* Déserts.

1960 *8 August: the revised* Déserts *is premièred at the ISCM Conference at Stratford, Canada, conducted by Frederik Prausnitz. Columbia Records issues its first LP recording of Varèse's ensemble works conducted by Robert Craft, including the two-channel stereo version of* Poème électronique *(MS 6146). September: Craft brings Varèse and Stravinsky together at the Waldorf-Astoria Hotel – their only meeting. October: Varèse begins work on the third version of the* Interpolations *for* Déserts. *He also revises* Arcana *for Craft's forthcoming recording.*

1961 *1 May: Robert Craft conducts the première of* Nocturnal I *(the incomplete form of* Nocturnal*), and the revised version of* Ecuatorial *in New York; Varèse receives a standing ovation. Ricordi publish the score of*

Déserts. *Early August: Varèse completes the fourth and final version of the* Déserts *Interpolations.* Arcana *and* Déserts, *conducted by Craft, are issued on Columbia MS 6362. Some time this year, in a fit of depression, Varèse destroys the manuscript of* Bourgogne, *unperformed since 1910. During the winter he suffers a serious bronchial infection.*

1962 *Varèse receives the Creative Arts Award from Brandeis University and is elected a member of the Swedish Academy. He continues slow work on the proposed* Nocturnal II, *but the bronchial trouble persists, with associated feelings of suffocation, and gravely reduces his capacity for work. During these final years he also manifests symptoms of arterio-sclerosis.*

1963 *Varèse receives the first Koussevitsky International Recording Award, for Craft's Columbia discs.*

1964 *23–26 January: Bernstein conducts four performances of* Déserts *at Lincoln Center. August: Varèse takes part in a Composers' Conference at Bennington College.*

1965 *31 March and 12 May: Varèse attends concerts of his works conducted by Ralph Shapey at Carnegie Hall, New York and in Chicago respectively. 23 July: he attends a performance of* Hyperprism *by the New York Philharmonic in their 'French-American' Festival. 21 August: receives the medal of the MacDowell Colony. 18 October: speaks at a memorial ceremony for Le Corbusier. 27 October: Varèse is admitted as an emergency to the Hospital of the New York Medical Center. After an operation the same day for intestinal blockage caused by thrombosis he contracts an infection and dies in the Hospital at about 5 a.m. on 6 November, aged almost 82. He is commemorated in several memorial concerts in Paris and New York, originally scheduled in celebration of his '80th' birthday that December.*

NOCTURNAL

The work which proved to be Varèse's last was commissioned by and dedicated to the Koussevitsky Music Foundation. *Nocturnal* is a setting of words and phrases taken from the novella *The House of Incest* by Anaïs Nin, interspersed – as in *Ecuatorial* and *Etude pour Espace* – with syllables devised by Varèse himself. Perhaps surprisingly, he made no attempt to utilize any of the electronic media he had so painfully mastered in *Déserts* and *Poème électronique*. But though he had long yearned for those media, and had now achieved extraordinary things with them, they did not dominate his consciousness or neutralize his scepticism. As he remarked during one of his 1959 Princeton lectures,

Grateful as we must be for the new medium, we should not expect miracles from machines. The machine can give out only what we put into it. The musical principles remain the same whether a composer writes for orchestra or tape.

The scoring of *Nocturnal*, therefore, is for soprano solo, a chorus of bass voices, and a small orchestra which, in its constitution, comes the nearest to a 'standard orchestra' of any of Varèse's late works. However according to Chou Wen-Chung – to whom fell the task of bringing *Nocturnal* to completion after Varèse's death, and who in his preface to the published score furnishes the only coherent account of its genesis – the composer's sketches show that his original plan had been to use 'a large wind and percussion ensemble, perhaps even with electronic sounds'.[1] (I take the vagueness of the words 'perhaps even' to mean that the sketches contain very few, or only very ambiguous, indications of an electronic componen.)

In the event, however, *Nocturnal* emerged with something approaching a standard 'small orchestra' instrumentation: 11 wind instruments (6 wood, 5 brass), plus piano, strings and, of course, a large body of percussion. This orchestra, with the solo soprano, suggests parallels with *Offrandes*, but the male chorus and the piano also evoke the sound-world of *Ecuatorial*. Since *Nocturnal* was put into shape in the early months of 1961 for a Composers' Showcase Concert given in his honour, it seems possible that the programme of this concert, which included *Offrandes* and the first performance of the new version of *Ecuatorial*, may have determined Varèse's choices.[2]

He seems to have intended to contribute a work of considerable proportions; but in fact, *Nocturnal* was very far from being completed by the date of the concert, and this world première, given at New York Town Hall on 1 May 1961, by the soprano Donna Precht and an ensemble conducted by Robert Craft, was only of a fragment,

---

[1] Chou Wen-Chung, Preface to the published study score of *Nocturnal* (New York: Colfranc Music Publishing Company, 1969), p. iii. Hereafter cited as 'Preface'.

[2] Chou, in the more informal medium of a public discussion (transcribed in Sherman Van Solkema, ed., *The New Worlds of Edgard Varèse*) comments (p. 89): 'I am willing to venture that it was not his first choice in terms of orchestration'.

extending to bar 94 of the posthumously-published score.[3] This fragment was merely the tip of the iceberg: for the 1961 *Nocturnal* seems to have represented simply the current form of a project which had been occupying Varèse since the early 1950s at least.

In October 1954, while preparing the tape interpolations for *Déserts* in Paris, he had spoken to Odile Vivier of his conception of a vocal work which he then called *Nuits*, and of his search for an appropriate text or group of texts. He was

choosing a poem of Henri Michaux, re-reading Novalis, and marking passages of *The Dark Night of the Soul* in a Spanish edition of St. John of the Cross, which never left his bedside table. He wanted, he told me, to create a synthesis with a very strong tension, at one and the same time erotic, mystic, spiritual and mysterious.[4]

In 1955 he reported to Vivier that he was now at work upon *Nuits*, and hoped that the première would take place in Paris. But by 1957 Varèse's intentions seemed to have changed. He spoke of the work in preparation as *Dans la Nuit*: it would be a setting of the poem of that name by Henri Michaux, for chorus, 15 brass instruments, percussion, organ, and two Ondes Martenots. He asked Fernand Ouellette to make a taped transcription of this poem into Morse code, apparently to try to discover a new rhythmic dimension in the words. In 1958, he was still searching for

strong texts, percussive words, the cries of the night considered in all their aspects. He approached Iannis Xenakis for Greek, specialists for contemporary poets, myself for Russian writers, the literatures of oral traditions, the texts of all existing liturgies. It all inspired him, as if he was bound to pursue the tireless, infinite, and indefinable quest of this Grail. He was prey to the anguish of establishing his text, of recovering the 'garamantic emeralds' of the word. His encyclopedic spirit, his nature of a Renaissance Man, inclined him to embrace as it were the totality of a subject before making his definitive choice.[5]

---

[3] According to Chou, loc.cit., Varèse had composed a few more measures, which were lost in the process of copying.

[4] Vivier, p. 174. As we have seen, Varèse had already turned to *The Dark Night of the Soul* for at least one passage in *Etude pour Espace*.

[5] Ibid., pp. 174–5. I do not know the source of the quoted phrase *émeraudes garamantiques*: in classical antiquity the Garamantes, mentioned by Herodotus, were a legendary people of central Africa.

Later still, in January 1961, he was using the title of the proposed Michaux setting, *Dans la Nuit*, as the working title for *Nocturnal* itself – which now drew its text from Anaïs Nin. The première of the *Nocturnal* fragment in May of that year in no sense brought the compositional prcess to a close. Varèse continued to work on extending it, but then abandoned this original version (which was to be re-designated *Nocturnal I*) for an entirely new form, *Nocturnal II*: this was to be somewhat longer than *Nocturnal I* but would use the same vocal forces and a text of similar character, again drawn from *The House of Incest*. The instrumental ensemble, Louise Varèse wrote to Vivier, was to be smaller 'to increase the tension. No strings except one double bass, woodwind, brass, harp and percussion'. This *Nocturnal II* seems to be identical with the work-in-progress which Varèse, up to the last months of his life, had come to refer to as *Nuit*. In a letter which Louise Varèse wrote to Ouellette in 1963, again listing the forces which Varèse was composing for, the bass chorus had been dispensed with and the orchestra had been reduced again, to 3 woodwind, 3 or 4 brass, double-bass and percussion. This work was apparently discussed by Varèse and Richard Dufallo for a New York Philharmonic concert in 1965, and it was actually announced by the Columbia New Music Group for its 1965–6 season, but it never emerged.

Although the Koussevitsky Foundation's commission for *Nocturnal* had been received as early as 1959, Varèse found it difficult to produce a score in time for the 1961 première. Indeed there never was an autograph full score; the score used in the performance was compiled by a copyist, working under pressure, directly from the composer's sketches, and was marred by numerous mistakes and omissions. Varèse had three reference copies made of this score, which he annotated extensively with a view to correcting and improving the fragment; he also continued to sketch later portions of the work. But in his failing state of health everything demanded greater effort, and *Nocturnal* seemed no nearer completion at his death.

Although it was soon clear that *Nocturnal* could never be completed in any way that would accord with Varèse's total conception, it was felt that the work must be made available in some concrete form. 'Since', as Chou Wen-Chung comments,

the original portion ends too soon and too abruptly, it was decided that what might be called a 'performance version' be made, with the original portion fully edited, incorporating Varèse's indicated changes and additions, and with a continuing portion added to provide formal balance and to include some of Varèse's sketched ideas not employed in the original portion.[6]

As Chou had been both a pupil and close friend of Varèse, he was the logical person to attempt the task, though on his own admission he was extremely reluctant, and it was over two years before Louise Varèse was able to persuade him. As he had anticipated, the assignment raised editorial and compositional problems of the most acute kind. The three reference copies of the copyist's score contain extensive indications of changes and addition 'of which some are specific, others have several alternatives, and still others bear no specified solutions'.[7] Moreover, as Chou discovered,

The comments on the three copies are often contradictory to each other, and I can say also that you find four-letter words on these copies where he apparently found himself very frustrated.[8]

Chou was nevertheless able to produce a scrupulously edited edition of the 92 bars of music represented by the copyist's score, often having recourse to the original sketches to resolve ambiguities and uncertainties. He then assembled a further 78 bars to provide *Nocturnal* with a satisfactory completion – following, as he has explained, two principles:

(1) continuation of some of Varèse's principal material of the original portion as suggested in the cryptic notes; (2) addition of new material from the few more elaborate sketches found so as to more fully illustrate his ideas for this work and his concepts in the use of vocal sounds. These two processes are mutually interpolated or superimposed as suggested in the cryptic notes and the nature of the material in question. All the details, whenever not specified in the sketches, are worked out according to the original portion or other sketches in which similar situations are found ... The added portion is purposely kept to the minimum length possible, just enough to include all suitable additional material and to provide structural coherence.[9]

The utilization of Varèse's sketches themselves was probably by no means as straightforward as this implies. Elsewhere Chou has commented that most of Varèse's surviving sketches

---

[6] Preface, p. iv.

[7] Ibid.

[8] Van Solkema, p. 89

[9] Preface, p.v.

are very 'sketchy'. You may have a rhythm, for instance, but nothing else. You may have the instruments, but without the dynamic levels, and so on. Furthermore, it is very difficult to identify the sketches ... [10]

He also observed that the task was

very frustrating: trying to put yourself in that person's shoes, so to speak ... is, to say the least, a frightening experience.[11]

Despite all these problems, Chou's conscientious performance of his difficult assignment has left us all in his debt, since he has made *Nocturnal* into a rounded and discussable whole. Even if its structure is not that which Varèse would have imposed upon it, and if it lacks the further development of the ideas which he would assuredly have wished to carry out, it is still a dramatically satisfying and performable piece of music, entirely Varèse in its materials and painstakingly true to his characteristic sound and style. Jonathan Bernard is of course correct to say that after the first 93 bars the work 'cannot be regarded as authentic'[12] at least for the purposes of analytical investigation of Varèse's compositional strategies. But the music which occurs after that point makes its own aesthetic and dramatic impact, and enlarges our view of the composer's expressive vocabulary.

In fact, perhaps precisely because of the penumbra of 'inauthenticity' which attaches to it, *Nocturnal* has received relatively few performances, and surprisingly little attention in the extant Varèse literature. It has been relegated almost unconsciously to the status of a 'minor' work, a fragment of no great significance for the overall view of Varèse's creative evolution. It is true that he does not seem to have considered that it would be his last composition, or any sort of testament (he spoke occasionally of the next project he wished to undertake, a work for large orchestra with electronics). Nevertheless it proves such a fascinating and deeply rewarding score that, in my opinion, it adds new dimensions to our understanding of his creative odyssey. It also, perhaps fortuitously, seems to close the circle of his life's work in an especially poignant fashion.

---

[10] Van Solkema, p. 90: in this context Chou is not speaking only of Varèse's sketches for *Nocturnal*, but it is clear that his comments include them.

[11] Ibid.

[12] Bernard, p. 243

Chou Wen-Chung has stated that 'except for the choice of words and instrumentation,' *Nocturnal I* and *Nocturnal II* 'are really one and the same, possessing the same ideas'.[13] He has also said that 'From these last years the titles *Dans la Nuit, Nuit, Nocturnal,* and *Nocturnal II* were all references to the same work'.[14] The qualification 'these last years' is significant here. Chou's comment just quoted is an amplification of an earlier one:

Towards the end of his life, in the years from 1961 to his death in 1965, he was fundamentally writing a single work, despite a number of titles he worked with. A number of people asked him to write a work at various times, and texts that he had in mind were changed, and so different titles emerged.[15]

As we have noted, *Dans la Nuit* was an initial working title for *Nocturnal I*. Yet it certainly seems possible to distinguish two prior and separate, though doubtless intimately interrelated projects: the work referred to as *Nuits* (in the plural), apparently planned on a large scale and drawing its text, like that of *Espace*, from a wide range of linguistic sources (c. 1954–58, say); and the – presumably fairly precisely imagined, to judge by the proposed instrumentation – Michaux setting *Dans la Nuit* (c. 1957), which grew out of it. Chou has commented that these works were 'soon abandoned as he realized he was more interested in the vocal and evocative qualities of individual words and phrases than in complete poems.'[16] Ouellette quotes some lines from Michaux's poem which in their repetitive, incantatory qualities suggest their suitability for use as isolated phrases—

> In the night
> In the night
> I have made myself one with the night
> With the limitless night
> With the night

—and in themselves these phrases strongly parallel parts of the text Varèse eventually fashioned from Anaïs Nin ('You belong to the night' / 'dark dark dark asleep asleep', etc.). They certainly confirm the

---

[13] Preface, page iv.

[14] In Van Solkema, ibid., p. 88.

[15] Van Solkema, loc. cit.

[16] Preface, p. iii.

seamless continuity of the imaginative impulse in both works, and indeed of all the multiform shapes of the project going back to the 1954 conception of *Nuits*. Whatever the text or the title, the music was concerned with night, with darkness, in its literal but also in its figurative and symbolic senses. One has the feeling – it has been palpable in *Déserts* and the *Poème electronique* – that Varèse, worshipper of the sun and stars, was returning to the 'black dream' of the night, first adumbrated half a century before in *Un grand sommeil noir*, to grapple once more with the inner darkness, with his own shadow-side, whence came his deep depressions and emotional violence. The published *Nocturnal* is a moving testimony to this process.

Anaïs Nin, who had associated with the Parisian avant-garde in the 1920s and 30s, and whose triangular relationship with Henry Miller and his wife June is one of the enduring icons of 20th-century literary passion, had been friendly with the Varèses for many years. Varèse had also known, and disliked, her father, the Cuban composer-pianist Joaquin Nin y Castellanos (1878–1949), who had been a fellow student at the Schola Cantorum and, like Varèse, resident in Berlin from 1908 onwards. His dislike was well founded: not only did Joaquin Nin[17] abandon his wife and children to marry a rich heiress, but we now know that he had an incestuous relationship with his daughter Anais. It is possible Varèse was aware of this, though she only revealed the fact publicly with the publication of her early diaries, two years after Varèse's death. This relationship was one of the cardinal experiences which fertilized her self-absorbed and self-analytical fiction, and was surely one inspiration for *The House of Incest*. Less a novella than prose-poem in the form of an interior monologue, the book was only published in 1949 (the year of her father's death), but had been written in 1935, at the age of 21, and was one of Anaïs Nin's most admired works; it had partly inspired a film by Ian Hugo, *The Bells of Atlantis*, and portions had already been set to music by the composer Carter Harman.

The text which Varèse culled from her book is an assemblage of isolated words and phrases, in an order which bears no particular relationship to the course of the original. Yet some of Anaïs Nin's own comments on *The House of Incest* are of considerable interest for the

---

[17] Nin y Castellanos is to be distinguished from his estranged son Joaquin Nin-Culmell (b. 1908), also a composer and Anaïs Nin's elder brother.

way in which she points up aspects of its imagery which clearly would have struck a responsive chord in the composer:

Images of split selves appear in *House of Incest*. The image of loneliness on another planet ... there is mention of crystals, precious stones ... 'all crushed together, melted jewels, melted planets'[18]

These aspects of the text might well have appealed to Varèse, with his fascination for crystals and astronomy. But there are no precious stones among the images he selected for his music. Loneliness, and the experience of a consciousness divided against itself, resonate from every line.

Omitting for the moment the onomatopoeic syllables with which Varèse interspersed Nin's words, and omitting also some repetition, the core of the *Nocturnal* text is as follows.

> you belong to the night
>
> I rise
> I always rise after the crucifixion
>
> dark dark dark
>
> bread and the wafer
>
> womb and seed and egg
> wailing of the unborn
>
> perfume and sperm
> I have lost my brother
>
> it grows again
> faces in the windows
> one window without light
>
> dark dark dark
> asleep asleep
>
> floating floating again ...
>
> crucifixion
> shadow of death
>
> I kissed his shadow

---

[18] *The Journals of Anaïs Nin, Volume 5* (1947–55), edited by Günther Stuhlmann (London: Peter Owen, 1974), p. 260.

In 1954 Varèse had told Vivier he was looking for a text synthesis 'with a very strong tension, at one and the same time erotic, mystic, spiritual and mysterious'. There can be no question that in these few lines he had found that synthesis. Night, darkness, sleep, dreams – related here, as throughout world literature, to death; images of sacrament and sex (sex as conception), self-division ('I have lost my brother'); alienation. The text is admirably stark and concentrated. But why did Varèse require precisely these elements?

One clue may be a word that does not occur in the sung text, but only in the title of Nïn's book (which would normally be printed wherever the text was printed): there is perhaps a suggestion that the sexual coupling which engenders the wailing unborn is, in fact, incestuous. And that suggests, not so much actual knowledge of Anaïs Nin's own experience of incest, but the archetypal myth of incest which Varèse had grappled with 50 years before – his own role as reflected in the figure of Oedipus, the father-slayer.

Varèse's violent hatred of his father was not exorcized when he broke free of the paternal tyranny. There is ample testimony[19] that it seared him throughout his entire life and probably underlay his recurrent, crippling depressions. Even in his late seventies, in his most anguished moments, he could be heard to mutter *'J'aurais du tuer ce salaud!'* (I should have killed that pig!). Thus in exploring night, via his chosen images from Nin's text, as an 'incestuous', sexually charged realm, Varèse was in one sense confronting his own Heart of Darkness, the source of a lifelong spiritual wound; in a word, of his own 'crucifixion'.

It is no surprise that he found the material so intractable, and had not resolved the struggle by the time he died. Yet as we shall see the musical result is not a defeat, nor even a tragedy, although tragic elements surely arise in the work's course. There is, rather, an increased clarity, lyricism and fantasy, laced with that characteristically sardonic humour that can arise so unexpectedly throughout Varèse's oeuvre. Fragment though it is, *Nocturnal* attains a final moment of balance, where all the contradictory passions of its creator are for an instant in equilibrium, if not (and never!) at rest.

Sound out of silence: a leap of an octave and a minor third, F to A♭, on oboe and piano, the F resonated by a bassoon, the A♭ picked up, prolonged and intensified by high muted trumpet and E♭ clarinet:

---

[19] See, for example, Ouellette, pp. 10–11; *LGD*, pp. 21–23

quiet, yet with a 'sharp attack' in the oboe, like a signal, or a cry (Ex.1).

Ex.1

The presence of the piano is reminiscent of *Ecuatorial*, and there are indeed many connexions between the two works, as between midday and midnight. The gesture itself recalls rather the opening of *Offrandes*, over a space of more than 40 years. Once again, as the text will later make clear ('faces in the windows'), we are in a sleeping city, in that peculiarly urban, big-city night whose wonder and loneliness Varèse's music so often and so vividly evokes.

The moment of stillness following the oboe's cry is shattered by a single percussionist playing a battery of four different-sized membrane drums (snare, field, tenor and medium bass) in abrupt, military rhythms. (Their pitches are of necessity relative; but the rhythmic motifs will be developed later with specific pitches, on timpani.) The drums' irruption introduces the first entry of the male chorus: threatening, chanted vocables, a sound from the edge of dream, or nightmare.

> *Wa ya you you*
> *Wa wa yao*
> *Ya ha ha ha you*

Varèse calls for a harsh, rasping sound, from the back of the throat, 'as though from underground': the men sing in two-part, half-voiced harmony at the bottom of their register, with a downward glissando on the final 'you' syllables. Their voices are lent a heavy phosphorescence by very low piano clusters, string drum (Lion's Roar) and low bass drum – all in rhythmic unison with the chorus – whose background is the dark shimmer of a large metal sheet being vibrated. Other percussion quietly punctuate. The whole effect is phantasmal, unbearably sinister.

The brass, resonated by piano, bassoon and double-basses, now make a dramatic entry, rapidly building up a low-lying chord-complex which they hold in the bass register against a soft quaver pattern in the percussion. The initial downward leap (trombone 2), octave plus minor third, is the inversion of Ex.1. The wind chord is then echoed, or rather 'ghosted', by a cluster of string harmonics in the highest register: the first (published) string chord Varèse had composed in almost 40 years (Ex.2).

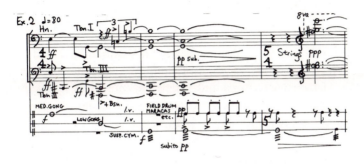

The aggregate sonority (for the piano sustains the low brass harmony) typically spans the heights and depths, with a central void in it – into which the membrane drums interpose their jagged rhythms, quiet now. The metal sheet's cold shimmer is heard again, as the background to irregular pulsations from a low wood-block, which Varèse directs to be played with yarn sticks, noting that its sound-quality should be 'liquid, like a drop of water'. Against the water-drops, Ex.1's signal-cry sounds out anew, on muted trumpet, echoed by two piccolos. The membrane drums speak again, their rhythms faster, more complicated. Ex.1 a third time, on E♭ clarinet. With the bold, simple strokes of a lifetime's experience, Varèse is etching a black dream-world.

The wood-block's last 'drop' now touches off a brief tutti fanfare build-up, developing the membrane-drum rhythms in the bass and Ex.1 in the treble, rapidly taking in all but two pitches of the total chromatic. Then it dies away on a high tone-cluster that refines itself down to a stratospheric C♯/D dissonance on E♭ clarinet and piccolo. Into the ensuing silence the chorus speaks:

> *you belong to the night*

The timpani, tuned to the five brass pitches of Ex.2 (the F♯ an octave higher), begins a long tattoo developing the rhythmic figures already established by the membrane drums. These soon join in with their relative pitches, and so too does a third percussionist, playing a set of five wooden tubes (or temple blocks). Each player fills in the others' pauses to provide a virtual continuum of percussion melody, continually varied in colour. Meanwhile wind instruments and strings build up crescendos and diminuendos of high note-clusters, instinct with tension. The passage climaxes in a sudden loud rhythmic unison from timpani, drums and wood tubes. Once more the metal sheet's low shimmer, and again the chorus, speaking:

you belong to the night

They start to sing the phrase – repeating it six times, insistently, as a kind of incantation, in a nightmarish muttering chromatic rise and fall (Ex.3). Melody instruments and percussion join in to intensify the figure; slight rhythmic variations, with an accelerando, tighten the repetitions until it sounds like a shouted curse.

It's altogether an extraordinary passage – horrifying, inhuman, yet with a grotesquerie that borders on the comic. (Like the mocking laughter through trombones which Varèse had used in *Arcana*.) This is the music made by things that go bump in the night; one thinks of Voodoo ceremonies. These low, black sounds are alien yet intimate, cold yet oppressive, as familiar and suffocating as family life.

The chorus's chromatic repetitions suddenly cease; thunder rolls on gong and timpani and dies away into a vibration of low percussion. Clear and free, the solo soprano's voice suddenly soars (Ex.4).

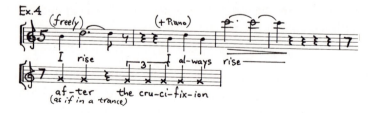

Her initial rising third echoes Ex.1, without its octave displacement; the minor ninth following it has been adumbrated in Ex.2, and opened the fanfare-tutti. The collapse into 'trance-like' speech immediately shows that the roles of soprano and the bass chorus are not to be cleanly and comfortably demarcated. All the music heard so far, striking though it is, has been essentially preludial, evocative scene-setting. With the entry of the soprano – the individual spirit – the main action commences. By implication it is an action of purgatorial struggle, between conflicting forces of light and dark, good and evil, sanity and madness. It also takes place, so to speak, in dream-time,[20] and incident now follows incident at a much accelerated pace.

First comes a new, brutal assault from the four membrane drums, and then an array of fist- and forearm-cluster smashes on the piano, blocking out a sound-space of more than five octaves. This coincides with a flurry of dark, ominous attacks and rolls from a large number of percussion instruments, topped off by an angry locust-chirr from high and low ratchets. The chorus, supported by strings, brass and woodwind, give vent to threatening cries in the motivic shape of rising minor ninth and falling minor third (we could regard this as a variant of Ex.2):

> *Dark! Dark! Dark!*
> *ah oh eh Hm*

Now ensues a kind of rapid recitative, half-sung, half-spoken, shared between solo soprano, low in her register, and chorus. The effect is of hallucinatory, disconnected phrases, as if echoing inside the skull during a fever – but also perhaps the responses in some ceremony of initiation, a rite, a mystery.

> SOPRANO: *o a o a oo a oo oo hm*
>   *bread and the wafer*
> BASSES: *womb and seed and egg*
>   *wailing of the unborn*
> SOPRANO: *perfume and sperm*
>   *I have lost my brother*

---

[20] We have Varèse's own authority for this interpretation, in a letter to Odile Vivier: 'The woman sings, speaks, howls, ululates, vocalises as if in a dream or a trance. The men: the nightmare voices surrounding the woman in her dream.' (op. cit., p.177).

The interest is entirely concentrated in the voices, with only an exiguous percussion and instrumental support to etch the phrases more clearly. Thus at 'wailing' the male chorus, doubled by cellos and basses, produce a rising phrase on 'wail-' including a dissonant quarter-tone, with a long glissando covering almost two octaves to their lowest register to speak the last syllable; and this is shadowed by an eerie rising-falling shake on the flexatone (here performing a task which Varèse might well, in an earlier score, have assigned to a siren).

The soprano's last two lines, marked 'dreamy' and 'softly spoken', are totally unaccompanied, self-absorbed. Silence; then she is startled – though still 'as if in a dream' – into a sudden vocalization (to the vowel-sound 'Ah'), rising the thematic minor third and then a ninth to a high B♮ – a scream of anguish or ecstasy (Ex.5), cruelly pierced by the stabbing entries of four woodwind.

This can be viewed as a direct development of Ex.1, the work's initial instrumental cry: although according to Ouellette,[21] Ex.5 (without its woodwind 'skewering') also exists in *Etude pour Espace*. Here it summons up a new burst of nightmare sounds from the chorus.

Soft but sinister, supported by the four membrane drums (now shared between two players) and low clusters in the piano, all in even quavers, the male voices take up a new syllabic pattern:

oomp' ts' oomp' ts' oomp' ts' ...

It might be a shuffling of feet, the pumping action of steam machinery, perhaps a heartbeat under stress. Over this pulse-rhythm the soprano (in unison with oboe and violas) starts to vocalize again to 'ah', but this time rising by small conjunct intervals into shapely, aspiring melody. Meanwhile the basses, divided in two parts, take up the text:

---

[21] Op. cit., p.164.

(1st HALF): *It grows again*
(2nd HALF): *It grows again*
(1st HALF): *Faces in the windows*
(TOGETHER): *One window without light*

Simultaneously the soprano's melody gains strength as it rises, woodwind and then trumpets doubling it an octave above and below, so that it rapidly assumes an epic, commanding character. The line's climactic leap of a seventh to high B♭ is a gesture which mingles anguish with a sense of triumph (Ex.6).

As a whole, this melody is a fascinating and characteristic Varèse construct. Its initial slow ascent of two conjunct semitones (related, of course, to Ex.3's manic 'you belong to the night' incantation) is the melancholy figure we have noted so often throughout the composer's oeuvre, and which had assumed such plangent significance as virtually the only 'thematic' element in *Poème électronique*. As its intervals widen, however, the melody becomes a note-series, typically embracing 11 tones rather than the full 12 (the 'missing' pitch, B♮, was the goal of the previous short vocalise and is also briefly present as a deep pedal in trombone 3). Reinforced at the dynamic peak by extra percussion (notably wood-block and guiro), this eloquent utterance fades back towards silence, with an atomized scatter of percussion rhythms, while the basses again mutter their '*oomp' ts*' ...' pulsation – which this time rapidly dies out.

The immediate result – and the last music Varèse himself prepared for performance – is a sonic structure as refined and evocative as anything he ever composed. As Ex. 7 shows, it is basically a slow-wheeling procession of luminous string chords, partly in harmonics, against hummed harmony in the bass voices, supported by clarinets; these two elements as background to a low-lying, sustained line in the soprano – essentially the 'conjunct semitone' figure again – doubled by oboe and violas *sul tasto*. As her words testify, she is still enwrapped in her dream:

Dark Dark Dark asleep asleep

In one sense this is very simple music, one of the most 'impressionistic', even Debussian, passages Varèse had written since as far back as *Amériques*. The chords, essentially an expansion of the harmony seen in Ex.2 (and in the tuning of the timpani, which itself refracted the music of the membrane drums) simultaneously into the higher and lower registers, are severely structured by an elaborate mirror-symmetry of motion around the soprano's line. The music's luminescent aura is further refined – and invested with an auditory equivalent of the soft, fuzzy quality of darkness one sometimes experiences on a summer night in the deserted alleyways of a big city – by the octave doubling of the upper voices in violin and cello harmonics, and by the tiniest percussion details: a *pianissimo* friction of sandpaper, and very quiet, yet staccato, impacts on a low bass drum. The mood created is, for once, almost peaceful, as if the night, for a brief space, is found to be acceptable and nurturing.

It is precisely here that the original portion of *Nocturnal*, as prepared for performance by Varèse, comes to an end: Chou Wen-Chung has indicated the precise break-off point in the published score by a dotted line; I do the same here in the last bar of Ex.7.[22] This whole 'authentic' portion of *Nocturnal* measures slightly more than 92 bars. Chou's 'continuing portion', whose nature and principles we have already discussed, completes bar 93 and adds a further 77 bars, although it should be said that in terms of the time taken in performance Varèse's original accounts for something like two-thirds of the whole.

The concluding 77 bars present passages which Varèse himself had elaborated during his labour on the work's continuation, together with Chou's realizations of sketches which were considerably more 'cryptic' – though as far as possible these realizations have been made to accord (perhaps, one reflects, more closely than Varèse himself would have done) with analogous passages in the opening portion. There are, in fact, a network of quite obvious correspondences in material and gesture between the two parts of the work. From that point of view the two parts surely establish an artistic unity, and the intimate, evocative atmosphere of *Nocturnal* is certainly convincingly maintained. That being the case, all the commentator can usefully do is to respect that unity, treating the last 77 bars as if they were indeed by Varèse, whatever marginal differences may arise in deep structure or the pace of rhetoric. Had Varèse lived to complete *Nocturnal* himself, his completion would undoubtedly have been different, though it would presumably have contained some of the same elements and perhaps some of the same specific passages. But Chou's completion is the nearest we will ever be able to come to Varèse's intentions.

Ex.7 has shown the moment of junction between the two parts of *Nocturnal*, for Chou's continuation begins after the first beat of bar 93 with a *pianissimo* tone-cluster on tremolo strings. It will be noted that the violas, though no longer *sul tasto*, reiterate the G pitch on which they had previously been doubling the soprano, who in fact sustains her G for a further two beats. Also, the scoring of the chord, with

---

[22] Chou has also commented (Preface, p.v), that 'For the 1961 performance, Varèse substituted the words "asleep, asleep" with "floating again" as temporary ending'. This remark is not perfectly clear, but I take him to mean simply that the words 'floating again' were set to the last four notes of the soprano line as shown in Ex.7, rather than that Varèse temporarily tacked on the quite independent setting of those words which we will shortly encounter in the course of Chou's completion of the score, and which may already have been in existence.

harmonics in first violins and cellos, echoes that of the rest of Ex.7; so the dovetailing is neatly and plausibly done. In the very next bar, however, a new element makes an appearance, as the strings' chord is sustained against a percussion music which in rhythm recalls the figures of the four membrane drums, but is entirely different in sound. Scored for bongos, cencerros, claves and maracas – only the last of which have so far been heard – it is altogether more exotic in effect.

It leads us directly back to the male chorus, with a brief variant of their first 'harsh, rasping' entry:

> *ha ha you*
> *hoo hoom*

The supporting scoring is almost exactly the same, but intensified and made heavier by the three trombones sustaining the notes of the piano's lowest cluster. As before, this music leads straight to a brass-and-piano fanfare, closely based on Ex.2 but transposed upwards by (mostly) a perfect fourth, and topped off by a raucous high thirteenth in clarinets and trumpet. Also as before, this chord-complex gives way to another in high string harmonics, with disjunct rhythmic commentary from three of the four membrane drums.

In one way this whole passage could be considered a kind of varied recapitulation of *Nocturnal*'s opening; though it is equally possible that Chou here presents alternative realizations of the same material. Certainly the sense of resumed struggle, of the inescapability of the black dream, is very strong, and this is now confirmed by the soprano's next words, heard against the still-sustained string chord—

> *Floating floating again*
> *a o a o a*

—although the actual line she sings, developing the conjunct-semitone figure but with seventh as well as semitone leaps, is new, with tremolos like distant thunder on low bass drum and the metal sheet.

The process of 'varied recapitulation' continues with the reappearance of the work's initial signal-cry – but the passage which is now built upon it so thoroughly transforms and recombines previously-heard elements that it amounts rather to far-reaching development. Ex.1, on piccolo and flute resonated by piano, is made into a double gesture, leaping its octave-and-minor-third span and then falling back to the initial tone (now A♯), only to leap again (to C♯). This melodic variant is integrated with a rhythmic variant in the bongos and maracas, itself introducing the soft repeated quavers in other percussion which were originally heard near the outset of the work.

Further variants of Ex.1 follow on muted trumpets, on oboe, and finally in its original form (though still using the A♯–C♯ pitches) on E♭ clarinet. Meanwhile the music of bongos, maracas, claves and cencerros fills out the long sustained tones, a kind of continuo of the tropical night. They are joined by membrane drums and other percussion, notably the metal sheet. This nervous, mysterious percussion activity is refined down to the irregular pulsations of the low wood block, struck with yarn sticks.

That instrument is not, as originally, marked 'like a drop of water', but the reminiscence of the former effect is clear; and as before, its solo 'drops', resounding in stillness, provoke a dramatic tutti outburst (Ex.8). This is largely unrelated to the one at the analogous point in

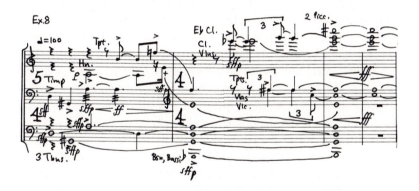

the work's opening portion. It begins with a heavy, imperious three-note figure on the timpani (sternly resonated by the trombones): an interval cell of tritone and minor ninth (which can also be found at the outset of Ex.2) that will assume continuing importance for the remainder of the work. From this opening the tutti builds up in typical Varèse fashion, accumulating pitches as it constructs a sustained chord which rises to span the full spectrum of the orchestra. Unusually, this tutti involves all 12 semitones (not the usual 10 or 11), but two of these (B♮ and F♮) have dropped out before the climactic 10-note chord has been consolidated. The low pitches of trombones, horn, bassoon and double basses are also soon subtracted; beneath the remaining tones the timpani sounds a sinuous, sinister glissando, a tritonal oscillation between the pitches E and B♭. It might be the moan of a beast, or of a great wind, and it carries with it a scatter of percussion noise and drumbeats – mysterious sounds emanating, as it might be, from the jungle, or the back streets. Flickering quintuplet rhythms on two woodblocks sound like a rattle of bones. From this point, the nightmare moves towards its climax.

The soprano lets out a low groan; and then, as stabbing minor ninths on the pitches F♯ and G pierce the air in woodwind, piano and violins, she groans again in a rising-falling curve, reminiscent of the sound of the flexatone earlier in the work. The bass voices, accompanied by percussion impacts and the inevitable metal-sheet shimmer, respond in their 'harsh, rasping' mode:

> *ha ha – hm*

The soprano, assailed by claves and membrane drums, expels air in a breathy puff.[23] The impression is of an anguished victim under attack, and the attack is now pressed home with frightening intensity.

Strings and high winds build up crescendo-diminuendo patterns out of sustained pitches: F♯, G♮, C♮, C♯, E♭, forming ninths and tritones in various orders but always at the same pitch-levels, with C♮ above middle C the lowest tone and the highest the C♯ two octaves and a semitone above it. Beneath the pain-throb of these tense, stratospheric sounds the percussion (especially wood blocks, claves, bongos and the various drums) batter out complex rhythmic and colouristic patterns, tending towards ever more rapid but more unified pulsations at climaxes. Meanwhile the male chorus, like a taunting, tormenting mob, launches a veritable fusillade of malefic phonemes; Varèse's marks of expression strive to create vocal effects that will seem wholly animalistic:

> (snarling): *who ho*
> (harsh): *ya!* (guttural): *whoo whoo sh!*
> (growling): *ga ra ya ga ra*
> *ya ga ra ha hoo*

---

[23] In the 1968 Vanguard recording the soprano Ariel Bybee in fact gives a third groan at this point, though somewhat less voiced.

The timpani, tuned as on its first entry to five pitches (the bottom four are raised a tone; the top one – B♮ – remains unchanged) interrupt for a single bar with a violent entry developing the tritone-and-ninth cell, and then the basses resume with the rest of the orchestra, the accumulating chord made frenetic by the feverish tremolo of all the strings, and supported by a terrific polyphony of militaristic rhythms in the percussion.

> (barking): *ba you ba a ba ee*
> *ha ba you boo*

The chorus cap this orgy of vocal violence with a vicious descending hissing sound. Again the timpani strikes in, developing the motivic cell – and again, as earlier in the work, its specific pitches are doubled in rhythmic unison by the relative ones of the membrane drums and the wooden tubes, with further simultaneous percussion contributions: a truly shattering outburst.

The soprano, '*hurlant*' (screaming), sings the single word 'Crucifixion!'. Yet, set as it is to an imperious variant of the timpani phrase from Ex.8, with an initial perfect fifth instead of the tritone, the word suddenly sounds not so much agonized as decisive, almost triumphant; and the basses, eschewing vocal effects for tonal definition, register agreement as well as threat (Ex.9).

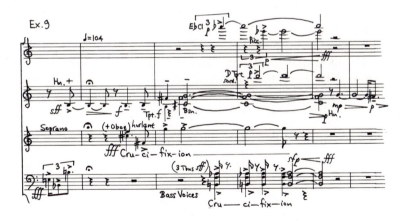

The role of the horn in this passage is significant. By resonating the final B of the preceding timpani outburst it has provided the thread of continuity; and its rise of a perfect fifth plus a semitone from F♯ to G is a mirror image of the soprano's descending fifth plus minor ninth. The F♯–G leap is thus transformed back into a simple semitone interval, and this figure is now passed quietly among horn, flute and clarinet.

From these unassuming beginnings is now built up a big, imposing tutti passage involving the full instrumental forces. Whether by Varèse's design, or Chou's decision of placement, it is the last such tutti in the work, and though in the nature of Varèse's mature discourse it lasts only a few seconds it is one of the most complex in his output, combining several elements in a vast synoptic sky-filling gesture. In the printed score of *Nocturnal* it lies very impressively across a double-page spread, which I reproduce overleaf as Example 10.

Despite its size the tutti only involves 10 of the chromatic pitches. The initial gesture, chord-building on trombones and piano, relates back to Ex.2, but is combined with a soaring melodic line on E♭ clarinet that stresses the re-expansion of semitones into ninths and sevenths and tritones. Then follow piano clusters with gong, as heard much earlier in the work 'after the crucifixion', but underpinned now by all bass instruments except for a rising-falling glissando in violas and divided cellos (an echo perhaps of the timpani glissando, or even the flexatone). While the high winds and strings exclaim the upper regions of the harmony (C and D trumpets on the D at the uppermost limit of their range), a last fragment of the membrane drums' music batters out against a pedal F♯ in the timpani, which eventually grows into a tremolo glissando as if in imitation of the low strings.

All in all, despite its extreme harmonic tension, this adds up to an impressive, even majestic wave of sound, which the male chorus tries to deflect with a raucous shout:

shadow of death

The huge chordal range sudenly shrinks to a small, tight fist of tones. On stopped horn we hear an eerie and melancholy line, spun out of the conjunct-semitone figure which initiated the soprano's vocalise in Ex.5. Its cluster of three pitches is doubled by divided violas, tremolo and *sul ponticello*. As we move into *Nocturnal*'s concluding bars (the final page of score, shown as Ex.11) the cluster is similarly echoed (a minor ninth above) by divided violins. This is a new form of the

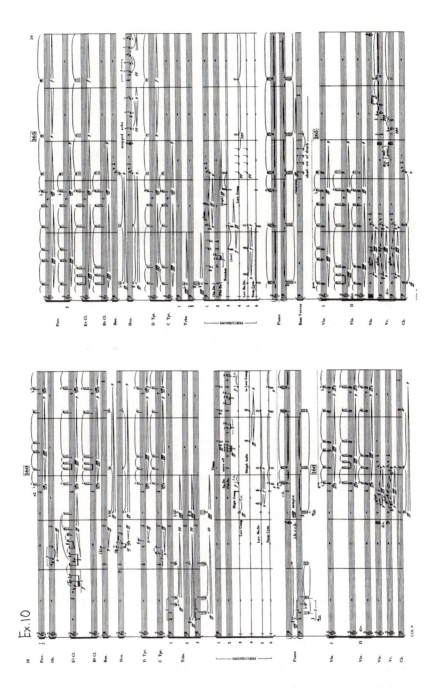

ambigious starlight, the faint and painful radiance, that occurs at the end of *Arcana*.

Ex.11

The soprano, 'as in a trance', slowly and deliberately intones the last words of the work:

I kissed his shadow

A brief, shocked silence: and then *Nocturnal* ends in a single 5/4 bar of violent instrumental exclamation. As seen in Ex.11, the last gesture in

Varèse's published output is harmonically a further development of the tritone-and-ninth cell, though the piano's cluster-chord encompasses all 12 pitches. But from the rhythmic aspect this furious outburst, with its dotted triplet figure and the trombone glissandi resonated by Lion's Roar, is essentially a new idea (just as Beethoven introduces a new theme in the final bars of his Ninth Symphony). So at the last, Varèse still surprises us; and the last sounds we hear are the resonance of the gong, bass drum and metal sheet, held on into silence.

It is difficult to evaluate the precise expressive significance of this ending (especially as it may not have been the ending Varèse himself intended). That final, brutal bar may suggest we should regard the words 'I kissed his shadow' as the symbol of some ultimate horror. But to me they seem something quite different: a positive act rather than a surrender, a suggestion of acceptance and reconciliation. The kiss is given both to the 'shadow of death' which the chorus has just evoked, and also to 'darkness' in all the many forms that *Nocturnal* has explored: the physical and fearful world of night, and the dark places of the heart, the mind, the soul. Being 'his' shadow it is not only Death's but the shadow of the lost brother, the shadow self, the inner daemon. The kiss signifies peace and even love, an ultimate gesture of tenderness and self-healing. The opposites are unified, light is reconciled with dark – and it is perhaps significant that the last bar's outcry, though violent, is nevertheless one of complete rhythmic unanimity. That Varèse could have composed these final bars – whether or not he would himself have made them the goal and ending of *Nocturnal* – suggests he had at least tasted victory in his own inner struggles; and that Chou should have placed them last shows a rare insight and sympathy with his late teacher. Chou clearly felt that *Nocturnal* was, for Varèse, partly an act of musical autobiography, for he has written that it encompasses

a world of sounds remembered and imagined, conjuring up sights and moods now personal, now Dantesque, now enigmatic ... could one, knowing Varèse's unique career, resist wondering about the line 'I rise, I always rise after crucifixion'? ... the liquid beat on the wood block, the shrill whistling of the winds, the tenacious shimmering of the strings – the insistent sound of a mass of shuffling feet, the flourishes of drumbeats, the sudden crashing outbursts. A phastasmagorial world? Yes, but as real as Varèse's own life.[24]

---

[24] Preface, p.iv.

The remaining few years of that life, when *Nocturnal* remained a fragment, failed – as so many years of his life had failed – to produce any substantial new work. Yet no-one could claim that his tortuous and frustrated career, his tiny output, had not produced sufficient music to ensure him immortality and transform the way that music may be heard and thought about. This music has still to be assimilated and understood. The painful eloquence that is the hallmark of all Varèse's works resounds throughout Chou's edition of *Nocturnal*; which demonstrates that Varèse had, fortuitously or not, brought his life-work to a fitting close. The wheel had turned full circle. The furious worshipper of the sun, the descryer of stars and speculator upon crystals, had hearkened to the inner voices which tried to call him back to the night. Wrestling with them in the darkness, he liberated himself – at least in his music – from the shadow of death.

Varèse's death removed from the New York arts scene a 50-year physical presence. Sociable and intensely interested in all that was going on, despite (or because of) the isolation of his creative endeavours, he was the most regular of attenders of opening nights, exhibitions and concerts. In an obituary, Benjamin Boretz wrote:

His interest in and involvement with the New York musical community was so unremitting that literally up to the very last moment his presence was an invariable and indispensable aspect of every important new-music concert. Moreover, there is hardly anyone who was ever a young 'advanced' composer in New York during the past thirty years who cannot count among his treasured professional experiences the remarkable sympathy and interest with which Varèse looked at his scores and listened to their performances.

We interacted professionally with him, we encountered him constantly in the homes of musicians and in his own, and it is indeed true, as *The New York Times*' editorial obituary so patronizingly noted, that he was loved and revered as a father figure by all of New York's *avant-gardes*, just as he was a monumental presence in the international artistic community.[25]

Varèse founded no school of composition; and by the time of his death, with modernism enthroned – temporarily – as a critically acceptable orthodoxy, it would hardly be possible to duplicate his achievement, far less its historic resonances.

---

[25] *The Nation*, 29 November 1965. Reprinted in *Music Columns from The Nation by Benjamin Boretz* selected and annotated by Elaine Barkin (New York: Open Space, 1991) p. 20.

His reputation, therefore, continues to stand high, but his influence has generally been diffuse rather solidly perceptible. The enormous advances in the *technology* of electronic music, in the decades since his death, do not seem to have called forth the whole new universe of sound and creative aspiration of which he dreamed. In many respects the most palpable catalyzations of the Varèsian aesthetic occurred not in the USA but in Europe, and in the immediate aftermath of his own late works. The composition that still – to the present writer – evokes most of the Varèsian vision and spirit of adventure, while logically extending *Déserts'* interplay of instruments and electronic tape into an actual counterpoint of the two media, was composed within Varèse's lifetime: *Collages*, the Third Symphony of his Catalan acquaintance Roberto Gerhard. Gerhard's highly individual late style, evolving out of rigorous Schoenbergian training and a native Miró-esque sense of colour and fantasy, came to treat sound in a manner as elemental, and as eloquently expressive of the tragedies of the human condition, as had Varèse.

Few of their younger successors could say the same. In Varèse they found instead a potent symbol of freedom, on many levels. Many younger composers have recorded the sheer excitement of their first encounter with a work of Varèse. For Brian Ferneyhough, *Octandre* struck him as 'the first truly modern work' he had ever heard. For John Cage and Morton Feldman, he was the prime exponent of music as an art of *sound* rather than notes: the composer who, above all others, lets the sounds 'speak' and by doing so *changes* his listeners.[26]

In Europe the younger composers' response to Varèsian liberation was more systematic (a paradox he himself might have relished). The young Karlheinz Stockhausen was undoubtedly impressed and influenced by the sounds and the ideas behind Varèse's works, and many of his early scores may legitimately be said to be part-responses to, and part-developments of, Varèsian concepts: *Zyklus* for solo

---

[26] See John Cage and Morton Feldman, *Radio Happenings I–V* (Cologne: MusikTexte, 1993) especially pp. 111–119. These are transcripts of conversations broadcast on WBAI New York City, 1966–67, thus in the immediate aftermath of Varèse's death. Cage elsewhere objected to Varèse's 'exploitation' of the sounds 'for his own purposes': he felt this showed him to be essentially 'an artist of the past. Rather than dealing with sounds as sounds, he deals with them as Varèse'. See John Cage, *Silence* (London: Marion Boyars, 1978), p. 84.

percussionist is a sort of one-man *Ionisation*, while fundamental to the whole concept of *Gruppen* for three spatially separated orchestras (1955–7) and its successors *Carré* for four choirs and orchestras (1959–60) and *Momente* for choirs, soloists and instrumentalists (1962–9) is the principle of 'sounds moving freely in space'. Stockhausen's *Gesang der Jünglinge* (1955–6) may justly claim to be the first important electronic music with a powerful expressive charge, and in this he even anticipated Varèse: though only, we may note, because he had speedier access to the technical resources. His combinations of electronics with instruments up to the late 1960s, in *Kontakte* (1960, with piano and percussion), *Mikrophonie I* (1964, for tam-tam sounds stereophonically transformed by microphones, filters and potentiometers) and *II* (1965, for choir, Hammond organ, ring-modulators and tape), and *Mixtur* (1964–7 for five orchestral groups, ring-modulators and sine-wave generators) all seem to realize aspects of Varèse's musical vision – though their principal expressive aims run in other, sometimes contrary directions, and their realization takes place at a length, and with a sometimes bewildering range of material, that Varèse would hardly have allowed himself. Despite a certain affinity of cosmic vision (Stockhausen, like Varèse, has been fascinated by Sirius – to the extent that he has claimed to originate from the planetary system of that star) his later work tends to be vitiated by his tendency to giganticism and solipsistic indulgence of his personal mythology, and his inability to compose a genuine musical argument rather than an assemblage of brilliant moments.

Varèse's influence is perhaps less easy to discern in the early output of Stockhausen's erstwhile friend and rival Pierre Boulez, despite the fact that he and Varèse shared a common French heritage. Though Boulez's works of the 1950s and 60s make some play with sound and space, it is perhaps only in *Poesie pour pouvoir* (1958; originally for orchestra and electronic tape, though eventually for three contrasted orchestras) and *Figures-Doubles-Prismes* (1958–68, for orchestra) that these concerns emerge with an authentically Varèsian forcefulness. More significant is his work since 1970 as begetter and administrator of the *Institut de Récherche et Coordination Acoustique/Musique* (IRCAM) in Paris, an organization specifically designed to harness technology and musical creativity under one roof. Here young composers may experiment with resources Varèse could only dream of, and develop their works in collaboration with scientific advisers; here new instruments and computer programmes with specific musical applications are constantly developed.

Immensely valuable though these operations are, it remains a question whether the artistic results have proved commensurate to the enormous investment of finance and ingenuity. Surely Boulez's own *Répons* (1981–4) – for keyboard soloists, chamber orchestra and a sophisticated computer-controlled electronic apparatus that mirrors, amplifies and modifies the instrumental sounds, allowing them to travel on predetermined paths in the auditorium by means of a complex loudspeaker array – could be claimed as a classic fulfilment of Varèse's dream of sounds 'open rather than bounded', 'moving freely in space'. Yet the aural effect of this brilliantly coloured and beautifully crafted music is essentially decorative, the decorations echoing and rebounding off one another to create a discourse whose precise substance remains hard to seek. More clearly than any other of Boulez's works, *Répons* reveals his essential roots in Debussian Impressionism, and how much closer he has stayed to those roots than did Varèse. Despite its very considerable qualities, such music – as Varèse said in another context – 'is the result of culture, and, desirable and comfortable as culture may be, an artist' – at least, we may silently qualify, a Varèsian artist – 'should not lie down in it'.[27]

Boulez's tendency to work on particular scores over decades, so that they become perpetual 'works in progress' recalls – though also from a 'cultured' perspective – Varèse's long frustration with such inchoate projects as *Espace*. But it is rather Boulez's contemporary Jean Barraqué, devoting his tragically short artistic career to the ideal of 'radical incompletion' with the physically inachievable project of *Le Mort de Virgile*, who actually created a music of Varèse-like urgency and passion, though his actual musical techniques are very different. In fact none of these composers considered themselves *primarily* followers of Varèse: their compositional techniques descended from Schoenbergian 12-note method, though by way of a 'post-Webernian' aesthetic of 'total serialization' which neither Schoenberg nor Webern

---

[27] The same observation applies to the more recent French tendency of *musique spectrale*, as exemplified in the music of Tristan Murail, Gérard Grisey and others, though their explorations of timbre for its own sake becomes, in the work of the Romanian Horatiu Radulescu, something akin to a Varèsian liberation of 'the inner life of the sound' in a context that suggests shamanic ritual.

might have considered a legitimate interpretation of their intentions (see above, p.330).

Among those who have chosen a differently radical path, Iannis Xenakis was an ardent supporter of Varèse from the time of *Déserts* and worked with him and Le Corbusier on the Philips Pavilion project that engendered *Poème électronique*. Approaching music from the vector of mathematics and architecture, he developed a 'stochastic' approach to sound based on statistical sampling (with the aid of computers) and probability theory. The creative results have been widely divergent in quality and appeal: as with many highly prolific composers, Xenakis can produce work that sounds cogent and exciting, or that merely appears endlessly to recycle the gestural content of his better music. It is ultimately in his sheer torrents of sound, as sound and nothing else; in the abrasiveness of his instrumental sonorities (no composer has more pungently achieved the 'sensation of non-blending'); and in the alignment of his sonic canvases with ancient ritual practices that Xenakis continues to sustain part of the Varèsian aesthetic.

In fact the nearest thing to a 'successor' to Varèse, were such a phenomenon possible, was probably the Venetian composer Luigi Nono. Though beginning, like most of the composers mentioned, in the post-Webernian forcing-house of Darmstadt serialism, from the first Nono combined his avant-garde language with a strong left-wing political impulse, in pieces such as *Il Canto Sospeso* and *Intolleranza*, which immediately moved it towards the urgent human dimensions of Varèse's work. He was also one of the most consistently daring experimenters with electronic tape for its expressive effect, both alone and in combination with voices or instruments. There have been many percussion-ensemble works since Varèse's *Ionisation*, but few have got closer to it in stature than Nono's hommage to an elder Italian master, *Con Luigi Dallapiccola* for six percussionists and live electronics. Especially in his last works, where he seemed continually to be patrolling and pushing back the borders between sound and silence, Nono most nearly approached Varèse in the sheer sense of existential adventure, of living out on a creative edge where there are no rules, only the ability to trust in right instinct. *A Carlo Scarpa, Architetto, ai Suoi Infiniti Possibili* or *No hay caminos, hay que caminar* – the titles themselves recall Varèsian tropes. *La lontananza nostalgica Utopica futura* (1988) for violin and tape – it is only so late in the century that there could be 'nostalgia' for the 'utopian future' – is both one of the most challenging works in the violin repertoire, and one of the most richly imaginative tape compositions since *Poème électronique* itself.

Yet few indeed of the supposedly 'revolutionary' late-century scores I have here briefly touched upon (Nono's works are the most honourable exceptions) do more, in sum, than to recycle the conceptual discourse of a modern music establishment. To turn from them to Varèse's own music is to be continually refreshed by the economy of his means and method, and above all the elemental nature of his message. Such qualities are occasionally present in the strongest works of Harrison Birtwistle, a composer for whom Varèse's music was a catalyst at a very deep level: yet even in the best of these, like the appropriately-named *Earth Dances*, Birtwistle remains a profoundly earthbound composer, a dealer in rock strata rather than crystals, a scryer of entrails rather than a speculator of the stars.

These names are the obvious ones among Varèse's scattered progeny, and their very diversity demonstrates how subtle and far-reaching, how much the opposite of a 'school', his influence has been. Yet with each of these composers, and with many others we could name, there will always be a reservation: what they bring of their own, of their view of music and culture, is not as fiercely pungent and mind-changing as Varèse's. Insofar as the 20th-century had a Beethoven, he is it. He has profoundly altered all our awareness of what music is and can be. I have attempted here to give a context for his vision, and suggest some of the sources of his extraordinary power. But in his creative discourse, in his language and themes, Varèse remains ultimately inimitable, modern music's scientific shaman, the one all alone.

Index